CHILD
Development

A Comprehensive Text for GCSE

Heather Brennand   Judith Fairclough
Valerie Hall   Eileen Nicholson   Enid Rees

Hodder & Stoughton

A MEMBER OF THE HODDER HEADLINE GROUP

Orders: please contact Bookpoint Ltd, 130 Milton Park, Abingdon, Oxon OX14 4SB. Telephone: (44) 01235 827720, Fax: (44) 01235 400454. Lines are open from 9.00 – 6.00, Monday to Saturday, with a 24 hour message answering service. Email address: orders@bookpoint.co.uk

Edexcel Foundation, London Examinations accepts no responsibility whatsoever for the accuracy or method of working in the answers given at the back of this book. The answers at the end of this book are the sole responsibility of the publishers and have not been provided or approved by SEG.

British Library Cataloguing in Publication Data
A catalogue record for this title is available from The British Library

ISBN 0 340 782722

First published 2001
Impression number   10 9 8 7 6 5 4
Year   2005 2004 2003 2002

Typeset by Multiplex Techniques Ltd, Orpington, Kent.

Printed in Great Britain for Hodder & Stoughton Educational, a division of Hodder Headline Plc, 338 Euston Road, London NW1 3BH by Printer Trento.

Contents

Part Two Care of the Child

Chapter 7 The Newborn Baby

Chapter 8 Post-natal Care

Chapter 9 Feeding and Nutrition

Chapter 10 Hygiene

Chapter 11 Environment

Chapter 12 Child Care Provision

Chapter 13 Child Health

Part Three Development of the Child

Chapter 18 Special Children

Part Four Key Skills/Coursework/ Exam preparation

Introduction

This book has been written primarily to support the new AQA specification for GCSE Home Economics: Child Development, although it will be of value to any student following similar GCSE and GNVQ courses looking for an up-to-date text book with a thoroughly modern approach.

The book is concerned with the growth and development of children from birth up to the age of five and is divided into three main sections for ease of reference.

Part One 'The Family' recognises the changing structures and wide variety of families today and focuses on the importance of the family unit in ensuring the growth and development of children. Additionally, planning for a family is investigated as well as the stages of pregnancy from conception to birth

Part Two 'The Care of the Child' begins with the post-natal care of the new baby and mother and examines the wider range of care needed for the growing and developing child.

Part Three 'The Development of the Child' examines how children develop and learn physically, intellectually, emotionally and socially. The importance of toys and play as well as other factors that may influence development is comprehensively covered. This section also looks sympathetically at the needs of special children, examining causes of disability and the support required by both children and their families.

Throughout the book the authors have sought to emphasise the interrelationship of the subject matter and within each section up-to-date information has been presented in a user-friendly and accessible way with clear cross-referencing. Each chapter has highlighted keywords and definitions at appropriate points within the text to enhance students' understanding and use of appropriate technical terminology. **Part Four** includes ideas on coursework, examination techniques and useful web sites. Questions at the end of each chapter enable students to test, extend and develop their knowledge and understanding, while activities are included which will help to develop the observation and research skills needed for coursework and examinations.

Many students on Child Development Courses will also be expected to demonstrate their competence in the Key Skills of Application of Number, Information and Communication Technology as well as the wider Key Skills of Improving own Learning and Performance, Working with Others and Problem Solving. Many of the activities suggested, along with the overall coursework requirement, will offer opportunities for the development of these skills and thus enable the required evidence to be generated.

Acknowledgements

The authors and publishers would like to thank Anne Wall, Sandra Brady and Janice Crooke at AQA for their advice and support.

Eileen Nicholson: I would like to acknowledge the Aitman family; the Enright family; the Gorrod family; The Farmhouse Nursery, Witney; Springfield School, Witney; Plantation Wharf Nursery; Sister Beatty from Pontefract General Infirmary and especially my husband, Jim Nicholson.

Enid Rees: I would like to thank my Mum, for her patience and encouragement in allowing me to read my work to her, and Miss Anne Giblin, former Head of Chemistry, for her advice.

Heather Brennand: I would like to thank St Wilfrid's CE Technology School; Dr Gina Mitchell; Catherine Tipton; Adrienne Shanon; my husband Dave and James and Rachael.

Valerie Hall: Thanks to my family: Ken, Samantha and Darren, also Wendy Burke and Sheila Calvert.

Judith Fairclough: To My Mum.

Part One
The family

In Part One we look at the nature of the family, pregnancy and birth.

In society there are many types and sizes of families, all unique, none perfect.

The family is one of the most important influences on the health, growth and development of the child. Having a child is a huge responsibility and should begin with planning and preparation to ensure the child has the best possible start in life.

Remember

Children deserve good parenting. Stability and love are key factors.

This section is about the family, its function and the different types of structure that exist in Britain today

The family is a group or unit of people that consists of a parent or parents, and their children, usually living together. The group of people are nearly always related by blood, marriage or adoption.

The family is a central part of British society and while there is a variety of different types of family that exist today, the family continues to perform many functions and needs to ensure the growth and development of their children.

Children have many needs and the cohesive family unit, whatever its type, must ensure a sound, stable environment is provided to enable children to flourish. The Tree of Life identifies many of the children's needs, however their basic requirements are:

- food
- shelter
- clothing
- care
- love
- safe, secure environment

Things to do

Select ten of the words from the Tree of Life below and put them in the order of priority you would choose from 1–10.

Figure 1.1 Children need many things to grow and develop and this starts and continues within the family

Children will learn what is expected behaviour, customs and values from the group of people closest to them. Children learn this social behaviour from family and friends. This is called Primary Socialisation.

Children will also learn other social rules from other people or sources – teachers, school, TV, radio, newspapers, etc. and this is called Secondary Socialisation.

Types of Family

Extended Family

A large family group, i.e. grandparents, parents, brothers, sisters, aunts, uncles, cousins who all live locally and support one another.

One-parent Families

One parent and children living together. Sharing responsibilities with birth parent is not always possible. Causes:

- divorce and separation
- death of one parent
- birth to single women
- parent ill or imprisoned
- parent works away for long periods.

Nuclear Family

Parents and their children live away from the rest of their family. There is no support or help from the family as they live too far away. More effort is required to keep contact with the family. Children are looked after by non-family members if parents work.

Residential Care Homes

Children without families or with parents who can't or are unable to look after children, may live in these homes.

Step Family

When a remarriage occurs, one or both partners may bring children from a previous marriage.

Adoptive Family

Parent/parents legally adopt a child/children. It is permanent.

Foster Family

Parents look after a child or children on a temporary basis. Children who may or may not have their own families live in other people's houses for a long or short period of time. They may return home at some stage.

The nature and make up of the family has changed considerably and attitudes to the traditional family structure vary.

The traditional British family consisted of a man and woman marrying, producing children and living near to the remainder of the family. This traditional family structure is known as the extended family.

⊃ Extended Family

This family contributed to the structure of the British society. The family unit lived in one house and very often the grandparents, aunts, uncles, cousins, etc., lived with the family, or close by.

⊃ Reasons for the Extended Family

◆ During the early part of the 1900s women had large families due to a lack of **contraception** and it was common to have nine or ten children.

Not all of the children survived, however, due to poor sanitation, housing, nutrition, health and medical care.

◆ The family was often poor and the couple could not afford to get married and live in a separate house, so they started married life living in their parents' home.

◆ Grandparents, if well enough, were able to help out with childcare, while the parents worked.

◆ Grandparents needed to be looked after and their children did this. The grandchildren were also expected to help out and look after their grandparents.

Today, this situation has changed and there has been a gradual move away from the extended family (see page 55) to the nuclear family (see the chart below).

(see page 55)

Key Words

Contraception ways of preventing pregnancy

Advantages	Disadvantages
• Family members can help out and look after each other.	• The family knows all your business.
• There is always someone available to look after the children when an emergency arises.	• Advice from interfering grandparents or parents may be given when not requested (This is how you should do it…).
• Advice is close to hand.	• There may be too many visitors in the home/lack of independence.
• There is close family bonding.	• There may be disagreements about how to bring up a child.
• The family members can enjoy each other's company.	
• The children can easily see if their parents are sick, or in need of assistance.	
• Grandparents see the grandchildren growing up.	
• Children have cousins to play with.	

There is evidence to suggest that extended families are not the norm. However, Pakistani and Bangladeshi families contain the highest number of dependent children, and usually have grandparents living with them. They also represent the smallest group of people living on their own. It is much more common for this ethnic group to have three generations living within the home. They also take greater responsibility for looking after the grandparents and elderly relatives.

Figure 1.2 An extended family today

⊃ The Nuclear Family

The nuclear family is the most common in British society. It is a smaller unit than the extended family, consisting of the parents and their children. This family may live a long distance from the other relatives and this may be desirable or not.

There are advantages and disadvantages to being in a nuclear family:

Advantages	Disadvantages
• There is no interference from other family members.	• Being away from parents and close family.
• The parents can make their own childcare provision.	• May miss family and close geographical location.
• The family can visit relatives when they choose to.	• Parents, grandparents and children will miss out on a close relationship (it will require more effort).
• Improved communication with telephones, mobile phones, e-mail, etc., so it is easy to keep in touch.	• Family members can't look after the children or help out the family in times of crisis.
• Improved transportation makes it easier to visit the family.	• Childcare will have to be paid for, i.e. childminder/nursery.
• Smaller family units/houses are more affordable.	• May be difficult to get to the family in times of crisis.

There are many reasons for the increase in nuclear families.

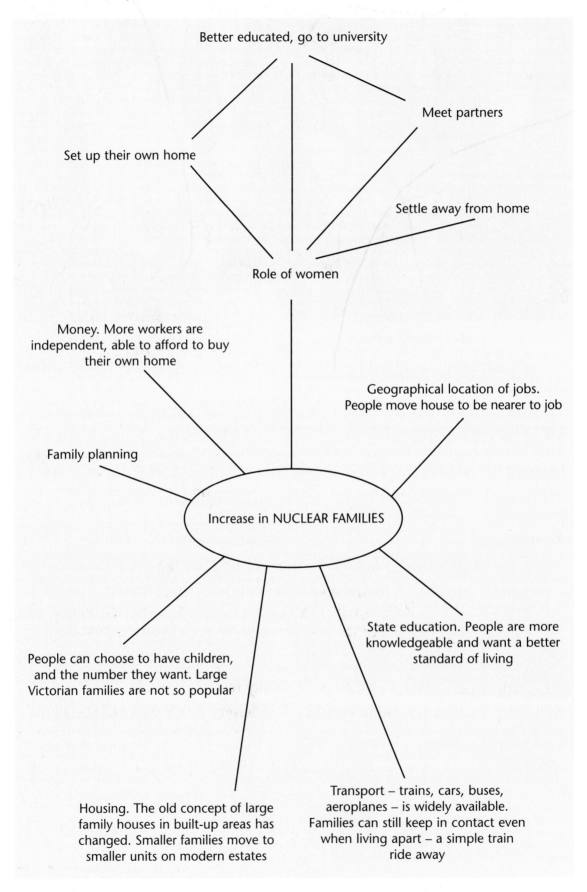

Better educated, go to university

Meet partners

Set up their own home

Settle away from home

Role of women

Money. More workers are independent, able to afford to buy their own home

Geographical location of jobs. People move house to be nearer to job

Family planning

Increase in NUCLEAR FAMILIES

State education. People are more knowledgeable and want a better standard of living

People can choose to have children, and the number they want. Large Victorian families are not so popular

Housing. The old concept of large family houses in built-up areas has changed. Smaller families move to smaller units on modern estates

Transport – trains, cars, buses, aeroplanes – is widely available. Families can still keep in contact even when living apart – a simple train ride away

Figure 1.3 A nuclear family

⊃ Step Families

Step families (or reconstituted families) are where lone parents, male or female, with or without children, join together and form a new partnership. This new partnership may result in:

◆ marriage
◆ co-habitation (living together)
◆ some dependent children
◆ more children

Step families bring with them very different issues for children from previous relationships. This will largely depend on the age of children, how many there are, size of the family home and many other factors.

Some issues:

◆ Younger children may adapt more easily to living with another family.
◆ Jealousy may be evident among the children, particularly if they are of a similar age.

◆ There may be confusion with roles – who is the disciplinarian? The birth parent or step parent?

◆ There may be animosity towards the step parent.

Some positive aspects:

◆ The family may have a better quality of life.

◆ There may be more money coming into the home if both partners are working.

◆ Parents have an adult relationship.

◆ There may be a new house, new start.

◆ Children will have a male and female role model.

Remember

It is estimated that lone mothers will remarry within five years. One in ten children lives with step parents.

⊃ One-Parent Families

One of the most significant changes in the family structure is that of the single parent household. The evidence is clear that one-parent families have more than trebled since 1961. Most single parents are mothers. (See table.)

% of lone parent households	
1961	3%
1998/99	11%

Source: Social Trends

	1972	1981	1991-92	Percentages 1998-99
Couple families				
1 child	16	18	17	15
2 children	35	41	37	36
3 or more children	41	29	28	26
Lone mother families				
1 child	2	3	5	6
2 children	2	4	7	8
3 or more children	2	3	6	7
Lone father families				
1 child	–	1	–	1
2 or more children	1	1	1	1
All dependent children	100	100	100	100

Figure 1.4 This table show the percent of dependent children living in different family types in Great Britain

Source: General Household Survey, Office for National Statistics: Social Trends 2000.

However, many people who are divorced and live alone often remarry creating a step family.

People become single parents because:

◆ they become widowed (one of the partners dies)

◆ they get divorced

◆ they separate from their partner

◆ the parent has never married and remains single after the child is born

◆ a parent may be imprisoned, or in a care home due to ill health

⊃ Lone Parents

Advantages	Disadvantages
• It may be better to be out of an unhappy relationship. The children will be less traumatised.	• The child will be lacking a father/mother figure and may not have a balanced viewpoint.
• The parent may be happier and more relaxed on their own.	• The children may grow up with problems associated with having one parent.
• The parent may find a new partner.	• One parent will find it considerably harder to support the family financially, emotionally and physically.
• The parent may be in a good position financially.	• The state is supporting one-parent families who find it difficult to cope.
• The atmosphere at home may be happier.	• The other parent is not readily available to share worries (although they may be contacted by telephone).
• The parent remains independent.	

There has been much debate about the effect single parents have had on the family.

Figure 1.5 A single parent family

⊃ ROLES WITHIN THE FAMILY

Figure 1.6 In the 1900s most women got married so they had someone to look after them

This section will identify the roles within the family, in particular the role of homes in British society and how this has changed during the last century.

During the early 1900s it was expected that working-class women would carry out domestic duties in the home, have children and care for them.

The wealthy women led a much more comfortable lifestyle. They were not expected to work. They entertained their husbands with musical recitals and passed the time of day with activities such as embroidery.

⊃ The Role of Women

The role of women now is very different from that of a century ago. There are many reasons for this:

◆ Acts of Parliament have been passed to give women (and men) legal rights.

◆ There is equal opportunity of education for both girls and boys.

◆ Society's attitudes towards women at work have changed.

◆ Nursery care provision and child minding have improved.

◆ Maternity leave and career breaks allow women to take time out with their families.

◆ Men's perceptions of women at work have changed.

◆ Working women have financial independence.

◆ Technological equipment has eased the burden on domestic chores, freeing time from the home.

◆ Industry and commerce recognises the valuable contribution of women.

◆ Food industry has responded to the changing family lifestyle with many convenience foods and products to make meal preparation easier.

◆ Women now have greater freedom.

Traditional Family Roles

Men:
- Were the breadwinners and took charge
- Controlled the money
- Spent time in the pub and other male societies, which excluded women
- Were often violent to women and children
- Were powerful and liked to be in charge and control the children.

Women:
- Provided many children
- Looked after the home and cared for the children
- Cooked, cleaned, washed and sewed for the family
- Worked in menial jobs to support the home, possibly taking in washing and ironing

Children:
- Children were sent out to work to bring in extra money
- Children were seen and not heard
- Boys were encouraged to be educated
- Girls were often allowed to stay at home to help their mothers rather than go to school. This created deep bonds between mothers and daughters.

Middle class women had a different life. They were not expected to work and often had help in the home like a nanny and cleaner.

When discussing roles of the family within the British Society there will be other factors affecting these roles:

    1. Status 2. Class 3. Money
    4. Attitudes 5. Traditions 6. Education

Modern Family Roles
- Husband and wife share the housework and childcare.
- They share leisure activities, and go out together.
- The family has meals out (at places geared to this).
- Both parties may be working, allowing luxuries such as two cars and holidays abroad.
- Partners operate independent roles alongside shared ones.
- Home improvement is completed by both partners.
- Children receive equal opportunity for education.
- Father seen as less authorative and a warmer, closer relationship has developed.
- Children's views may be listened to.
- Many labour-saving devices in the home to allow for more leisure time for all the family.
- Parents on the whole are more educated and therefore have different standards and expectations in the home.
- Children are expected to help out in the home.

⊃ 'MILLENNIUM' FAMILY IN BRITISH SOCIETY

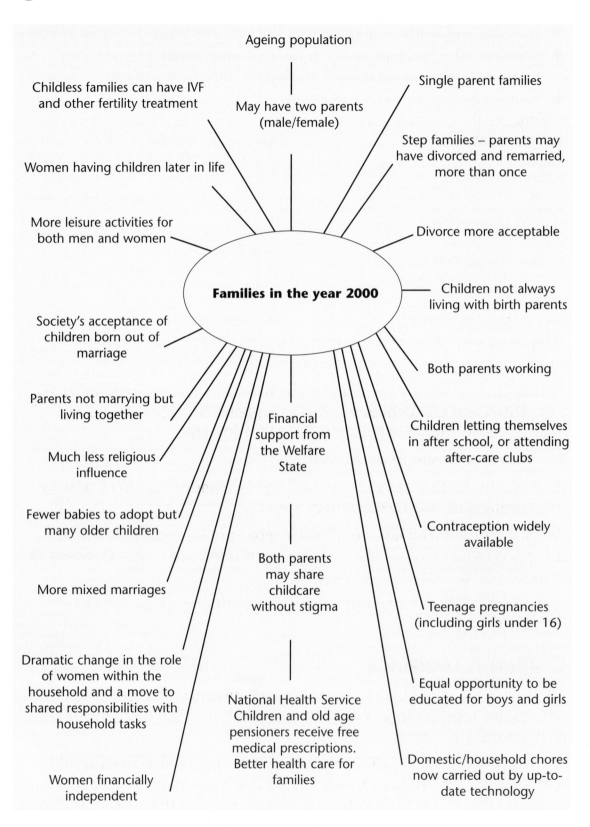

Ageing population

Childless families can have IVF and other fertility treatment

May have two parents (male/female)

Single parent families

Step families – parents may have divorced and remarried, more than once

Women having children later in life

More leisure activities for both men and women

Divorce more acceptable

Families in the year 2000

Children not always living with birth parents

Society's acceptance of children born out of marriage

Both parents working

Parents not marrying but living together

Financial support from the Welfare State

Children letting themselves in after school, or attending after-care clubs

Much less religious influence

Fewer babies to adopt but many older children

Contraception widely available

More mixed marriages

Both parents may share childcare without stigma

Teenage pregnancies (including girls under 16)

Dramatic change in the role of women within the household and a move to shared responsibilities with household tasks

Equal opportunity to be educated for boys and girls

National Health Service Children and old age pensioners receive free medical prescriptions. Better health care for families

Women financially independent

Domestic/household chores now carried out by up-to-date technology

AGEING POPULATION

The ageing population describes a situation where people are living longer and have an average life expectancy of well over 70 years (see table). Many people are not only experiencing grandchildren, but great-grandchildren as well.

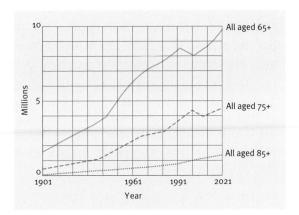

Figure 1.7 The elderly population: past, present and future

Reversing Roles

Parents look after and care for their children when they are young. They often help their children to start a home, babysit, lend money and help decorate as they enter retirement age.

As they become elderly the emphasis switches to their children (more often a daughter) and grandchildren offering support. The support may be financial, help with cleaning, going out on trips, etc.

The roles above seem to keep reversing.

However, in the times of the extended family grandparents lived near to their family and looking after them was easier.

Today there are many families who are separated by great distances and support is harder to give. Communication is improved with telephones to keep in regular contact.

In the year 2000 we have seen a massive growth of nursing homes for the elderly.

WHAT IS MARRIAGE?

Marriage is a legally-binding commitment between a man and woman who wish to live together in a permanent relationship. It can be a religious or civil service.

At the beginning of the 1900s it was expected that most women would marry. People who did not marry were called spinsters (women) and bachelors (men). For various reasons women felt that they had little choice over many issues (see section on Role of Women) and that marriage was a 'security ticket'.

The traditional view of marriage in Britain was to find a suitable match for a couple, the joining together of two families. This is a little like the Asian culture of arranged marriages in Britain where a suitable man is found for the woman. The families meet and if accepted the marriage will go ahead and the love will happen as they grow in their relationship. People also tended to marry others of equal social status.

Today, however, some people have a romantic view of marriage and expect all the trimmings and a 'good party'. Some marriages are still based on religious beliefs, although many people consider love to be the most important factor.

Until the early part of the 1970s society still considered that marriage was the expected route for couples and it was not very common for people to have lived together (co-habited) before marriage as a trial. Living together without getting married was considered 'sinful' or wrong and frowned on particularly by the older generation and those people with religious and moral beliefs.

Despite the number of people living together today, marriage remains the usual partnership between men and women. However, this includes people who remarry as well as their first marriage (see Figure 1.8).

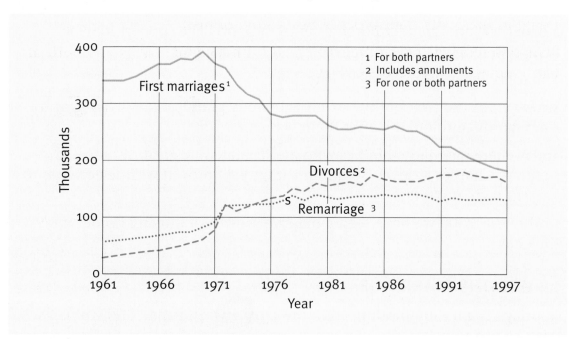

Figure 1.8 Marriages and divorces in the UK

Source: Social Trends 2000

⊃ DIVORCE

Divorce is where the legal marriage between a man and a woman ends. This is carried out in a court of law and is much easier to obtain than it was before 1971.

Divorce was not common during the early 1900s and adultery (a sexual relationship with another partner) was the only grounds for divorce until 1938.

The graph on page 14 shows the sharp rise in the number of divorces after the 1971 Divorce Act and again after 1984, when The Matrimonial and Family Proceedings Act enabled couples to get divorced within one year, as opposed to three years.

In 1997 seven out of ten divorces were awarded to women on the grounds of unreasonable behaviour. The most common reason for men divorcing their wives in 1997 was adultery.

One in three marriages during the 1980s ended in a divorce. Today the divorce rate has levelled out, because there are fewer people getting married and therefore fewer people to get divorced.

During the last 20 years there is much evidence to suggest that children are living in many different types of home environment.

A high percentage of children are living with a couple but one or both of the couples are divorced. See Figure 1.9.

England & Wales				Thousands
	1971	1981	1991	1998
Under 5	21	40	53	40
Aged 5-10	41	68	68	68
Aged 11-15	21	52	40	43
All aged under 16	82	159	161	150
All couples divorcing	74	146	159	145

Figure 1.9 Children in families of divorced couples: by age of child

Source: Office for National Statistics

The Effects of Divorce on Children

All children will be affected by divorce, some will be able to deal with it better than others. This will depend on:

◆ the age of the child (younger children seem to be more adaptable than teenagers)

◆ how the child has been treated

◆ the reasons for the divorce

The list below highlights some of the feelings children can have about divorce:

◆ Divorce may be a relief to the children if parents have been constantly arguing, violent or hurting one another.

◆ Alternatively, it may make the children feel very insecure.

◆ The family may be struggling financially if one parent has been left alone.

◆ The children may be missing the parent that has gone.

◆ Seeing the parent they are living with very upset can also upset the children.

◆ The children may have had to move out of their home.

◆ The children may have definite views on marriage from their own personal experiences.

◆ It may cause difficulties for the children having only one parent as a role model.

◆ The children may get caught up in custody battles, which may cause them great emotional stress.

LIVING TOGETHER

Co-habitation means living together and today there are many more people living together before marriage, or instead of marriage.

The views and attitudes of society towards people living together has changed. The 1960s and 1970s saw many changes and influences giving people (particularly women) greater sexual freedom with more easily accessible contraception and the **legalisation** of abortions.

Evidence suggests that the only two per cent of people in the late 1960s lived together before their

Great Britain		Percentages
	Males	Females
16-19	1	8
20-24	18	27
25-29	39	39
30-34	44	35
35-39	36	29
40-44	31	26
45-49	28	16
50-54	17	16
55-59	18	12
All non-married (aged 16 to 59)	26	25

Figure 1.10 Cohabitation

Source: Social Trends 2000

marriage. During the 1990s this trend totally reversed and most people lived together before marriage.

It is expected that the trend to live together, whether it results in marriage or not, will continue to rise.

Possible negative effects of the breakdown of 'The Family'

◆ Single parents may not get support from another adult.

◆ The parent who remains with the children becomes exhausted, sometimes 'hitting out' at a child when they are at 'cracking point'.

◆ Children may accept this family type as the 'norm' and then choose a single-parent option for themselves, e.g. 'My mum had a baby at 16, got a flat and managed on state benefits and help from her own Mum'.

◆ There may be a lack of discipline within the household, with too much to do and not enough time to spend with the children.

◆ It may be more difficult or not financially viable to work as a single parent.

◆ There is no one to look after the elderly who are living longer, and more private nursing homes are emerging (draining pensioners' life savings).

◆ Children may not ever sit down together to eat a healthy meal around a table. The art of conversation and socialising is an important part of development.

◆ One wage coming into a house as opposed to two could lead to financial problems, and perhaps burden on the Welfare State.

◆ Step families may create their own problems, requiring large accommodation when two sets of children join together. If they are of a similar age, much rivalry could take place between the children, creating a lack of harmony within the household.

◆ There is no extended family to support isolated nuclear families.

⊃ CULTURAL VARIATIONS

The family in Britain today is not as straightforward as it was during the first half of the twentieth century. After the Second World War the British Government actively encouraged a cheap labour force to come over to this country from places such as India, Pakistan and the West Indies. After the war there was a shortage of people required to work in industry and there was a surge in the number of immigrants (people who moved from another country to live in Britain) who came to this country. This trend continues today.

These people sometimes came from different cultural backgrounds and brought different dimensions to family life in Britain.

⤵ What is a culture?

A culture is a set of norms, beliefs and values that belong to a group, which make them different from another. It is also acceptable within a given culture to follow certain traditions.

Traditions are certain patterns of behaviour that you carry out within the family because your family has always 'done it that way'.

For example, in your household a turkey may be roasted and eaten on Christmas Day as a celebration of the Christian religion and the birth of Jesus. For some families who are not Christian, for example Muslim, celebrating Christmas will have little meaning since they do not celebrate the birth of Jesus.

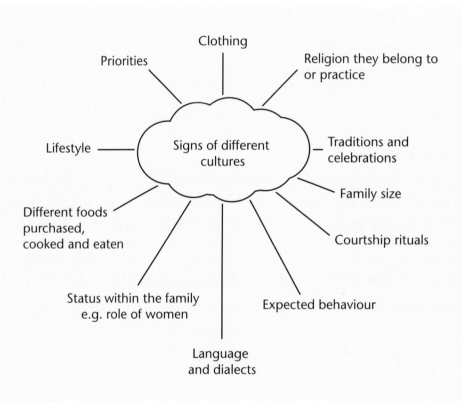

Signs of different cultures

- Clothing
- Priorities
- Religion they belong to or practice
- Lifestyle
- Traditions and celebrations
- Family size
- Different foods purchased, cooked and eaten
- Courtship rituals
- Status within the family e.g. role of women
- Expected behaviour
- Language and dialects

Multicultural society

Britain is a multicultural society. This is particularly evident in certain pockets of the UK. For example, there are large Asian communities in cities such as London, Manchester, Blackburn and Middlesbrough.

Whilst it may appear within these cities that there are large numbers of Asian people living in Britain, in fact they are a minority (that is, a very small percentage of the total population in Britain).

What actually distinguishes these groups of people is the colour of their skin. However, there are many groups, such as the Italians who have settled in this country but are not so easy to see as being different.

Sociologists refer to these minority groups of people whose culture is different from the culture of the people living in the dominant society as **ethnic groups** or **ethnic minorities**.

When ethnic groups join another culture they have to mix within the culture of that country, e.g. go to school. This can very often lead to a situation where the children are 'between two cultures'. For example, being westernised during the day at school and returning home to a different language and culture after school.

Discrimination

To discriminate is to make a difference between things. For example, to choose not to give a person a job simply because of their skin, colour, sex, age etc. There are laws to protect the people living in the British society from this discrimination.

Acts and Milestones that have given Women Greater Power and Equality

 # Time Line

1970 *Equal Pay Act* equal pay for equal work – in reality this did not always happen

1974 *Sex Discrimination Act* it became illegal to **discriminate** in the UK in jobs, housing, training and provision of goods and services. Discrimination against women was against the law

1975 *Equal Opportunity Commission* set up to ensure that the Equal Pay Act and the Sex Discrimination Act were put into practice

Employment Protection Act protected women and ensured they were given maternity leave and pay

1976 *The Commission for Racial Equality* made it illegal to discriminate on grounds of race

1976 *Domestic Violence Act* gave greater legal protection to women suffering violence in the home.

ADOPTION AND FOSTERING (THE ALTERNATIVE FAMILY)

This section will look at and examine the issues surrounding adoption and fostering

Children who cannot live with their own family may have to find an alternative family. This could be either short-term or permanent. There are two ways of finding such a family:

◆ adoption
◆ fostering

Adoption

What is Adoption?

◆ Adoption is a legal procedure where all the responsibilities of the child's 'birth parents' are transferred to the adopters.
◆ It provides a permanent new family for children whose own parents can't bring them up.
◆ Once a child is adopted all legal ties with the birth parents are broken.
◆ The child/children usually take the name of the new family.
◆ Adoption can be changed back only in rare or exceptional circumstances.

Figure 1.11 A family with an adopted child

⊃ Who Can Be Adopted?

Many people may think that only babies are available to adopt. However, this is not the case today. In fact, there are very few babies available. 'In 1995 only 322 children below the age of one were adopted.'

There is a variety of reasons which explain this low number of babies available for adoption:

◆ Before the contraceptive pill was introduced into Britain in 1961 there were fewer reliable alternative methods of contraception available for women. As a result unplanned and unwanted babies were born and placed for adoption.

◆ Women today have more choice with regard to contraception. It is widely available to both sexes through family planning centres and Brook Advisory Services and as a result there are fewer unplanned babies available to adopt.

◆ **Abortion** is legal and more easily available.

◆ Attitudes towards single parents have changed, and the State has made it easier for one-parent families to survive by promoting support through the Welfare State, such as the single parent allowance.

Despite this there are many older children available for adoption, including children with disabilities, and ethnic minorities (who need the same background). In addition, there are brothers and sisters who need to stay together rather than be split up.

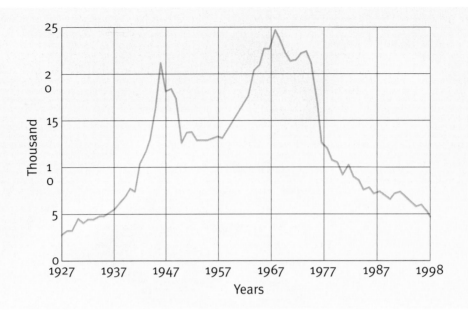

Figure 1.12 Children Adopted In England and Wales To 1998 (Crown Copyright 2000)

Source: Social Trends 30 (2000)

Adopters

Couples who wish to adopt may do so for a variety of reasons.

◆ They may be unable to have a child naturally for medical or health reasons.

◆ They may have had numerous failed attempts at IVF treatment and can no longer afford or wish to carry on with this route.

◆ They may have one or more children of their own and feel their family is incomplete. Perhaps for medical and emotional reasons they cannot have another child naturally.

◆ A couple or family may wish to give a home to a child who has no parents.

◆ A couple may wish to adopt children from a previous marriage (this is not as simple as it seems because it severs the child's legal links with their other birth parent and the wider family).

The Baby Issue

Since there are very few babies for adoption the adoption agencies and social services can be rather selective in their choice of parents and often insist on the following:

◆ The upper age limit of the couple is between 35 to 40 years.
◆ The couple should have been married for at least three years.
◆ Some agencies will not accept people who have been divorced.

⟁ Children with Special Needs and Older Children

There are many children who are older or with special needs and it is much easier for older or single people to adopt one or more of these children. This is because the adoption agencies' view is:

◆ Older parents have more experience.
◆ Single parents may have more time.
◆ Where a loving family already exists it will provide stability and a role model for the children.

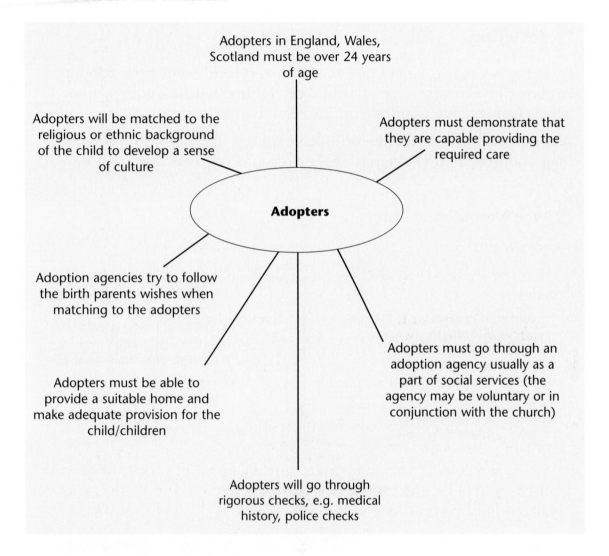

Adopters in England, Wales, Scotland must be over 24 years of age

Adopters will be matched to the religious or ethnic background of the child to develop a sense of culture

Adopters must demonstrate that they are capable providing the required care

Adopters

Adoption agencies try to follow the birth parents wishes when matching to the adopters

Adopters must go through an adoption agency usually as a part of social services (the agency may be voluntary or in conjunction with the church)

Adopters must be able to provide a suitable home and make adequate provision for the child/children

Adopters will go through rigorous checks, e.g. medical history, police checks

⟁ Advantages of adoption

◆ It gives the adopters a family and such joy.
◆ It enables children without stability and family to enjoy a good home life.
◆ It provides opportunities for children who may never have had the chance to experience them.
◆ It ensures children are not sent from one children's home to another.

◆ It gives the children a sense of real belonging.

◆ There is less of a burden on the state resources.

Rights of the Child

In 1975 the Children's Act gave rights to the adopted child. This Act ensured that at the age of 18 the child could see the birth certificate of the mother, giving her name, occupation, date of birth and address at the time of the birth. If details of the father are available, then this information may also be given.

Fostering

Fostering is not permanent and that is how it is different from adoption. Fostering involves the care of a child or children within another home, when the birth parent or parents are unable to look after them.

When a child is fostered the birth parents keep their responsibilities for their children, and will help to make decisions for them while they are in foster care.

Who Needs Foster Care?

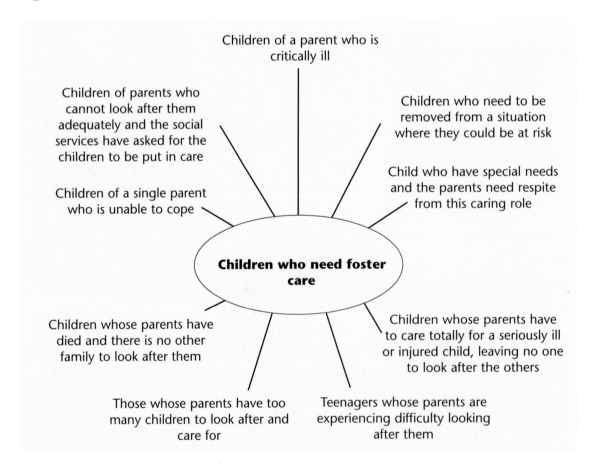

Figure 1.13 A respite carer

Types of Fostering

Fostering can be long- or short-term depending on the individual family circumstances.

◆ Short-term is usually about three months.
◆ Long-term could be for weeks, months or years.

Short-term Fostering

Short-term fostering is used when the parent/parents are unable to cope with their children for only a few weeks. An example would be if the mother has had a serious operation from which she will make a good recovery but has no family or friends who can help out during this time. As soon as she is fit again, she will be able to look after her children.

Advantages of short-term fostering

◆ Children can visit their parent/parents.
◆ The children know it is only a temporary measure.
◆ It enables the family to remain together in the long-term, but gives parents time to get over illness, breakdown, or exhaustion from caring for a child with special needs, for example.
◆ The birth parents/parents know that their children are in safe hands.

Long-term Fostering

Long-term fostering may occur with children whose birth parents do not wish them to be adopted but who are unable to cope with them on a regular basis. It could be a situation where a short-term fostering placement has extended into a long-term placement, initially hoping to integrate the children back with their parents. Sometimes the children may not be allowed to return to their parents if the parents are unfit to look after them.

Advantages of long-term fostering

◆ The children have stability with one family by not being placed in several different homes.

◆ They can have contact with their birth parent/parents, therefore they know where they have come from and who their parents are, and the curiosity that can exist with adoption does not always happen.

◆ A good home with opportunities may enable children who would otherwise not have had these chances to succeed and do well within a different environment.

◆ It provides a stable environment until the children are of an age that they can make decisions themselves.

◆ Some financial assistance may be given.

Fostering can be carried out by couples who are married or living together, and single parents.

However, people with a criminal record would not be allowed to foster.

⊃ Disadvantages of Fostering

Short-term and long-term

◆ If children have come from a stable background and there is no one else to look after them they may be very homesick.

◆ Even if the situation is not good at home, the children may be very unhappy to be away from their parents.

◆ There are varying types of foster homes and some are more desirable than others.

◆ Children are suddenly thrown into a situation with strangers and may have difficulty settling.

◆ Other children from the foster home may have difficulty with the foster children, particularly if, for example, a streetwise teenager comes into the home and influences the habits of a sheltered child.

◆ Children may have to move on if the fostering arrangement is not working. This could affect the stability of the children.

◆ Children in foster homes may experience a better standard of living then they are used to. When it is time to leave, they may have difficulty adjusting to their own home.

◆ The age gap of the foster parents in relation to the children needs to be considered. For example, if a foster mother is 21 years old and a teenage child aged 15 comes into the house, it could create problems.

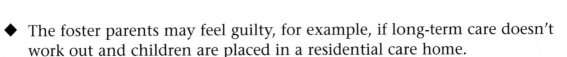

- The foster parents may feel guilty, for example, if long-term care doesn't work out and children are placed in a residential care home.
- There may be deep attachment between foster children and foster parents, particularly those who have been long-term fostered. If children choose to return to their parents (blood ties are very strong) this could be hurtful to the foster parents.

Foster parents need not live in a large house or have a large income. Foster parents, unlike adoptive parents, may have some financial assistance from the state.

Who can be a Foster Carer?

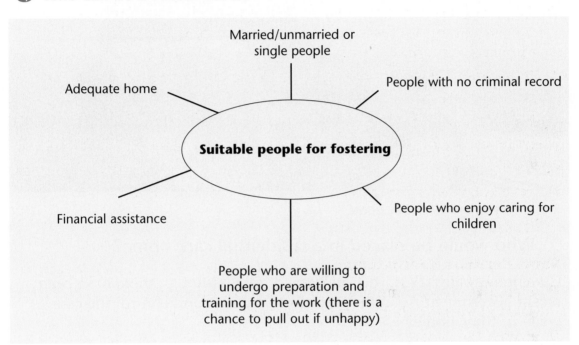

Married/unmarried or single people

People with no criminal record

Adequate home

Suitable people for fostering

People who enjoy caring for children

Financial assistance

People who are willing to undergo preparation and training for the work (there is a chance to pull out if unhappy)

Remember

Fostering can be a most rewarding experience, its main aim being to support the family in need and to place that child back with its family successfully, not to replace the child's family.

RESIDENTIAL CARE HOMES

Residential care homes are usually run by Social Services and are situated all over the country. The purpose of these homes is to look after children who are unable to remain with the birth family.

- Children who have been orphaned (their parents have died)
- Children who have problems such as drug or alcohol dependency, whose parents are unable to cope with them

◆ Children whose parents cannot control them

◆ Children who are neglected by their parents

◆ Children who are at risk from abuse in the family home, e.g. physical, sexual or emotional abuse

Figure 1.14 A residential care home

⟳ Who would be placed in a residential care home?

Care homes can vary in their delivery of care, although there have been recent government recommendations to regulate and control the care given in these homes.

Advantages

◆ Children are looked after by professionals.

◆ It provides an adequate shelter with and food and basic essentials.

◆ It may allow a cooling-off period for a child from a home environment.

◆ It provides immediate care for a child who may have been abused.

Disadvantages

◆ Children may be very unhappy away from the family.

◆ The children do not have a home environment.

◆ There are many shared facilities.

◆ It may lack the privacy of the children's own home.

◆ There are strict regulations.

◆ Children may miss the physical bonding with their parents.

Questions

Question 1

a What is a family?

b Define the following family types
   i extended
   ii one-parent
   iii nuclear
   iv step

c Describe six present day trends within the UK family lifestyle.

d Design a chart to list some of the advantages and disadvantages of different family types.

e Explain possible reasons for the increase towards a nuclear family type.

Question 2

a Suggest two events which could result in a child being brought up by one-parent.

b Identify two ways in which the family life of children, in a single parent family may differ from that of children with two parents.

c What effect may it have on the children of two families who join together and form a step-family?

Question 3

a Design a chart that depicts the changes in the role of women during the early 1900's and compare this to the role of women today.

b Describe how the father's role may have changed within the family household today.

c How have women gained greater equality of opportunity?

Question 4

Using a spray diagram, design a chart of your own which reflects family life today in British Society.

Question 5

a What does the ageing population mean?

b i Describe the shift towards the increased number of nuclear family

  ii What role do many grandparents carry out today?

c What are the advantages and disadvantages of grandparents taking on the role of carers for their grandchildren?

Question 6

a Explain briefly what is marriage.

b Why is there a trend for people to marry at a slightly older age?

Question 7

a What is divorce?

b List some of the effects divorce may have on children from those families.

c List five reasons for the increased number of divorces in our society.

Question 8

a What does the term 'co-habitation' mean?

b During the 1960s a very small percentage of people lived together before marriage, in today's society most people live together before marriage. Why has this changed?

Question 9

a Give four negative effects of the breakdown of the traditional family.

Questions continued

Question 10

a Define the terms

   i   adoption

   ii fostering.

b Explain why there are few babies available for adoption today.

c Give four important facts about the people who would be able to adopt.

d What is the main aim of fostering?

e Who needs to be fostered?

f Explain the difference between long and short term fostering.

g List four advantages and disadvantages of fostering.

Question 11

a What is a residential care home?

b Which children may be placed in a residential care home?

c Give two advantages and disadvantages of a child being placed in a residential care home.

Question 12

a Define the following terms

   i   culture

   ii tradition

b Identify and list six signs of cultural differences.

c What do you understand by the phrase 'a multicultural society'?

d What is an ethnic group?

e i What is discrimination?

   ii Give an example of discrimination and how people in Britain are protected from this.

Extension Questions

Interview parents, grandparents and family about their family life; roles within the family and how they have changed from their childhood. Try to get a range of age groups and find out what opportunities they had e.g. to go to school, university, get a job, pursue a career etc.

Write a short report and present your findings to the group.

⟳ FAMILY WORDSEARCH

N	O	I	T	P	O	D	A	E	I	R	K	C	Y	J
O	F	O	Y	T	I	R	U	C	E	S	Q	S	T	U
I	M	O	X	Q	E	M	M	R	X	B	V	X	M	H
T	A	M	S	M	Y	T	J	O	T	S	H	Z	Q	J
A	R	E	I	T	G	T	S	V	E	W	J	K	N	B
S	R	A	S	A	E	O	Q	I	N	B	T	Q	Z	I
I	I	G	J	N	P	R	P	D	D	J	P	P	D	G
L	A	I	T	N	E	D	I	S	E	R	I	I	D	P
A	G	N	L	B	V	T	O	N	D	A	B	C	I	E
I	E	H	M	I	O	L	H	Y	G	E	U	V	Y	N
C	E	Y	L	E	L	F	A	M	I	L	Y	J	H	R
O	M	K	I	V	U	O	M	A	T	C	T	I	A	K
S	B	D	U	F	S	H	M	U	X	U	O	I	G	R
G	L	E	L	Z	Z	J	R	H	N	N	I	D	C	T
O	G	P	X	D	L	E	G	O	X	J	U	P	V	Y

Adoption	Love
Culture	Marriage
Divorce	Nuclear
Extended	Residential
Family	Security
Fostering	Socialisation

2

Planning a Family

In this section we will consider various factors that may influence the planning of children within the family

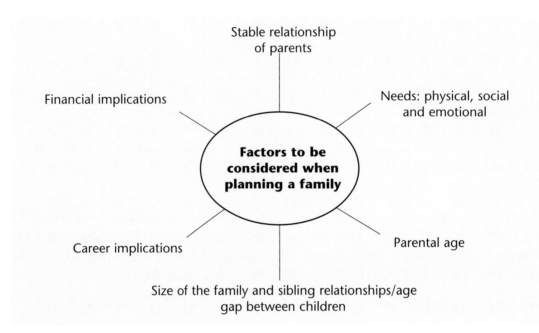

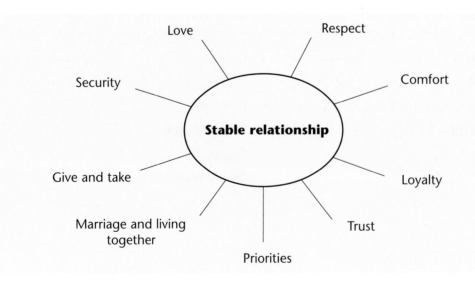

⊃ FACTORS TO BE CONSIDERED WHEN PLANNING A FAMILY

When planning to bring a new life into the world it is important that the baby is 'wanted'. However, it is also important to recognise that many children are not planned but their parents are still able to bring them up well.

Having a baby to hold really is a miracle of life and the birth of a baby can be one of the most glorious experiences of the parents' lives. However, it will bring about much exhaustion, lack of freedom and time for a partner as this little human being is totally dependent on the parents. This overwhelming sense of responsibility can be quite terrifying, yet some parents take it in their stride.

⊃ A STABLE RELATIONSHIP

A stable relationship between the partners is most important when bringing a child into the world. The word stable suggests that the relationship is steady, secure and happy. It is a relationship based on love, trust, caring for and sharing with one another. The relationship allows the couple to talk openly about any worries, concerns and thoughts while preparing for the role of parenthood.

In a loving, caring relationship, it is important that both partners consider what each other would like and respect each other's feelings. If one partner desperately wants children and the other doesn't, it could lead to a difficult time where the parents may end up resenting one another.

Some people consider bringing a child into the world for the wrong reasons:

◆ to improve a faltering relationship
◆ because the mother may feel her body clock will run out
◆ grandparents hinting they are waiting for the big day
◆ to escape a difficult situation at work
◆ pressure from friends to have a baby
◆ romantic notion about 'cute' babies

It is important to have the baby for the right reasons.

⊃ CHANGE IN LIFESTYLE

Many parents insist that a baby is not going to change their lifestyle, although evidence suggests that it does.

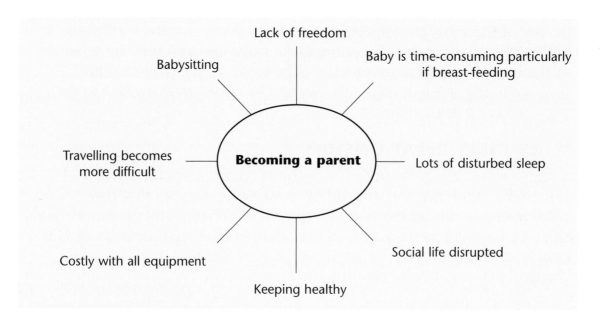

⊃ PARENTAL AGE

There have been various trends which suggest that women used to marry younger and have a family in their early twenties. Today this has changed and the average age of women having babies is 27. There is also a trend for women to have their babies at an older age – between 35 and 39 years of age.

Possible reasons for this trend for women to have their first children in their thirties may be:

◆ they get married later
◆ they have attended further education courses
◆ they have pursued a career
◆ they have been achieving financial security
◆ contraception has given them freedom of choice

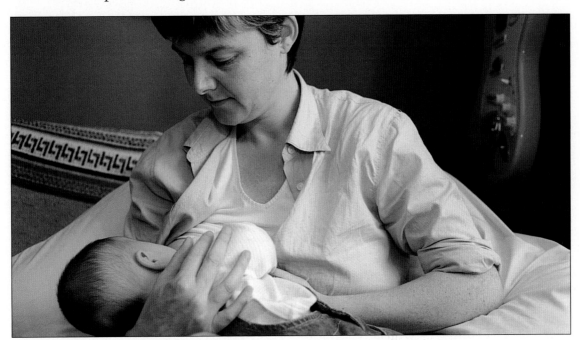

Figure 2.1 An older first-time mother

Dr Neil Sebrie from the Harris Birthright Centre for Foetal Medicine at Kings College Hospital, London, said:

Forty or fifty years ago if you were having a baby in your forties it often meant that you were from a disadvantaged background and were having your seventh or eighth child, which was why you were more likely to be at risk. Today, however, mothers in their late thirties are more likely to have planned their pregnancy, be in a stable relationship and be socially and financially secure. (1996)

Whatever the age of the parent it is a very responsible decision to bring a child into the world and one that can be underestimated.

Very often there is a romantic association with having a cute little baby and the pleasure of decorating a nursery. The fact is that having a child is a huge responsibility: it is tiring, time consuming, encroaches on your freedom and one day this baby will grow into a teenager.

Figure 2.2 Fertility rates: by age of mother at childbirth in the UK

Live births per 1,000 women						
	1961	1971	1981	1991	1997	1998
Under 20	37	50	28	33	30	31
20–24	173	154	107	89	75	74
25–29	178	155	130	120	105	102
30–34	106	79	70	87	89	90
35–39	51	34	22	32	39	40
40 and over	16	9	5	5	7	8
All ages[3]	91	84	62	64	60	59

[1] Live births to women aged under 20 per 1,000 women aged 15 to 19 at last birthday.

[2] Live births to women aged 40 and over per 1,000 women aged 40 to 44.

[3] Total live births per 1,000 women aged 15 to 44.

Source: Office for National Statistics: General Register Office for Scotland; Northern Ireland Statistics and Research Agency.
Source: Social Trends 2000

Remember

Becoming a parent is for **life**

⊃ The Mother

The mother's age is of concern when planning a child because the quality of the mother's eggs depletes as she gets older as does her ability to conceive.

Once a woman has passed through the **menopause** (her reproductive cycle stops) she is unable to have any more children.

It is a personal choice at what age a mother would choose to conceive a child with her partner. It will also depend on their personal circumstances.

⊃ The Father

The father can continue to produce sperm until he dies and provided he is capable of sexual intercourse he can father a child into old age. While one could argue that this may not be fair on the child who will have an elderly father, it is physically possible.

Being a younger parent

Advantages	Disadvantages
• The parents may be fitter and healthier.	• The parents may be less secure financially.
• Their life expectation is greater.	• They may not have the confidence to look after a young family.
• The mother's body may recover more quickly.	• They may resent not having a career which brings financial security.
• The parents will have more energy and be less tired.	• Both parents may feel too young to be stuck at home and may not have the money to go out socialising like they used to.
• The mother may have the baby before a career.	• They may not feel ready for the responsibility of a young family.
• She will be young enough to pursue qualifications and career after having a family.	• They may not feel secure and settled in the relationship.
• The grandparents may be young enough to look after and enjoy the grandchildren, to help with care, etc.	• They may not have had time to get their home organised and secure.
• There is less risk of having a Downs Syndrome baby if the mother is under 35.	

Being an older parent

Advantages	Disadvantages
• The couple may already have children and enjoy having a child in later life which may be more relaxed than previous experiences.	• There is a much higher risk of having a Down's Syndrome baby if the mother is over 35.
• They are likely to be more secure financially.	• The parents may have chosen to have family at a younger age, and may feel resentful that parenthood is about to start again, having begun to pursue a career, etc.
• They will be more mature and more patient.	• Older people get more tired and don't have the same energy levels as when they were younger.
• They may not be particularly worried about missing out on a social life.	• The mother's body may take longer to get back in shape.
• They will have been able to have a career, travel, etc, if they wanted to, and won't feel resentful about missing out.	• Children may be embarrassed because the parents may look a lot older. Other children (friends) may mistake them for grandparents.
• Parents may feel more content and settled with a baby in later life.	• The amniocentesis test carries with it a risk of miscarriage.
• Antenatal screening tests are available, e.g the amniocentesis test so that early detection of genetic abnormalities, e.g. Downs Syndrome, could be acted on.	• Older parents may find the teenage years more difficult.
• They will have more experiences of life.	
• Age is less linked to ill health.	

⊃ Contraception

The chart below demonstrates the wide variety of contraception available to men and women today and the popularity of each method of contraception. (Details of contraception can be found on page 39).

Figure 2.3 Contraception: by method used

Great Britain				Percentages
	1976	1986	1995-96	1998-99
Non-surgical				
Pill	29	23	25	24
Male condom	14	13	18	18
IUD	6	7	4	5
Withdrawal	5	4	3	3
Injection	..	..	1	2
Cap	2	2	1	1
Safe period	1	1	1	1
Spermicides	..	1	–	–
Surgical				
Female sterilisation	7	12	12	11
Male Sterilisation	6	11	11	12
At least one method	68	71	73	

¹By women aged 16 to 49, except for 1976 which is for women aged 18 to 44.

Source: Family Formation Survey and General Household Survey, Office for National Statistics (Source Social Trends 2000)

The statistics suggest that the contraceptive pill remains the most used method of contraception, followed by the male condom.

ADVANTAGES AND DISADVANTAGES OF CONTRACEPTION

This section will give information on how to prevent pregnancy by using contraception.

Key Words

The word **contraception** is made from two words: **contra** which means against, and **ception** meaning to conceive.

Non-surgical methods

The Progesterone-only Pill (POP)99% effective (no oestrogen) – prevents ovulation and implantation)

Advantages

- 99% effective
- Can help relieve pre-menstrual tension (PMT) and very painful periods
- Taken orally

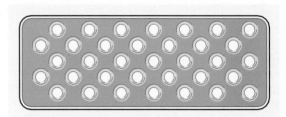

The progesterone only pill

The Combined Pill ('the pill') 99% effective (progesterone and oestrogen) – prevents ovulation and implantation

Advantages

- It does not interfere with the sex act
- It can help to ease painful periods by making them shorter, lighter and less painful
- It can help to relieve pre-menstrual tension
- It protects against different types of cancers, i.e. cancer of the ovary and cancer of the womb
- Protects against some pelvic infections
- It reduces the risks of fibroids, ovarian cysts and breast disease that is not cancer

Disadvantages

- There may be side effects such as headaches, weight gain or loss, nausea, breast tenderness or mood changes
- Forgetting to take the pill will remove its effectiveness

⊃ Male and female condom (barrier method, preventing sperm and egg meeting)

Advantages

◆ The man can take responsibility for contraception
◆ Both male and female condoms provide protection against sexually transmitted disease

Disadvantages

◆ The male condom can only be used on an erect penis, and this can often impair enjoyment of the sex act
◆ The thin rubber of the male condom can be split, making it unsafe – sperm can seep through the damaged condom without anyone realising it

   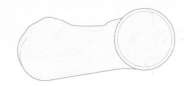

The male condom is 98% effective   The female condom is 95% effective

⊃ Intra-uterine Device (IUD) 98-99% effective (Coil, prevents sperm reaching the egg, discourages implantation)

Advantages

◆ It works as soon as it is inserted
◆ It works for three to ten years depending on the type used, and if fitted under the age of 40, it can stay in until menopause

Disadvantages

◆ Periods may be heavier or longer, or even painful
◆ The IUD can move, and sometimes it can come out

⊃ Withdrawal Method (male withdraws penis avoiding ejaculation in female)

Advantages

◆ This is often practised by people who cannot use other methods
◆ It is fairly reliable, as long as the man is not 'carried away'

Disadvantages

◆ Often, even if both partners are careful, a little semen could leak from the penis
◆ This can often leave partners frustrated because the penis has to be withdrawn before ejaculation takes place

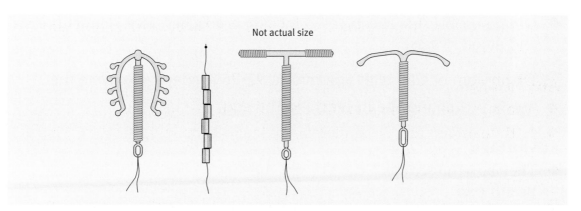

Not actual size

A selction of IUDs

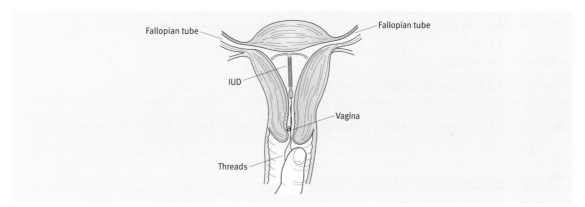

Fallopian tube   Fallopian tube

IUD

Vagina

Threads

An IUD in the correct position

⟳ Cervical Mucus Method (female observes mucus changes from white to clear/wet when ovulating)

⟳ Temperature Method (rise in temperature can be recorded after ovulation)

Advantages

◆ It is useful for those who for medical reasons cannot use other methods

⟳ Contraception Injection 99% effective (prevents ovulation and implantation)

Advantages

◆ A woman does not have to think about other methods of contraception for up to 12 weeks

◆ It does not interfere with sexual intercourse

◆ It can be used even if the woman is breast feeding

Disadvantages

◆ Periods can often become irregular or stop

◆ Some women gain weight

◆ Other possible side effects could include headaches, acne, tender breasts and mood swings

⊃ Diaphragm or Cap with Spermicide 92-96% effective (covers the cervix preventing sperm reaching the egg)

Advantage

◆ They have no serious health risks
◆ They can often help to prevent both cervical cancer and some sexually transmitted disease

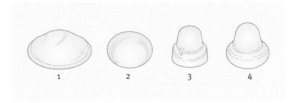

A diaphragm

Disadvantages

◆ Putting the diaphragm or cap in place can interrupt sexual intercourse
◆ It can take quite a long time for a woman to learn how to insert both correctly

⊃ Safe period (Calendar Method)

Advantage

◆ It is a method which is often favoured by religious sects and those who believe that other (unnatural) methods should not be allowed

Disadvantages

◆ If a woman's cycle changes, she may need to recalculate
◆ It is too unreliable to be used on its own, and is often used as a crosscheck with other methods
◆ Depends on accuracy of people involved

⊃ Implant over 99% effective (prevents ovulation and implantation)

Advantage

◆ The implant lasts up to three years, during which time no one has to think about contraception

Disadvantages

◆ A doctor has to put the implant in the arm, like having an injection, and it can be difficult to remove
◆ Side effects may include headaches, acne, weight gain, tender breasts, mood changes and irregular bleeding

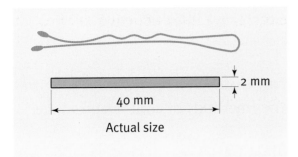

An implant

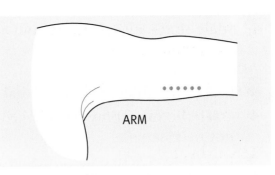

ARM

Postition in arm

⊃ Spermicides (helps to destroy sperm)

These are used with other forms of contraception such as the cap.

⊃ **Surgical methods**

This section deals with the permanent methods of contraception. It involves surgery both for males and females and, since both are irreversible, couples have to be quite certain that this is the option for them.

⊃ Female sterilisation over 99% effective

Advantage
◆ As with the vasectomy, this operation is permanent
◆ Once the operation has worked, no other form of contraception is necessary

Disadvantages
◆ The Fallopian tubes could rejoin, making the woman fertile again
◆ Some other form of contraception must be used up to the time the woman is sterilised and until she has had her first period afterwards.

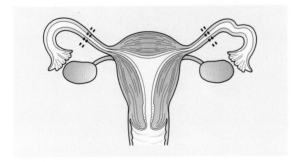

How the Fallopian tubes are blocked

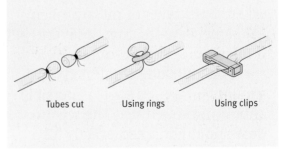

Tubes cut   Using rings   Using clips

Some of the ways the Fallopian tubes can be blocked

⊃ Male sterilisation (also known as vasectomy) 99% effective

Advantages

◆ It does not interfere with sexual intercourse

◆ Once the vasectomy has worked, other methods of contraception are not necessary

◆ It is more effective then female sterilisation

◆ It is a simple operation

Disadvantages

◆ It usually takes a few months for all the sperm to disappear from the semen. Therefore until the man has had two semen tests after the operation, he should use other forms of contraception

◆ The tubes could rejoin and the man could become fertile again

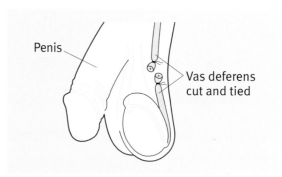

Penis

Vas deferens cut and tied

The male reproductive tract

⊃ EMERGENCY CONTRACEPTION

If sexual intercourse has taken place, and no method of contraception was used at all, or the couple think that the method they are using has failed in some way, then they can use emergency contraception. There are two methods of emergency action that can be taken: emergency pills and copper IUD (see page 40).

⊃ Emergency Pills

Emergency contraceptive pills must be taken within three days (72 hours) of unprotected sex. They are more effective the earlier they are taken. Both types of pill are taken the same way. The first dose (one pill if taking progestogen only pill) or two pills (if taking combined pills) should be taken as soon as possible after unprotected sex. The second dose should be taken exactly 12 hours later. Both sets of pills:

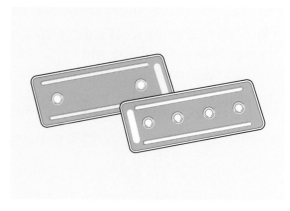

The progestogen-only pills (top) and the combined pills (bottom)

◆ stop an egg from being released and delays ovulation

◆ stop a fertilised egg settling in the womb.

Advantages

◆ They are effective and statistics tell us that 95 per cent of all women who take them do not become pregnant.

◆ Most women can take them.

Disadvantages

◆ The woman may feel sick, although this is less likely with progestogen-only pills.

◆ The pills may not be effective if the first dose is taken more than 72 hours after unprotected sex.

◆ The pills could also fail if the woman forgets to take the second dose.

◯ WHERE TO GO FOR HELP

This section deals with finding information about methods of contraception, and where to go for help and advice.

◆ There should be lists of GPs in libraries, Post Offices, Advice Centres, Health Authorities and Health Boards.

◆ Doctors who give contraceptive advice have the letter 'C' after their names.

◆ Details of the nearest family planning or sexual health clinic can be found in any telephone directory, health centre, hospital, advice centre or from a midwife or health visitor.

◆ Young people can phone the Brook Advisory Service on:

Brook Advisory Service: Freephone: 0800 018 5023 (London)

Administration Centre: 020 7284 6070 (London)

Birmingham 0121 643 5341.

◯ STOP PRESS

The latest news of the male pill is that it is a mixture of both testosterone and progestogen. It will be another five years before research is completed, and we assume that it will then be safe to be administered. The male pill is expected to be almost 100 per cent effective.

Remember

• There are many different types or methods of contraception and different methods suit different people at different times of their lives.

• Most contraceptives need to be prescribed by a doctor.

• All contraceptives are free, via your Health Clinic, but you may prefer to purchase them if you do not want the clinic or your doctor to know!

• Only barrier methods protect against sexually-transmitted diseases.

There is no doubt that contraception has given women the freedom of choice to:

♦ limit family size
♦ choose the age of conception
♦ plan a career
♦ gain an education/further education
♦ provide a quality standard of living
♦ be financially independent
♦ be in control

⊃ Teenage Pregnancies in the UK

There is also an increased trend for young teenagers in the UK to become pregnant (See Figure 2.4). In fact the UK has one of the highest rates of teenage pregnancies within the EU.

It is the aim of the Social Exclusion Unit (1999) to attempt to reduce by half the number of women under 18 years of age having a baby. The government is also supporting this aim.

The statistics demonstrate that these teenage pregnancies will occur outside marriage (Social Trends 2000).

Prior to the 1960s and 1970s it was unusual for a woman to give birth outside marriage, however, as society relaxed its attitudes to children born out of wedlock, the numbers began to grow steadily from the 1970s.

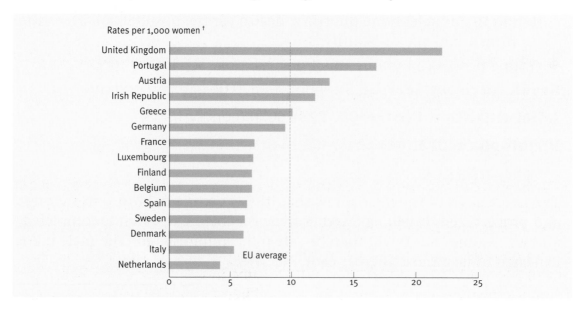

Figure 2.4 Teenage pregnancies

Source: Eurostate; Office for National Statistics
Source: Social Trends 2000

Many of these teenagers are below the legal age of 16 to have sexual intercourse. The question raised is: are these young women capable emotionally of the responsibilities of parenthood?

⊃ SIZE OF THE FAMILY

Once a child has been born into a family the parents may feel strong urges to produce a sibling (a brother or sister) for the child, or they may have quite the opposite feelings.

May wait until first child is more independent

Career plans

Plenty of/little money

Mother too exhausted to have more children

Lots of space to have more children

May have been a great experience the first time and the parents wish for a large family

Difficult birth has made mother nervous of having more children

First child born by IVF treatment – may not be able to afford further treatments

Factors affecting the desire to have more children

May not want an only child

Contraception

Choice may have been taken away with a difficult/ complex first birth

May be life-threatening to the mother to carry another baby

Inability to conceive a second time

May be family pressure to try before ready

⊃ Changes in the Size of the Family

Women at the turn of the century had large families of between 10 and 15 children. They continued to get pregnant into their forties as contraception was available only to the wealthy.

After contraception, particularly the contraceptive pill, was made widely available, and the Abortion Act of 1969 came into force, families became smaller. Today the average number of children per family is two to three.

One advantage of having a smaller family is that the whole family will benefit from a higher standard of living.

Early 1990s	115 live births per 1000 women
1998	less than 60 live births per 1000 women

Source: Social Trends 2000

The Age Gap Between Sisters and Brothers

It is not always possible to choose when to have a baby as the exact time of **ovulation** can be difficult to pinpoint. However, some couples are able to conceive at the first attempt.

It is physically possible for a woman to become pregnant as soon as her periods return, which means that she could conceive two children within a year.

The current average age gap is three years.

As mentioned previously, some parents remarry creating step families. If they choose to have a family there may be a larger gap between the children's ages.

What is the Best Age Gap?

There is no correct answer to this question, it will depend on many factors. Here are some advantages and disadvantages:

Small age gap 1–2 years

Advantages	Disadvantages
• All baby equipment can be used with the second child.	• If poor pregnancy may be no-one to look after the demanding toddler.
• Having the children close together means less time away from a career in the long run.	• Mother may not have recovered physically and emotionally from the first birth.
• Children will probably have common interests, and choice of toys they wish to play with.	• Mother could find two children in nappies without independence exhausting.
• Double buggies will make mobility easier.	• If the gap is around two and a half years, jealously may be at its height and the toddler may have temper tantrums.
• May both have a sleep at the same time in the afternoon.	• Children over two may feel their world has fallen apart because they are no longer getting the attention they had before the baby was born.
• With a very small age gap the children are unlikely to be jealous of each other.	• Older child may favour father or try to get mother's attention by asking for a drink as soon as she starts to feed the baby.
• Children will always remember being around one another and having someone to play with.	• Some children who are jealous regress in their behaviour and may start wetting the bed.
	• Toddlers may need to be watched as they may have a tendency to try to hurt the baby.
	• Could be very expensive with two childcare places to pay for.

Bigger age gap 3–4 years +

Advantages	Disadvantages
• Mother may be more physically and emotionally recovered from the first pregnancy.	• The toys and games that are played with will be different because of the bigger age gap.
• Toddler may be old enough to go to a pre-school group or school, allowing the mother time with the newborn baby.	• Younger children may pester and want the older child's games.
• An older child will understand what is happening and enjoy the prospect of having a sister or brother.	• Small pieces from games, e.g. K'NEX, Lego, may be around for the baby to pick up.
• Mother will be able to give the same attention to the newborn as the older child received.	• Children may not develop common interests.
• Parents may feel more confident and enjoy the second baby more.	• It will prolong the early years and may affect the mother's career plans.
• Parents may be financially more secure. Mother may have returned to work and saved money in anticipation of the pregnancy.	
• May only have one childcare place to pay for if the other child has started school.	

⊃ The Only Child

Some couples have just one child, either as a matter of choice or other reasons:

◆ Financial (not enough money and support more children)

◆ Not enough space for more children

◆ A partner may have left the home

◆ The mother may have suffered severe **postnatal depression** after the first child

◆ The child may have been conceived with IVF treatment. No money left for further attempts

◆ The parents may want to devote attention to one child only

◆ The mother may not be able to conceive a second time

Advantages	Disadvantages
• It is easier to look after one child.	• The child may have difficulty sharing and mixing with other children. This would have to be encouraged by the parents.
• Parents are able to give the child a lot of attention.	• The child may be lonely.
• It is less costly.	• The child may be spoilt.
• There is no sibling rivalry.	• The child may be demanding and seek attention.

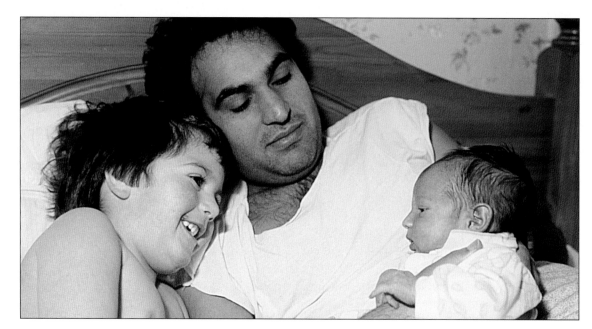

Figure 2.5 Meeting a sibling for the first time

Multiple Births

For some women fertility treatment may be the only option to have children. If they have three fertilised eggs put back into the uterus and they all implant, this would result in triplets (three babies).

Sometimes twins will occur naturally and suddenly the size of the family increases. Women who have had one set of twins are more likely to have another set of twins.

WORK AND THE FAMILY

The effect of women working alongside men, with equal career opportunities and salaries, has changed the traditional family lifestyle. While there are men who choose to alter their career paths and possibly take a career break or stay at home, it still remains the fact that women, because of their ability to give birth, have to be absent from work (time dependent on the chosen length of **maternity leave**) to have the baby and adjust to feeding and caring for the new family. **Paternity leave** is the only time the father is allowed off work.

Getting the Balance Right!

There is no right or wrong choice for parents, it is simply the best to suit the family circumstances at the time. However, it is still usually the mother who stays at home, or works part-time, and looks after the family.

Key Words

Maternity/paternity leave
Paid time off work for mothers/fathers

Full-time work

Advantages	Disadvantages
• The parent can continue and keep up to date with a career so that they do not lose confidence.	• The mother is not in control of the care of the children.
• She can enjoy the companionship of other colleagues and adults.	• She has little time to see the children if they are dropped early at a nursery and picked up late.
• She gets out of the house and away from mundane chores (she may pay someone to do ironing/cleaning).	• She may feel too tired to give the children attention after work.
• She may have felt depressed, lonely and unhappy at home.	• She may be too tired to pursue leisure activities after work and childcare.
• She feels refreshed with her children when returning from work and can give them 'quality time'.	• She may feel she is missing out on milestones that the children achieve.
• A significant wage/salary will be coming into the home.	• The children may have a greater attachment to the childminder/ grandparent or whoever is caring for them.
• The family may be able to afford extra luxuries, e.g. holidays.	• The mother misses the children.
• The mother will be financially independent.	• The mother may not be happy with the childcare provision and worries about it.
• She may be able to own and run a car giving her independence.	• There is little time to foster friendships with other mothers or fathers, or go to toddler groups, etc. during the day.
	• The children may eat dinner late or have ready-made meals if the parent does not return home from work until late.
	• She may worry about the pressures of work and find it difficult to relax.

Part-time work (This could range from a few hours to days.)

Advantages	Disadvantages
• Continuation with a career to keep up to date so that returning to full-time employment will be an easy transition.	• The expectations of work and the family are demanding and some times it is hard to get the balance right, e.g. working on the days off to catch up.
• The employer may be flexible about the hours of work.	• The parent does not belong to either lifestyle – the full-time working parent or the one who stays at home.
• The parent can have precious time with the children which can be made very special.	• The parent has to be careful that days off are not totally spent on household chores when time could be spent with the children.
• The parent still remains in control of some of the children's days, routine and stimulation.	• There may not be sufficient income to allow for luxuries, may be a big change in lifestyle.
• This sometimes enables a parent to attend toddler groups, social mornings, make friends with other parents of small children and make local contacts.	• The wage may only just cover childcare costs (so the reason to work would not just be financial).
• It gives the parent time to relax.	

Advantages continued	Disadvantages continued
• It enables activities to be undertaken on days off, e.g. swimming lessons. This could ease the pressure at weekends which could be family time. • The parent has the best of both worlds, keeps their confidence, mixes with adults at work and other parents. • The parent has time on days off to catch up with chores, etc. • The parent may be able to keep some financial independence, e.g. to run a car.	• There may be no flexibility with days off. If the parent is asked to work for a small number of hours in the day, it may not be worth working part-time when costs, e.g. travel and childcare, are taken into account.

Staying at home

Advantages	Disadvantages
• The parent is in total control of the children's routine, who they mix with and stimulation required. • The parent can enjoy and build a close special bond with the children every day. • The parent has time to visit and socialise with other parents who have children of a similar age. • This enables friendships to develop between parents as well as between the children. • The parent may have time to help out with other parents and their children who in turn will help them out (this saves money). • The parent may receive some financial assistance from the government. • There is time to keep the home and family happy and organised. • The children can eat a well-prepared meal, when they come home from school. • May have taken a recognised career break, which has refresher days to keep in touch with the job.	• There is little income coming into the house. • The parent may feel lonely and depressed away from work colleagues and misses adult conversation. • They may live far away from their family which makes loneliness worse. • They may feel isolated if there is no money to run a car. • There may be little money to socialise or pursue hobbies. • The parent may lose confidence and feel it is hard to return to work. • The parent may have spent a long time training for a career and feels it has been wasted.

Figure 2.6 Arriving at the childminder's home

Questions

Question 1

a What factors should be considered when planning to have children?

b What do you understand by the term a stable relationship?

c List four reasons which may not be the most positive ones to choose to bring a child into the world.

d How may the parents lifestyle be effected by the birth of a child?

e List <u>six</u> important needs of a child.

Question 2

a Women are choosing to have their first child at a slightly older age. Give possible reasons for this trend.

b Select and record four advantages and four disadvantages of having a baby as

   i   a young parent

   ii an older parent

Question 3

a What has made it possible to plan for a family?

b Explain why contraception has given men and women greater freedom to plan a family.

Question 4

a What is a sibling?

b What reasons may a parent with one child give to

   i   have more children

   ii no more children?

Question 5

a What advice would you give to a mother who is considering the age gap between her first child and having another baby?

b List four advantages and four disadvantages of having an only child.

Question 6

a Design a simple chart which will identify the advantages and disadvantages of

   i   Working full time

   ii Working part time

   iii Staying at home with the family

Questions continued

Question 7

a What is the meaning of the word contraception?

b Describe **two** barrier methods of contraception

Question 8

a What are 'natural' methods of contraception?

Question 9

a Why is it important to plan a family (Give your own views).

b Give details of at least **six** pieces of advice you would give to someone, to help prevent an unwanted pregnancy

Question 10

How do the following methods help with preventing a pregnancy in an emergency?

- The emergency Pill
- The IUD Coil.

Extension Questions

Essay: In an ideal situation discuss what factors you would consider to be the most important when choosing to bring a child into the world

Things to do

Interview parents both male and female and find out what they chose to do in respect of work, after having children. Why did they make these choices? It may be if interest to ask grandparents who may have experienced different attitudes from society than those of today.

Record your results and present then in the form of a written report.

⟳ PLANNING A FAMILY WORDSEARCH

N	O	I	T	A	C	U	D	E	A	X	I	X	J	K
O	M	C	H	I	L	D	R	E	N	T	T	R	L	U
I	R	U	V	U	A	C	X	R	W	F	C	F	H	V
T	K	E	V	I	I	G	W	T	P	F	E	K	N	Z
P	Y	B	E	C	C	T	G	A	B	D	S	J	N	S
E	V	T	O	R	N	T	R	D	U	R	J	K	I	N
C	S	G	I	L	A	E	Z	F	N	F	M	B	Y	Z
A	Y	U	Q	L	N	C	X	T	V	R	L	S	P	M
R	E	L	A	T	I	O	N	S	H	I	P	J	D	M
T	T	P	F	P	F	T	Q	P	N	Z	X	M	T	H
N	I	F	A	E	O	A	R	G	Z	T	L	L	Y	I
O	K	J	M	P	R	N	H	E	N	F	W	D	Z	E
C	O	C	W	A	D	D	E	R	F	F	L	Q	S	F
P	E	S	P	Z	I	I	C	M	T	J	J	H	S	N

Career   Financial
Children   Menopause
Contraception   Parent
Education   Relationship
Fertility   Sibling

3

Reproduction

This section will concentrate on the development of the male and female reproductive systems through puberty.

From the moment a child is conceived, the female ovary of an unborn foetus will have many immature eggs stored within its tiny ovaries. However, it is not until a male and female begin the development of their reproductive organs that intercourse may take place and a new life can begin. When children reach **puberty** they will enter a transitional period from childhood to adulthood. **Adolescence** is the growth spurt in the mind and puberty is the growth spurt of the body. This can be a difficult time for young people who are not only seeing physical changes occurring within their own bodies, but also coping with the emotional strain of what can be for some adolescents quite a traumatic time.

Puberty often starts at about 11–13 years and is usually earlier for girls than boys. However, we are all individual and it could occur much earlier or much later for many. This may depend on factors such as heredity, diet and environment, to name a few.

HORMONES

During puberty **hormones** (chemical messengers) are produced from **endocrine glands** whose job is to signal changes within bodies that will transform them from a child to an adult. It is important to understand these changes to understand how a child is made.

THE FEMALE ANATOMY

During the menstrual cycle, the lining of the uterus goes through four stages. These are:

1) The lining of the uterus is shed. This is when menstruation occurs, and will only happen if the egg is not fertilised.
2) A new lining for the uterus is started.

Key Words

Hormones	Chemical messengers.
Endocrine glands	These are ductless glands which secrete hormones that have a particular job to perform, to enable our bodies to grow and develop properly.
Adolescence	Growth spurt in the mind.
Puberty	Growth spurt of the body.

3) The lining of the uterus has become much thicker, and is ready to receive a fertilised egg.

4) If the egg is not fertilised, the lining of the uterus begins to break down again. (The cycle moves back to stage 1.)

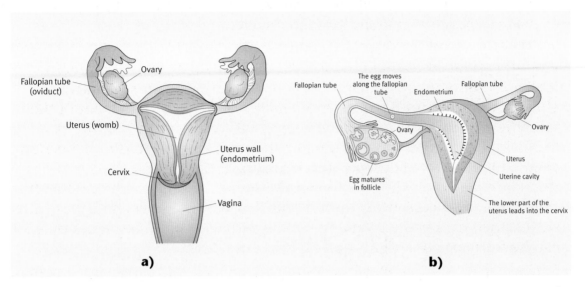

Figure 3.1 The female reproductive system a) front b) side

⟳ THE FEMALE REPRODUCTIVE SYSTEM

◆ A female usually has two **ovaries** which are the female sex glands controlling the hormones oestrogen and progesterone. Once a month the ovaries produce eggs, known as **ova** (a single egg is an **ovum**). This is known as **ovulation**.

◆ The **uterus** is pear-shaped and hollow with strong muscular walls called the amnion and the chorion. The uterus is capable of nurturing the unborn child and growing to incorporate the developing foetus.

◆ The uterus (womb) lining (endometrium) is capable of enriching with blood during the receptive phase (see figure 3.4) and of breaking down when no fertilised egg is implanted.

◆ The **Fallopian tubes (oviducts)** are two tubes that lead from the uterus. The egg that is released each month will travel down this tube and it is here the sperm will swim to and fertilise an egg.

◆ The **cervix** is a strong muscle between the uterus and **vagina**. The cervix is capable of holding in the unborn child. Normally the cervix is closed with only a small opening to allow **menstrual** flow to leave the body and semen to enter.

◆ The vagina is a tube about 10–12 cm long, which extends to the cervix at the neck of the uterus and exits the body.

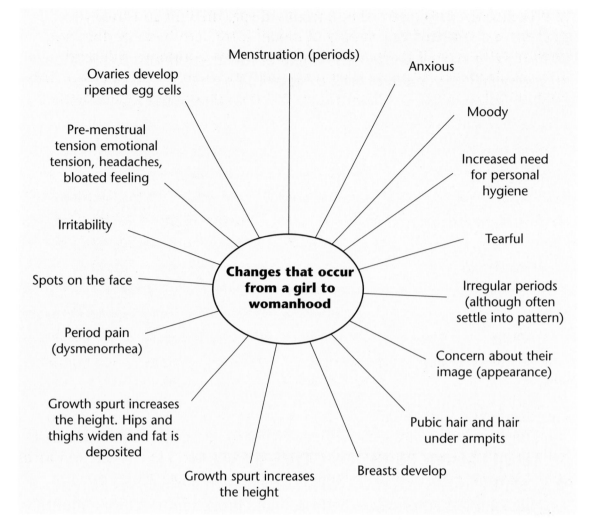

Menstruation (periods)

Ovaries develop
ripened egg cells

Pre-menstrual
tension emotional
tension, headaches,
bloated feeling

Irritability

Spots on the face

Period pain
(dysmenorrhea)

Growth spurt increases
the height. Hips and
thighs widen and fat is
deposited

Growth spurt increases
the height

Anxious

Moody

Increased need
for personal
hygiene

Tearful

Irregular periods
(although often
settle into pattern)

Concern about their
image (appearance)

Pubic hair and hair
under armpits

Breasts develop

**Changes that occur
from a girl to
womanhood**

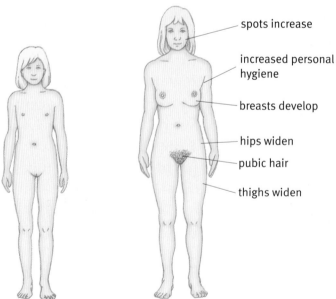

spots increase

increased personal
hygiene

breasts develop

hips widen

pubic hair

thighs widen

Figure 3.2 Female development

In preparation for the arrival of a fertilised egg, the lining of the uterus thickens with an enriched supply of blood. If the fertilised egg does not implant (attach itself to the uterus wall) then the hormones will send messages from the lining of the uterus (endometrium) to break down. This is commonly known as a period. This can last approximately 5–7 days.

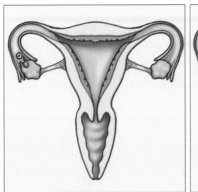 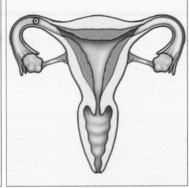 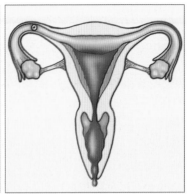

Figure 3.3 Uterus when normal

Figure 3.4 Uterus with thickened lining

Figure 3.5 Uterus expelled lining

The female hormones which are carried via the blood stream are oestrogen and progesterone. Oestrogen is responsible for the development of the female sex organs. Progesterone (the pregnancy hormone) works in conjunction with oestrogen and other hormones controlling the menstrual cycle.

⟳ The Menstrual Cycle

This usually occurs every 28 days, although it can be longer for some women and shorter for others.

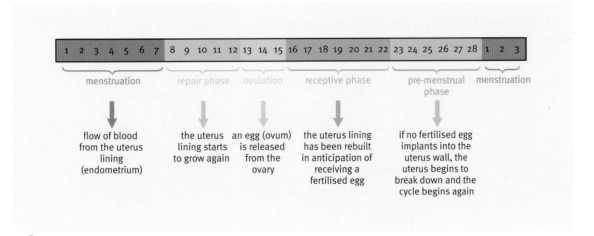

Figure 3.6 Menstrual cycle chart

A woman is considered fertile once the menstrual cycle has started. This will continue until a woman reaches approximately 45–55 years of age. When this cycle stops or slows down it is known as the 'change of life' or the **menopause**.

Key Words

Cervix	neck of the uterus.
Fallopian tube (oviduct)	transports the female eggs from the ovary to the uterus. Fertilisation takes place here.
Menopause	often known as the change of life, when a woman's reproductive cycle stops.
Menstruation (Period)	uterus lining breaks down and there is a small flow of blood from the vagina.
Ova	female eggs produced from the ovary.
Ovary	female sex gland.
Ovulation	a female egg is released from an ovary.
Ovum	a single female egg.
Uterus	place where the foetus (baby) develops.
Semen	a milky white nourishing fluid containing sperm.
Vagina	the opening of the female reproductive system, where sexual intercourse (coitus) takes place, sperm are deposited and a flow of blood exits the body (a period).

THE MALE REPRODUCTIVE SYSTEM

The main hormone stimulating physical sexual development of the male is testosterone. In addition to the physical changes it affects emotional development, bringing about great periods of uncertainty and extremes of feelings from depression to great excitement.

The male reproductive organs

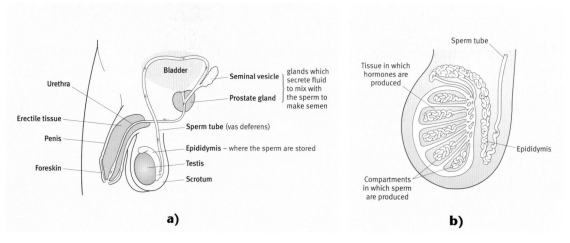

Figure 3.7 a) The male reproductive system (front) b) the male reproductive system (side)

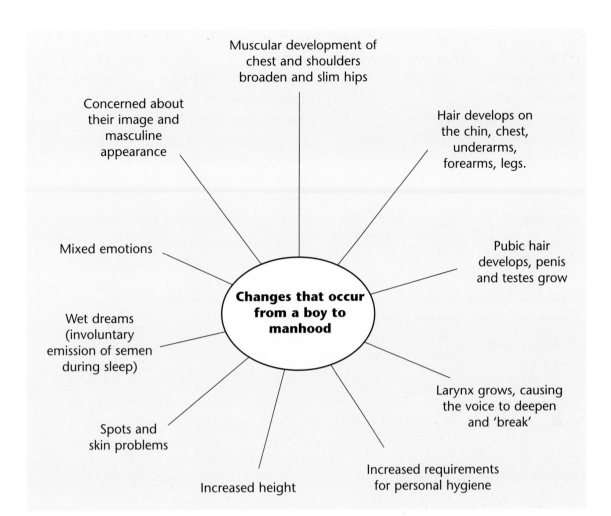

Muscular development of chest and shoulders broaden and slim hips

Concerned about their image and masculine appearance

Hair develops on the chin, chest, underarms, forearms, legs.

Mixed emotions

Changes that occur from a boy to manhood

Pubic hair develops, penis and testes grow

Wet dreams (involuntary emission of semen during sleep)

Larynx grows, causing the voice to deepen and 'break'

Spots and skin problems

Increased requirements for personal hygiene

Increased height

The male equivalent of the ovaries are the **testes**. Sperm are produced in the testes and then the testes produce the male hormone testosterone.

The testes are stored within the **scrotum**, a pouch below the pelvis. This enables the sperm to be stored outside the body at a temperature of 35°C.

When the male is sexually aroused sperm will travel along the **sperm tube** and pass the **seminal vesicle** which stores and produces seminal fluid. This fluid mixes with the sperm producing semen.

In order that sexual intercourse can take place the penis must be sexually stimulated. Its limp/flaccid state will engorge with blood causing the **penis** to go hard. This is called an erection.

Key Words

Testis (testes)	sperm are made here.
Epididymis	sperm are stored here.
Sperm tube (vas deferens)	sperm travel along this tube.
Seminal vesicle and prostate gland	glands secreting substances that mix with sperm to provide semen.
Urethra	where semen and urine exit.
Penis	capable of becoming erect.
Foreskin	covers the top of the penis.
Scrotum	bag that stores the testes.
Ejaculation	emission of the semen containing sperm from the penis.

Questions

Question 1　Explain the following terms:

　　i)　endocrine glands

　　ii)　adolescence

　　iii)　puberty.

Question 2　List four changes that may occur during puberty for:

　　i)　male

　　ii)　female.

Question 3　Name two female hormones which help to control the menstrual cycle.

Question 4　Explain where i) sperm and ii) female eggs are made.

Question 5　Identify when ovulation takes place during the menstrual cycle and explain what happens.

Question 6　Give two reasons why menstruation might stop for some time.

Question 7　What is testosterone?

Question 8　Explain:

　　i)　where sperm are made and stored

　　ii)　at what temperature sperm should be stored.

Question 9　Explain how semen can be produced.

Question 10　What is male erection and what is its purpose?

REPRODUCTION WORDSEARCH

C	O	N	T	R	A	C	E	P	T	I	O	N	C	D
N	C	W	O	L	X	K	O	I	Z	V	B	O	D	M
H	E	K	R	I	D	Q	U	L	U	D	J	I	U	S
X	O	M	V	D	T	J	I	L	V	N	N	T	S	A
S	U	R	E	T	U	A	A	K	S	N	Z	A	J	I
S	E	A	M	S	E	T	S	E	T	T	D	U	U	W
C	L	Q	O	O	I	R	G	I	C	O	S	R	P	R
D	U	Q	D	O	N	N	W	Y	L	I	Y	T	U	I
O	Z	Z	N	V	X	E	E	E	D	I	W	S	B	S
C	G	L	O	G	C	V	S	P	O	Q	R	N	E	I
Z	Q	Q	C	I	H	C	A	B	H	O	K	E	R	L
L	T	Y	A	D	E	M	A	G	V	N	K	M	T	E
K	I	I	B	N	D	T	C	U	H	X	M	O	Y	S
Q	M	Y	C	J	V	N	U	Q	K	O	X	U	O	A
A	Q	E	G	P	B	C	F	K	W	D	Q	E	E	T

Adolescence

Cervix

Condom

Contraception

Hormones

Menstruation

Ovulation

Penis

Pill

Puberty

Semen

Sterilisation

Testes

Uterus

Pre-conceptual Care

In this chapter, we will look at a period of time before conception takes place, It is a time for both partners to agree on such things as diet and exercise. By reducing known risks such as poor diet, alcohol and smoking they are helping to create the very best conditions in which an embryo can grow and develop into a healthy baby.

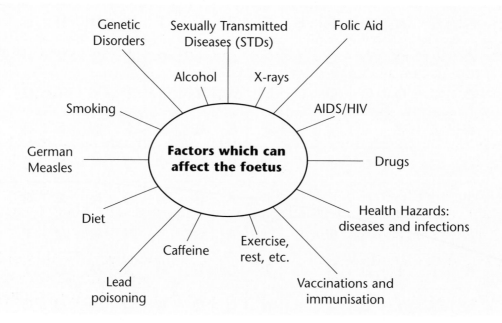

The environment in which the embryo and subsequently a **foetus** grows will have a tremendous impact on its life. Above is a spidergram of these factors which could effect the development of the foetus.

⊃ EXERCISE

The fitter and healthier the mother is both before and during pregnancy, the better she will be able to cope. Being pregnant puts a great deal of strain on the body, and being aware of this, and actually doing something to prepare for it, will undoubtedly help both mother and baby. Nowadays we recognise that exercise is not only beneficial, but necessary too, providing it:

◆ is regular (before and during pregnancy)

◆ does not overtire the mother (during pregancy see page 138)

◆ is in moderation (before, but particularly during, pregnancy). Activities such as cycling, horse-riding, walking and swimming can all be carried out, as long as they are planned with care and common sense. It is important to stress that the mother can continue with her chosen activity until she feels uncomfortable, particularly during pregnancy itself.

DRUGS

When the word 'drugs' is used, people usually think of heroin and cocaine. Here, we will look at drugs that are considered to be harmful and those that are not. Technically speaking, all medicines are drugs – a drug being any substance that has some effect on the workings of the body. So two very simple definitions of drugs are:

◆ *Medicines* are given or prescribed by a doctor to people for the sole purpose of treating a disease.

◆ *Drugs* as we think of them are not necessarily given or prescribed, but are usually taken illegally for the effects they have.

Whether it is medicines or habit-forming drugs all may be harmful to the mother before and during pregnancy.

Medicines known to be harmful to an unborn baby are travel sickness pills and some antibiotics. Pain relievers such as aspirin, paracetamol, etc. should be taken with caution.

Social drugs, i.e. those that are habit forming (addictive), should not be taken, even before a woman conceives. Such addictive drugs can easily enter the baby's blood stream and subsequently make the baby addicted as well. The baby then has to be weaned off them at birth.

Research into drug-related problems before and during pregnancy shows that:

◆ Marijuana (even though it is known as a 'soft' drug) interferes with the normal production of male sperm and the effects of taking such a drug take between three and nine months to wear off.

◆ The baby of an addicted mother may have a low birth weight.

◆ Hard drugs such as heroin, cocaine, morphine and cannabis can damage the chromosomes both in the sperm and ovum, which will ultimately lead to abnormalities in the baby's development.

◆ Usually, an addictive woman causes her baby to have withdrawal symptoms from the drugs immediately after the birth, in the same way as an adult has withdrawal symptoms.

◆ Fumes from some solvents and glues are also extremely harmful.

> # *Remember*
>
> A woman who is hooked on heroin, cannabis, glue sniffing or any similar addictive substance, should consult either her doctor or get help before trying to conceive.

SEXUALLY-TRANSMITTED DISEASES (STDs)

Many STDs can affect conception. For instance

Non-specific Genital Infection

◆ Urethritis – infection of the urethra
◆ Vaginitis – infection of the vagina
◆ Cystitis – infection of the bladder.

These are liable to hinder conception.

Trichomoniasis (Trich or TV)

The cause of this infection is a small **parasite** (a protozoa) which infects both the vagina and the urethra. It is a very common complaint. This disease occurs only in women and would make sexual activity painful.

Genital Warts

These warts can appear anywhere on either the vagina or the penis. The main cause is a virus, similar to that which causes common skin warts. This disease occurs only in women and would make sexual activities painful.

Gonorrhoea (The Clap)

This disease is extremely common and tends to occur in very young people. It is an infection that can be spread only through sexual intercourse. Unless cleared by antibiotics or injections, these symptoms can lead to both the sperm ducts and oviducts becoming infected, and this in turn can cause sterility.

Syphilis (The Pox)

Nowadays we hear very little of syphilis but need to be aware of it because it is one of the most dangerous of all sexually-transmitted diseases, particularly if left untreated. It has a habit of spreading to other parts of the body, causing heart disease, blindness, deafness, insanity and even death. A woman who is thinking of becoming pregnant, and is suffering from syphilis and has allowed the infection to be untreated, can easily pass on the infection to her unborn child.

Key Words

Venereal diseases   these refer to diseases in the sex organs which have become infected.

Sexually-transmitted diseases   infection of the sex organs spread by sexual intercourse.

Infection   see chapter on child health.

Genital   this term is used to describe the external (outside) sexual organs.

Remember

Any type of infection requires time to develop. Just because symptoms have not appeared does not mean that an infection has not begun. Some people do not develop any symptoms, for example, not all women who have gonorrhoea suffer symptoms, and not all men who have contracted herpes suffer from sores.

X-RAYS

It is not a good idea for a woman planning to become pregnant to be subjected to X-rays, or any form of radiation, unless it is absolutely necessary, i.e. if the mother's life is at risk. This is because any developing baby (foetus) will be rapidly making new cells and X-rays and radiation rays will destroy new or healthy cells.

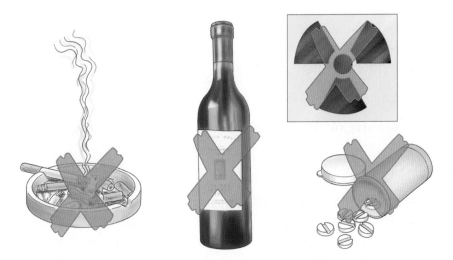

Figure 4.1 These can harm the unborn baby

AIDS/HIV

AIDS is short for Acquired Immune Deficiency Syndrome. The virus known to be the cause of AIDS is Human Immunopathic Virus (**HIV**).

A women who is planning to be pregnant who is affected with the virus may pass the infection to her unborn child.

Key Words

Foetus when a baby is conceived, and after developing for a month, the baby at this stage is known as an embryo. At this stage also, the embryo has a tail, and other parts which appear to look as though they might develop into gills. When the embryo is 2 months old, it has now grown sufficiently to resemble a human form, and it is at this stage that the word embryo is replaced with foetus (or fetus). Main bodily structure are more or less in place at the foetal stage, and the heart is beating.

AIDS the letters stand for Acquired Immune Deficiency Syndrome. It is a disease whereby the white blood cells are no longer able to function efficiently. White blood cells are often called white corpuscles, or leucocytes, and their sole function is to protect the body against infection. When AIDS occurs, these white cells are no longer able to resist infection, and so the person can easily be infected with many types of germs. The infected person tends to have enlarged lymph nodes, and sometimes a particular type of cancer which affects the skin. The virus which causes AIDS to occur in the first place is known as HIV.

AIDS is caught by:

◆ having sexual intercourse with someone who has the HIV virus;

◆ coming into contact with infected blood. (This is why the disease if often found among drug addicts who use infected needles for injecting.)

HIV the letters stand for Human Immunopathic Virus. Blood tests can show whether a person is HIV-positive. If someone is HIV-positive, they can in time develop the illness AIDS (see definition).

Antibodies these are substances which the human body is capable of producing in response to antigens. An antigen is any substance which can stimulate the production of antibodies. For instance, antigens can be in the form of germs, vaccines, or food. Each different antigen has the ability to stimulate the production of the type of antibody which in turn will destroy that antigen. Antibodies are:

◆ molecules of protein

◆ found in blood, tissue and lymph nodes

◆ are made by the white blood cells

Their sole function is to destroy germs.

Immunity a human body is capable of resisting infection in many ways. When a person is immune to a particular disease, the white blood cells work alongside the antibodies, destroying germs which they recognise. The degree of immunity can vary from

◆ total immunity – all germs destroyed

◆ partial immunity – insufficient immunity to prevent the disease, but enough antibodies to make the disease less severe

◆ no immunity – if the germs invade the body, infection usually follows.

Foetal trauma is a term referring to the foetus during the birth process. Occasionally during labour the baby's blood may be sampled. These procedures can endanger the baby by making it go into a kind of shock. This not only prolongs labour for the mother, but can cause harm to the baby itself.

AZT a drug given to treat patients who are HIV-positive. It is given orally to pregant women who are HIV-positive, as it can protect the foetus from infection. The baby will then be regularly scanned for growth checks.

GERMAN MEASLES (RUBELLA)

German Measles is one of the most common of all childhood diseases. It is often referred to as Rubella, because it is caused by a virus of the same name.

Women who are thinking about having a baby should find out from their doctor whether or not they are immune to German Measles. If they are not, the doctor can **vaccinate** against it. After being vaccinated, and provided that the vaccination was successful, a woman should wait for about three months before trying to conceive.

A woman who comes into contact with a person infected with, or suspected of having, German Measles should tell her doctor immediately. The doctor will then arrange for the woman to have a blood sample which will be tested for antibodies. The result will determine whether or not the woman needs to be treated.

VACCINATIONS AND IMMUNISATION

Shortly before conception, and certainly during pregnancy, it is advisable for a woman not to be immunised. However, there are exceptions and these are:

◆ If the mother-to-be has been exposed to infectious diseases.

◆ If she is to travel outside the UK, and therefore requires typhoid or cholera protection.

In either case, the woman must first contact her doctor and be advised as to whether or not the vaccination is necessary.

One the mother has been vaccinated, the vaccine goes into her bloodstream.

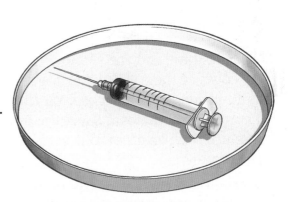

◆ Poliomyelitis vaccine/ protection should be sought before conception because the disease can be extremely severe during pregnancy.

Figure 4.2 Syringe used in vaccination

CAFFEINE

Tea, coffee, cola and cocoa all contain a substance called caffeine.

Caffeine is a stimulant and can cause feelings of restlessness, fatigue or increased heart rate in some people. These symptoms may cause harm or discomfort before and during pregnancy, so it is best if the woman reduces the amount of caffeine she takes into her body. She can do this by drinking weaker tea/coffee or by leaving it out altogether and drinking mineral water or fruit drinks.

⊃ LEAD POISONING

Lead is a toxic (poisonous) substance and is present in drinking water and petrol. It can also be found in old pipework and old paint.

⊃ What is Spina Bifida?

Spina bifida is a defect where one or more parts of the vertebrae (spine) do not fully develop. This allows a section of the spinal cord to remain exposed. It is possible for the condition to occur anywhere along the spinal cord, but it is more usual for it to happen quite low down the back.

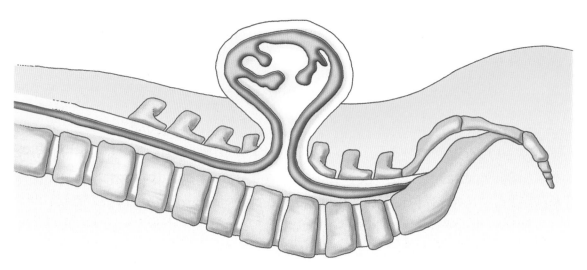

Figure 4.3 Exposed spinal cord resulting in spina bifida

Both the spine and the vertebral column start from a flat layer of cells. The edges of these cells come together to form a tube. This tube is the hollow cavity inside the spinal cord. Within approximately four weeks from the time of conception, the cord itself, the bones surrounding it and the vertebrae close up. High levels of folic acid in the mother's blood, particularly at the start of pregnancy, are vitally important if the neural tube is to close.

◆ Whatever the age of the mother, all babies are at risk of developing spina bifida and other neural tube defects, such as hydrocephalus.

◆ A mother experiencing a first pregnancy is just at risk as a healthy mother, who has already given birth to healthy children.

◆ Women who have had several children are particularly vulnerable because they have had little time to top up their folic acid levels before they are pregnant again.

◆ Women who have had one child with Spina Bifida are far more at risk than women who have given birth to 'normal children'.

◆ Folic acid is mainly found in fruit and vegetables. The latest government guidelines suggest that everyone should eat at least five portions of fresh fruit and vegetables per day.

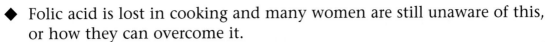
◆ Folic acid is lost in cooking and many women are still unaware of this, or how they can overcome it.

◆ A strict regime of healthy foods including those rich in folic acid in the diet of a woman pre-conceptually and/or during pregnancy is absolutely essential so as not to place the baby at risk (see page 74).

CONTRACEPTION (FAMILY PLANNING)

The majority of methods can be stopped immediately, but there are two which require some thought before this can happen.

The Pill

Women who wish to become pregnant are advised to stop taking the pill up to a month before they start trying to conceive. This is to allow the woman to menstruate (have a period) at least once normally before she becomes pregnant. Occasionally, a woman will become pregnant immediately after she has stopped taking the pill. Some evidence suggests that a woman is much more fertile at this stage. If a woman has miscarried before, or has had experience of low fertility, then possibly this way could be ideal for her.

A woman who thinks that she may be pregnant while still taking the pill should see her doctor. This is because some types of pill contain very high doses of progestogen which could interfere with the development of the embryo in the first few weeks.

Intrauterine Device

This method is sometimes abbreviated to IUCD or IUD, or called the Coil, and it works by irritating the lining of the uterus, so that it is almost impossible for a fertilised egg to implant itself on the lining.

It is recommended that the IUD is removed before conception, as removing it after the woman is pregnant could increase the risk of a miscarriage. If the woman becomes pregnant while the IUD is in place, it usually comes away with the placenta after the birth.

HEALTH HAZARDS I

Women who suffer from such diseases as

◆ epilepsy
◆ heart disease
◆ kidney disease
◆ asthma
◆ STD
◆ AIDS
◆ diabetes

should not assume that they will never become pregnant but that does not mean that they can go ahead with a pregnancy without any advice at all.

Women with such conditions or diseases should talk things over with their doctor, so that all through the pregnancy they can manage both disease and pregnancy in the most effective way possible.

Key Words

Asthma is a common respiratory problem where a person finds breathing difficult. This is as a result of the airways to the lungs narrowing. This occurs when the muscles in the walls of the airways go into a spasm causing the mucus lining the airways to swell up and secrete more mucus.

Heart Disease is a defect in the functioning of the heart

Diabetes is a condition that occurs when the pancreas is unable to produce sufficient insulin to help cope with the glucose (sugar) level.

Kidney disease is a defect of the functioning of the kidneys.

Epilepsy is a brain disorder characterised by a temporary loss of consciousness

Renal dialysis if one or both kidneys are diseased, their function of removing toxic (poisonous) substances from the blood is severely impaired.

Renal dialysis is a process where a person with such a condition is attached to a dialysis machine, which performs the functions the kidneys are unable to.

⊃ HEALTH HAZARDS II

A woman who is thinking of conceiving or who is already pregnant should care for her body by eating good, wholesome food with all the necessary nutrients (see section on Diet). However, she could easily put herself and her growing baby at great risk if the food she is eating is contaminated by bacteria. Below are the most hazardous of food-related risks.

◆ Salmonellosis

◆ Toxoplasmosis

◆ Listeriosis

⊃ Salmonellosis

This is an infection from the Salmonella bacteria and is usually traceable to raw eggs and raw chicken. Salmonella can be avoided only if the food is cooked thoroughly at high temperatures.

⊃ Toxoplasmosis

An infection of this nature is caused by a **parasite**, which could be present in:

◆ raw or undercooked pork and steak

◆ unpasteurised milk

◆ the faeces of cats and dogs.

In the mother, this parasite would cause mild flu-like symptoms, but it can be very harmful to an unborn child, causing foetal brain damage and blindness. It could even result in the mother aborting the foetus. The third stage of pregnancy (third trimester) appears to be the most dangerous and vulnerable time.

The parasite Toxoplasma is found in the faeces of animals, often cats, however most people with this disease have caught it by eating undercooked meat.

Listeriosis

Listeria can be contracted through eating some chilled foods and also by direct contact with infected live animals, particularly sheep. If the mother is infected with this disease, it will pass into the baby's blood stream, and can lead to stillbirth, spontaneous abortion or the child could be born dangerously ill. Symptoms are similar to those of flu, i.e. a high temperature, sore throat, aches, pains, diarrhoea and abdominal pains.

Pasteurising temperatures normally destroy these bacteria but if the food becomes infected and is then refrigerated, the bacteria will continue to grow. For this reason pregnant women should avoid chilled foods especially if they are after their 'best by' date.

Dysentery

This disease is dangerous, particularly once the woman is pregnant, because it can cause **dehydration**. The infection is usually carried in the **faeces** of a person who is already infected, and its symptoms are severe diarrhoea and abdominal pain. There are two types of dysentery: amoebic dysentery which is usually found in the drinking water of tropical countries, and bacterial dysentery. In this country, any dysentery infection will normally be caused by bacteria. The main cause is an infected person failing to wash their hands thoroughly after visiting the toilet, and then promptly handling food.

GENETIC COUNSELLING

Genetics and genetic disorders are dealt with in much more detail later on in the book. A woman who is thinking of becoming pregnant will be offered genetic counselling, particularly if she falls into any of the following categories.

◆ If she has a history of repeated miscarriages.
◆ If there is a blood relationship between the mother and her partner, for example, they may be cousins.
◆ If a woman has previously given birth to a child with a genetic disorder, e.g. cystic fibrosis, or a child with a chromosomal disorder such as Down's Syndrome.

◆ If a woman's previous child was born with a congenital defect, e.g. **a club foot**.

◆ If there is a family history of mental handicap or other abnormal developments.

A woman and her partner owe it to their unborn child to seek advice and counselling, if any of the above categories apply.

Key Words

Club foot a condition where a child is born with the sole of one or both feet facing either downwards and inwards, or upwards and outwards.

⟳ DIET

The diet of a mother particularly in the pre-conceptual stage is important and should be taken seriously. The mother owes it to her baby to be as healthy as possible. This is the only provider of healthy nutrients to her baby, and she should therefore take full responsibility to ensure that her baby receives the very best nourishment. Research carried out into the mother's diet during pregnancy has shown that what she eats during her pregnancy affects not only the unborn child but also the child after it has been born.

⟳ FOLIC ACID

Under normal circumstances, a woman's level of folic acid is removed from her blood fairly quickly. During pregnancy, it is removed via her kidneys at *four times* the normal rate. Therefore it is essential that the mother eats folic acid-rich foods, or takes folic acid supplements every day, so she does not place her developing baby at risk. A woman's level of folic aid should be topped up even before she conceives – the recommendation is three months before trying for a baby.

◆ A daily dose of 400 micrograms (mg) is recommended.

◆ Folic acid capsules come in 400 mg doses, so one capsule per day should be taken from three months before conception, until the baby is born (term).

◆ A folic acid milk drink is readily available from chemists for women who dislike taking capsules or tablets. One carton of this milk contains the daily requirement of folic acid.

◆ There is very little danger of women overdosing on folic acid, but large doses may interfere with the absorption of it into the blood stream.

◆ Women who have had a child with neural tube defects should have 4 mg of folic acid daily before and during later pregnancies.

Folic acid comes in several forms:

Food with High levels of folic acid	Foods with Medium levels of folic acid	Food that are fortified with folic acid
Liver, Brussel sprouts	Soya beans	Some breads
Kidney, Spring greens	Potatoes	Most cereals
Beef extract, Kale	Lettuce	
Broccoli, Spinach	Peas	
Green beans	Wholemeal bread	
Yeast extract	Cauliflower	
Leafy green vegetables are very good, particularly the darker green ones	Chick peas	
	Oranges plus orange juice	
	Baked beans	
	Parsnips	

The words Folic Acid continue to give rise to a great deal of confusion, because they are often called by other names – all derivatives of the word folic. A collective name, i.e. FOLATES is therefore given to any word, which is a derivative of the word Folic. Do not be surprised to see either of the following words, and be sure that they all mean the same thing.

Folic acid is also known as:

◆ folate and

◆ folacin (this word is used occasionally on food labels)

During pregnancy the need for folic acid is greatly increased, particularly in women who have been taking oral contraceptives (the pill) for a long time. A pregnant woman deficient in folic acid is likely to become **anaemic**, and this gives rise to other problems including premature delivery, **spontaneous abortion**, low birth weight baby, or a malformed baby. The most obvious type of malformation is spina bifida or anencephaly. These are both neural tube defects. In simple terms, this means that the metabolism of the foetus is not developing at a normal rate.

⊃ FERTILITY AND INFERTILITY

Key Words

Fertility means the ability to have children. It is regardless of gender, and so being fertile is dependent on both male and female developing their sex characteristics correctly. This happens during puberty, i.e. between the ages of 12 and 16 in girls, and around 14–18 in boys. Changes that occur at puberty are started off by the pituitary gland, which in turn triggers the adrenal or sex glands to produce hormones.

Infertility means being unable to conceive. There could be many reasons why people are infertile, and it could affect either partner. When it does happen, both partners need to be examined thoroughly by a doctor, and they also need to be given helpful yet sensitive advice.

Nowadays, a great deal can be done for couples who are unable to have a baby. Some of the reasons for infertility are detailed below.

MALE	
Reasons for infertility	**Treatment**
A blockage of one or both of the vas deferens – tubes which connect the testicles to the seminal vesicles (sperm is stored here). This blockage could be the result of a sexually-transmitted disease.	Drugs
Ejaculation failure. Sometimes men find that they do not ejaculate at the same time as a female's orgasm.	Counselling
Very low sperm count. This could occur if the man works with pesticides or metals such as lead, mercury, etc. Tight underwear and overheating are two other causes.	Drugs counselling
Testicular failure. This is a rare condition when the semen contains no sperm.	Tends to be untreatable
Poor diet. A poor or unhealthy diet can result in a low sperm count.	Better diet – plenty of fresh fruit and vegetables. Plenty of exercise, sleep, etc.
FEMALE	
Hormonal imbalance. An ovarian cycle is almost completely dependent upon the correct balance of hormones. If there is too much or too little of either one of them, an egg will not be produced.	Fertility drugs
Fibroids. These are totally benign (non-cancerous) growths within the uterine walls. They are more likely to occur in women aged 35 and over.	Surgery to remove the fibroids
Blocked Fallopian tubes. These could be due to a sexually-transmitted disease, miscarriage or a pregnancy that has been terminated.	Surgery to unblock tubes
Endometriosis. This is a condition where patches of the lining of the uterus are found in the ovaries, the pelvis, Fallopian tubes, etc.	Laparoscopic surgery

The list below suggests ways in which couples can increase their chances of conceiving a baby:

◆ Women should take 0.4 mg of folic acid daily.

◆ Neither partner should smoke.

◆ Partners need to be fairly clear of sexually-transmitted diseases.

◆ A healthy diet is essential for both partners.

◆ Both partners should be aware of their drinking allowances, i.e.:

　◆ not more than 2 units per week for women;

　◆ not more than 7 units per week for men.

◆ Very overweight women should try to reduce their weight.

◆ The woman should not use temperature charts to work out her fertile time as this could cause stress.

◆ Men should wear loose-fitting undergarments to allow air to circulate around their testes. They should also avoid become overheated.

Questions

Question 1

a What is folic acid?

b Explain its importance in the diet of a pregnant woman.

c What are the dangers of not ensuring that there is sufficient folic acid in her diet?

Question 2

a Does an expectant mother need to eat for two? Explain your answer.

b Which of the nutrients should she avoid in large amounts?

c Which parts of the body are particularly affected by the increasing weight?

Question 3

Name three factors that can affect the health and well-being of an unborn child. Make detailed notes about each one.

Question 4

a What is Rubella?

b Why is it so important that a pregnant woman does not come into contact with someone suffering from Rubella?

Question 5

Describe three health conditions, e.g. diabetes, which a pregnant mother might have, and how will they affect both the mother and the unborn baby.

Question 6

Discuss each of the following in terms of:

a the effect on the mother

b the effect on the unborn child.

　◆ sexually-transmitted diseases (STDs)

　◆ drugs (both over-the-counter and social drugs such as marijuana).

Question 7

Describe in some detail the effects of the following food poisoning hazards on both the mother and the unborn child.

a Salmonella

b Toxoplasmosis

c Listeriosis

Question 8

A healthy diet is essential for a woman wanting to conceive.

Discuss the above statement, with particular reference to those women who are vegetarians.

Pregnancy

This section will determine how conception takes place, embryonic formation, implantation and the development of the foetus. It also covers multiple pregnancies and genetic inheritance.

CONCEPTION

The miraculous moment when a male sperm penetrates and fertilises a female ovum (egg) is known as **conception**. For conception to occur the mother and father need to be sexually stimulated, enabling sexual intercourse (coitus) to take place.

The urge to reproduce is a strong and natural way to continue a species. It can also be a loving and caring way of expressing emotions to a partner.

During sexual intercourse the male penis will become erect and will be placed inside the female vagina. At the height of sexual stimulation the penis will ejaculate sperm inside the vagina, usually at the top near to the cervix. This will enable the sperm to swim (propelled by their tails) towards the uterus and into the Fallopian tubes. The sperm will meet with a female egg and fertilisation will take place within the Fallopian tube (oviduct). The ovum can live for 12 to 24 hours after being released from the ovary. Sperm can survive for up to 72 hours inside the woman's body. To increase the chances of conception intercourse should take place the day before ovulation so that the sperm will be waiting in the Fallopian tube when the egg is released.

Ovum

Figure 5.1 A ripe ovum released from the ovary travels down the Fallopian tube. Jelly-like coating to prevent egg sticking to the sides of the Fallopian tube.

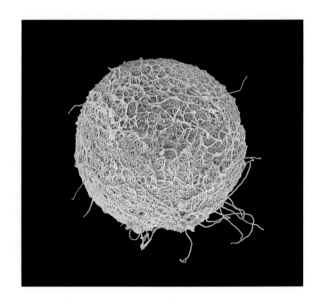

Figure 5.2 A sperm 1/25th of a millimetre long. Its long tail is able to move from side to side enabling it to swim up the vagina, through the uterus to the Fallopian tube

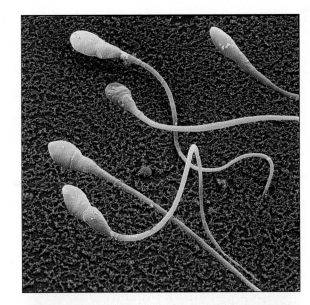

Figure 5.3 Sperm attempting to penetrate an ovum

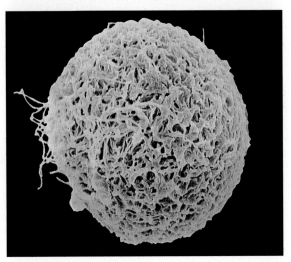

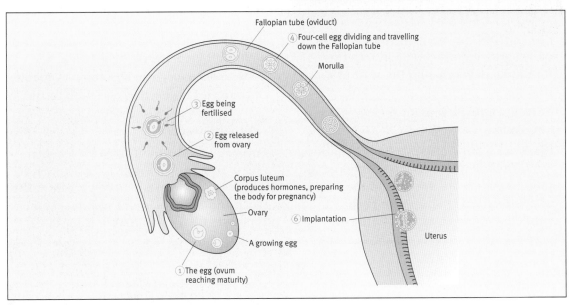

Figure 5.4 Ovulation, conception and implantation

1 and **2**. _Ovulation_ – a ripened egg is released from the ovary on about the fourteenth day of the menstrual cycle. The fringe-like projections of the Fallopian tube will encourage the egg to travel down the Fallopian tube.

3. _Fertilisation_ – once a successful sperm penetrates the egg no other sperm can enter. It no longer requires the tail, which is discarded. The sperm and egg fuse and become one cell.

4. _Morulla_ – the egg divides rapidly and begins to look like a blackberry.

5. _Blastocyst_ – four to five days after conception a cell mass forms a tiny hollow ball of new tissue called the blastocyst.

6. _Implantation_ – once the fertilised egg has reached the uterus it will embed itself into the enriched lining that awaits it. When the egg is firmly attached conception is complete. The outer cells of the **embryo** settle into the uterus lining and link with the mother's blood supply. This will eventually form the **placenta**. Other cells will develop into the **umbilical cord** and different parts of the baby's body.

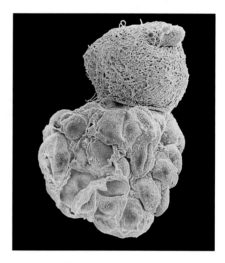

Figure 5.5 Blastocyst

Once conception has taken place the female hormones oestrogen and progesterone increase, causing the lining of the uterus to have a good blood supply, the breasts to enlarge and the ligaments to relax.

Key Words

Conception the moment when a male sperm and a female egg join together forming a new cell, and the start of a new baby

Coitus another name for sexual intercourse

Placenta a large disc-shaped organ, deep red in colour, which enables oxygen and food to pass to the foetus and to get rid of carbon dioxide and waste products (sometimes known as the afterbirth)

Umbilical cord a pale white twisted cord with red blood vessels, which links the baby to the placenta. The cord is capable of transporting oxygen and food to the baby and takes away carbon dioxide and waste products.

Embryo the technical term for a baby less than seven weeks old. During these weeks all of the major development takes place and at the end of seven weeks a complete baby in miniature is formed.

⊃ MULTIPLE PREGNANCIES

What are twins? Normally one egg is fertilised and develops in the uterus. However, twins occur when either one egg fertilises and splits into two cells forming **UNIOVULAR TWINS** or two eggs are released, fertilised and produce **BINOVULAR TWINS.**

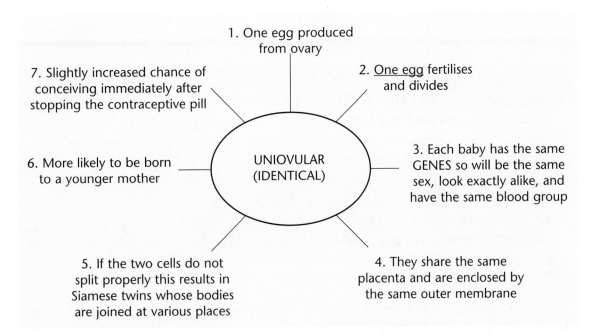

1. One egg produced from ovary

2. <u>One egg</u> fertilises and divides

3. Each baby has the same GENES so will be the same sex, look exactly alike, and have the same blood group

4. They share the same placenta and are enclosed by the same outer membrane

5. If the two cells do not split properly this results in Siamese twins whose bodies are joined at various places

6. More likely to be born to a younger mother

7. Slightly increased chance of conceiving immediately after stopping the contraceptive pill

UNIOVULAR (IDENTICAL)

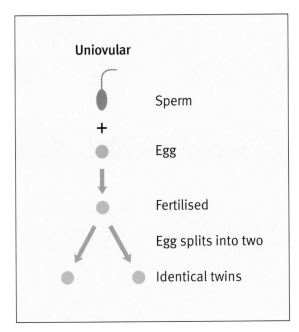

Uniovular

Sperm

+

Egg

Fertilised

Egg splits into two

Identical twins

Figure 5.6 Uniovular twins

Key Words

Genes these are carried on thread-like structures called chromosomes and determine our inherited characteristics, such as blue eyes

Figure 5.7 Identical twins

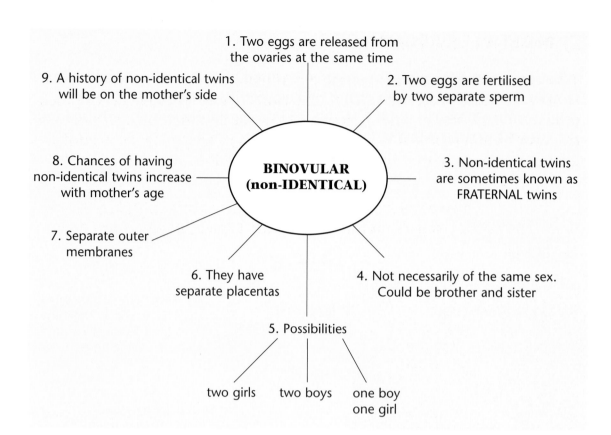

1. Two eggs are released from the ovaries at the same time

9. A history of non-identical twins will be on the mother's side

2. Two eggs are fertilised by two separate sperm

BINOVULAR (non-IDENTICAL)

8. Chances of having non-identical twins increase with mother's age

3. Non-identical twins are sometimes known as FRATERNAL twins

7. Separate outer membranes

6. They have separate placentas

4. Not necessarily of the same sex. Could be brother and sister

5. Possibilities

two girls   two boys   one boy one girl

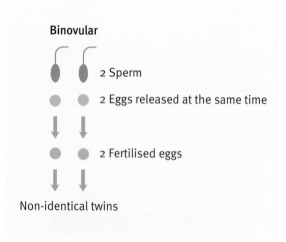

Binovular

2 Sperm

2 Eggs released at the same time

2 Fertilised eggs

Non-identical twins

Figure 5.8 Binovular twins

Figure 5.9 Quads

Position in the Family

Twins often fight to be recognised especially if they are dressed alike, treated the same and referred to as 'the twins'. Early language development of twins can be slower, and sometimes they develop their own way of communicating (not real words) with each other. They may be less likely to gain individual attention or gain masses of attention and another single child can be left out.

There is a much greater chance of multiple births with fertility treatment. More eggs could result in multiple births, e.g. triplets, quads, quins or sextuplets.

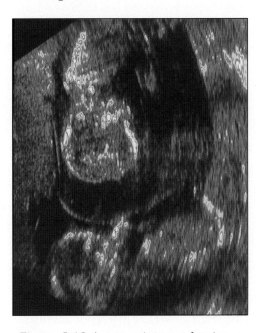

Figure 5.10 A scan picture of twins

Early Signs of a Multiple Pregnancy

◆ More obvious symptoms of pregnancy (see page 86) at a very early stage
◆ The uterus enlarges quickly and becomes uncomfortable
◆ Excessive vomiting
◆ Increased desire to urinate

Issues with a Multiple Pregnancy

◆ More than one baby may lead to a premature labour because of pressure on the uterus.
◆ More ante-natal check-ups are attended so that complications can be dealt with quickly.

◆ Twins can be delivered in the normal way although a **Caesarean** may often be necessary.
It will depend on the position of the babies.

◆ Triplets would inevitably require a Caesarean section to ensure the safe delivery of the babies and for the mother's health.

◆ Support for parents worrying about coping with twins can be found from The Twins and Multiple Births Association (TAMBA).

Key Words

Uniovular twins identical twins.

Binovular twins non-identical twins. Sometimes known as fraternal twins.

Caesarean section where the mother's abdomen is cut open and the baby is lifted out. The wound is stitched back together.

⟳ HEREDITY

The study of **heredity**, why we are as we are, is called genetics.

All human cells contain 46 **chromosomes** except the sex cells, the sperm and the ova. The sex cells contain only 23 chromosomes and at conception they join together to become one, forming a **zygote** with 46 chromosomes.

Each individual chromosome is a thread-like structure that carries information which will determine the appearance, growth and function of a new life. Each chromosome carries several thousand **genes** and each gene is responsible for part of the human make-up, e.g. hair colour, hair texture, height, etc. Of the 46 chromosomes, two will determine the sex of the child. Some sperm contain a Y chromosome and some an X chromosome, while the ova always contain an X chromosome. When the egg and sperm join together if an X and a Y chromosome meet a boy baby is formed.

Sperm chromosome	+	Ova chromosome	=	Sex of baby
Y	+	X	=	YX boy baby
X	+	X	=	XX girl baby

Abnormalities in the make-up or numbers of chromosomes can lead to common disorders (see Chapter 18).

⟳ Chromosomes in Sex Cells and Fertilisation

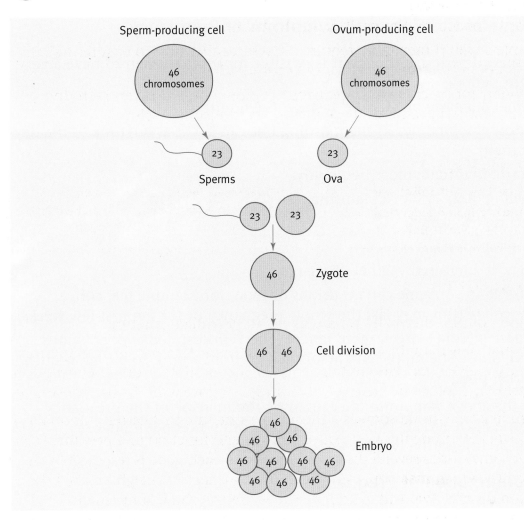

Figure 5.11 Chromosomes in sex cells and fertilisation

Key Words

Chromosomes 23 thread-like structures from a male sperm and 23 from a female egg.

Heredity studying genetics.

Zygote a fetilised egg cell created by the sperm and egg

⊃ PREGNANCY

⊃ Some of the Signs and Symptoms of Pregnancy

◆ A missed period, although it is possible for some women to have a very light period.

◆ A metallic taste or 'strange' taste in the mouth.

◆ Sickness sometimes in the morning but can occur at anytime of the day or night.

◆ Desire to urinate more frequently.

◆ Feeling dizzy and even fainting.

◆ Feeling exhausted.

◆ Constipation.

◆ Slightly increased vaginal discharge.

◆ Unable to consume certain drinks or food, for example tea, coffee, chocolate (this may last the whole pregnancy or for the first few weeks).

◆ Breasts become larger, more tender. The veins can look very obvious and 'blue'. The nipple and areola can go from a pink colour to a much darker pink.

All of the above symptoms are caused by the increase in the pregnancy hormone PROGESTERONE. The symptoms often become milder or disappear around the twelfth week of pregnancy.

⊃ Confirmation of Pregnancy

Figure 5.12 Awaiting results of a preganancy test

For couples who have planned a pregnancy, confirming they are pregnant can be an euphoric time, filled with excitement and anticipation. For others it may be a more difficult time particularly if the pregnancy is unplanned.

⊃ How to Test for Pregnancy

◆ The most common way of detecting a pregnancy is by obtaining a urine sample in a clean container from the mother after she has missed the first day of her period. The urine is mixed with various chemicals and is able to detect the presence of the pregnancy hormone GONADOTROPHIN.

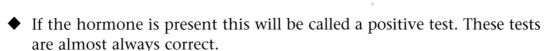

◆ If the hormone is present this will be called a positive test. These tests are almost always correct.

◆ However, a negative result may not be correct and a re-test may be required two weeks later. This is because there may have been insufficient levels of gonadotrophin to read with the test.

◆ A test can be carried out by a GP or for a small charge by the Brooks Advisory Service, British Pregnancy Advisory Service or the Family Planning Clinic. Local chemists will charge a fee for a test.

◆ Home pregnancy testing kits are now widely available and can be purchased from chemists and large supermarket chains. Advantages of these tests are that they give instant results, using a midstream sample of urine. They also enable women to carry out the test in private. However, the test instructions must be read and followed accurately or a false reading may occur. A disadvantage is that they are rather costly.

⊃ Home Pregnancy Tests

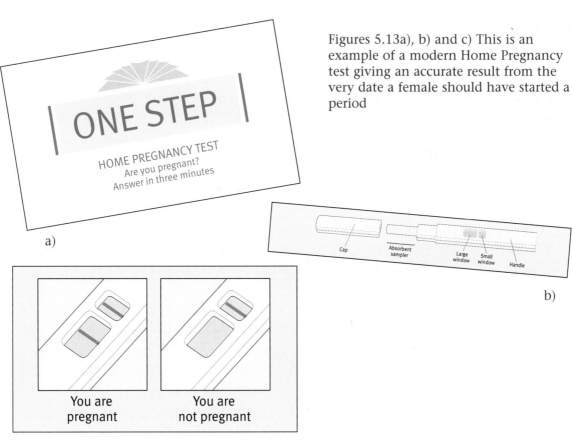

Figures 5.13a), b) and c) This is an example of a modern Home Pregnancy test giving an accurate result from the very date a female should have started a period

⊃ Estimated Date of Delivery

The first thing parents usually want to know is when their baby will be born.

PREGNANCY CALENDAR

You can use the chart below to find your expected date of delivery and work out your crucial weeks. Pick out the date of the first day of your last period from the figures in light type.

Your due date is immediately underneath in bold. Always remember that this is just an estimate, and you are unlikely to deliver on that exact day.

| January | 1 2 3 4 5 6 7 8 9 10 11 12 13 14 15 16 17 18 19 20 21 22 23 24 25 26 27 28 29 30 31 |
| Oct/Nov | 8 9 10 11 12 13 14 15 16 17 18 19 20 21 22 23 24 25 26 27 28 29 30 31 1 2 3 4 5 6 7 |

| February | 1 2 3 4 5 6 7 8 9 10 11 12 13 14 15 16 17 18 19 20 21 22 23 24 25 26 27 28 |
| Nov/Dec | 8 9 10 11 12 13 14 15 16 17 18 19 20 21 22 23 24 25 26 27 28 29 30 1 2 3 4 5 |

| March | 1 2 3 4 5 6 7 8 9 10 11 12 13 14 15 16 17 18 19 20 21 22 23 24 25 26 27 28 29 30 31 |
| Dec/Jan | 6 7 8 9 10 11 12 13 14 15 16 17 18 19 20 21 22 23 24 25 26 27 28 29 30 31 1 2 3 4 5 |

| April | 1 2 3 4 5 6 7 8 9 10 11 12 13 14 15 16 17 18 19 20 21 22 23 24 25 26 27 28 29 30 |
| Jan/Feb | 6 7 8 9 10 11 12 13 14 15 16 17 18 19 20 21 22 23 24 25 26 27 28 29 30 31 1 2 3 4 |

| May | 1 2 3 4 5 6 7 8 9 10 11 12 13 14 15 16 17 18 19 20 21 22 23 24 25 26 27 28 29 30 31 |
| Feb/Mar | 5 6 7 8 9 10 11 12 13 14 15 16 17 18 19 20 21 22 23 24 25 26 27 28 1 2 3 4 5 6 7 |

| June | 1 2 3 4 5 6 7 8 9 10 11 12 13 14 15 16 17 18 19 20 21 22 23 24 25 26 27 28 29 30 |
| Mar/April | 8 9 10 11 12 13 14 15 16 17 18 19 20 21 22 23 24 25 26 27 28 29 30 31 1 2 3 4 5 6 |

| July | 1 2 3 4 5 6 7 8 9 10 11 12 13 14 15 16 17 18 19 20 21 22 23 24 25 26 27 28 29 20 31 |
| April/May | 7 8 9 10 11 12 13 14 15 16 17 18 19 20 21 22 23 24 25 26 27 28 29 30 1 2 3 4 5 6 7 |

| August | 1 2 3 4 5 6 7 8 9 10 11 12 13 14 15 16 17 18 19 20 21 22 23 24 25 26 27 28 29 30 31 |
| May/June | 8 9 10 11 12 13 14 15 16 17 18 19 20 21 22 23 24 25 26 27 28 29 30 31 1 2 3 4 5 6 7 |

| September | 1 2 3 4 5 6 6 7 8 10 11 12 13 14 15 16 17 18 19 20 21 22 23 24 25 26 27 28 29 30 |
| June/July | 8 9 10 11 12 13 14 15 16 17 18 19 20 21 22 23 24 25 26 27 28 29 30 1 2 3 4 5 6 7 |

| October | 1 2 3 4 5 6 7 8 9 10 11 12 13 14 15 16 17 18 19 20 21 22 23 24 25 26 27 28 29 30 31 |
| July/Aug | 8 9 10 11 12 13 14 15 16 17 18 19 20 21 22 23 24 25 26 27 28 29 30 31 1 2 3 4 5 6 7 |

| November | 1 2 3 4 5 6 7 8 9 10 11 12 13 14 15 16 17 18 19 20 21 22 23 24 25 26 27 28 29 30 |
| Aug/Sept | 8 9 10 11 12 13 14 15 16 17 18 19 20 21 22 23 24 25 26 27 28 29 30 31 1 2 3 4 5 6 |

| December | 1 2 3 4 5 6 7 8 9 10 11 12 13 14 15 16 17 18 19 20 21 22 23 24 25 26 27 28 29 30 31 |
| Sept/Oct | 7 8 9 10 11 12 13 14 15 16 17 18 19 20 21 22 23 24 25 26 27 28 29 30 1 2 3 4 5 6 7 |

Figure 5.14 A pregnancy chart

◆ Calculating the estimated delivery date (EDD) of the baby will require a pregnancy calendar like the one above. Calculations are made using an average 28-day cycle, therefore this is only a rough guide.

◆ A pregnancy lasts about 266 days from conception to birth.

◆ Conception on average takes place on the fourteenth day of the cycle.

◆ To calculate the EDD count 266 days + 14 from the first day of your last period = 280 days

◆ An average pregnancy is 40 weeks although it can range from 38 to 42 weeks.

MISCARRIAGE

The medical term for miscarriage is **SPONTANEOUS ABORTION.** This means the loss of the foetus from the uterus before the twenty-eighth week of pregnancy or prior to viability (the ability of the foetus to survive outside the uterus without support from medical intervention).

The majority of miscarriages occur within the first ten weeks. Also, a woman may miscarry without knowing that she was ever pregnant. Therefore a number of women may not seek medical advice. However, it is estimated that approximately 30 per cent of all pregnancies end in miscarriage.

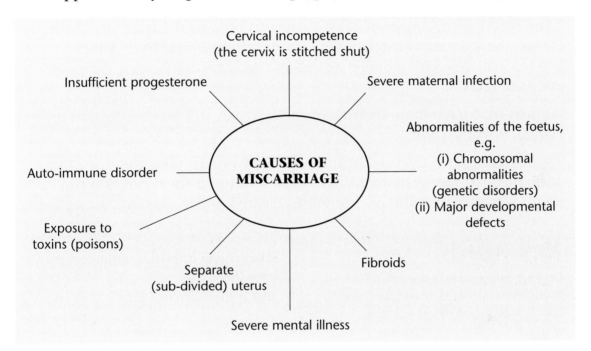

Signs and Symptoms of Miscarriage

◆ Heavy bleeding from the vagina.

◆ Cramp-like period pain from mild to severe.

◆ Light bleeding may occur, caused by a low-lying placenta or cervical erosion. These pregnancies may continue until full term.

◆ Spotting blood accompanied by severe pain may indicate a miscarriage or an ectopic pregnancy (where the implantation has taken place in the Fallopian tube). This is a most serious condition.

◆ Gush of clear or pinkish fluid may indicate that the amniotic sac has ruptured (broken).

There are different types of miscarriage.

◆ Threatened abortion – the foetus remains alive and does not come out of the uterus despite vaginal bleeding.

◆ Inevitable abortion – the foetus has died and is therefore expelled (sent out) from the uterus. Sometimes it is not complete and the foetus/placenta do not all come away.

◆ Missed abortion – despite the foetus having died it remains intact in the uterus with the placenta.

⊃ Prevention of the Miscarriage

When a woman is in danger of having a miscarriage she will be advised to have complete bed rest to reduce the blood loss. However, in some instances there may be little that can be done to stop it happening.

If the cervix is incompetent, (it is unable to hold in the contents of the uterus) the woman would have the cervix stitched shut to make it stronger. Bed rest will be recommended as well as medication that may help the uterus to relax.

Women who have more than three miscarriages will be investigated to find out the possible cause.

If a miscarriage occurs the hospital will carry out an ultrasound scan to find out if the foetus has died. This may result in a short hospital stay where the woman will have her uterus cleared under a general anaesthetic.

Key Words

Ectopic pregnancies are when the foetus develops in the Fallopian tube. This is a very dangerous situation.

Miscarriage is the loss of the foetus from the uterus.

EDD is the Estimated Date of Delivery.

⊃ Parents' Feelings

When parents suffer the loss of a baby, even during the early weeks of pregnancy, it may be traumatic particularly if the baby was desperately wanted.

◆ A mother may worry whether or not she will ever have a normal, healthy baby.

◆ A mother may feel guilty: was there something she did to cause the miscarriage?

◆ A mother may want to try to become pregnant again immediately, although some doctors advise waiting for at least three menstrual cycles.

◆ Some parents may be realistic about the loss and feel that it was not preventable.

◆ Parents can contact the local miscarriage support group.

◆ Other people may not understand the need to mourn and come to terms with the miscarriage.

Most women who have had a miscarriage will go on to have a normal healthy pregnancy.

⊃ ANTE-NATAL CARE

This section will deal with the role of ante-natal care and the types of care available.

Ante-natal care, as it suggests, is the care of the mother and her unborn baby/babies before the birth takes place.

Ante-natal care is good in this country and widely available to all pregnant women. Employers must, by law, allow pregnant women to attend ante-natal classes, without losing pay. There are many aims to ante-natal care – here are some of them:-

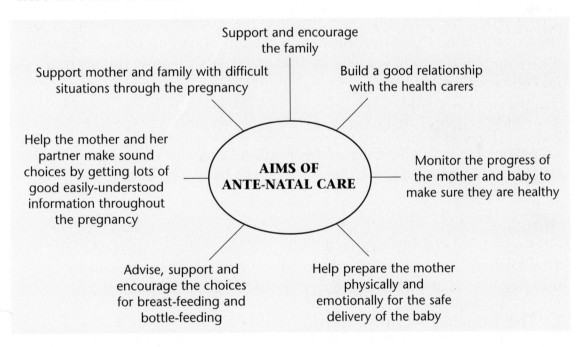

Another role of ante-natal care is to carry out tests that with today's advanced technology will help to detect any problems with the mother and her unborn child. Often treatment can be given to prevent further problems and ensure the pregnancy is healthy. More details regarding the specific types of testing will be discussed later on page 110.

Types of Ante-natal Care

There are different types of ante-natal care available largely depending on the area in which you live.

Shared

The GP (general practitioner) and community midwife will share the case with a consultant obstetrician. This means that some ante-natal checks will take place at the local doctor's surgery or health clinic and others at the hospital where more specialist equipment is available.

Full Consultant

This is where the consultant obstetrician will take on the case of the mother although more often than not a team of junior doctors and midwives will care for her. It is only when problems arise that the consultant will become more involved.

Community

This is where the ante-natal care will take place at the health centre or GP's surgery and will often be monitored by a team of community and hospital midwives and the local GP. The mother often gets to know the team of midwives well.

Domino

This type of care is where the midwife will take care of the mother at home but will go into hospital with her, deliver the baby, and come home with the mother afterwards.

Home

This is where the mother will have care from within the community midwifery team at home, and may choose to have a home birth.

The Booking Appointment

Once the pregnancy has been confirmed the GP will arrange the Booking Appointment. It is at this point that the type of ante-natal care will be decided, although it could change if complications arose, or if certain types of care were not available.

The Booking Appointment may be at a hospital, ante-natal, clinic, home or at the GP's surgery. It is usual for this to be carried out by a midwife. The midwife will ask a lot of questions at this visit and it is her role to gather as much information as she can regarding the mother, her medical history, etc.

The following summarises the role of the midwife at this booking appointment.

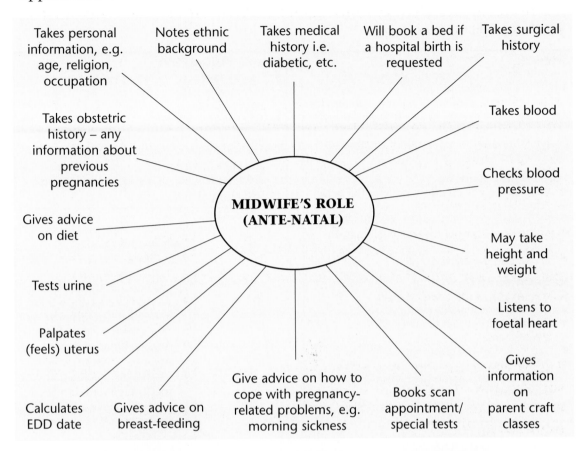

Takes personal information, e.g. age, religion, occupation

Notes ethnic background

Takes medical history i.e. diabetic, etc.

Will book a bed if a hospital birth is requested

Takes surgical history

Takes obstetric history – any information about previous pregnancies

Gives advice on diet

Tests urine

Palpates (feels) uterus

Calculates EDD date

Gives advice on breast-feeding

Give advice on how to cope with pregnancy-related problems, e.g. morning sickness

Books scan appointment/ special tests

Gives information on parent craft classes

MIDWIFE'S ROLE (ANTE-NATAL)

Takes blood

Checks blood pressure

May take height and weight

Listens to foetal heart

Figure 5.15 A midwife takes the medical history at the booking appointment

There are a number of specialist people that the pregnant woman may come into contact with depending on the health of the woman and her medical history. The chart below summarises the role of each Health Care professionals:

Midwife
A highly skilled and trained practitioner whose role is to be qualified to look after an expectant mother through a normal pregnancy, labour and after the birth. They are qualified to give drugs. Most are working in both the community and hospital. Must visit the mother for the first 10 days then HV takes over

Community Midwife
- Will visit the house before and after the birth
- Attached to GP's practices
- May give antenatal classes at the GP's surgery
- May deliver home births and in GP/midwife units
- Involved in the domino system

Hospital midwife
- Will see you at the antenatal clinic
- May deliver a straightforward birth
- Complications would require a DR's involvement
- Will look after you on the post natal ward
- Will give advice on feeding, caring for the baby, and checking on the general health of the mother

Health Visitor (HV)
- Usually nurses who have opted to work in the community looking after family health from birth to death
- 10 days after the birth, the HV will make a visit to see the mother and baby
- She will continue to visit until the mother is fit and will encourage the mother to come to the child health clinic to get the baby weighed and checked over

Paediatrician
- A doctor who has specialised in the care of babies, children and teenagers
- As soon as the baby is born in hospital a paediatrician will check the baby thoroughly
- A home birth baby may never see a paediatrician
- Often a neonatologist as well specialises in the care of newborn babies who are in the special care baby unit

Gynaecologist
- A highly specialised doctor whose role is to treat problems of the woman's reproductive organs
- Works closely with obstetricians and may be a consultant in this field also
- Assists couples with fertility problems (see section on infertility)

Specialist people who will look after the pregnant woman and after the baby is born

Obstetrician
- A doctor who has specialised in the care of women during pregnancy, labour and birth
- A consultant obstetrician will care for hospital births
- Consultants tend to deliver babies when there are complications (usually a midwife will deliver a baby)

General Practitioner (GP)
- This is a family doctor
- Usually the first person a woman goes to, to confirm her pregnancy
- Some GPs run their own antenatal clinics
- Shared care involves the joint responsibility of antenatal care between the hospital and the GP
- GP involved with home births and deliveries in GP/midwife units
- GP will pay a visit when mother and baby return home

Physiotherapist
- An obstetric physiotherapist has been trained to look after the physical needs of the pregnant woman during labour and postnatally
- Attends antenatal and aquanatal classes
- Advises on breathing techniques and, exercises to tone the muscles to regain shape after the birth

Dietician
- A highly qualified part of the medical team who will give nutrition advice on any special diet or need
- Particularly involved with women who are diabetic or develop diabetes through pregnancy

THE PLACENTA

The placenta develops during the first 12 weeks of pregnancy and is the means by which the foetus breathes, eats and disposes of its waste products. The placenta links the blood supply of the mother to the baby.

The placenta develops from the **chorion**. It is firmly attached to the lining of the woman's uterus and is connected to the baby by the umbilical cord. By the end of the 40 weeks of pregnancy the placenta is about 2.5 cm thick, 20 cm wide and weighs approximately 500 grams, and is deep red in colour. Shortly after the baby is born the placenta (afterbirth) is expelled from the uterus. This is known as the third stage of labour or the placental stage.

The placenta transfers oxygen from the mother's circulation to the foetus's circulation and removes waste products form the foetus's blood to the mother's blood for excretion by her lungs and kidneys. The placenta also conveys nutrients from mother to baby.

The mother's blood and baby's blood never mix. The baby's blood flows via the umbilical cord to the placenta, where it enters tiny blood vessels that are arranged in finger-like projections called **chorionic villi.** These chorionic villi are surrounded by a pool of the mother's blood and the exchanges take place.

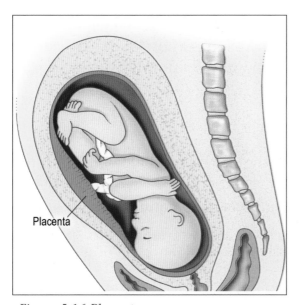

Figure 5.16 Placenta

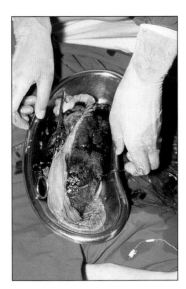

Figure 5.17 Placenta after the birth

Key Words

Chorion the outermost layer of cells that develops from a fertilised egg.

Chorionic villi Blood vessels where nutrients/waste are exchanged between mother's and baby's blood.

Amniotic fluid

Inside the uterus there is a sac, known as the amniotic sac, which contains the developing embryo and the foetus. The main purpose of the sac is to ensure that the foetus can grow safely. The warm fluid inside the sac is very important and without it the foetus would have difficulty continuing to grow.

The main functions of the amnoitic fluid are:

◆ to enable the foetus to float freely in the early stages, allowing limbs to stretch and flex

◆ to keep the foetus at a constant warm body temparature of approximately 37°C

◆ to protect the foetus from knocks, jolts, falls and bangs, acting like a cushion

Other factors

1. The foetus may drink a little of the amniotic fluid and this is safe and healthy.

2. Although most of the waste products are taken out via the umbilical cord, a small amount of urine may pass out of the foetus into the amniotic fluid.

⊃ DEVELOPMENT OF THE FOETUS

⊃ Week 6

Figure 5.18 The embryo is the size of a grain of rice

⊃ Embryonic facts (four weeks after conception)

◆ Embryo is 4–6 mm ($\frac{1}{4}$″) from crown to rump
◆ Embryo floats in a fluid-filled sac
◆ A tiny heart beats, seen as a bulge on the front of the chest
◆ Eyes and inner ears begin to form
◆ Four limb buds begin to develop
◆ Simple brain, spine and cerebral nervous system develop
◆ Internal organs, blood, bone muscle and blood vessels begin to develop

⊃ Pregnant Woman

◆ No visible signs
◆ Breasts may be uncomfortable
◆ Areola and nipple begin to darken
◆ Tiredness and irritability caused by the pregnancy hormone progesterone
◆ Morning sickness gets worse, some women feel sick all day
◆ Some have experience of light bleeding or spotting
◆ May need to urinate more frequently due to increased hormones

⊃ Week 8

At eight weeks the foetus is the size of a strawberry and the uterus is the size of a pear.

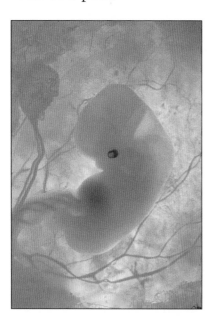

Figure 5.19 Foetus at 8 weeks

⊃ Foetus facts (six weeks after conception)

◆ The embryo is now called a foetus

◆ Measures 2.2 cm (1") from crown to rump

◆ The foetus has heart valves

◆ Spine and neural tube are rapidly developing (hence the importance of taking folic acid to prevent spina bifida)

◆ Foetus moves around

◆ Arms, legs, shoulders, elbows, hips and knees are detectable

◆ Fingers and toes are forming although joined by webs of skin

◆ Middle part of baby's ear will have developed. Responsible for balance and hearing

◆ Eyes are starting to form

◆ All the major organs are present in simplistic form

⊃ Pregnant Women

◆ Sickness and nausea. This could be severe

◆ Weight gain 0.5 – 1kg (1 – 2 lb)

◆ Breasts are tender, enlarging and blood vessels form under the skin.

◆ Pain down the back of the legs caused by pressure on the sciatic nerve from the growing uterus

- ◆ Slight thickening of the waist
- ◆ Increased need to pass urine caused by the pressure on the bladder.
- ◆ Constipation caused by increased levels of progesterone causing the bowel to slow down
- ◆ Very tired caused by a increase in the pregnancy hormone progesterone
- ◆ Affects a woman's feelings towards intercourse. Some people avoid sex and others feel the need for more
- ◆ Mother must continue to take folic acid until week 12 of the pregnancy to prevent spina bifida

⊃ Week 12

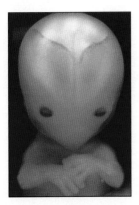

Figure 5.20 Foetus at 12 weeks

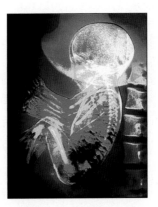

Figure 5.21 Back of foetus spinal cord showing

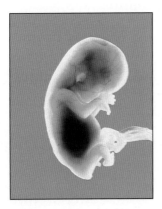

Figure 5.22 The foetus at 12 weeks

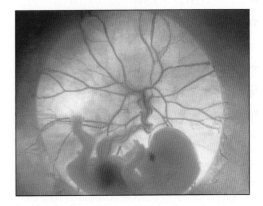

Figure 5.23 In amniotic sac

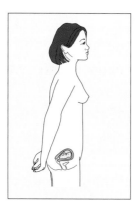

Figure 5.24 12 Weeks

⟲ Week 12

⟲ Foetus facts (ten weeks after conception)

◆ Foetus is approximately 6 cm ($2\frac{1}{2}$")from crown to rump and 9–14 g ($\frac{1}{2}$ oz) It would fit into the palm of your hand
◆ Foetus looks like a human, it is fully formed in miniature
◆ Foetus can swim and make a fist
◆ Foetus is moving but cannot be felt
◆ Organs, muscles, limbs, bones and sex organs are well developed
◆ Heart is beating strongly and fast (twice as fast as an adult's)
◆ Foetus can suck thumb
◆ Foetus is sensitive to heat, touch, light and sound
◆ Takes sips of the amniotic fluid
◆ Fingers and toes separate and nails begin to grow
◆ Eyelids cover the eyes which will remain closed for three months
◆ Head becomes more rounded
◆ Hiccups, and can open and close mouth

⟲ Pregnant Woman

At 12 weeks the foetus cannot be felt although some 'flutters' (foetal movements known as quickening) may be felt at 16 weeks

◆ Breasts will be heavier and tender
◆ Top of uterus can be felt above the pubic bone
◆ Thickening of the waist
◆ Sickness may begin to ease
◆ Pressure on the bladder is not so great so the desire to pass urine should be less

◆ Hormonal changes may make the mother emotional

◆ Constipation

◆ The lung, heart and kidneys will be working harder due to the increased blood circulation in the mother's body

⊃ Week 24

⊃ Foetus Facts

◆ Foetus measures 21 cm (8″) in length and weighs around 700 g ($1\frac{1}{2}$lb)

◆ Substantial weight gain

◆ The UK recognises 24 weeks as legally viable for a baby to survive outside the uterus (termination after this date is illegal unless severe abnormalities are evident)

◆ Chances of survival would be reasonable in the neonatal intensive care unit (NICU) although the lungs would be inactive and would require ventilation

◆ Face is fully formed

◆ Soft nails

◆ **Vernix** (white greasy substance) forms

◆ **Lanugo** (downy hair covering the foetus) forms

◆ Hair grown on head

◆ Skin is red and wrinkled

◆ Eyelids fused together (open during the twenty-sixth week)

◆ Bones are starting to harden

◆ Exercises vigorously

◆ Fingerprints have formed

◆ Has definite periods of sleep and waking

◆ May respond to loud noises or music

⊃ Pregnant Woman

◆ May have gained 4-4.5 kg (8–10 lb) and is putting on weight at a more rapid rate

◆ The fundus (top of uterus) is about 5-7 cm (2–3″) above the navel and a definite bulge can be seen

◆ Can feel the foetus kicking, somersaulting and turning

◆ May feel the foetus change position

◆ A clear heartbeat can be heard by the midwife

◆ Often 'blooms' at this stage with excellent skin, nails and hair, due to hormones

- Some women notice a change in skin pigmentation (more common in dark-haired mothers)
- Gums may bleed and feel a little swollen
- Water retention and puffy hands can be a problem
- Stretch marks develop
- May experience back ache. Should wear flat shoes if possible
- Heartburn and shortness of breath, mother needs to sit up straight
- Uterus pressing on the bladder causes discomfort and the need to urinate frequently.

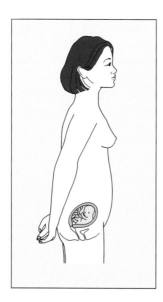

Figure 5.25 Diagram demonstrating the size of the foetus in relation to the female body

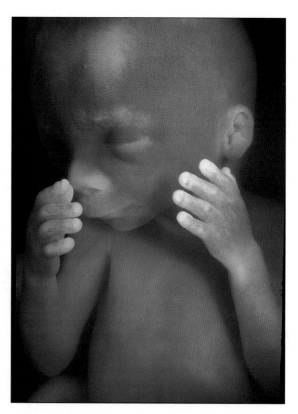

Figure 5.26 This unborn foetus is covered in lanugo and vernix at about 22–24 weeks. The lanugo and vernix often disappear before the birth

Figure 5.27 Foetus at 24 weeks - fingers and fingernails formed

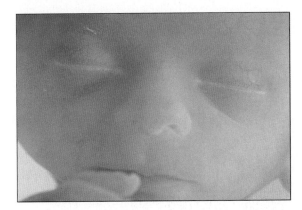

Figure 5.28 Sucking thumb

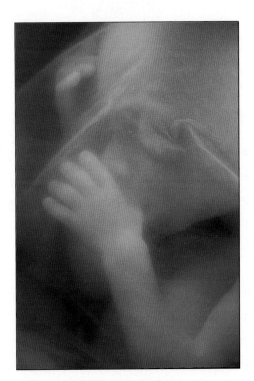

Figure 5.29 In amniotic sac

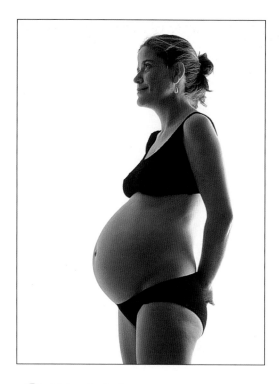

Figure 5.30 A pregnant woman at 36 weeks

⊃ Week 36

⊃ Foetal Facts

- ◆ Weighs around 2.5kg (5 lb) length 33.5 cm (13″)
- ◆ Hair may have grown about two inches
- ◆ The foetus has put on weight and has a more rounded appearance
- ◆ Skin is pink
- ◆ The head may have dropped into the pelvis ready for birth. This is called engaging
- ◆ Nails have grown on fingers and toes
- ◆ Testicles descend in a boy
- ◆ Foetus will gain 28 g (1oz) per day from now on
- ◆ Foetus would have an excellent chance of survival if born early
- ◆ Vernix and lanugo disappear

⊃ Pregnant Women

- ◆ Once the foetus drops into the pelvis and the height of the foetus lowers, the mother may find the indigestion and breathlessness disappear
- ◆ Continued need to pass urine
- ◆ Legs may feel swollen and heavy. Needs to sit with her legs up
- ◆ Skin is stretching and itchy, stretch marks may develop
- ◆ Ribs can feel uncomfortable

- May not feel the foetus move as frequently because of restricted space
- Varicose veins may be a problem.
- May be a little anxious prior to the birth
- May have difficulty sleeping

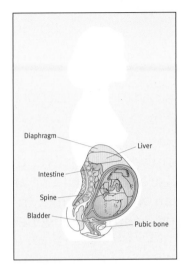

Figure 5.31 Foetus at 36 weeks in relation to mother

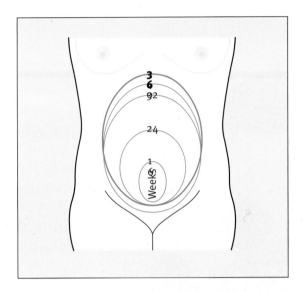

Figure 5.32 Height of the **fundus**

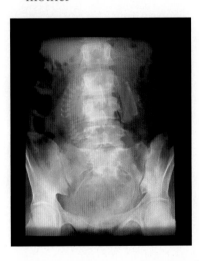

Figure 5.33 Picture showing the foetus in relation to the mother

Key Words

Vernix a white greasy substance that covers the baby. Its purpose is to protect the baby's skin while in the uterus.

Lanugo fine, downy hair that covers the foetus from the fifth month of pregnancy.

Fundus the height of the uterus measured by feeling the mother's abdomen. It often indicates the stage of pregnancy.

⟳ THE MIDWIFE

Whilst there are many other health care professionals involved with the pregnancy – it is the midwife who is likely to have the most contact with the expectant mother, her partner and family.

Figure 5.34 Midwife in hospital

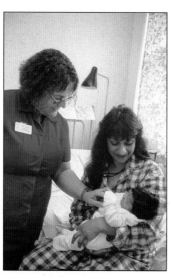

It is most likely that a midwife will deliver the baby unless complications arise and it would be at this point that an obstetrician will be brought in to perform sections, forceps, ventouse deliveries (see Chapter 6).

Figure 5.35 Holding the new baby

Choice of ante-natal classes

The purpose of the antenatal classes are to prepare the expectant mother and her partner for the pregnancy, birth and beyond.

Who runs the classes:

◆ Midwives (most common)
◆ Obstetricians
◆ Birth teachers by National Childbirth Trust (NCT)

Partners

Some partners do not wish to be involved, they may feel daunted by all the pregnant mothers, embarrassed about the nature of the childbirth, scared of 'blood', etc. However, the partners should be encouraged to support the expectant mother and to be prepared for the weeks ahead. Partners can learn how they can help the woman throughout the pregnancy.

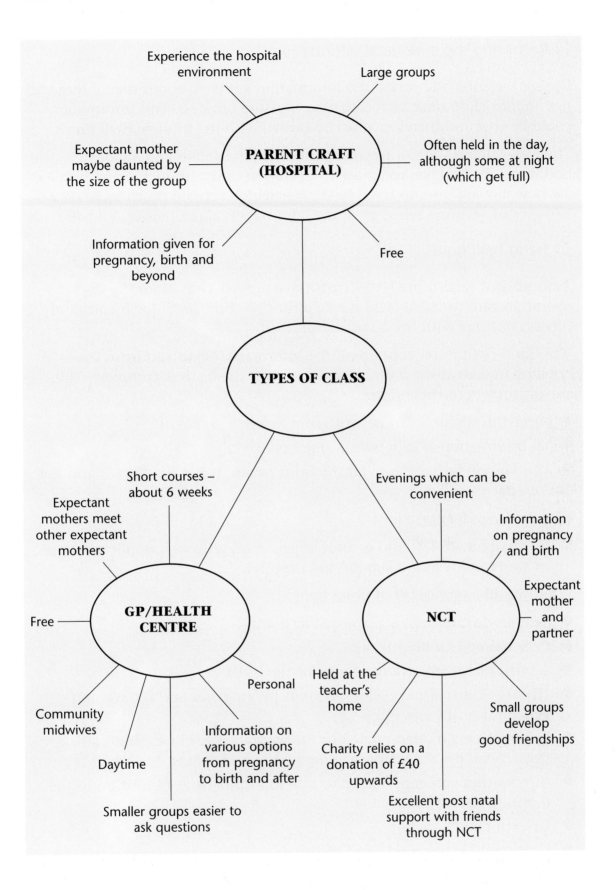

Experience the hospital environment

Large groups

Expectant mother maybe daunted by the size of the group

PARENT CRAFT (HOSPITAL)

Often held in the day, although some at night (which get full)

Information given for pregnancy, birth and beyond

Free

TYPES OF CLASS

Short courses – about 6 weeks

Evenings which can be convenient

Expectant mothers meet other expectant mothers

Information on pregnancy and birth

Free

GP/HEALTH CENTRE

NCT

Expectant mother and partner

Community midwives

Personal

Small groups develop good friendships

Daytime

Information on various options from pregnancy to birth and after

Held at the teacher's home

Charity relies on a donation of £40 upwards

Smaller groups easier to ask questions

Excellent post natal support with friends through NCT

⟩ Recording the ante-natal information

During the antenatal period the information gathered about the mother and her unborn child must be recorded to measure progress. This information could be vital and therefore must be carried with the mother at all times.

There are various ways of recording the antenatal details and a more traditional method was using the co-operation card; although many hospitals are now moving towards hand-held notes which contain much more detail and give the woman access to all the information about herself and baby.

⟩ Hand-held notes

A number of Healthcare NHS Trusts have moved away from the co-operation card to Hand-Held notes; although some areas have both and others continue with the co-operation card.

The Hand-Held notes contain all the information gathered from the booking in date at the ante-natal clinic until the birth is complete. There are <u>advantages</u> to these notes:

◆ more information can be written in detail

◆ all information is kept within one booklet

◆ the woman has access to all the information regarding herself and her unborn baby

The main <u>disadvantage</u> is:

◆ If the notes are lost and cannot be replaced, although duplicate copies of scans and tests are kept by the hospital.

<u>What would a typical set of notes contain?</u>

◆ Telephone numbers, e.g. the delivery suite

◆ Personal and family history

◆ A birth plan with arrangements for the birth

◆ History of menstrual cycles, previous pregnancies and the woman's general health

◆ Information gathered related to the woman, e.g. blood group, urine tests, blood pressure, any swelling of feet and hands, and weight

◆ Information gathered related to the unborn baby, e.g. position in the uterus, heartbeat, movement

◆ Growth charts

◆ Ultrasound scan reports and pictures

◆ Hospital admissions

◆ Infant feeding

◆ Post-natal period.

The notes and birth plan should be available for the midwife if it is a home birth, or taken into hospital with the woman when she goes into labour.

What is a birth plan?

A birth plan has been designed to enable the woman and her partner to make informed choices about the baby's birth. The midwife will discuss with the expectant mother and possibly father what options are available and the woman will write down her preferences on the chart.

The birth plan is meant to be the ideal situation, although births do not always go according to plan. It is a good idea to have thought about a number of the following questions well beforehand.

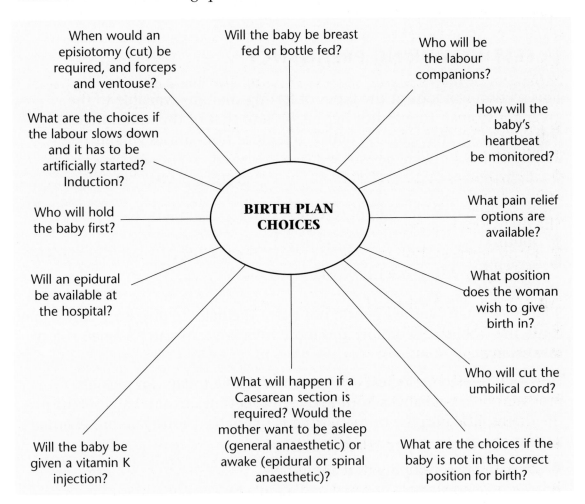

The woman and her partner may make several choices in response to the birth plan, but it is also a good idea to have an open mind and enable changes to take place if the need arises.

Key Words

Ante-natal before birth

Health visitor a qualified nurse who opts to look after the health of the family in the community

Paediatrician a specialist doctor who cares for babies, children and teenagers

Obstetrician a specialist doctor who cares for women during pregnancy, labour and birth

Physiotherapist a trained healthcare professional who uses exercise, massage, etc. to help people to regain their health

Consultant a senior doctor leading a team in hospital known as Mr, Mrs or Miss

Dietician a health care professional who gives nutritional advice

General practitioner qualified family doctor

Gynaecologist a specialist doctor who cares for women of any age and their reproductive organs

Midwife a highly qualified practitioner (may be a nurse) who looks after the pregnant woman, delivers babies and visits the home for 10 days after the birth

TESTING DURING PREGNANCY

This section will look at the types of testing that are available to the pregnant woman to monitor her health and that of the unborn baby. Further testing that can also detect genetic abnormalities will also be discussed.

There are three main types of testing:

◆ routine
◆ screening
◆ diagnostic

Some of the tests carried out do not harm the baby in any way, others may cause the woman discomfort and more invasive tests carry a small risk of miscarriage.

However, the technological equipment available today can pick up problems before a baby is born and can sometimes treat a baby whilst in the uterus. The purpose of the testing is to enable healthcare professionals to find out if:

◆ the baby is developing as it should be
◆ and that the woman continues to be healthy

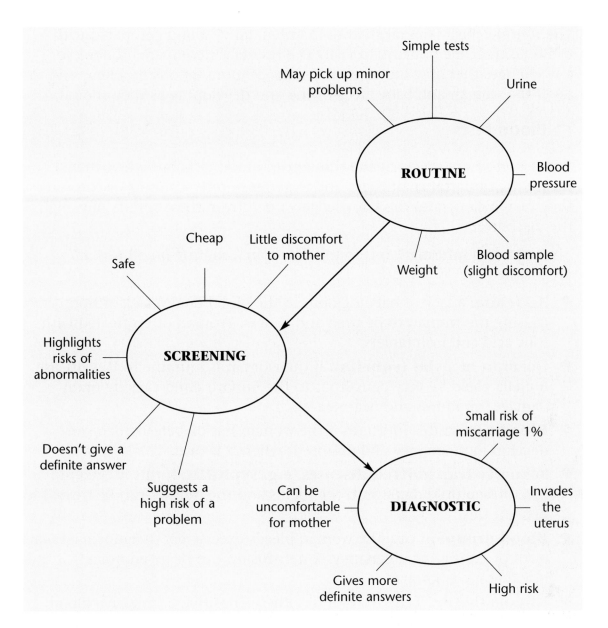

Routine tests

Routine tests are carried out during the antenatal period to monitor the baby and woman and to check that everything is progressing as it should be.

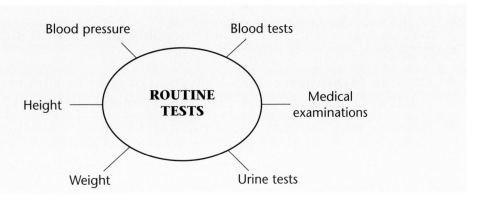

The routine checks are taken at each antenatal visit and compared with those taken at the booking-in visit. The results are compared to look for any changes that may indicate early signs of more serious problems and to see if the woman and baby are growing and developing as they should.

Blood tests

Some women are scared at the thought of blood tests but when they realise the importance of them and experience only a minor discomfort they may believe that the knowledge gained from these results outweighs the discomfort.

The following information is found out from a routine blood test in pregnancy:

- **Anaemia:** a lack of haemoglobin in the blood due to lack of iron, causing the woman to be tired and listless. Woman often treated with folic acid and iron tablets.

- **German measles (rubella):** if the woman is immune to this disease. Rubella could be very dangerous to the unborn child causing brain damage, blindness and deafness.

- **Blood sugar:** this indicates if the woman has diabetes which can develop in pregnancy and disappear when it is over.

- **Sexually-transmitted diseases. e.g. syphillis:** if this is evident it can cause untold damage to the foetus and the mother can be treated to prevent this.

- **Blood group:** in case the woman bleeds excessively (haemorrhages) at birth or during the pregnancy. A transfusion can be given quickly if the blood group is known.

- **Rhesus factor:** if the woman has Rhesus positive or negative blood

- **Hepatitis B and C:** this virus causes liver disease. Both are treatable if the woman is found to have the infection.

- **HIV:** the woman can pass this to the baby via the placenta or through breastfeeding. Advice can be offered.

Urine tests

A small sample of urine is tested by the midwife. They will indicate the following:

- **Protein (albumen):** sign of infection or possibly a more serious condition later on in pregnancy, pre-eclampsia (see page 124)

- **Glucose (sugar):** may indicate diabetes known as gestational diabetes during pregnancy. It is controlled by diet and possibly insulin.

◆ **Ketones:** may happen when the woman has hyperemesis (excessive vomiting) which will require hospital treatment. The woman may be dehydrated requiring a drip to replace fluids and glucose. If left the woman could go into a coma and die (ketosis).

Height and weight

The height often gives the midwife an indication of the pelvic size. Height over 160cm (5ft) and more than size 3 shoe indicate a normal sized pelvis. The weight will be taken initially to use as a base line to compare the weight of the woman as the pregnancy progresses (some areas do not weigh the woman).

◆ **Weight loss:** baby may have stopped growing, mother may be ill.

◆ **Weight gain:** sign of pre-eclampsia if excessive.

Most women will gain between 10-12.5kg (22-28lbs) during a normal pregnancy.

Blood pressure

This is again compared with the blood pressure measured during the booking-in visit.

◆ **Significant rise:** may indicate pre-eclampsia.

Medical examination

This is usually carried out by the midwife and involves:

◆ **Feeling the abdomen:** to check the position, size of the foetus and whether it fits with the EDD.

◆ **Listening to the heartbeat of the foetus:** this checks for any irregularity in the heartbeat. Normal heartbeat of a foetus is 110-150 beats per minute.

◆ **Checking legs:** these are checked for swelling, and signs of varicose veins.

Testing for abnormalities

Improved technology has enabled doctors to detect and diagnose some abnormalities of the developing foetus. This may sound a simple straightforward procedure, however it can involve the woman and her partner with many weeks of worry waiting to find out the results of the tests.

However, the tests can confirm that the baby is developing well and without abnormalities which is reassuring for the parents. If a problem is detected the woman and the partner then may have to decide whether or not to go ahead with a termination (to get rid of the unborn foetus). Some parents would not consider this option and therefore choose not to have further tests, which may carry a risk of miscarriage.

Women have the right to refuse screening tests. Some do, because they would not consider a termination. Others choose to have the tests even though a termination would be out of the question, so that they could prepare themselves and their family for the future.

⊃ Screening tests

The following are examples of screening tests used during the pregnancy:

- ◆ Ultra-sound scans
- ◆ Nuchal fold scan
- ◆ AFP test (Alphafetoprotein)
- ◆ Serum screening

AFP test

What is it?

- ◆ A test which measures how much alphafetoprotein is in the woman's blood
- ◆ A blood test will be taken from the woman between the 15th and 18th week of pregnancy

High APF
- ◆ Maybe further than 18 weeks pregnant
- ◆ Twins
- ◆ In rare cases a problem with the spinal cord called spina bifida

Low APF
- ◆ Less than 15 weeks pregnant
- ◆ Indicates the baby has Down's Syndrome (higher risk with older women)

Advantages	Disadvantages
◆ May indicate the need for a diagnostic test without going straight to this risky procedure ◆ It's like a warning test ◆ Woman has not put her baby at risk ◆ It's a simple blood test procedure	◆ It only suggests that Down's Syndrome is a possibility ◆ The only way to be certain is to have cells from the foetus collected and tested ◆ Could cause worry to the woman for no reason

Nuchal Fold Measurement (ultrasound)

What is it?

- ◆ This is a new test and is not widely available in this country
- ◆ It is called a nuchal translucency measurement
- ◆ The test looks at the fold of skin on the back of the babys neck which is thicker in babies who have Down's Syndrome
- ◆ To give a positive result a diagnostic test would be offered (see next chart)

Advantages	Disadvantages
◆ It is not invasive to the woman ◆ No risk of miscarriage as a result of the test ◆ It claims to have approximately 90% detection rate (in combination with specific blood tests)	◆ Not widely available in all hospitals ◆ Only available in the larger more central hospitals ◆ It is not conclusive ◆ It only indicates that it is possible

Ultrasound scan
What is it?

◆ An ultrasound scan will give a picture on a tv type screen of the baby. The picture will be black and white and the parents may find it difficult to identify the baby
◆ Usually the woman requires a full bladder, she will lie on her back, gel will be placed on her abdomen, and a hand held scanner will be rubbed back and forth on the abdomen until a picture appears on the screen
◆ Much information is gathered from the screen related to the baby's size, and any major abnormalities
◆ Checks how many babies the woman is having and confirms the EDD
◆ Checks the position of the placenta

Technological Advancements
Doppler Ultrasound

◆ A new 3D scanner giving a three dimensional picture of the baby
◆ Not widely available
◆ Capable of measuring the blood flow to the uterus and baby
◆ Advantages may be that women who may have a risk of problems such as pre-eclampsia or very small babies

Advantages

◆ It is very safe and does not affect or harm the baby
◆ Does not hurt the woman, only the discomfort of a full bladder
◆ Exciting for the parents to see a heartbeat and shape of their baby
◆ Encourages the woman to bond early in the pregnancy as it becomes reality
◆ Enjoyable experience
◆ Can indicate abnormalities
◆ Can tell the sex of the baby
◆ Can pick up multiple pregnancies

Disadvantages

◆ None known
◆ Although scanning does not take place all the time as a precautionary measure

Serum screening

This test is used to detect abnormalities that may occur with the unborn foetus e.g. Down's Syndrome. The tests are sometimes known as:

◆ Triple or Barts test (three tests)
◆ Double test (two tests)

The tests are slightly different and it combines the result of

◆ AFP
◆ Estriol (see AFP test)
◆ Human chorionic genadotrophin

If the results are negative it means that it is unlikely that Down's Syndrome is present. A positive result means a higher chance of Down's Syndrome is likely. If a woman is at a higher risk she will be offered an amniocentesis.

⊃ DIAGNOSTIC TESTS

The two main diagnostic tests available are:

◆ Amniocentesis
◆ Cordocentesis

The amniocentesis test is more widely available than the CVS and there has been concern about the risk factors involved with it. Some evidence suggests the risk of miscarriage with CVs is similar to amniocentesis.

⊃ Amniocentesis

Why would the test be offered?

◆ To women over the age of 37 years due to a higher risk of carrying Down's Syndrome babies
◆ If the AFP serum screening or nuchal fold scan indicated that there was a high risk of Down's Syndrome.
◆ Ultrasound scan has detected an abnormality
◆ History of genetic disorders such as Down's Syndrome

⊃ The test

The test is carried out with the help of an ultrasound scan. It is very important so that the position of the baby and the placenta are known. A hollow fine needle is passed through the skin of the abdomen, uterus wall and amniotic sac, and some amniotic fluid is drawn off and sent away to be tested. If this needle went into the placenta or foetus it might cause abnormalities. It is carried out between the 15th and 17th week of pregnancy.

The test is able to detect:

◆ Down's Syndrome
◆ Viral infections
◆ Sex of the baby (Important fo some sex-related genetic disorders, see Chapter 18)
◆ Lung developments of the foetus
◆ Neural tube defects, e.g. spina bifida

Amniocentesis

Advantages	Disadvantages
◆ If abnormality detected parents can prepare for the birth of this child	◆ Take 2–5 weeks to get the results
◆ Some problems may be sorted out in the uterus	◆ Length of time waiting for the results is very worrying for parents
◆ Parents who may choose to terminate have the choice	◆ Once an abnormality is detected the foetus could be 20 weeks and the woman has felt the movements in the uterus, which may make a termination of the pregnancy harder
◆ Parents may continue the pregnancy in a relaxed manner if it is proven to be free of some abnormalities	◆ A termination at this stage would require the woman to go through labour
	◆ Risk of miscarriage of a healthy baby
	◆ Foetus or placenta could be pierced or damaged
	◆ If woman does not believe in a termination, she may refuse an amniocentesis rather than risk a miscarriage
	◆ Membranes are punctured

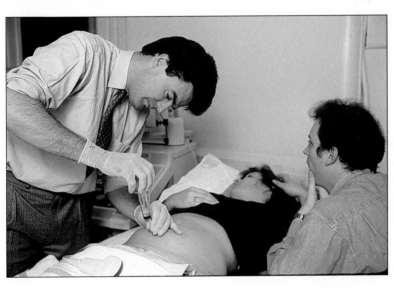

Figure 5.36 Amniocentesis

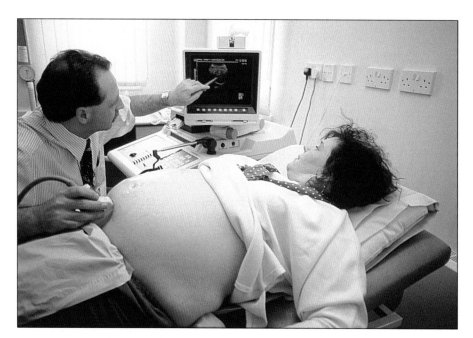

Figure 5.37 Ultrasound Scan

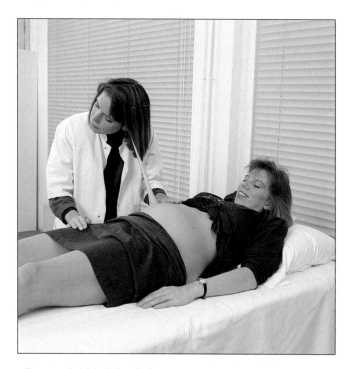

Figure 5.38 Midwife listens to the foetal heart

Cordocentesis

This test is carried out when urgent information is needed and usually after 20 weeks of pregnancy.

Test

The test is carried out (using an ultrasound scan) by passing a needle into the abdomen and the umbilical cord to obtain blood cells from the baby.

The blood cells will give the following information:

◆ Chromosomal problems

◆ Anaemia affecting the baby's blood

◆ Rhesus disease and if a blood transfusion is required

Key Words

Amniocentesis a diagnostic test carried out by extracting amniotic fluid to confirm certain genetic abnormalities

Down's Syndrome a genetic hereditary disorder present from the time of conception. One extra chromosome is present causing physical and mental disability

Ultrasound (scan) sound waves bounce off the mother's abdomen relaying a black and white picture on a screen showing the baby's internal organs

---

PROBLEMS DURING PREGNANCY

This section will look at some of the common minor problems/discomforts associated with pregnancy. It will also consider some of the more serious complications that can arise during pregnancy.

Minor problems

Pregnancy is the most natural physical condition for women and the majority of women enjoy a healthy pregnancy and a safe birth. However, there are times during pregnancy that they see considerable **physical** and **emotional** changes which may be of a minor nature, or could if not **monitored** correctly develop into serious more complicated issues

Below are some of the minor physical problems that a pregnant woman may encounter:

The following chart briefly highlights possible causes of these minor complaints and how they can be improved.

Minor Problem	Possible Cause	Solutions
Sickness at various times of the day	◆ Hormone imbalance (disappears after 12th week of pregnancy) ◆ Severe sickness known as hyperemesis is more serious; a doctor should be consulted and requires urgent treatment	◆ If during the morning get up slowly, try a dry biscuit before you get up ◆ Try ginger, flat Coca Cola, small snacks ◆ Hospitalisation to rehydrate the woman due to lack of fluids
Feeling faint	◆ Due to lowered blood pressure ◆ Moving quickly can have a brief effect on the blood supply to the brain ◆ Blood sugar level may have dropped	◆ Eat smaller meals more frequently ◆ Don't eat too much high sugar foods causing a rise in blood sugar, extra insulin and then a rapid blood sugar drop ◆ Head between the knees or lower than legs
Cramp	◆ Calf muscles contracting shortening caused by a lack of salt and calcium and potassium	◆ Avoid high heels ◆ Consult the doctor if it becomes serious ◆ Massage the affected area
Breathlessness	◆ Happens towards the later stages where the baby presses on the diaphragm. Disappears after 36th week when the head engages ◆ Sign of anaemia	◆ Sit or lay more upright ◆ Rest
Heartburn	◆ Burning feeling from the stomach into the throat caused by too much acid ◆ Hormonal effects	◆ Take care taking antacids, consult a doctor ◆ Sit up in bed ◆ Small meals frequently ◆ Avoid pies and fatty foods
Dental	◆ Gums become inflamed and may bleed	◆ Brush teeth and floss more often ◆ Visit the dentist regularly, it's free
Varicose Veins	◆ Swollen veins in the legs (can be in the vulva) ◆ Increased weight ◆ Pregnancy hormones relax the blood vessel walls	◆ Avoid standing ◆ Keep moving ◆ Don't cross legs ◆ Good support tights ◆ Elastic stockings
Urine leakage	◆ Coughing, sneezing and laughing can cause the urine to leak ◆ Towards the end of pregnancy and after the birth ◆ Weak pelvic floor muscles	◆ Pelvic floor exercises ◆ Aqua natal classes – exercise strengthens the pelvic floor

Minor Problem	Possible Cause	Solutions
Frequent urination	◆ Passing water more often is caused by hormones in early pregnancy ◆ Later months pressure on the bladder ◆ With pain or burning may indicate ◆ Infection	◆ Empty bladder regularly ◆ Visit doctor if pain or burning
Swollen ankles	◆ More common in later months ◆ If other swelling i.e. face and hands, could be pre-eclampsia	◆ Put feet up ◆ Don't wear tight socks, etc. ◆ Walking ◆ Rotate ankles ◆ See GP if other swelling occurs
Numbness	◆ Tingling like pins and needles can be felt in the arms and legs ◆ Pressure on nerves from the uterus as it grows	◆ Lie on side ◆ Prop up with lots of pillows ◆ Consult GP if it becomes extreme
Unable to sleep	◆ Worry about the responsibility of parenthood, the birth ◆ Uncomfortable ◆ Baby kicking ◆ Require the toilet	◆ Relaxing bath ◆ Breathing exercises ◆ Lots of pillows ◆ Music ◆ Warm drink ◆ Reading ◆ Massaging (partner)
Backache	◆ More common in later pregnancy ◆ Extra weight and enlarged uterus cause muscular strain ◆ Hormones ◆ Could be a kidney infection	◆ Avoid straining the back ◆ Pick up sensibly, bend the knees ◆ Sit in a straight high backed chair ◆ Lots of pillows ◆ If kidney infection consult GP
Piles (haemorrhoids)	◆ Varicose veins of the back passage (rectum) caused by strain when constipated ◆ Pressure on the circulatory systems	◆ Bleeding: go to GP ◆ Drink lots of fluid ◆ Exercise ◆ Creams can be applied ◆ Ice pack
Tiredness	◆ The first three months are tiring as the baby forms ◆ The last three months are tiring due to the weight of the baby ◆ Other children to look after ◆ Work	◆ Relax, and gain as much sleep and rest as possible ◆ Ask for help with domestic chores

Minor Problem	Possible Cause	Solutions
Flushing and sweating	◆ Hormone changes ◆ Blood flow to the skin increased	◆ Keep air circulating in the bedroom ◆ Cotton clothing ◆ A fan ◆ Cool baths
Constipation	◆ Inability to pass faeces is caused by the hormone progesterone ◆ Relaxes the wall of the intestine and doesn't work as well	◆ High-fibre foods ◆ Lots of fluid (water) ◆ Exercise
Thrush	◆ A white thick discharge from the vagina ◆ Itching ◆ Soreness ◆ Bleeding ◆ Painful to urinate	◆ A pessary and cream from the GP ◆ No soap ◆ Plain yoghurt ◆ No tight clothing around the vagina

⊃ Complications around the pregnancy

There are occasions when some women during their pregnancy may have or develop complications that require close monitoring and special care. It is possible through antenatal care that a serious condition may be discovered, which could save the woman's and baby's lives. This highlights the importance of attending the antenatal clinics and classes.

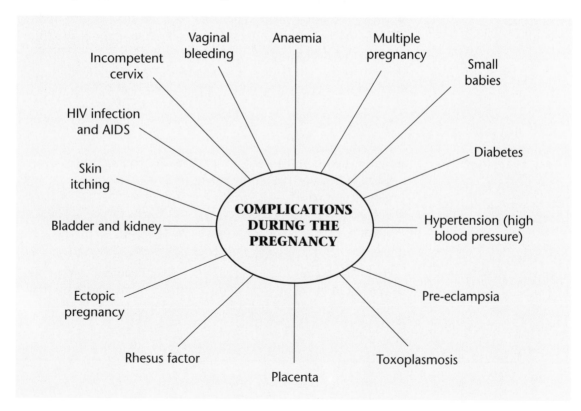

ANAEMIA

- Mother very tired and lethargic
- Mild or severe

Cause

- Lack of iron required to help make red bloods which transports oxygen to the cells of the body to re-use energy

Treatment

- Iron and folic acid tablets
- More foods containing iron, e.g. red meat, cabbage, spinach

INCOMPETENT CERVIX

- This is where the neck of the uterus – the cervix – is weak and cannot hold in the contents of the uterus causing a miscarriage

Treatment

- A small stitch will be put across the cervix to keep it closed
- Towards the end of the pregnancy it will be removed

TOXOPLASMOSIS

- This is caused by a germ which is found in meat and cat faeces
- The woman may develop flu like symptoms
- It is possible for the disease to pass through the placenta to the unborn child

Cause

- Woman eating undercooked meat infected by the germ
- Woman has contact with faeces of a cat
- It can cause a miscarriage or stillbirth, premature baby, baby may develop problems with the brain and eyes, causing learning disabilities and blindness

Treatment

- Prevention
  1. Cook meat well
  2. Avoid raw eggs, unpasteurised milk or dairy products
  3. Wash soil from all vegetables
  4. Don't handle cat litter trays or wear gloves to handle
  5. Good personal hygiene
- Woman may be given antibiotic if detected early

DIABETES

◆ Some women develop diabetes during pregnancy and sugar is present in the urine and disappears after the pregnancy

Cause

◆ Some women who have high sugar levels may have true diabetes which means that their body has a problem producing insulin which controls the blood sugar

Treatment

◆ Adjustment of insulin to keep blood sugar levels even
◆ Careful diet

PLACENTA

◆ May be bleeding from the vagina
◆ Bleeding from the vagina with pain, known as:-

ANTE-PARTUM HAEMORRHAGE

Cause

1. PLACENTA PRAEVIA – where the placenta lies across the cervix blocking it, and the baby cannot deliver normally
2. PLACENTA ABRUPTIA – where some of the placenta was separated from the uterus

Treatment

Placenta Praevia – hospitalisation and immediate care, possibly the delivery of the baby
Placenta Abruptia – this is a very serious condition and requires immediate hospitalisation because the oxygen supply to the baby can be seriously affected

HIGH BLOOD PRESSURE

◆ Sometimes known as pregnancy-induced hypertension maybe a sign of pre-eclampsia

Pre-Eclampsia

◆ Symptoms include:
   1. High blood pressure
   2. Swelling face, hands and legs
   3. Protein in the urine
   4. Excessive weight gain
   5. Severe pain in the abdomen later on during the pregnancy
   6. Severe headaches

Cause

◆ Unknown
◆ It is very serious and can cause the baby to have a reduced oxygen supply
◆ It is dangerous because the woman may develop fits (convulsions)
◆ Maternal death

Treatment

◆ Bed rest
◆ Cut down salt in the diet
◆ Drugs to lower blood pressure
◆ Severe signs would require hospitalisation
◆ May be required to deliver the baby as soon as possible

BLADDER AND KIDNEY

◆ Pain passing urine, chill, fever, blood in the urine, possibly a burning sensation
◆ A pain in the lower back, rapid heartbeat, vomiting and headaches

Causes

◆ Cystitis – is a bacterial infection causing the bladder to be inflamed
◆ Kidney infection

Treatment

◆ Some antibiotics are safe during pregnancy, prescribed by the GP
◆ If kidney infection, call a doctor immediately

RHESUS FACTOR

- The issue is whether the woman's red blood cells carry a protein called the Rhesus Factor
- The problem arises when the woman is Rhesus Negative (approx 15%) and the baby's blood is RH (Rhesus) positive
- The baby may carry RH positive blood
- The woman produces antibodies which destroy the baby's red blood cells and if not treated the baby could die. This disease is known as **HAEMOLYTIC DISEASE**

Causes

- During pregnancy a small amount of the baby's blood crosses the placenta and RH positive blood enters the woman's blood
- The woman's blood thinks that there is something foreign in the blood, and the woman produces antibodies to fight it
- There are not enough antibodies to harm the first baby but it could seriously harm any further babies

Treatment

- A blood test early in pregnancy of the woman, or after
  1. Miscarriage
  2. Abortion
  3. Amniocentesis
  4. CVS tests
- If the first baby is RH positive and the woman is RH negative the woman will be given a protective vaccination called Anti-D to destroy any of the baby's blood cells in the woman's blood so that they cannot harm any other babies

SKIN ITCHING

- Itching over the body and limbs in the last three months can indicate a serious liver complaint (Including Jaundice)

Treatment

- Usually the woman is treated to prevent serious problems
- May require inducing the baby early

MULTIPLE PREGNANCIES

- Twins/triplets are the most common
- A greater risk of anaemia, pre-eclampsia and babies lying breech, or transverse

Causes

- The additional work the woman's body has to cope with

Treatment

- Regular antenatal checks
- Increased rest from 32 weeks
- If complications arise a Caesarean may be required

ECTOPIC PREGNANCY

- There is severe pain in the abdomen when pregnant
- There may be bleeding or not

Cause

- A fertilised egg has implanted itself into one of the fallopian tubes instead of the uterus
- This is not the correct place and is very dangerous
- Sometimes caused by a damaged tube

Treatment

- A serious condition which will require hospital treatment
- May lead to removal of the Fallopian tube
- Detected early, other techniques possible

SMALL BABIES

Babies not growing are known as 'small for date' babies

Causes

- Woman who smokes, poor diet
- Placenta not working (sometimes in diabetic women)

Treatment

- Close monitoring blood flow
- If baby distressed or has stopped growing the baby will be born early either by Caesarean section or induction

VAGINAL BLEEDING

◆ This may be a sign of a miscarriage if it is before 28 weeks

Cause

◆ Placenta problems

Treatment

◆ Any risk to the placenta (which is the baby's lifeline) could be dangerous, and the doctor will hospitalise the woman
◆ A blood transfusion may be required
◆ Slight bleeding may require the woman to rest

HIV INFECTION AND AIDS

◆ Acquired Immune Deficiency Syndrome, caused by Human Immune Deficiency Virus (HIV)
◆ The woman can pass this virus to her unborn child

Treatment

◆ Anti-AIDS drugs
◆ Planned Caesarean
◆ Woman advised not to breast feed

⊃ A HEALTHY LIFESTYLE DURING PREGNANCY

This section will consider how to ensure that the pregnant woman and her unborn child continue to grow, develop and maintain good health.

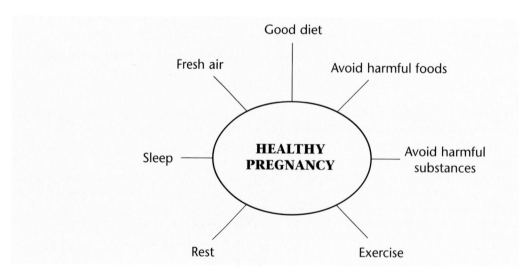

One of the best starts to any pregnancy is to have considered and carried out all the sound advice previously discussed within the pre-conceptual section of this book. Much of that advice should be carried out throughout the pregnancy together with the information gathered from this section.

⊃ EATING YOUR WAY THROUGH PREGNANCY!

This section will concentrate on the specific needs of the pregnant woman and her unborn baby.

The woman and her unborn baby require specific foods for a healthy and well-balanced diet throughout the pregnancy and after the birth. The following specific nutrients and examples of how to obtain these nutrients will contribute to a healthy pregnancy.

ANIMAL PROTEIN

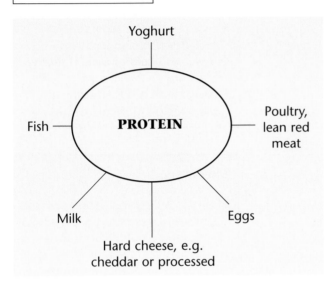

Check it out!

✔ Always choose lean cuts of meat
✔ Always cook meat thoroughly
✔ Grill meat and fish rather than fry it
✔ Eggs fresh, should be thoroughly cooked
✔ No soft cheeses

☆ A good idea is to read the label of pre-packed foods to check if they are suitable

Protein – is required for growth and repair

PLANT PROTEINS

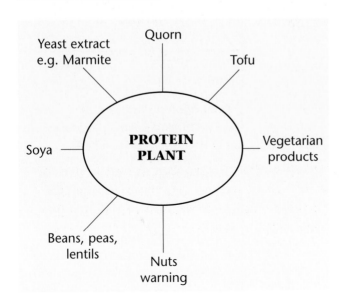

Check it out!

✔ The Department of Health advise PEANUTS and PEANUT products to be avoided whilst pregnant and breastfeeding. A higher risk of the baby developing a peanut allergy
✔ A dietician would be able to advise a woman with specific advice

☆ A good idea is to look for the vegetarian logo

VITAMIN C

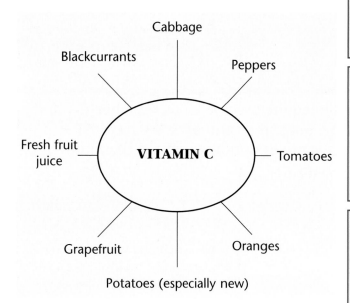

Cabbage

Blackcurrants

Peppers

Fresh fruit juice

VITAMIN C

Tomatoes

Grapefruit

Oranges

Potatoes (especially new)

☆ A good idea is to steam or microwave fresh vegetables, better still eat them raw, to keep the vitamin C. Try smoothies, fresh fruit cocktails!

Check it out!

✔ Vitamin C is lost during storage, preparation and cooking
✔ Eat fresh fruit and vegetables
✔ Twice as much vitamin C is required during pregnancy

Vitamin C

◆ Aids (helps) the absorption of IRON into the bloodstream
◆ It will also help to build a strong placenta
◆ Assists with healthy gums, prevents them from bleeding

IRON

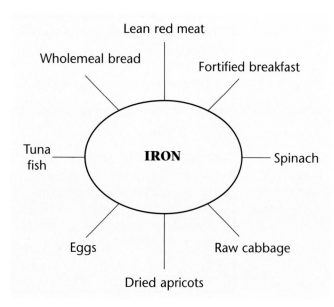

Lean red meat

Wholemeal bread

Fortified breakfast

Tuna fish

IRON

Spinach

Eggs

Raw cabbage

Dried apricots

Check it out!

✔ Liver is an excellent source of iron but avoid this because it contains very high amounts of vitamin A which could harm the baby Warning! Do not eat liver or liver products

☆ A good idea is to eat iron-rich foods with foods high in vitamin C to get the most iron from the food for your baby

Iron

◆ Is important to produce haemoglobin which produces the red bloods responsible for carrying oxygen to all living cells in the body
◆ The foetus takes iron from the woman to store in its liver for after the birth, lasting 4-6 months (reason – no iron in milk!)
◆ The extra blood required for the woman and baby

CALCIUM

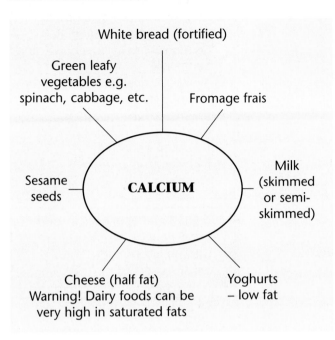

White bread (fortified)

Green leafy vegetables e.g. spinach, cabbage, etc.

Fromage frais

Sesame seeds

CALCIUM

Milk (skimmed or semi-skimmed)

Cheese (half fat) Warning! Dairy foods can be very high in saturated fats

Yoghurts – low fat

Check it out!

✔ Fortified means enriched foods by adding certain nutrients. It could be a legal requirement or carried out by the manufacturer because they choose to
✔ Many breakfast cereals are fortified with calcium
✔ Twice as much calcium is needed

☆ A good idea is to choose dairy products that are low in fat, e.g. skimmed milk, low fat cheese

Calcium

◆ Makes sure the bones and teeth of the foetus develop correctly which start to form in the 8th week of pregnancy
◆ Woman requires it because the calcium in her bones and teeth used up by the baby

FOLIC ACID

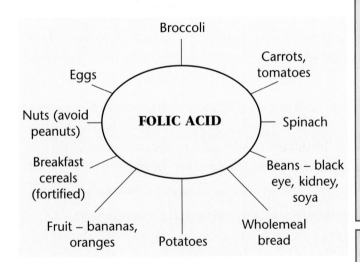

Broccoli

Eggs

Carrots, tomatoes

Nuts (avoid peanuts)

FOLIC ACID

Spinach

Breakfast cereals (fortified)

Beans – black eye, kidney, soya

Fruit – bananas, oranges

Potatoes

Wholemeal bread

Check it out!

✔ To prevent spina bifida it is essential to take folic acid before conception
✔ The Department of Health has produced a report recommending that all flour is fortified with folic acid to reduce further the number of children with spina bifida
✔ The important aspect is to have lots of folic acid before conception and during the first 12 weeks of the pregnancy when the spine will develop

☆ Before conception take folic acid tablets and for the first 12 weeks of the pregnancy – see GP or midwife

Folic acid

◆ It is essential before conception because pregnant women do not always know exactly when they have conceived
◆ Folic acid helps to form the neural tube correctly which forms the spine and brain. This condition is known as spina bifida where the spine can split and cause various degrees of disability

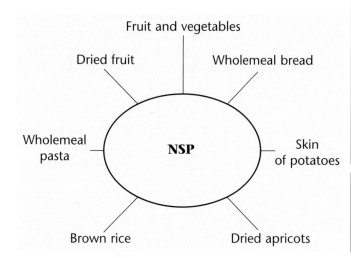

| FIBRE (NSP – NON STARCH POLYSACCHARIDES) |

Check it out!

✔ Constipation can be a problem for the pregnant woman due to hormones causing the bowel to be sluggish
✔ Avoid constipation near the time of birth. After the birth it can be traumatic if the mother is constipated and has a sore perenium from stitches
✔ Bran can stop your body absorbing essential nutrients

☆ A good idea is to have a good daily supply of NSP but discuss it with the GP or midwife if it becomes serious

NSP

◆ Is NOT a nutrient
◆ It is very important to gather and collect all the waste material from the digestive system and to help to get rid of it on a regular, daily basis from the body

⊃ The Vegetarian Mother

More and more women are opting for a vegetarian diet, and as long as they are sensible and aware of the dangers, there is no reason why they cannot continue with such a diet.

If a mother is on a vegetaian diet, as long as she eats dairy products, both she and the baby can remain healthy. However, she should increase both her protein and calcium intakes. This can easily be achieved by eating more dairy products, e.g. at least three or four eggs per week, and a pint of skimmed milk per day.

A very real problem arises if the mother is a vegan (strict vegetarian). A vegan does not eat animal products, which are rich in vitamin B12. Since this vitamin is vital for the growth and well-being of a foetus, as well as being essential for the mother during breast-feeding, the mother must either add milk and eggs to her diet, or take vitamin B12 supplements. This will have to continue throughout pregnancy and breast-feeding.

Remember

♦ A healthy diet is essential for a pregnant woman.

♦ Throughout pregnancy a growing foetus will require the woman to increase her protein requirement by 30 per cent.

♦ Carbohydrates can also cause obesity (weight increase). They fool the body into thinking it can take more. Do not let them fool – they are empty calories. The carbohydrates that are long lasting are the complex variety.

♦ Fats are fine, as long as they are eaten in moderation. Look for Omega 3-type fats especially during pregnancy.

♦ Vitamins and minerals are vital to the health and well-being of woman and baby.Throughout pregnancy a growing foetus will require the woman to increase her protein requirement by 30 per cent.

♦ A pregnant mother needs to increase her calorie intake by 500 calories per day during pregnancy. Both pre-conceptual weight and weight gained during pregnancy will ultimately affect the health of the child.

⊃ Tips for a healthy diet during pregnancy

⊃ Check it out!

✔ Eat a well-balanced diet

✔ Avoid foods that are high in saturated fats

✔ Try to grill or roast foods rather than fry them

✔ Look for the label with the healthy eating logos and choose less fat if possible

✔ Avoid excessive amount of sugar and chocolate

✔ Drink lots of water and fresh fruit drinks

✔ Avoid alcohol and caffeine

✔ Avoid processed foods which are high in salt, sugar and fat, and have lots of coded colourings, flavourings and preservatives

✔ Learn to read the label, look at the nutritional label and the contents. Choose wisely avoiding foods with additives

✔ Avoid cook chill foods, pre-cooked chickens (see page 132)

✔ Look for low salt products, since salt is related to problems such as sweating, and pre-eclampsia

⊃ Foods that may harm the unborn child

The following foods should be avoided or prepared and cooked correctly otherwise they could cause serious problems for the unborn child!

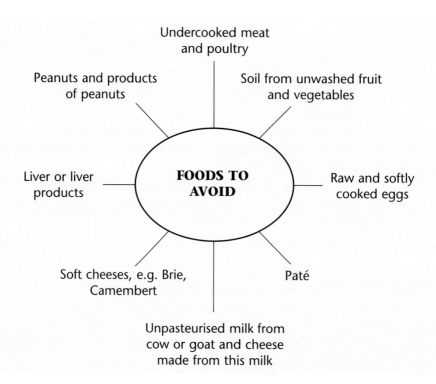

HARMFUL FOODS			
FOOD	PROBLEM	CAUSE	EFFECT ON UNBORN BABY
Raw meat, poultry	◆ Meat not cooked thoroughly ◆ No blood should be visible Take care at barbecues!	◆ Parasite called TOXOPLASMA causes toxoplasmosis, an infection that the mother gets causing mild, flu-like symptoms	◆ Miscarriage ◆ Still birth ◆ Brain damage
Fruit and vegetables	◆ Soil not washed off fruit and vegetables ◆ Take care eating out, particularly in foreign countries	◆ As above	◆ As above
Eggs	◆ Raw and softly cooked eggs which do not destroy the bacteria ◆ Foods containing Raw eggs	◆ The salmonella bacteria which can cause severe food poisoning	

HARMFUL FOODS			
FOOD	PROBLEM	CAUSE	EFFECT ON UNBORN BABY
Paté, unpasteurised milk (goat or cow) and products of this milk, e.g. goat's cheese, Brie, Camembert and Stilton.	◆ The foods are not heated to a high enough temperature to destroy the listeria bacteria found in these foods ◆ It can survive at temperatures above 4°C (domestic recognition is 1-4°C)	◆ Listeriosis is a very rare disease which can cause severe problems for the unborn baby	◆ Severe illness ◆ Miscarriage ◆ Still birth
Cook chill products	◆ Cook chill foods are not thoroughly reheated		
Liver/liver products	◆ Too much vitamin A	◆ Excessive vitamin A will remain in the body and has a toxic effect on the baby	◆ Birth defects
Peanuts/peanut products	◆ Allergic reactions to the nut	◆ If parents or children have an allergy, hayfever, eczema, asthma, more risk of a peanut allergy	◆ Passing the risk of this allergy to the baby

Dos and don'ts of food safety

◆ Food to be reheated should reach boiling or high temperatures and should only be reheated once.

◆ Always wash hands immediately after using the toilet, and certainly before touching food.

◆ Cover any cuts with a plaster (preferably blue so that it can be seen if it falls into the food).

◆ Food that has already been defrosted should not be refrozen.

◆ Ensure that frozen foods, particularly meats such as chicken are thoroughly defrosted before being cooked.

◆ Do not allow raw meat and eggs to come into contact with other foods.

◆ Different preparation areas or chopping boards should be used for different foods to avoid cross contamination.

◆ 'Blown', dented or rusty tinned foods should be thrown away and not used.

◆ Food that looks slightly strange or smells odd should be thrown away.

◆ Clean utensils and cutlery should be used to prepare all food. It is a good idea to use certain knives for specific tasks.

Harmful substance	Effect on foetus intake	Treatment/ways to reduce
Smoking – nicotine and other poisonous substances	◆ Reduces the amount of oxygen and nutrients received ◆ Greater risk of still birth, premature birth and low birth weight ◆ Breathing problems ◆ Increased risk of cot death	◆ Give up smoking before conception ◆ Change habits ◆ Distractions/new hobbies ◆ Help and support of partner
Alcohol	◆ Heavy drinkers (more than 6 units a day) can cause their babies to have 'foetal alcohol syndrome'	◆ Drink in moderation or cut out completely ◆ Try healthy fruit cocktails, milkshakes
Illegal drugs, e.g. amphetamines, cannabis, ecstasy, heroin, LSD, tranquillisers	◆ Very harmful to the baby ◆ Greater risk of miscarriage, stillbirth	◆ Stop before conception ◆ Seek medical advice
Medicines and prescribed drugs	◆ May cause abnormalities of the foetus	◆ Speak with the doctor or dentist before taking medication

◯ SMOKING

Smoking is one of the most damaging factors to the health and development of an unborn child.

When a pregnant woman smokes, some of the chemicals in the smoke pass from her lungs into her blood stream, and then to the placenta. At the placenta, the chemicals pass from the mother's blood stream to that of her unborn baby. Two of the harmful chemicals in smoke are nicotine which will make the baby's heart beat much faster and carbon monoxide (a poisonous gas) which replaces oxygen in the blood. The baby will then receive less oxygen than it needs and will not grow as well as it should. Other risks involved include:

◆ the possibility of miscarriage, stillbirth or

◆ placental damage where the baby does not receive the nourishment it needs to grow

◆ a low-birth weight baby. Women who smoke 20 or more cigarettes a day throughout pregnancy generally have smaller babies. The average birth weight of their babies is approximately 200 g (8oz) less than the norm.

◆ a higher risk than normal of foetal abnormalities.

◆ poor growth and learning difficulties. Children of heavy smokers are often found to have these conditions. (Development tests have been carried out proving this.)

Children born to heavy smokers, and those who are subjected to a great deal of smoke in their homes, are more likely to suffer from bronchitis, pneumonia and other chest infections. Some research shows that this passive smoking can be a contributory factor towards leukaemia and other types of cancers. An unborn baby's health can also be damaged by passive smoking (inhaling other people's smoke) if the woman is in contact with it during pregnancy.

For the sake of her unborn baby, a woman should not smoke at all. She should cut down on her smoking, or consider giving up even if she is only thinking about having a baby. However, if a woman finds it difficult to break the smoking habit, she can reduce the harmful effect by:

◆ taking fewer puffs

◆ smoking less of each cigarette

◆ not inhaling

◆ buying only low-tar brands

◆ cutting down on the number of cigarettes smoked each day

Remember

Rest is particularly important during pregnancy and the woman should try to put her feet up for about one hour each morning and each afternoon. A good night's sleep is also essential.

◌ ALCOHOL

Much research has and is being carried out into the effects of alcohol on the mother before, during and after pregnancy.

Alcohol is also a danger to the unborn baby. When a pregnant woman drinks alcohol, it passes into her bloodstream. Once there, it crosses the placenta and enters the baby's bloodstream as well. Risks to the unborn baby include:

◆ mental retardation

◆ retarded growth

◆ damage to the brain and nervous system, i.e. congenital abnormalities. This is now known as Foetal Alcohol Syndrome

◆ the possibility of **stillbirth**

◆ alcohol addiction – it is a well-known fact that an alcoholic woman's baby be born addicted

These conditions would not become apparent until the baby was born.

The wisest course of action for the woman would be to avoid alcohol altogether, both pre-conceptually and during pregnancy. However, the occasional drink during pregnancy is harmless. It is only when drinking becomes regular that it may interfere with the baby's development.

A HOP, SKIP AND JUMP THROUGH PREGNANCY

This section will look briefly at the importance of exercise, fresh air, sleep, rest and relaxation during pregnancy.

Whilst it is important to consider what foods are necessary for a healthy pregnancy, and what substances are harmful for the woman and her unborn baby there are other essential aspects to help her have a healthy, enjoyable pregnancy.

The following aspects which may contribute to a healthy pregnancy are:

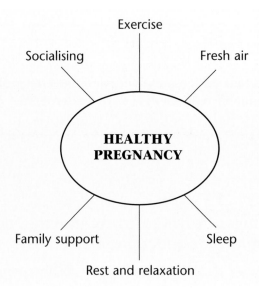

Exercise

It is important not to treat the pregnancy as an illness and to exercise throughout the pregnancy.

The advantages are:

◆ reduces stress
◆ helps to maintain a steady weight gain
◆ an easier pregnancy and labour
◆ helps the mother to get her figure back

⊃ Aqua-natal classes

These must not be confused with <u>ante-natal</u> classes. They are usually held at the local swimming pool and are taken by an obstetric physiotherapist with the assistance of the community midwives. The advantages are:

◆ a good way of meeting mums-to-be and making friends

◆ usually held when there are few other people in the pool

◆ qualified professionals who instil confidence

◆ less strenuous on the joints of the body exercising in water

◆ concentrates on the places that matter, e.g., strengthening the pelvic floor muscles, etc.

◆ concentrates on breathing exercises that assist with the labour

◆ getting to know better the community midwives

◆ socially good to have a 'cup of tea' afterwards and ask any questions to the professionals

◆ usually the same physiotherapist will run a post-natal exercise class (not in water)

Figure 5.39 An aqua-natal class

⊃ Exercising during pregnancy

◆ Don't push the body too far
◆ Start gently

Carry on with usual activities such as swimming or walking, or start these for a short time and build up gradually

◆ At any exercise class, tell the teacher if pregnant
◆ Rest if feeling dizzy, in pain or tired
◆ Drink fluid to avoid becoming dehydrated
◆ Avoid horse riding and skiing and waterskiing
◆ Dance classes are a good idea

⊃ Backache

During pregnancy the posture of the woman changes and it can cause the woman to stick out her bottom, causing the back to overarch. This contributes towards backache, together with the pregnancy hormones which cause the muscles and ligaments to relax which means that they could very easily be strained.

Check it out!

✔ Protect the back by not making sudden movements
✔ Don't bend over to pick up something, kneel or squat
✔ Turn on the side from a lying down position and get up gradually
✔ Stand tall, tuck in bottom, lift out chest
✔ Carry objects or lift from a squatting position
✔ Sit up straight in a chair supported by a cushion

☆ A good idea is to practise squatting particularly if this position is to be used during the labour.

⊃ Pelvic floor

This is very important, the pelvic floor refers to the 'hammock' of muscles that support the bowel, bladder and uterus. The muscles go softer and are capable of stretching so that the pelvic floor becomes weaker with the pressure of the baby as it grows. This can cause a few problems:

✔ Urine leaking out when sneezing, coughing, laughing
✔ A heavy feeling between the legs

⊃ Strengthening the pelvic floor

◆ Try to exercise this muscle frequently throughout the day, it can be done anywhere

◆ Try to imagine stopping the urine coming out in mid-flow, or pulling a tampon into the vagina

◆ Try to imagine stopping a bowel movement, squeeze the muscles

◆ Hold the muscles for a few seconds then let go

> ☆ A good idea also is to sit and rotate the feet in different directions, to reduce swelling, and prevent cramps in the calf.

⊃ Rest and relaxation

It is very important to rest and relax during pregnancy and listen to the body. It will help to reduce stress and one of the ways is to take the mind off those aspects most worried about.

Ways to relax:

◆ watch television

◆ read books

◆ listen to music or the radio

◆ take exercise

◆ massage, reflexology

◆ a walk in the park

◆ visit friends

◆ phone a friend

◆ go out for a meal with partner

◆ take up a hobby - china painting, crossstitch, sing in a choir

◆ join a local group

◆ 'retail therapy' – shopping

◆ gentle yoga

◆ talk over worries with partner

◆ partner to help with household chores

Relaxation positions

◆ use pillows to support legs and bump and head

◆ don't lie flat on the back sit upright

Breathing

◆ breathing exercises will help to stop over- breathing (hyperventilating)

◆ breathe in through nose and out slowly from the mouth

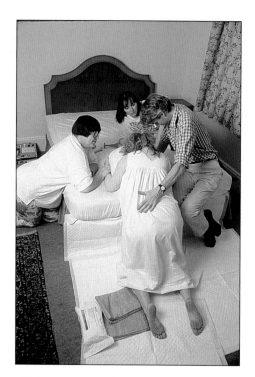

Figure 5.40 Pillows used for support

Figure 5.41 Practising breathing techniques

Sleep

The pregnant woman may feel very tired during the first trimester (first 12 weeks) of the pregnancy as the baby develops fully and feels unable to carry out everyday tasks, particularly if she is suffering with sickness. This is a time to listen to the body and to sleep as much as possible.

Often the 2nd Trimester (12-24 weeks) is one where the woman 'blooms', has most energy and sleeps quite well. However, during the 3rd Trimester (23-40 weeks) the baby is growing fast and often decides to wake up at night when the woman is trying to sleep, by kicking, pushing. Also, the bladder requires emptying more regularly so this disturbs sleep. Try adopting some relaxation positions, using lots of pillows to support the bump and legs. Try to have a sleep in the afternoon or put up one's feet, and close one's eyes to some pleasant music.

Fresh Air

Lots of fresh air with steady, gentle walking will help the pregnant woman to sleep more soundly.

Questions

Question 1

a) What is conception?

b) Explain the process of ovulation

c) Describe the journey of the sperm from the time of production to the moment of conception.

d) Define the following
   i) Blastocyst
   ii) Implantation
   iii) Embryo

Question 2

a) Define the following
   i) Uniovular twins
   ii) Binovular twins

b) Explain how the following are formed
   i) Uniovular twins
   ii) Biovular twins

Use diagrams to illustrate your answer

c) Who maybe more likely to have twins?

d) List four early signs of a multiple pregnancy?

e) What issues may occur with a multiple pregnancy?

Question 3

a) Define the following terms
   i) heredity
   ii) zygote
   iii) gene
   iv) chromosome

Question 4

a) List six signs and symptoms of pregnancy

b) Explain how a pregnancy can be confirmed

c) How is the estimated delivery date calculated

Question 5

a) What is the medical term for miscarriage?

b) When do the majority of miscarriages occur?

c) List eight causes of miscarriage?

d) Give four signs and symptoms of miscarriage?

e) Explain how a parent may feel who has suffered a miscarriage?

Question 6

a) What is ante-natal care?

b) List three aims of ante-natal care.

c) Using a spray diagram, identify the role of the midwife at the mother's booking in appointment.

Question 7

a) The placenta is a vital organ to the mother and her unborn baby. Using diagrams to illustrate your answer, explain why.

b) The umbilical cord is a lifeline to the unborn baby, describe its functions.

c) Give four reasons why the amniotic fluid is important to the unborn baby.

Question 8

a) After conception takes place many changes occur for the mother and her developing unborn baby. Copy the table below, using the headings suggested as guidelines to discover and record at least six facts at each stage of development for
   i) developing embryo/foetus
   ii) pregnant women.

Stage of embryo/foetal development	Embryonic/foetal facts	Pregnant Women Facts
4 weeks		
8 weeks		
12 weeks		
24 weeks		
36 weeks		

Questions (continued)

Question 9

a) What is the purpose of ante-natal classes?

b) Explain the different type of ante-natal classes available to the expectant mother and her partner.

c) What are the advantages of hand held notes?

d) What is the birth plan?

e) Suggest five points an expectant mother might choose to include in her birth plan.

Question 10

a) What are the three main types of test carried out on the expectant mother during the ante-natal period?

b) What is the purpose of carrying out these tests?

c) List the routine tests that are carried out on the expectant mother.

d) During the pregnancy routine blood testing will take place. Explain what information can be found from these tests.

e) List three conditions a urine test can indicate to an expectant mother.

f) How is a screening test different to a diagnostic test?

g) How are the following tests carried out and what information can be obtained from them:
  i)   amniocentesis
  ii) ultra-sound scan

Extension Questions

1) Design a Healthy Pregnancy booklet aimed at pregnant mothers. Include the following information in the booklet -The importance of:
◆ Healthy diet
◆ Avoiding harmful foods
◆ Exercise
◆ Rest
◆ Sleep
◆ Fresh air

2) Match the following sentences together:

1. Protein is required	to help form the spine and brain.
2. Folic acid is taken before conception	reaction which can pass to the baby.
3. Calcium is required	and cook chill products cause Listeriosis.
4. Vitamin C helps	during pregnancy to prevent constipation.
5. Liver is an excellent source of iron	carry a parasite causing Toxoplasmosis.
6. Fibre or NSP is very important	Iron to be absorbed in the bloodstream.
7. Listeriosis can cause	but should be avoided as it contains too much vitamin A which is harmful to the baby.
8. Unwashed fruit and vegetables and raw meat	for healthy bones and teeth.

Extension Questions (continued)

9. Peanuts can cause an allergic	a miscarriage or still birth.
10. Pate, un-pasteurised milk	for growth and repair.

3) Design a chart to highlight the complications that can occur during the pregnancy. Use the following headings as a guideline.

Complication	Cause	Treatment

4) A mother may suffer minor problems during the pregnancy. Design a chart to highlight ten problems, their possible cause and how to put it right.

⊃ PREGNANCY WORDSEARCH

S	I	S	E	T	N	E	C	O	I	N	M	A	S	L
I	E	N	N	M	S	E	T	E	B	A	I	D	W	I
S	C	G	R	O	E	J	D	G	C	S	S	K	P	L
O	G	H	E	I	I	H	I	W	P	G	X	L	Z	B
I	V	E	F	O	O	T	C	M	C	H	V	E	O	G
R	Z	A	U	L	T	R	A	S	O	U	N	D	T	L
E	E	R	K	E	P	L	C	X	O	G	A	Z	A	S
T	R	T	Q	M	C	A	I	S	A	N	X	T	N	W
S	J	B	J	E	G	T	L	I	K	L	I	D	X	C
I	B	U	E	U	C	A	O	T	U	P	E	M	N	K
L	O	R	D	I	W	N	F	P	S	J	K	R	O	T
F	P	N	L	K	T	E	X	O	I	P	T	I	V	D
R	G	W	Y	V	P	T	H	Y	H	C	N	W	L	R
B	F	F	G	A	A	N	A	E	M	I	A	R	E	I
R	F	K	S	X	F	A	R	S	Y	F	F	T	E	M

Amniocentesis
Anaemia
Antenatal
Diabetes
Domino scheme
Ectopic
Folic acid

Heartburn
Hospital
Listeriosis
Pre eclampsia
Relaxation
Ultra sound

⊃ BIRTH ARRANGEMENTS

> This section will consider the various options available for an expectant mother to choose where to have her baby, the advantages and disadvantages of each option and pain relief

One of the first issues an expectant mother faces once she has adjusted to the fact that she is pregnant is where to have the baby. What are the choices available and which will be the best for her?

The choices may depend on a number of factors:

◆ Complications with previous deliveries

◆ Complications with the health of the expectant mother, e.g. if she is diabetic

◆ Personal circumstances (there may not be anyone to help with the baby) such as living on her own

◆ The expectant mother's personal feelings

◆ Medical advice

There are three main choices of where to have the baby and these are highlighted in the chart below:

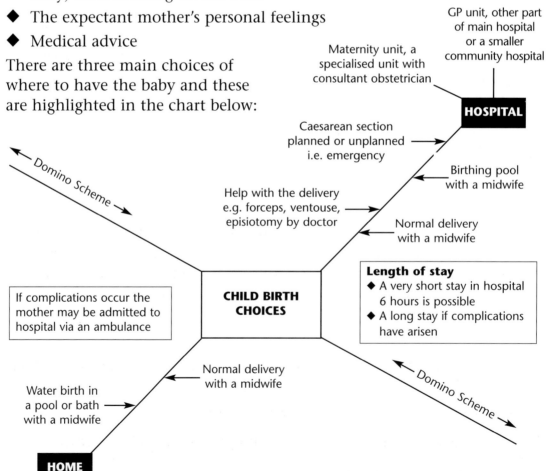

GP unit, other part of main hospital or a smaller community hospital

Maternity unit, a specialised unit with consultant obstetrician

HOSPITAL

Caesarean section planned or unplanned i.e. emergency

Birthing pool with a midwife

Help with the delivery e.g. forceps, ventouse, episiotomy by doctor

Normal delivery with a midwife

Domino Scheme

CHILD BIRTH CHOICES

If complications occur the mother may be admitted to hospital via an ambulance

Length of stay
◆ A very short stay in hospital 6 hours is possible
◆ A long stay if complications have arisen

Normal delivery with a midwife

Domino Scheme

Water birth in a pool or bath with a midwife

HOME

There are many advantages to having the baby at home and in hospital and it would seem that the Domino Scheme combines most of the advantages of both. However, there are circumstances where medical advice will be given to the expectant mother which may make her seriously consider the option of delivering the baby safely in hospital.

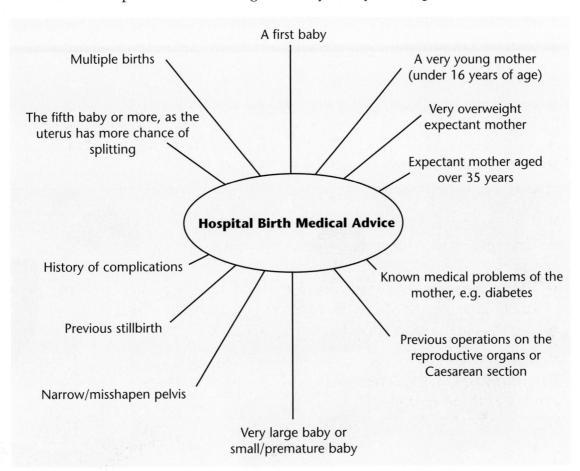

Home Birth

In Britain during the 1950s approximately one-third of all expectant mothers chose to have their babies at home. By the mid 1980s the number had dropped to around one per cent. Today this figure has risen very slightly because expectant women are considering a home birth as an option. It is still more unusual and the trend is to have babies in hospital.

Arranging the Home Birth

Some GPs are reluctant to support this and only agree if no complications have occurred with a previous birth and the expectant mother is in excellent health.

The following are requirements for a home birth:

◆ A room that is clean, hygienic and has good temperature control

◆ A midwife must be booked

◆ A table for the midwife's equipment which will include:
  ◆ A birth delivery pack (bought one month prior to EDD)
  ◆ Oxygen
  ◆ Gas and air
  ◆ Resuscitation equipment to clear a baby's airways and assist breathing
◆ A comfortable bed for the mother
◆ A cot and equipment for the baby
◆ Plastic sheets to protect the floor, carpet, etc.
◆ Buckets: one for waste and another for the placenta
◆ Plenty of hot water

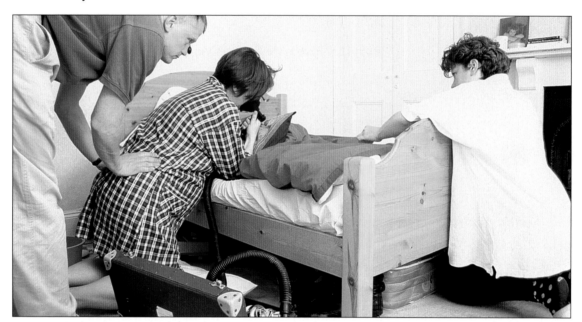

Figure 6.1 Woman and midwife at a home birth

⊃ Hospital Birth

During the 1950s over half of all births were taking place in hospital and by the mid 1980s 99 per cent of women were having their babies in hospital. The main reason for this change is that there is a lot more advanced, technological equipment today which has saved the lives of both mother and baby. There is always the worry with a home delivery that, if something goes wrong, there may not be enough time to get to hospital to save the mother or baby.

⊃ Arrangements for a Hospital Delivery

◆ A team of midwives will have already been dealing with the expectant mother during antenatal visits and it is likely that one of these will be on duty for the delivery of the baby.

◆ A consultant obstetrician will be available.

◆ An anaesthetist will be available if an epidural is required.

◆ The baby will be delivered within the maternity unit, which comprises antenatal wards, labour wards, operating theatres, postnatal wards and special care baby units.

Key Words

An obstetrician is a doctor who specialises in the care of pregnant women during the labour and immediately after the birth.

⊃ Birth in a GP or Midwife Unit

This type of unit can be separate from the hospital, as part of the maternity ward.

⊃ Arrangements

◆ A community midwife would deliver the baby

◆ It is more personal than a hospital and delivery

◆ If it is part of the main hospital and help will be nearby if an emergency arises

◆ It is not an option for those women who have had problems with the pregnancy of previous deliveries

◆ It is usually very low-key technically, with not a lot of obvious equipment about

ADVANTAGES HOME BIRTH	ADVANTAGES HOSPITAL
• The family can be involved particularly if there are other children.	• Trained staff are available particularly if a problem or emergency arises.
• The woman will be more relaxed in her own home with familiar surroundings without lots of people watching the birth.	• If a baby becomes distressed then the equipment and staff will be immediately available to deal with the situation, which could save the baby's life.
• No transportation is required (unless a complication arises).	• Forceps, ventouse and Caesarean deliveries would have to be carried out in hospital.

ADVANTAGES HOME BIRTH continued	ADVANTAGES HOSPITAL continued
• The midwife can bring TENS, gas and air, and pethidine to the house.	• It is only possible to have an epidural as pain relief in hospital. This has to be administered by an anaesthetist.
• There is the possibility of hiring a birth pool to have a water birth at home.	• An emergency Caesarean section to save the baby and possibly the mother's life could only take place in a hospital. This may require a general anaesthetic.
• Minimal monitoring is needed by the midwife.	
• There is the freedom to move about anywhere within the home.	• The mother and partner feel reassured by the 'safe environment' and secure that if an emergency arose they would be in the best place.
• A midwife could perform an episiotomy if required and stitch and repair the wound at home.	
• The mother can determine her own routines and meal times.	• After the birth the mother has the constant support of the midwives to assist with breast feeding and any worries.
• She may experience less interference from the medical staff and be able to deal with her newborn baby as she sees fit.	• Midwives can give the mother a break by taking the baby to the nursery.
• She can possibly build up a good relationship with the midwife who will deliver the baby at home.	• The mother will not become exhausted by having too many visitors.
	• She will be comforted by the other mothers who have shared experiences and worries.
	• There are no worries of home life, the telephone ringing, visitors arriving unexpectedly, shopping, cooking, cleaning, combination of both etc.

Domino Scheme

The midwife will look after the expectant mother at home until it is necessary to accompany her to hospital to deliver the baby. Provided there are no complications she will go home with the mother and baby about six hours after the birth.

Advantages

◆ The mother will remain within the comfort and familiarity of her own home for as long as possible.

◆ She experiences relaxed labour at home knowing the midwife is present.

◆ She is reassured that she will be safe and secure within the hospital environment for delivery.

◆ She will be able to return home quickly to her partner and family shortly after a straightforward labour to enjoy the new baby together, knowing the midwife is available if needed.

⊃ PREPARATION FOR THE BABY

Planning and preparing for the arrival for a new baby can be an exciting time, particularly for those expecting their first baby. Although it is possible for the parents to find out the sex of their baby before it is born, some parents do not choose to know whether it is a boy or a girl. They may, therefore, choose equipment, furnishings and decor that would be unisex (suitable for a boy or a girl). If parents are preparing for their second or subsequent baby, there is good chance that some of the equipment and furnishings could be used again.

COST
- Shop around for sale items
- Parents/friends may complete the decorating
- Obtain second-hand items
- Items may be passed between families
- Borrow items
- Get value for money
- Obtain good quality items
- Consider financial assistance from the state

NOTE: Check the safety of items that are not purchased as new.

SUITABILITY
- May choose colours that would suit both boys and girls
- Decor may be chosen to last more than the first years of babyhood
- Curtains may have black-out lining
- Items that may have a dual purpose e.g. three-in-one pram carry cot, pram and pushchair
- Compact units for changing

Factors to consider

SAFETY
- Check for safety kitemarks
- Electrical items should have BEAB approval
- Lead-free paint should be used
- Flame retardant fabrics and furnishing should be used
- There should be no sharp edges or corners on equipment
- Use safety protection e.g. socket covers on electrical sockets
- Make sure the correct electrical wiring has been carried out
- Use non-toxic materials

HYGIENE
- All surfaces should be easy to clean
- Fabrics should be easy to launder
- Wallpaper should be wipeable
- Removable mattress covers, pram covers etc. should be used

SLEEPING

- Carry cot
- Cot bumper
- Moses basket
- Cot/cot bed
- Mattress
- Blankets (no duvets until 1 year old)
- Waterproof cover
- No pillows
- Baby intercom
- Swinging crib

FEEDING

- Steriliser, microwave steam, electrical free-standing steam, cold water, sterilising solution
- Nipple cream
- Maternity bra
- Breast pads (disposable/washable)
- Bottles, teets, bottle brush
- Formula feeds
- Kettle

Physical preparations and equipment

TRANSPORTATION

- First car seat
- Travel system (1st car seat and pushchair in one)
- Pram
- Net to cover pram for protection from insects
- Three-in-one carry cot, pram and pushchair
- Twin pushchair
- Raincovers
- Sunshade canopy
- Baby sling
- Cozytoes for pushchairs to regulate the temperature
- Changing bag

ROOM

- Baby changing mat
- Bouncing cradle or rocker
- Changing unit or box with toiletries, nappies, barrier cream and cotton wool
- Suitable lighting/lamps and night light
- Chair to feed baby
- Thermometer to keep constant temperature
- First toys
- Adequate heating
- Curtains
- Wallpaper/paint
- Top and tail bowl
- Baby bath

CLOTHING

- Cotton
- Sleepsuits
- Scratch mits
- Socks
- Bootees
- Hat
- Outdoor sleepsuit
- Cardigans
- Vests

NOTE: Further details of feeding can be found in Chapter 9, and of clothing in Chapter 11.

⊃ Choosing items in preparation for the baby

There are many choices available for the baby, and it can be quite difficult deciding which piece of equipment would be best. It is important to look around and compare prices from different shops. Very often, grandparents or other relatives may offer to help and support financially with larger items. The most important factor regarding second-hand items passed on or purchased is that a thorough check is made to ensure that it is safe. Many friends and relatives may purchase gifts for the new baby.

⊃ What physical preparations may need to be considered?

The baby will require:

- a small room to sleep in (or space in parents' room)
- furnished and decorated nursery
- something to sleep in
- adequate means of transportation
- suitable feeding equipment

- adequate clothing
- feeding equipment, if bottle feeding
- changing items
- baby bath
- nappies

The expectant mother must prepare herself a few weeks prior to the EDD in case the baby arrives early. It is a good idea to prepare a hospital bag even if a home delivery is planned, in the event of an emergency.

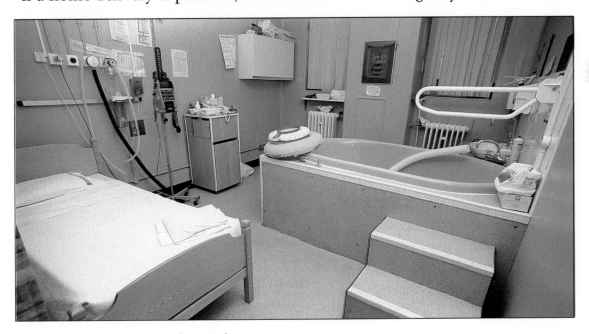

Figure 6.2 A GP unit in a hospital

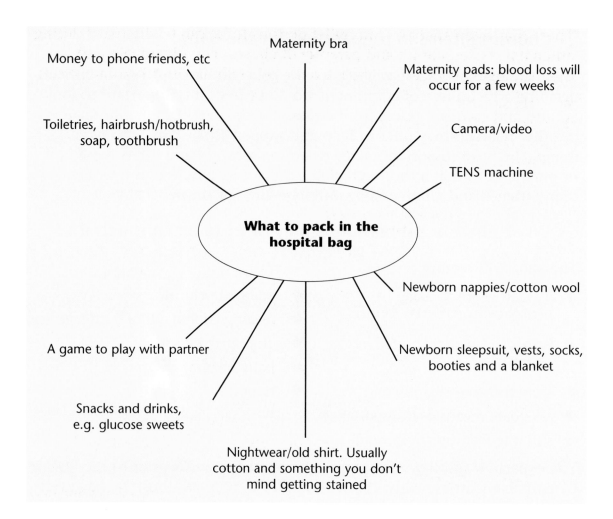

Maternity bra

Money to phone friends, etc

Maternity pads: blood loss will occur for a few weeks

Toiletries, hairbrush/hotbrush, soap, toothbrush

Camera/video

TENS machine

What to pack in the hospital bag

Newborn nappies/cotton wool

A game to play with partner

Newborn sleepsuit, vests, socks, booties and a blanket

Snacks and drinks, e.g. glucose sweets

Nightwear/old shirt. Usually cotton and something you don't mind getting stained

⊃ TYPES OF PAIN RELIEF

This section will examine the various pain relief options during labour.

The main purpose of pain relief during labour is to ease the pain and discomfort the expectant mother may experience, ensuring that the baby is unharmed.

As the EDD gets closer an expectant mother will begin to focus on such questions as:

◆ Will labour hurt?

◆ Will I show myself up screaming with pain?

◆ How will I cope with the pain?

◆ How will I make the best choice for the baby and myself?

Some expectant mothers aim to have as little interference as possible during labour whereas others are happy to consider as many pain relief options as possible. There is no doubt that the more relaxed and active a woman can be during labour, the easier labour will progress, since tension can cause greater pain as the muscles contract.

There is a wide variety of pain relief options these can be discussed during antenatal classes, clinics and parentcraft classes. The advantages and disadvantages of the types of pain relief generally fall into two categories:

◆ those which use drugs
◆ those which are drug free

⊃ Pain relief options

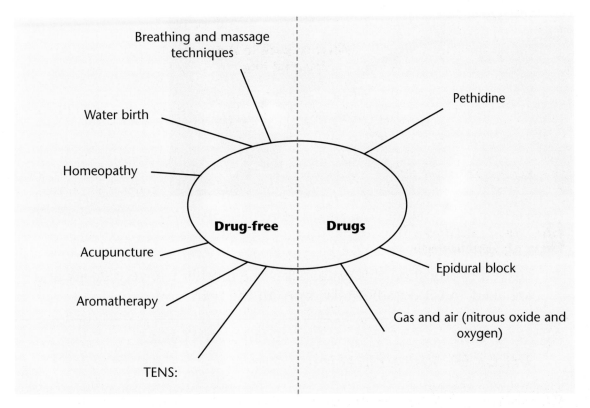

There are a number of advantages and disadvantages to consider when selecting the type of pain relief for labour. Although an expectant mother and her partner may have investigated fully all the options available, written them into the birth plan and felt happy with their choice, it maybe wise to keep an open mind, since their views may change as labour progresses.

⊃ Pain Relief with Drugs

Pethidine (drug)

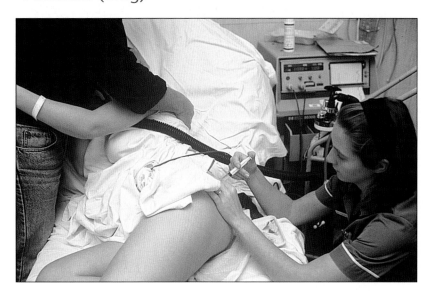

Figure 6.3 Injecting pethidine

How it Works

◆ Given by injection this drug makes the mother feel very sleepy and relaxed, but it does not take away all the pain.

ADVANTAGES	DISADVANTAGES
• It makes the muscles relax	• The drug crosses the placenta and if given too close to near the birth a) causes the baby to be sleepy which can delay breast feeding or b) could affect the baby's breathing
• The pain is more bearable because mother feels confident	
• It is more useful during the early stages of labour, allowing the mother to rest and sleep	• The mother does not feel in control
	• The mother can feel drowsy and disorientated

◗ Gas and air (entonox – drug)

How it works

◆ A mixture of nitrous oxide (laughing gas) and oxygen

◆ Inhaled through a mask or by a mouthpiece

◆ Provides a distraction for the mother and a focus away from the pain However, it does not take away all the pain

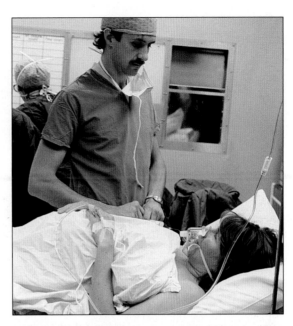

Figure 6.4 Using gas and air during labour

ADVANTAGES	DISADVANTAGES
• Mother controls how much of the drug she wants	• Does not take away all the pain
• Feeling quickly wears off when the mother stops breathing it in	• Some women do not like the feeling of a mask over their face (sometimes a mouthpiece can be used)
• Gas and air takes only a few seconds to start working	• It can make the mother feel sick, lightheaded and a 'little drunk'
• It can be used safely as pain relief in a water pool	• Not as useful during the second stage of labour where the mother has to push her baby out
• Provides a distraction for the mother	
• It will not harm the baby	
• It can also be used when an epidural is being administered and when a mother is being stitched after an episiotomy	

◗ Epidural block (local anaesthetic)

How it works

◆ This is carried out by an ANAESTHETIST, a doctor giving pain relief.

◆ The mother will be asked to curl up like a ball or lie on her side and keep very still.

◆ A local anaesthetic will be injected at about waist level.

◆ The anaesthetist will find the correct space in the spine to place a hollow needle containing a fine plastic tube (catheter) which will be left in place and taped to the mother's back. The needle is removed.

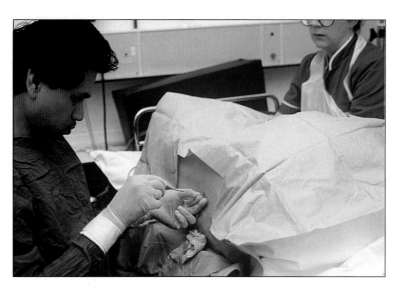

Figure 6.5 An epidural

◆ The liquid anaesthetic is then injected into the space in the spine where the nerves of the uterus, birth canal and spinal cord meet. The mother will not feel pain because the brain will not receive the messages.

◆ It can take up to one hour before the mother feels completely numb from the waist down, therefore it may need to be planned in advance.

◆ This method is useful during a long, difficult and painful labour.

ADVANTAGES

- This takes away all of the pain from the waist downwards

- The mother will be calmer and feel less stressed which will benefit the baby

- Unlike the after effects of pethidine the mother will not feel drowsy after the birth

- A walking epidural, which uses less local anaesthetic, will enable a mother to move about and possibly walk with help. These are becoming more widely available in hospitals

- If timed correctly the epidural can begin to wear off and a mother can assist with the second stage of labour

- If the epidural is still effective after the birth, the mother could be stitched if necessary

DISADVANTAGES

- After labour some mothers wished they had experienced how a contraction felt and feel cheated

- Often forceps are required to assist the delivery

- There is a slight rise in the number of Caesarean sections.

- A complication may occur with one in 100 cases where the anaesthetist places the needle in the wrong place, causing fluid to leak out of the spinal cord. This causes a very severe headache which can last for a week. This could affect the early days with the newborn baby particularly if the mother is attempting to breast feed

ADVANTAGES continued	DISADVANTAGES continued
• A Caesarean section could be given under epidural	• Electronic foetal monitoring will be required (see monitoring during labour later in this chapter). This means that the mother is unable to move about and is restricted to lying on her back. This can slow down labour and the baby's oxygen supply
	• An intravenous drip will be required because epidurals lower the blood pressure and the drip helps to keep the blood pressure high.
	• A catheter maybe fitted in the urinary tract because the mother will not be able to pass urine.
	• Some women suffer from backache for a long time afterwards.
	• Epidurals are not always effective.
	• The mother cannot feel contractions and therefore has to rely on the midwife to tell her when to push.

◗ Drug Free Pain Relief

TENS – Transcutaneous Electrical Nerve Stimulation

How it works

◆ Small electrodes are placed on to the skin on the back where nerve messages travel.

◆ Using a small monitor the mother can control pain by pushing a button that causes electrical impulses to be sent through the electrodes.

◆ The impulses interfere with the pain messages and ENDORPHINS are released. These are the body's natural pain – relieving chemicals.

◆ A TENS machine may need to be hired if it is going to be used at home.

ADVANTAGES	DISADVANTAGES
• It is useful during the early stages of labour, giving the mother something to focus on	• The TENS machine can become less effective as the first stage of labour progresses
• It can be used at home	• If the pain becomes intense it may have little effect

ADVANTAGES continued	DISADVANTAGES continued
• The mother can control it	• The mother is unable to take a bath or shower
• There are no side effects to the mother or baby as it is external	• TENS cannot be used during a water birth
• The mother can move about freely	

Breathing Techniques

How it works

◆ A mother may learn to control the timing of contractions and the breathing techniques through aquanatal classes, and other antenatal classes, yoga, etc

ADVANTAGES	DISADVANTAGES
• This gives the mother a focus and can distract from the pain and help her to feel relaxed	• This will not take away the pain
• It does not affect or harm the baby or mother	• If a mother panics she may totally forget all that she has learnt
• The partner can assist with such techniques prior to and during the birth	

Water birth

How it works

◆ The mother enters a special pool provided by the hospital (or they can be hired privately) which is filled with warm water and kept at a constant temperature.

Figure 6.6 Water birth

ADVANTAGES	DISADVANTAGES
• The muscles of the back and abdomen relax	• There is a possible risk of infection
• Encourages the release of endorphins	• The midwife may not be able to monitor the baby as effectively
• The partner can enter the birthpool and help	• This does not take away all the pain

Homeopathy

How it works

◆ These are natural products which may use herbs. An example is caulophyllum (blue cohosh) which reduces the length of labour.

ADVANTAGES	DISADVANTAGES
• Before the birth a homeopath can supply a number of natural remedies to be used during labour	• None are known

Acupuncture

How it works

◆ At specific energy points fine sterilised needles are placed under the skin.

◆ The needles are placed along MERIDIANS (lines in the body) where the Chinese believe the Chi energy flows.

ADVANTAGES	DISADVANTAGES
• This helps to relieve pain and relax the body • It encourages the production of endorphins	• The angle of the needles makes it difficult to sit or lie down

Aromatherapy

How it works

◆ Essential plant oils

All of the above must be carried out or taught by qualified therapists.

ADVANTAGES	DISADVANTAGES
• Different oils are used for different reasons, for example frankincense helps the body to relax	• The oils must be mixed by qualified aromatherapist as some are considered unsafe during birth

Figure 6.7 Aqua-natal class

Key Words

Inhale	To breathe in (gas and air)
Injection	Giving a medicine/drug in liquid form, by putting a needle into the skin/vein of a person and forcing the contents of the syringe into the whole body
Anaesthetic	Artificially preventing a feeling of pain by giving gases or injecting drugs
Anaesthetist	A doctor who specialises in giving anaesthetics
Local anaesthetic	Taking away the feeling of pain in a small area only, e.g. the back, a thumb, etc, by injecting a drug
Catheter	Fine plastic tube
Endorphins	The body's natural pain-relieving chemicals
Drip	A hollow needle attached to a bag of fluid containing, for example, drugs, is put into a vein
Forceps	Two curved blades are put into the birth canal around the baby's head and the baby is gently pulled out

⊃ THE BIRTH

> The section will examine the signs and symptoms and three stages of labour.

The word 'labour' suggests physical and mental **hard work**. In this case it is used to describe the process of childbirth from the start of uterine contractions to the delivery of the baby.

Most expectant women and their partners approach the time around the EDD (Estimated Date of Delivery) with great anticipation, excitement and apprehension, wondering what life will be like after they have brought home their newborn child. It is also a time when the mother may go over the EDD and begin to worry whether everything is all right. In fact the EDD is only a guideline and very few babies actually arrive on this date. It is quite normal for a baby to be delivered between 38 and 42 weeks of pregnancy.

Labour is divided into three stages and is triggered by changes in hormones (chemical messages). The main aim of labour is to ensure that the muscular contractions of the uterus cause the cervix to open to 10 cm in diameter, which enables the baby's head to drop down to the vagina to be born.

⊃ Signs and Symptoms of labour

◆ **Braxton Hicks Contractions:** these are practice contractions where the abdomen becomes tight and then relaxes. When the contractions become stronger and last longer it is a sign that labour may have started.

◆ **Waters breaking**: this is when the bag of water (amniotic fluid) surrounding the foetus bursts. It maybe a trickle or large gush. At this stage the woman will be advised to go to hospital to prevent a risk of infection.

◆ **Show:** this may happen as labour starts. It is a blood-stained plug of mucus that comes away from the cervix, as the cervix becomes wider (dilates). There should not be a loss of blood. The purpose of this plug is to seal off the uterus during the pregnancy. As the cervix dilates the plug comes away.

◆ **Diarrhoea**

◆ **Backache**: a mild period-type pain which will increase and become more regular.

◆ **Nausea or vomiting**

Most women will recognise the signs of labour, however it would be advisable to telephone the hospital or midwife if there was any doubt. At this point an expectant woman will either go to the hospital, or if she has arranged a home confinement the midwife will make a visit, to prepare for the first stage of labour.

Hospital Confinement

◆ The expectant woman (and her partner) will report to the admission desk

◆ She will either be admitted to the antenatal ward if she is in the early stages of labour or the delivery suite if the labour is more advanced.

◆ The expectant woman will be assessed by a midwife. She will have her temperature and blood pressure taken, her abdomen felt, and will be connected to a foetal heart monitor which will record the baby's heartbeat as well as her own.

◆ A vaginal examination will establish how dilated the cervix is.

◆ The midwife will examine and discuss the birth plan, the chosen options for pain relief, and the position the expectant mother wishes to give birth in.

◆ A midwife will ask her to put on a hospital gown or an old one of her own.

Position of the Baby

Before the birth of a baby the midwife will be able to feel the mother's abdomen to find out which position the baby is in. An ultrasound scan will also give this information.

The usual position for a baby to be delivered is with the head down (see below). The head becomes engaged in the pelvis ready to descend down the birth canal.

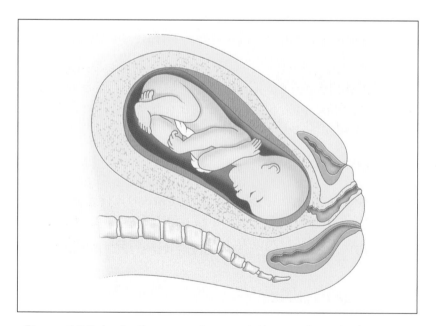

Figure 6.8 Baby in the normal presentation ready to be born

However, there are other positions that the baby may lie in and although it may be possible for the doctor to attempt to turn the baby, sometimes they resume their original position.

Alternative Positions

Breech: Babies in the bottom or feet first position can be delivered vaginally although they can cause problems. Often forceps are used to deliver the head quickly.

Transverse: The baby lies across the abdomen.

Oblique: The baby lies at an angle in the abdomen.

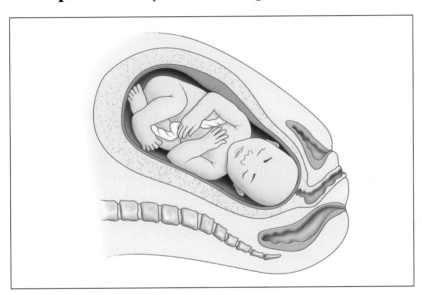

Figure 6.9 Baby about to be born at oblique angle

It is obvious that babies presenting themselves in the above positions may require assistance during the delivery. A transverse or oblique presentation would require a Caesarean section, as would the breech baby if the delivery was proving difficult or the mother requested it.

Positions during labour

Unless she has been hooked to a monitor or given an epidural the mother should try to keep as mobile as possible. While it is more common to see women lying on their beds during labour there are other positions which may be more comfortable, such as:

Positions for the First Stage of Labour

Sitting Upright
Sit on a chair, facing the back. Keep the knees apart and rest the head on folded arms resting on a cushion. Alternatively, sit on the edge of the chair (facing forwards) with legs apart and hands on knees.

Kneeling

Kneel on a pillow and place a cushion on a small table or chair. Lean on the cushion.

Standing

Keep upright and lean towards the partner or wall. The partner can massage the back.

All Fours

Kneel down on hands and knees either on a mattress or on the floor. Rocking the pelvis backwards and forwards may help.

Keep Moving

Changing positions may add a distraction and help with the pain.

Kneeling Forwards

Kneel over a bean bag or a pile of cushions with legs apart. This position will help if the mother has a 'backache' labour.

Lower Back Massage

Figure 6.10 Active birth

⊃ Positions for the Second Stage of Labour

Sitting Slightly Upright

Sometimes gripping the thighs and keeping the chin down may help.

Squatting

This opens up the pelvis and uses gravity to push out the baby. It can be very tiring on the legs.

Kneeling

This is a good position because it also uses gravity but is not so tiring. Kneeling on all fours may also be an option and takes the pressure off the back.

The Three Stages of Labour

The First Stage

This begins with early symptoms showing that labour has started. Its purpose is to open up the cervix gradually.

- The waters (amniotic fluid) may break.

- Contractions tighten and shorten, become stronger, more regular and last longer, and at this stage more pain relief is required.

- The mother is asked to be as active as possible, to try to remain upright and take a warm relaxing bath.

- The mother may adopt various positions rather than lie on her back although she may be restricted by the type of pain relief she has chosen.

- With a first baby this stage could take 12 to 15 hours until delivery.

- Contractions gradually open up the cervix until it is fully dilated to a width of 8–10 cm.

- If the head has not already engaged in the pelvis it will do so now.

- Towards the end of this stage the contractions can become intense and the mother may become agitated.

- This stage can cause sweating, vomiting, shivering and loss of bladder and bowel control caused by the pressure from the baby's head.

- The Transition Stage: links the first and second stages of labour and it is here that the contractions speed up and become very intense.

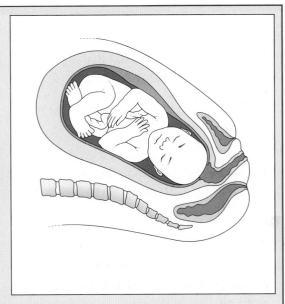

Figure 6.11 Cervix almost dilated

⊃ The Second Stage

This begins when the cervix is fully dilated and ends with the birth of the baby. This stage can take about one hour and can be exhausting for the mother.

- The partner can rub the mother's back, massage and give words of encouragement.

- Once the cervix has fully dilated to 10 cm the vagina and cervix become one and are called the birth canal.

- The baby's head will now be able to move down the birth canal.

- During this stage each time a contraction starts the mother will push down. This is helping the baby move along the birth canal.

- The mother should rest between contractions.

- Once the head can be seen the midwife will ask the mother to stop pushing and blow out to allow the baby's head to be born gradually. When the head can be seen at the vaginal opening this is known as CROWNING.

- It is important for the head to be born slowly so that the perineum (skin between the vagina and the rectum) does not tear.

- Once the head has been delivered, the hard work is over.

- Some babies require the mucus to be cleared from the mouth and nose, and others require some oxygen.

- The baby's body will be turned to allow one shoulder at a time to be delivered.

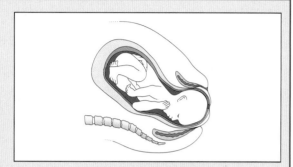

Figure 6.12 The baby's head can now move down the birth canal

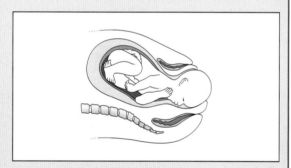

Figure 6.13 Crowning

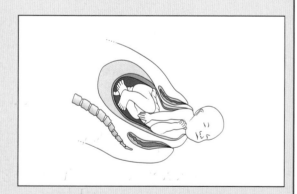

Figure 6.14 The head is delivered

- The rest of the body then slides out easily.

- The umbilical cord is clamped and cut and this ends the second stage of labour.

- The baby can be placed straight on to the mother's stomach if that is what she has requested.

- The baby may be a little messy with blood and perhaps the white greasy substance called VERNIX will be evident.

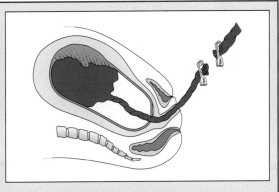

Figure 6.15 Umbilical cord is clamped

The Third Stage

This stage begins when the baby is born and is completed after the membranes, cord and placenta have been delivered.

- This is the shortest stage.

- After the baby has been born, more contractions will push out the placenta (afterbirth).

- This process could last between 20 and 60 minutes. To speed it up the midwife may give an injection of **syntocin** which causes the uterus to contract and prevents heavy blood loss.

- At this stage if a tear has occurred or a cut (episiotomy) was required because the perineum would not stretch, the midwife will carry out the stitching using a local anaesthetic.

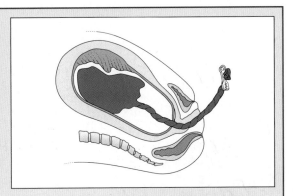

Figure 6.16 Placenta being delivered

Examination of the Placenta

A thorough examination of the placenta will take place once it has been expelled (pushed out). It will be dark red, like liver, weigh 470g (1lb) and be the size of a large dinner plate. It should be intact (complete) as it is dangerous to leave any inside the mother as this could cause an infection or a haemorrhage (large blood loss). The placenta belongs to the mother and if she wishes to keep it she can. It is most common in this country that the hospital will dispose of the placenta.

⊃ After the baby is born

These are some comments made by mothers, fathers and other relatives after the birth.

I felt exhausted but elated.
Mother.

We were relieved that the baby was in good health.
Partner.

I had a girl and now I have a boy. It's wonderful.
Mother.

I cried!
Grandparent

I was shaking as the baby came quickly in the end.
Mother.

I couldn't believe that after all the months of waiting I was finally a mother. I was high!!
Mother.

I held my daughter tight with such pride, happiness and joy to be the first to cuddle her.
Father.

My baby was placed on to my stomach and within minutes I felt the strength of my newborn suckling on my breast.
Mother.

I was worried when I saw my partner in pain but amazed to see how quickly she recovered when I handed her our baby.
Partner.

Although I missed the birth because of complications I was happy and confident to leave it in the capable hands of the professionals – and relieved to see my healthy baby boy!
Father.

I missed the moment of birth as my wife had me in a headlock.
Father.

Key Words

Birth Canal	where the vagina, cervix and uterus become one channel.
Confinement	the period from the beginning of labour to the birth of a child.
Contractions	the muscles of the uterus shorten and tighten gradually becoming stronger, more frequent and effective.
Crowning	where the baby's head can be seen at the entrance to the vagina.
Dilate	to widen or open the cervix gradually in response to contractions of the uterus.
Perineum	the skin between the vagina and the anus.
Transition Stage	the stage of labour that links the first and second stage.

TECHNOLOGY AND MEDICAL ASSISTANCE DURING THE BIRTH

This section will look at how technology today can help with the safe delivery of a newborn baby.

Technology can be defined as scientific knowledge and skills that can be applied practically. Today, technology helps to ensure that all babies have a very good chance of being born safe and well. It is because of advancements in technology that few women nowadays lose their children, or their own lives, while giving birth. The infant death rate in the early 1900s was very high and many women had large families, perhaps nine or ten children but only a few would survive until their first birthday.

While childbirth is one of the most natural aspects of life, it is possible for complications to arise and for science to be needed.

Reasons to Assist with the Delivery

Figure 6.17 A midwife assists

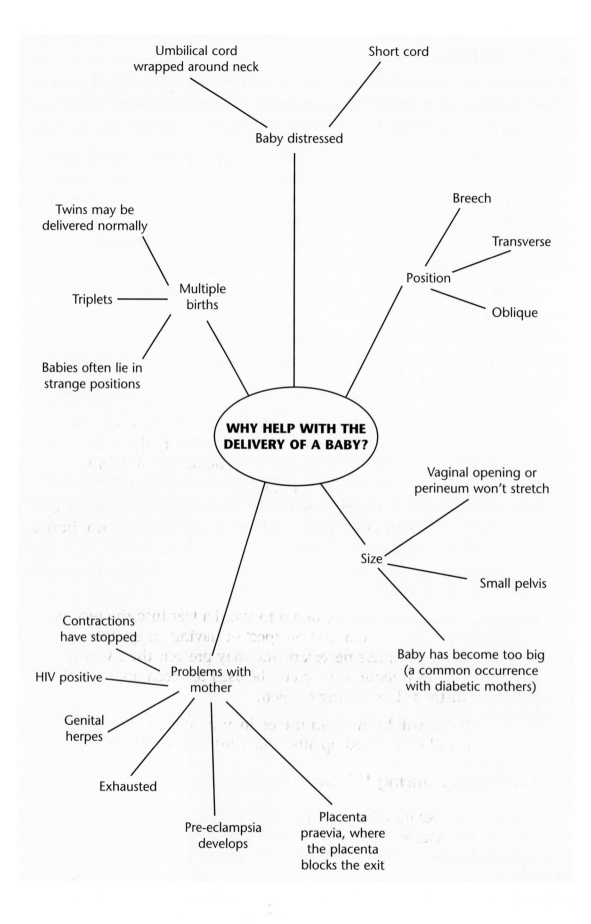

Umbilical cord
wrapped around neck

Short cord

Baby distressed

Breech

Transverse

Position

Oblique

Twins may be
delivered normally

Triplets

Multiple
births

Babies often lie in
strange positions

**WHY HELP WITH THE
DELIVERY OF A BABY?**

Vaginal opening or
perineum won't stretch

Size

Small pelvis

Baby has become too big
(a common occurrence
with diabetic mothers)

Contractions
have stopped

HIV positive

Problems with
mother

Genital
herpes

Exhausted

Pre-eclampsia
develops

Placenta
praevia, where
the placenta
blocks the exit

⊃ Induction

Sometimes a doctor will decide that a woman needs to have her labour artificially started. This is called induction or being induced.

Reasons for inducing birth

◆ The mother's contractions have started and then either slowed down or stopped.
◆ The mother has high blood pressure.
◆ The baby is failing to grow and thrive.
◆ The mother has gone over her EDD by one to two weeks. After this time the placenta becomes less efficient in supplying oxygen.

⊃ How Does the Induction Take Place?

1. By pessary, or gel which is inserted into the vagina. This works by softening or ripening the cervix. This can take more than one attempt. Once labour has been triggered it usually progresses as expected.
2. The hormone (syntocin) is placed into the body by setting up a drip into the mother's arm. This can have quite a dramatic effect, causing the mother to go into labour quickly without a gradual build-up of pain. Labour can be slowed down by controlling the flow of the drip.
3. Breaking the waters. An instrument (amni hook) is used to break or rupture the membranes surrounding the baby to allow the amniotic fluid (waters) to be released and trigger off labour. This does not hurt as the membranes contain no nerves.

⊃ Episiotomy

An episiotomy is a cut in the perineum to avoid a tear into the rectum. Many women are frightened at the prospect of having an episiotomy. This is not performed unless necessary and may prevent the risk of a serious tear to the perineum. It may also be used to speed up the delivery if the baby is distressed or lacking oxygen.

A local anaesthetic will be given in the perineum prior to the cut being made. The cut will be stitched up after the third stage of labour.

⊃ Monitoring During Labour

When a mother goes into the early stages of labour, she will be monitored by the midwife either at home or in hospital to ensure that the baby's heartbeat is regular and that it is not distressed. The midwife will know if the baby is distressed because the heartbeat will be too fast or too slow. The heart rate of a baby is approximately twice the speed of the mother's. If the heartbeat goes down it may be that the blood vessels of the placenta are being squashed.

There are three main ways to monitor:

Listening

- The midwife listens using a foetal stethoscope which looks like a trumpet, or a hand-held electronic device using ultrasound.
- Only the midwife can hear the heartbeat, not the mother.

Continuous Foetal Monitoring – External

- Two electrodes are strapped to the mother's abdomen using stretchy bands.
- This measures the baby's heart rate.
- It also measures contractions – how long they are and the gap between them.
- The mother will have to lie or sit for this monitoring.

Internal

- A tiny electrode is placed through the vagina onto the scalp of the baby (or bottom if breech).
- This can only be used if the waters have broken.
- The mother will have to lie quite still for this type of monitoring.

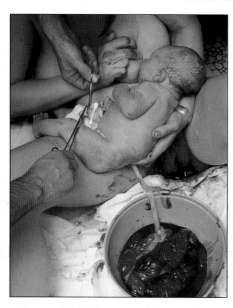

Figure 6.18 Placenta delivered

Figure 6.19 The new baby

Key Words

Pelvic Floor   the 'hammock' of muscles that contain and support the pelvic contents, e.g. uterus, ovaries, Fallopian tubes, bladder and lower bowel

The issue of monitoring will be discussed during ante-natal classes. If all is going well then it may happen from time to time. However, if a doubt exists about the baby's condition the internal scalp monitor will gave a clearer, more accurate picture of what is happening.

There are a number of advantages and disadvantages to monitoring:

ADVANTAGES	DISADVANTAGES
If there is a problem with the heartbeat and the baby is distressed, emergency treatment such as a Caesarean section can be carried out immediately to save the baby's life.	It can prevent mother being active and walking about.
When mother feels tired it can reassure her and keep her going.	The heartbeat monitor can affect people emotionally and make them feel scared.
It gives an indication that all is well, which can be very comforting.	The internal monitor can be painful to insert for the mother and has to be placed on to the baby's scalp.

Forceps

The main reasons for using forceps are:

◆ The mother is exhausted

◆ The mother and/or baby are showing signs of stress

◆ The baby is in a breech position, or it is a premature birth, and the head requires protection

◆ The mother has had an epidural and can't feel when to push the baby out

The forceps are two curved metal instruments a little like sugar tongs. The mother will be given a local anaesthetic and an episiotomy. The forceps are placed into the birth canal and around the baby's head, allowing the doctor to pull gently with each contraction and assist the delivery.

This instrument can leave some bruising and red marks on the baby's face. The mother's cervix must be fully dilated to use this instrument.

Ventouse Extraction

Figure 6.20 Vacuum extractors used in Ventouse extraction

Sometimes known as a vacuum suction, this can be used for similar reasons to a forceps delivery although the cervix does not have to be fully dilated. It is not suitable for a breech or premature baby because in such deliveries the baby's head needs to be protected.

A small cap connected to a vacuum pump is placed on to the baby's head and used to pull out the baby. This may cause a slight swelling and bruising on the baby's head and sometimes the top of the head may be a little misshapen. All of these symptoms will gradually subside.

Caesarean Section

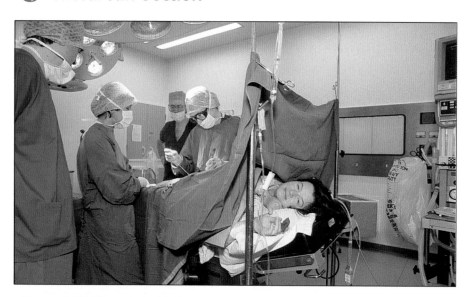

Figure 6.21 Caesarean Section

A Caesarean section is a surgical operation where a bikini-line cut is made into the mother's abdomen and uterus, and the baby is lifted out. The operation got its name from Julius Caesar whose own mother died during childbirth, and her uterus was opened to pull him out. Sometimes Caesareans are planned for the following reasons:

◆ If the mother is having a multiple birth.

◆ If the baby is too large to pass through the pelvis (this sometimes happens with diabetic mothers).

◆ If the mother's pelvis is misshapen or deformed.

◆ If the placenta is covering the entrance to the birth canal and the baby cannot emerge without the placenta tearing and haemorrhaging (bleeding). This is known as placenta praevia.

◆ If the mother is HIV positive. This is to protect the baby from infection.

◆ If the mother has active genital herpes (cold sores on the vagina), this can seriously affect newborn babies.

◆ If the baby is in a difficult position.

◆ If the mother has fibroids or an ovarian cyst.

⊃ Elective Caesarean Section

A planned Caesarean is known as *elective* and can be carried out using a local anaesthetic, such as an epidural or spinal block. This means that the mother will be conscious (awake) for the operation but will feel nothing from the waist down.

ADVANTAGES	DISADVANTAGES
• No after effects of a general anaesthetic, e.g. sickness, drowsiness.	• The mother has not experienced a 'normal' delivery and may feel cheated.
• The father or partner can be present	• She is likely to be very sore after the operation and may find breast-feeding uncomfortable.
• The baby can be held by the mother straight away.	• The mother may be unhappy to have a scar but these usually heal quickly and are rarely visible.

⊃ Emergency Caesarean Section

An emergency Caesarean section may be needed for the following reasons:

◆ The foetal heart rate could drop, which may cause a lack of oxygen to the foetus.

◆ The mother may be very distressed after a long labour which is not progressing.

◆ If the mother is bleeding this might indicate placenta problems.

◆ If the mother has very high blood pressure.

◆ If the umbilical cord falls down ahead of the baby.

If the mother has had an epidural as a form of pain relief for her 'normal' delivery and it is still effective then she could go ahead with an emergency Caesarean section as previously mentioned.

However, there is not always time to set up an epidural and a general anaesthetic is given instead.

ADVANTAGES	**DISADVANTAGES**
• The baby is delivered safely.	• The parents may miss the birth completely.
• The mother's life may have been saved.	• They may feel robbed of those first precious moments.
• If the mother was scared she would know nothing about the operation.	• The mother may feel sick and drowsy after the anaesthetic.
	The scar usually fades within three to six months and most parents feel that it was worth the discomfort to ensure the safe delivery of their child.

Key Words

Breech	the baby is lying bottom or feet first in the birth canal.
Episiotomy	a J shaped cut in the perineum to make the vaginal opening larger.
Induce	to start off labour artificially
Ventouse Extraction	a vacuum pump is attached to the baby's head to help pull the baby out from the birth canal.

Questions

Question 1

a) What child birth choices are available to the pregnant woman?

b) Some women are advised to have their baby in hospital.

   List eight reasons why this medical advice may be given.

c) Where is a woman most likely to have her baby today?

d) Describe a GP or midwife unit.

e) List six advantages of having a baby
   i) in hospital
   ii) at home.

f) Describe the Domino scheme and give four advantages of this to the expectant mother and her family.

Question 2

a) Name three pain relief options that are
   i) drugs
   ii) drug free

b) Using the headings suggested below, design a chart which will identify four types of pain relief; how they work and two advantages and disadvantages of each.

Type of pain relief	How it works	Advantages	Disadvantages
A. Gas and Air (ENTONOX)		1. 2.	1. 2.
B.		1. 2.	1. 2.

Questions continued

Question 3

a) Identify and describe four signs and symptoms that labour has started.

b) What position should an unborn baby present itself in before a 'normal delivery'?

c) What alternative positions may an unborn baby be lying in before delivery?

d) A number of women lie on their back during the first stage of labour; what other positions could they find helpful?

e) How may a squatting position during the second stage of labour assist with the delivery of the baby?

Question 4

Design a chart to describe the three stages of labour.

Question 5

Why would it be dangerous for some of the placenta to be left inside the uterus?

Question 6

Describe the feelings a new mother and father may have after the birth of their child.

Question 7

a) List six reasons why a woman may need help with the delivery of the baby.

b) Explain what induction means and why it is carried out.

Question 8

a) What is an episiotomy?

b) Explain why an episiotomy may be carried out.

Question 9

a) How can the unborn baby be monitored during the labour?

b) Give two advantages and two disadvantages of monitoring during labour.

Question 10

a) Explain what the following are, giving reasons for their use

i) forceps

ii) Ventouse Extraction

b) What is a Caesarean section?

c) Why may a Caesarean section be planned?

d) What are the advantages of an Epidural Caesarean?

e) Give five reasons why an emergency Caesarean may be carried out.

Things to do

Question 10

a) Carry out a survey to discover:

i) How many fathers were present at the birth.

ii) What role did the father/partner play during the birth?

iii) Ask the mother how the father/partner helped during the birth.

b) Interview a mother about her experiences of childbirth, and write up your findings as a case study.

Health Services Personnel

Define the role of the following Health Care Professionals who assist with pre-conceptual care, pregnancy and the mother, baby and family after the birth.

a) Community midwife and hospital midwife

b) Health visitor

c) General Practitioner (GP)

d) Gynaecologist

e) Obstetrician

f) Paediatrician

g) Physiotherapist

h) Dietician

i) Neonatologist

Part Two
Care of the child

In Part Two we will look at the early development of the child, and the care needed and support available to help them to progress.

Remember

From the moment of birth a parent becomes a carer, nurse, teacher, provider and protector. Help is available from a wide variety of sources.

The newborn baby

In this section we will look at:

◆ the routine tests that are carried out on a newborn baby

◆ the reflex actions of a newborn baby

◆ the appearance of a newborn baby

◆ the senses of a newborn baby

◆ how to handle a newborn baby

◆ sleep and the newborn baby

◆ special care babies

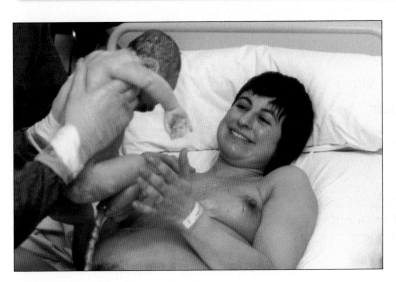

Figure 7.1 Mother and baby immediately after birth

A new born baby will usually be handed straight to the mother so she can hold her baby closely. It is a very emotional time for both parents and their child and if all appears well the medical personnel will give the parents a few moments with their baby before the first health check is carried out.

Immediately after birth babies will be given a number of routine checks. These checks are carried out by an experienced midwife or a doctor.

⟳ APGAR TESTING

Between one and five minutes after they are born babies will be examined to check their Apgar score. The Apgar test is carried out to ensure the lungs and heart are functioning and the responses are sound. Each of the five elements shown below is given a score of nought to two. A score of over seven means the newborn baby is in excellent condition. If the score is under four the baby may require some resuscitation.

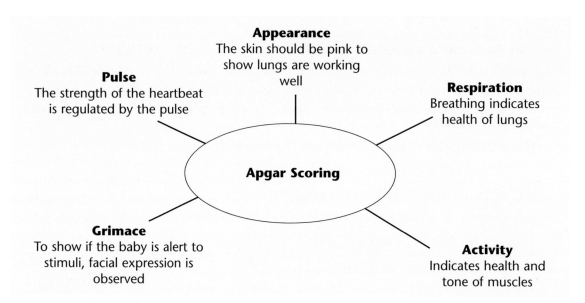

The table shows the scoring system using the Apgar Test.

	0	1	2
Appearance	Blue or pale arms and legs	Body pink and blue	Completely pink
Pulse	No pulse	Under 100 beats per minute	Over 100 beats per minute
Respiration	Absent	Slow and irregular	Breathing well
Activity	Limp and floppy muscles	Some movement, bending of arms and legs	Active/Moving
Grimace	No response to stimulus	Small movement or whimper to stimulus	Vigorous crying

Other checks that take place immediately after birth are:

◆ making sure the facial features and body proportions are normal

◆ checking the spine for defects

◆ examining the anus, legs, fingers and toes

◆ checking the umbilical cord has two arteries and one **vein**

◆ weighing the baby (average 3.5 kg/7 $\frac{1}{2}$ lb)

◆ measuring head circumference (average 35 cm)

◆ measuring body length (average 50 cm)

◆ checking the baby's temperature (average 37°C)

When these initial tests have been carried out babies will be left to get used to their new world.

⊃ OTHER TESTS

Within 24 hours a **paediatrician** will carry out a more detailed examination. The parents will be encouraged to attend the examination so they can ask the doctor questions and discuss any queries they may have. The examination generally begins at the head and moves down to the toes.

⊃ Head and Neck

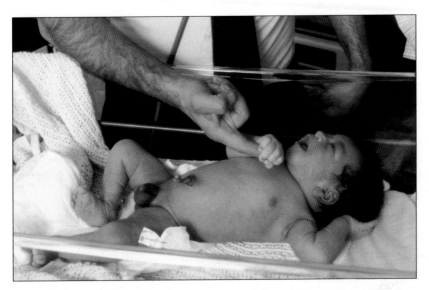

Figure 7.2 A paediatrician carries out checks on a one-day old baby

The neck will be checked for cysts or swellings and the mouth for abnormalities such as a **cleft palate**. Although rare, some babies are born with a tooth. If this happens the tooth is likely to be removed because there is a risk it may fall out and be swallowed.

The eyes, ears and nose will be checked and the fontanelle and skull bones looked at. The fontanelles are generally known as the 'soft spots' and are the areas where the skull bones have not yet fused together in order that the head may pass easily down the birth canal.

⊃ Chest and Heart

The heart and lungs will be checked with a stethoscope. Many babies' hearts make odd sounds in the days immediately after birth because the workload of the heart increases substantially when they are controlling their own circulation. These odd sounds will normally disappear very quickly.

⊃ Arms and Hands

Each arm will be checked for a pulse and for strength and movement. The doctor will look at the palms of the hands. Two major creases are normal. If there is only one the doctor will look for other physical abnormalities.

⊃ Abdomen

By pressing gently on the abdomen the size and shape of the liver and spleen will be assessed. It is not unusual for these to be slightly enlarged. The lower spine and anal area will also be checked for **congenital abnormalities**.

Key Words

Arteries	blood vessels carrying oxygenated blood from the heart around the body.
Cleft Palate	a slit in the roof of the mouth.
Congenital Abnormalities	abnormalities that are present at birth.
Paediatrician	a doctor who specialises in the treatment of diseases in children.
Stethoscope	an instrument used to listen to sounds within the body, such as the heart and lungs.
Veins	blood vessels that carry de-oxygenated blood towards the heart. Veins are thinner than arteries.

Hips, Legs and Feet

The test to check the hips is called Barlow's test. It is used to find out whether the head of the thighbone is unstable or lying outside the hip joint. The test is carried out by laying the baby on his/her back with the feet pointing towards the doctor. Each leg will be checked for size and length and then each hip will be gently flexed and moved away from the midline of the body with backward pressure. If the hip is prone to **dislocation** a click can be felt. If the hips do dislocate, treatment will begin to correct the problems because if left untreated it can lead to problems later in life. Treatment usually includes **manipulation** and perhaps a **splint**. Barlow's test does not hurt the baby but many babies cry at the unusual movement. Sometimes a baby's ankle may be turned in. This can also be corrected by manipulation or a cast.

Nerves and Muscles

The baby's arms and legs will be put through a range of movements to check they are not too stiff or too floppy. This tells the paediatrician about the condition of the nerves and muscles. The paediatrician will also check that the baby's inborn reflexes are present and that head control is normal.

At the end of the first week two further tests are likely to be carried out on the baby:

PKU Test or Guthrie Test

PKU stands for phenylketonuria. This is a rare disorder that prevents the baby from **metabolising** a chemical called phenylalanine, which is present in most protein foods including milk. Babies are given the Guthrie test routinely to check the levels of phenylalanine in the blood by pricking the heel and obtaining a blood sample. If phenylketonuria is diagnosed the baby will be given a special milk substitute, and at weaning a very low protein diet will be recommended.

⊃ Thyroid Function Test

The thyroid function test is carried out to check if the thyroid gland is producing the hormone thyroxin. Thyroxin is needed for normal growth and development. Low levels of thyroxin may lead to poor growth. The condition is easily remedied by giving the baby regular supplements of the hormone as early as possible. The test is a simple blood test, like PKU.

Key Words

Dislocation	bones meeting at a joint are displaced (put out of position)
Manipulation	skilful handling
Metabolising	when food is broken down by chemical and physical changes enabling the body to grow and function
Splint	a rigid support to maintain the hips, legs or feet in a set position

⊃ REFLEX ACTIONS

Babies display a number of movements called reflexes or reflex actions. Movements of this kind are inborn and made automatically without thinking. The most important reflexes are:

- swallowing and sucking
- rooting
- grasping
- walking
- startle
- falling
- blinking

⊃ The Swallowing and Sucking Reflex

When a finger is placed in the mouth babies will automatically suck, so when the breast or teat is put in the mouth they respond by sucking then swallowing. Occasionally babies are born with sore fingers because they have sucked them while still in the womb. This reflex will disappear after about six months.

⊃ The Rooting Reflex

When a finger is gently stroked across the face, babies will turn their head as if in search of a nipple or teat. This reflex will disappear after six weeks.

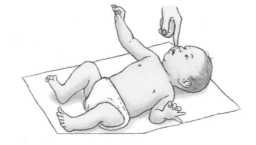

The Grasp Reflex

Babies will automatically curl their fingers round an object when it is placed in the palm of their hand. This reflex will disappear at about three months.

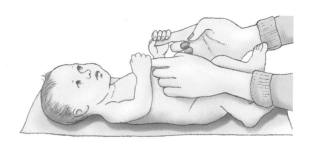

The Walking Reflex

When held in a standing position with the soles of the feet touching a firm surface babies will make stepping movements and attempt to straighten their bodies. This same reflex will cause babies to 'step up' if their shins are placed against a firm surface. This reflex will have disappeared by six months.

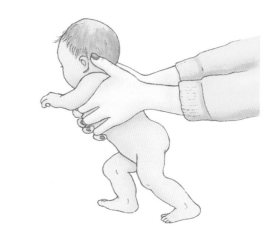

The Startle Reflex

When loud noises or bright lights startle babies they will close their hands into fists, bend the elbows to bring the arms towards the shoulders and they may cry.

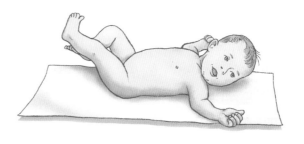

The Falling Reflex

This reflex is also known as the 'moro' reflex. Sudden movements affect the neck and make babies feel that they may be dropped. This feeling causes them to open their hands wide and throw their arms back, then bring the arms together as though they were catching a ball.

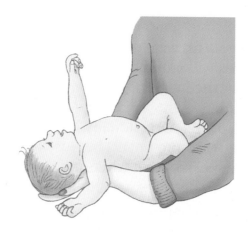

The Blinking Reflex

Newborn babies respond to light and touch by blinking. When a light is shone directly into babies' eyes they will blink.

THE APPEARANCE OF A NEWBORN BABY

The soft spot or fontanelle can be seen where there is a pulse beating beneath the scalp

The umbilical cord has been clamped and cut. It will shrivel quickly and drop off within a few days

Eyes may be puffy and closed most of the time

There may be a fine covering of hair on parts of the body. This is called lanugo and will soon fall off. Some babies have a full head of hair, while others are bald

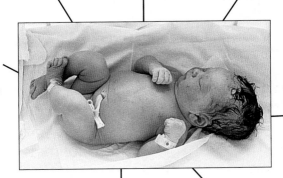

There may be small white spots on the face. These are called milia and are caused by the temporary blockage of small **sebaceous glands.** They will disappear within days of their own accord

The skin may be covered in a whitish lard-like substance called vernix which acted as a natural barrier cream while the baby was in the womb. The vernix is often left on the baby as a natural protector rather than being washed off

The arms and legs will remain bent, close to the body as if the baby were still in the uterus

Birthmarks

Birthmarks are harmless and do not cause the baby pain. Most birthmarks are just abnormal collections of small blood vessels under the skin.

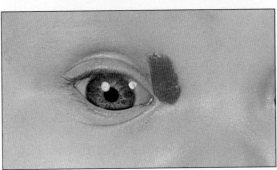

Stork Bites

These are small pink blemishes often found on the eyelids or nape of the neck. These discolorations fade with time and leave no visible marks. They are also known as salmon patches.

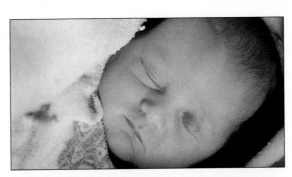

Strawberry Marks

These may first appear as small red dots but can grow quite quickly early in the baby's life to give red raised lumps. However, they will shrivel and disappear without scarring by the time the baby is two years old.

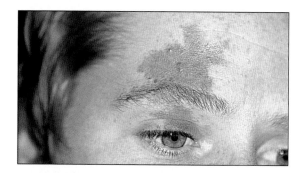

Port Wine Stains

These bright red or purple marks caused by **dilated capillaries** can appear anywhere on the body. They are permanent but can be camouflaged with makeup or removed with laser treatment.

Mongolian Spots

It is very common for dark-skinned babies to have a harmless blue/grey discoloration around the buttocks or on the back. The mongolian spots fade naturally.

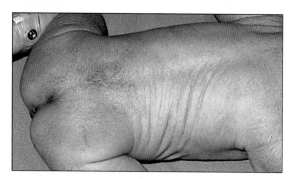

Key Words

Sebaceous glands   glands in the skin that secrete an oily substance
Dilated capillaries   enlargement of very small blood vessels

THE SENSES OF A NEWBORN BABY

Senses collect information and bring it to the central nervous system. At birth a baby possesses the following senses:

- vision
- hearing
- smell
- taste
- touch

These senses will become more refined as the baby develops.

Vision

It is believed that babies' eyes have been developing since the very early weeks of pregnancy and by the twenty-sixth week they can be opened and shut. At birth babies can see but eyesight is limited: they can focus on objects between 25 and 30 cms away, so it is very important to hold babies closely when talking to them. Outside this range, objects may appear blurred and fuzzy. In the early days babies like to look at faces, lights and patterns and strong contrasting colours will attract them. Newborn babies with white skins usually have blue-grey eyes, while babies with dark skin usually have brown eyes. The colour of the eyes will change over the first few months. True colour may not be defined until as late as 12 months.

Figure 7.3 New mother and newborn baby

The eyes will be examined as part of the six-week developmental check. Babies at this stage will be expected to focus on a face and follow a moving object. Many babies appear to have a squint, where the eyes move independently of each other. This is normal as they are still gaining control of the eye muscles.

Hearing

Long before babies are born they are able to hear and can recognise familiar sounds. These sounds will be very comforting during the birth and will be recognised among the great jumble of sounds after the birth. The most recognisable and comforting sound for babies is their mother's voice and they can easily pick this out from other voices.

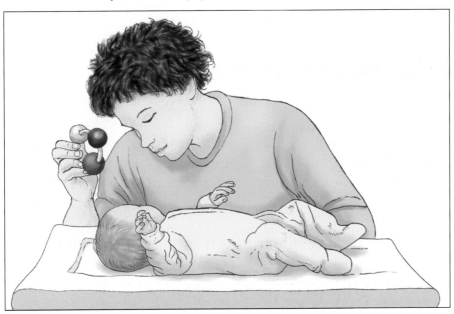

Figure 7.4 Newborn baby's hearing being checked

To encourage the development of hearing it is important that babies are talked to. Hearing is an essential part of speech development. By the age of six months babies will be able to associate sound with a cause, and be able to locate the direction from which sound is coming.

To check babies are hearing well, stand behind them and clap your hands, ring a bell or click your fingers and they will turn round in response to the sound.

⊃ Smell

Newborn babies are sensitive to smell. They recognise the scent of their own parents/carers quickly and will be comforted by familiar smells. Babies who are breast-fed will smell the milk when near the breast and try to root for the nipple. If babies come into contact with an unpleasant smell they will try to turn away from it.

⊃ Taste

Babies show that they find tastes pleasant or unpleasant by facial expression or by trying to expel the taste from their mouths.

⊃ Touch

New babies are very sensitive to touch. As we know they are comforted by close human contact, and like to be cuddled and stroked.

⊃ HANDLING A NEWBORN BABY

Newborn babies appear very delicate and fragile but in fact they are quite robust. Babies need to be handled carefully but with confidence to give them a feeling of security and comfort.

At first babies seem floppy all over and need to be supported from head to toe. They love to be held close to another body, to feel a heartbeat and hear a reassuring voice. Babies should be handled slowly, gently and quietly.

⊃ Picking up a Baby Face-to-Face

◆ Slide one hand, palm up, under the baby's bottom and lower back.

◆ Slide the other hand, palm up, under the baby's head making sure the weight is being fully supported.

◆ Slowly lift the baby up making sure the head and neck are kept in line with the back.

Picking up a Baby From the Side

◆ Slide one hand under the baby's neck and head and the other under the bottom.

◆ Ensure the full weight is supported then slowly scoop the baby towards you keeping the head and neck in line with the back.

Figure 7.5 Dad holding baby in the crook of the arm

Carrying the Baby

It is very important that when newborn babies are being carried they should be safe, the head should be held and the length of the body supported: Below, two different safe ways of carrying babies are described.

◆ It is safe to carry babies by holding them against the upper part of the chest with the head nestling against your shoulder. One hand should be supporting the back and the bottom and the other should support the head.

◆ Another safe way is to carry babies by cradling the head in the crook of a slightly inclined arm. The lower arm, wrist and hand will support the rest of the baby's body. The other arm can be used as additional support for the bottom and legs.

⊃ Using a Sling

Many parents prefer to carry their baby in a sling. A sling is a lightweight fabric support, providing a comfortable way of transporting a young baby. There are a number of points to take into consideration with its use:

Advantages	Disadvantages
The baby feels close and secure.	If the parent falls or trips, the baby could be injured.
The baby receives warmth from mother/parent.	Heavy shopping cannot be placed on a pram and would have to be carried.
The baby can look outwards and inwards.	The baby may become too hot or too cold.
Some designs can be worn on the back or front.	As the baby becomes heavier it may affect the posture of the mother.
Leaves mother's hands free to push a young sibling in a pram, or hold a toddler's hand.	
Access to shops, particularly those without lifts, is much easier, because hands are free to carry shopping.	

When choosing a sling:

◆ look for a sling which is made of a strong washable fabric
◆ try it out to make sure it is easy to put on correctly, and is comfortable for the wearer and the baby
◆ ensure the sling supports the baby's head and neck and the straps are wide enough to support the baby's weight

Figure 7.6 Father with baby in sling

SLEEP AND THE NEWBORN BABY

The amount of sleep a newborn baby needs varies from baby to baby and probably from day to day. Babies are individuals and will adopt their own routine but it is not unusual for some babies to sleep 20 of the 24 hours in each day, waking only if they are hungry, cold or uncomfortable.

Initially babies are not aware of night and day but they gradually notice that there are more sounds and movements during the day and use this as a wakeful time. Night-time is seen as a quieter time but parents should be warned that baby's evenings may not begin until after 10.00 pm.

Where Should Babies Sleep?

Over the first few weeks it is ideal if the baby can sleep in a seat, carrycot or crib which is portable. This will enable the baby to be moved around the home, and taken out shopping and visiting without being disturbed.

Figure 7.7 Baby seat

Figure 7.8 Moses basket

Figure 7.9 Carrycot with chassis

Some newborn babies are likely to share their parents' bedroom for the first couple of months. The parents are sure they can always hear if the baby needs comfort and giving nightfeeds is easier if the baby is close at hand. If and when babies have their own room, it must be kept warm because babies cannot regulate their body temperature. A suitable room temperature is between 16°C and 20°C. A night-light or dimmer switch is useful so babies can be checked without switching on a main light, which might disturb them.

In the daytime it is good for babies to sleep outdoors. They should be wrapped up according to the weather and should be visible at all times. If it is sunny the pram should be in the shade, or a sun canopy or parasol should be used. The hood of a pram can act as a windbreak and a cat net should always be used.

Tips to Settle Babies to Sleep

◆ For the first weeks babies like to be swaddled (wrapped up tightly). The feeling of being tightly enclosed as they were in the uterus makes them feel secure.

◆ Give a comfort suck of breast or bottle.

◆ Darken the room.

◆ Have a musical mobile over the cot.

◆ Gently rock the pram/cot or lovingly stroke the head, back or limbs.

◆ Some babies settle if they are carried around being held closely so they feel the warmth and the heartbeat.

Sleeping Position

Young babies should be placed on their back to sleep with their head turned to one side, so any regurgitated milk (milk that has been swallowed then brought back into the mouth) can trickle from the mouth. Once babies are able to turn over and move around in the cot they will adopt the position in which they feel most comfortable.

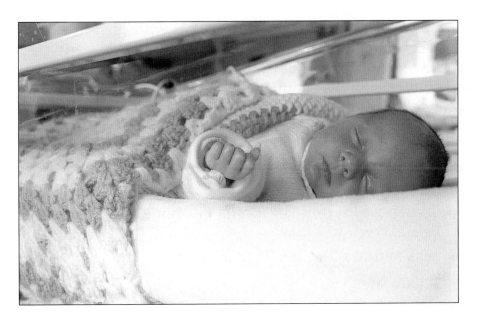

Figure 7.10 Newborn baby sleeping on back

Sudden Infant Death Syndrome (SIDS)

Sudden Infant Death Syndrome is commonly known as cot death and is the sudden and unexplainable death of a baby under six months old.

As the cause of cot death is not known it is impossible to give carers advice on prevention. Risk factors have been identified and continuing research will perhaps ultimately give an answer, which will prevent the unexpected deaths of over 500 infants each year.

The following guidelines are recommended to reduce the risk of cot death:

◆ always place babies on their back to sleep

◆ avoid babies coming into contact with tobacco as it is believed that babies whose parents smoke before and after birth are at risk from SIDS

◆ do not let babies become overheated either from the heat of the room, or too much clothing or bedding

◆ if babies appear to be feverish take off clothing or blankets to cool them down and always seek medical advice if you think the baby is unwell

SPECIAL CARE BABIES

Some babies need extra care when they are born and may be taken to a special care baby unit (SCBU). By far the most common reason for babies to be taken to special care is if they have been born prematurely or pre-term. These are terms used to describe babies who are born less than 37 weeks into the pregnancy. One in 18 babies in Britain is premature. Today, with the great advances in technology and the highly-skilled and dedicated teams in special care baby units, babies born as early as 22 weeks can survive.

From approximately 12 weeks into pregnancy babies are already formed but the next 28 weeks are spent maturing. Therefore, babies born early are going to need help for their maturation to continue before they can survive independently outside the womb.

Premature babies often have:

◆ weak muscle tone and do not show much movement

◆ low calcium, iron and blood sugar levels

◆ sealed eyes

◆ underdeveloped lungs which cause breathing difficulties. This is known as respiratory distress syndrome (RDS)

◆ an inability to suck and swallow

◆ difficulty in digesting milk

◆ lack of ability to regulate body temperature

◆ a yellow tinge to the skin (jaundice)

◆ red and wrinkled skin

◆ a disproportionately large head in comparison to the rest of the body

◆ a weak immune system which means the body cannot defend itself adequately and there is an increased risk of infection

If the parents have been to antenatal classes they will probably have seen the special care baby unit, so if their baby needs special help they will already be familiar with the unit. Special care baby units can initially be very daunting places with so many incubators, monitors and IV lines, with a high ratio of doctors and nurses to babies.

⊃ Special Care Baby Unit Equipment

⊃ Incubators

An incubator is an enclosed thermostatically-controlled cabinet made of transparent material with a 'lid' that opens and 'port-holes' in the side. The incubator filters and humidifies the air and maintains a constant temperature.

Ventilators

Ventilators help babies to breathe until the lungs are mature enough to cope on their own.

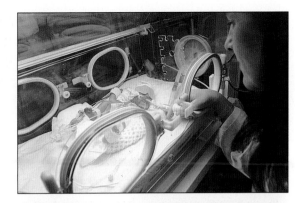

Monitors

Monitors are soft sensors that can be attached to the baby's skin. These sensors can monitor breathing, the heartbeat and the amount of oxygen in the blood stream. The sensors are linked to monitors/display screens. If the signals suggest the baby needs attention, an alarm bell sounds to alert staff.

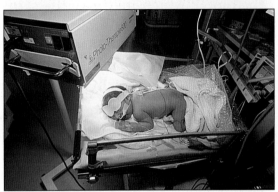

Intravenous Lines

IV Lines, as they are commonly known, are needles connected to tubes that pass measured doses of fluid and drugs directly into the baby's system. The tubes are connected to a pump which regulates the flow. Babies who are unable to digest food naturally may be fed intravenously.

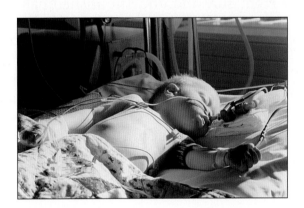

Nasogastric Tube

If a baby is unable to suck and swallow, food may be given by a tube, which goes up through the nose and down into the stomach. If the mother of a premature baby wishes to breast feed her baby she can express (squeeze out) her milk and it can be fed to the baby in this way.

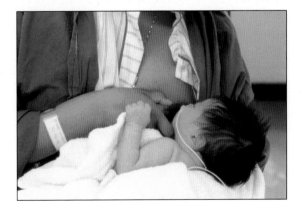

⊃ Light Therapy

Light therapy units are usually placed above an incubator and are used to treat jaundice. Jaundice is not a disease but is caused by the breakdown of red blood cells a couple of days after the birth.

This causes an excess of bilirubin in the blood, which may give the skin a yellowish tinge. Bilirubin is usually excreted by the liver but the premature baby's liver may take a week or so to be working fully and so clear the jaundice.

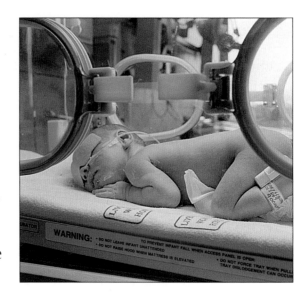

⊃ **Low Birth Weight Babies**

Low birth weight babies are those who weigh less than 2.5 kg at birth. Some low birth weight babies may be full-term but are naturally small. Premature and undernourished babies may well need special care.

⊃ Effect on the Family when a Baby is in Special Care Baby Unit

Having a baby in the Special Care Baby Unit can be traumatic for parents, who after months of waiting for the arrival of the newborn child, with hopes and dreams of taking the baby home to the newly-decorated nursery, find that life becomes centred around hospital visits and nights sleeping at the hospital bedside.

The family may be unable to recognise that a baby has been born and don't acknowledge it in the usual way

Tiredness/exhaustion/ stress and strain on the whole family

Mother/father/siblings may not be able to hold the newborn baby

The family become attached to the doctors and nurses and they become an extension of the family

Mother may have had a Caesarean section and be unable to visit the baby immediately

Effects on the family

Mother may not be able to breast feed the baby but could express the milk for feeding

Some premature babies are only in hospital for a short time, others for quite a long period, and uncertainty about the future can strain relationships

Constant ups and downs as the baby struggles to survive

Father may attempt to carry on his work schedule, then visit hospital after work, with little time for 'normal life'

Other siblings will require looking after by extended family or partner if mother is at the hospital

Young siblings may find it difficult to cope with mummy/daddy being away from home and begin to feel insecure

Questions

Answer the following questions:

1   Name the five elements which give the total Apgar score.

2   What is the average weight of a newborn baby?

3   Barlow's test is used to check what?

4   Name the seven reflex actions.

5   Why do small babies often appear to squint?

6   What are senses?

7   Careful handling of newborn babies is very important. Why?

8   Give five guidelines which should be followed to reduce the risk of cot death.

9   What is a premature or pre-term baby?

10 Give the term used to describe a baby whose birth weight is under 2.5kg.

Match the beginnings to the ends.

11	When a newborn baby is carried	lightweight fabric supports
12	Slings are	clothing and blankets to cool them down
13	Babies should be wrapped up	their backs to sleep.
14	Young babies should be placed on	the head and the length of the body must be supported
15	If a baby appears feverish take off	according to the weather.

Give the full definitions of the following abbreviations:

16 PKU

17 SIDS

18 SCBU

19 Collect a number of pictures of newborn babies and make a poster with captions to point out the characteristics of a newborn baby.

20 **Extension work**

Make a leaflet which could be available at the Special Care Baby Unit of your local hospital. The leaflet could explain to visitors the facilities which are used in the unit. People who could help you with this may include teachers, local midwife, health visitor, local SCBU or parents who have experience of SCBU.

⊃ NEWBORN WORDSEARCH

U	W	N	M	S	C	J	I	S	X	H	N	C	C	H
Y	B	Q	S	K	R	A	M	H	T	R	I	B	L	S
X	T	H	J	G	N	I	T	O	O	R	O	M	Y	E
H	O	E	A	N	N	Z	B	B	C	W	Z	N	C	M
X	G	L	U	I	Q	W	E	U	A	P	G	A	R	B
I	U	L	N	P	L	E	M	L	V	X	S	J	Z	Z
E	N	E	D	S	N	F	K	W	F	F	Z	R	L	Z
E	A	N	I	A	E	I	L	T	V	W	P	Q	Y	F
O	L	A	C	R	N	Z	S	M	E	B	T	K	H	C
V	H	T	E	G	X	S	K	I	P	N	U	E	M	O
X	I	N	R	E	V	G	G	U	O	M	L	H	L	F
A	C	O	L	A	O	H	T	G	N	E	L	H	R	
E	F	F	J	Q	T	G	F	V	F	S	V	C	Z	F
G	E	M	P	R	U	S	M	H	V	E	S	O	D	H
R	D	X	B	P	N	O	W	X	R	L	D	I	W	W

Apgar	Moro
Birth marks	Newborn
Circumference	Reflex
Fontanelle	Rooting
Grasping	Startle
Jaundice	Vernix
Lanugo	Walking
Length	Weight

Post-Natal Care

In this section we will look at the post-natal examination and **post-natal** depression, bonding, why babies cry and how the midwife or health visitor can help the new mother.

During pregnancy most expectant mothers will have imagined what life with a newborn baby will be like. It is easy to fantasise but sometimes reality is a little more difficult to live with. A baby can take up so much time and energy but new mothers also need to care for themselves and keep fit and healthy. New mothers must never be afraid to seek help and advice from partners, from family or from medical personnel.

If the baby has been born in hospital, a midwife will always be on hand to offer help and advice. When the mother returns home a midwife attached to her general practitioner's (GP's) practice will visit daily until the baby is ten days old. The midwife who makes a home delivery will continue to visit the mother and baby for the next ten days.

After the first ten days the care of the mother and baby becomes the responsibility of the health visitor. A health visitor is a nurse who has midwifery experience and has also gained further qualifications in family health and child development. The health visitor will make an initial visit and will then call from time to time to check all is well. The health visitor will give the mother a contact number where advice can be asked for if there is a problem.

Key Words

Post-natal refers to the first six weeks after the birth of the baby.

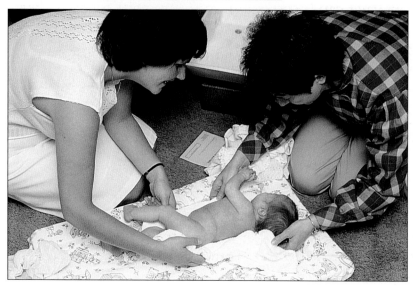

Figure 8.1 A health visitor with a new mother at home

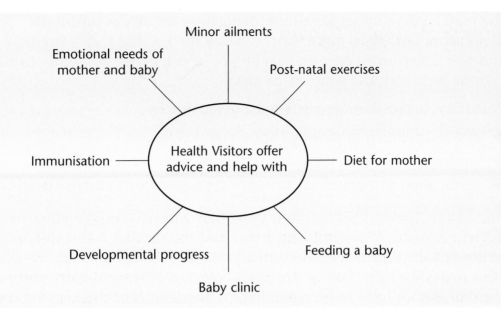

Remember, health visitors are there to help. The new mother must never be afraid to ask questions, however simple they may seem. Finding out the answer to a problem will give the new mother added confidence.

⊃ POST-NATAL DEPRESSION

It is very common during the week following the birth for the new mother to feel miserable and down for a day or two. This is not post-natal depression. This is commonly known as 'baby blues' and it comes about because the mother's hormones are actively trying to return to their normal pattern which has changed during pregnancy. She is also getting little sleep and may be very tired after a long, hard labour and she may be worrying about how she is going to cope with a new life.

Baby blues usually disappear as rapidly as they appear and as long as the new mother has plenty of love and understanding around her, she will realise her feelings are natural. A partner can be very supportive during these early days and it is sensible for him to take paternity leave when the mother and baby return home rather then when they are in hospital. Paternity leave is a statutory right for working fathers. They are currently allowed to take up to five days away from work with full pay at any time around the birth of a new baby (2 weeks of paid paternity leave from 2003).

If the baby blues continue for more than a few days and the new mother appears

◆ constantly tired   ◆ unable to cope
◆ wakeful and agitated   ◆ lacking in emotions
◆ tearful for no apparent reason ◆ resentful and angry towards the baby
◆ withdrawn and almost vacant   ◆ to have nightmares
◆ unaware of the track of time

she may be developing long-term depression known as post-natal depression. Post-natal depression is when the mother feels extremely sad and low. She is overtaken by a feeling of hopelessness and often thinks she cannot cope with the simplest of tasks.

Post-natal depression can usually be overcome by:

◆ close support from partners and extended family
◆ getting advice from the general practitioner and health visitor
◆ medication (progesterone injections, progesterone **suppositories**)
◆ psychiatric treatment

If the post-natal depression continues and the mother is not responding to treatment she may be admitted to a psychiatric hospital for more intensive treatment. Most psychiatric hospitals have a mother-and-baby unit so that the pair do not have to be separated for any length of time as this could seriously damage the bonding process which may already be jeopardised.

⊃ PUERPERIUM

Birth to six weeks is known as the puerperium. During the puerperium:

◆ the uterus is expected to have shrunk back to normal size
◆ any soreness around the perineum should have disappeared
◆ any stitches should have dissolved and wounds healed
◆ post-natal bleeding should have cleared
◆ minor problems like constipation, backache and haemorrhoids will have cleared up
◆ post-natal exercise should be done to help pelvic and abdominal muscles to return to normal

At the end of the puerperium the mother and baby will have a check up known as the post-natal examination. This examination can be carried out by a GP or by a doctor at the hospital where the baby was delivered. Babies are checked to ensure they are in good health and thriving.

The post-natal examination of the mother will check:

◆ her weight
◆ her blood pressure
◆ her urine
◆ that the reproductive organs have returned to size
◆ her emotional condition (looking for signs of post-natal depression)
◆ that any cuts or tears to the perineum have healed and all stitches have dissolved

The doctor will also offer a routine smear test and volunteer contraceptive advice.

After the first six weeks everyone tends to leave the mother and baby to settle into a routine. It is advisable to adopt a routine which suits both the mother and baby and to be flexible. No one expects her to be perfect and to know all the answers, so she still has the support of the health visitor and her GP, but words of encouragement from partners, relatives, neighbours and friends are always needed. Mothers still need time for themselves and time to spend with their partner, so they should arrange for someone reliable to look after the baby occasionally.

NEWBORN BABIES CRY!

Babies do not cry to exercise their lungs. If a newborn baby cries it is a sign that something is wrong. A carer will quickly learn to distinguish between different cries.

Remember at this stage, crying is a baby's only way of communicating.

Babies cry because of	To comfort babies
Hunger	If babies are bottle-fed and it is more than two hours since the last feed, they may be hungry again and could need another feed. If babies are breast fed it is difficult to judge how much food they have had and they should be offered a feed.
Thirst	Babies often cry because they are thirsty, not hungry. A new baby can be offered a drink of previously boiled water from a bottle.
Temperature	If babies are too hot or too cold they may cry. If a baby looks hot loosen any tight-fitting clothing and fold back or take off some covers.
Soiled nappy	Some new babies do not like lying in a soiled nappy. Change the nappy to make them comfortable.
Tiredness	Sometimes babies become over-tired and are fractious and irritable. Some babies respond to being picked up and loved while others prefer to be left alone to fall asleep.
Colic (abdominal pain)	This is one of the most common causes of crying in the early days. It often occurs in the evening, when babies may have continuous bouts of screaming pulling their legs up to their tummy. The baby will probably find comfort in being held closely and comforted. Infant colic usually stops at around three months old.
Fear/Insecurity/Loneliness	Babies can cry if they are frightened by a loud noise. They may be bored if put in a pram or cot where they are not able to see anything. They will respond if picked up and cuddled tightly then sat in a bouncing cradle or propped up in a pram or pushchair.

Hints on Soothing a Baby

If young babies continue to cry for no apparent reason carers can:

- rock them in their arms or in a rocking chair
- hold them tightly and talk or sing quietly
- lay them across the knee and gently rub their back
- play some music (low noises are preferable to high-pitched sounds)
- offer a comforter (a sterile dummy)

The benefits of a comforter

Figure 8.2 Young baby with dummy

In the early days a dummy often provides a form of comfort to a baby. As long as the dummy does not replace human forms of comfort such as love and cuddles it is not harmful. A comforter can be a great source of security when no one is around – for example, a baby may wake in the night and be comforted with the dummy without disturbing anyone else, before drifting back to sleep. After the first few months babies often have a favourite blanket, garment or soft toy which acts as a comforter.

BONDING

Bonding is the process in which strong psychological and emotional ties are established between a parent and a newborn child. It is an essential and very basic part of a baby's emotional development.

Bonding is a two-way process in which baby and parent respond to each other's gestures and expressions. Bonding is not instant. It is built up during the first months of life.

A difficulty to bond between a parent and child is not unusual and may occur if the baby is very ill or premature and in a special care baby unit where it is not easy for the parents to handle the baby, although the medical team will encourage this as much as possible. Bonding problems can also occur if the parent's own family experiences did not show them good parent/infant relationships.

It is widely believed that lack of bonding at this very early stage can lead to emotional difficulties for the child in later life.

One of the most instinctive feelings a mother has when her baby is born, is to hold the baby to the breast. The baby's rooting and sucking reflexes begin, creating a close skin-to-skin contact with the mother. This can be an overwhelming experience for the mother, creating a special bond. However, this close bond will also occur with the baby who is bottle-fed, since skin-to-skin contact is made with a simple gesture such as touching cheek to cheek.

Key Words

Suppositories – Medication in a solid form that can be inserted into the vagina or rectum.

Figure 8.3 Father and baby bonding

Questions

Answer the following questions:

1 What period of time does post natal refer to?

2 Describe briefly the role of the health visitor.

3 What are the 'baby blues'?

4 List five signs which may indicate a mother is suffering from post-natal depression.

5 How many weeks after birth would a woman expect a post-natal check?

6 How do new born babies communicate?

7 Give three ways to try and calm a crying baby.

8 What is bonding?

9 Why may bonding be difficult if a baby is in a SCBU?

10 Name three items which may be used as comforters to a baby.

Questions continued

Match the beginning to the end

11 | The health visitor will give the mother a contact number | as long as it does not replace love and hugs.

12 | A sensible time to take paternity leave | is when a mother feels low and is overtaken by feelings of hopelessness.

13 | Post-natal depression | is known as puerperium.

14 | Birth to six weeks | where advice can be sought if there is a problem.

15 | A dummy is not harmful | is when the mother and baby return home from hospital.

16 Sue and Colin have just had a baby daughter Olivia, they also have a son Stephen who is five. Colin is self employed and cannot afford time away from work, Stephen goes to the local primary school. Sue and Colin's parents have offered help as has neighbour Pat. Sue is showing signs of post-natal depression. Discuss in depth how best you feel the parents and Pat could help Sue and Colin in the coming days.

17 Olivia cries a lot. Imagine you are a health visitor, explain the advice you would give her parents to try and calm her.

Feeding and Nutrition

In this section, we will look at feeding babies and young children.
To do this successfully, we must examine the following topics:-

- breast and bottle milk
- the different stages of weaning
- the importance of nutrients and daily requirements of each one
- establishing a healthy eating pattern
- likes and dislikes of children
- controlling children's diet

It is very important for the mother to look after herself in many ways before, during and after pregnancy, particularly regarding her diet. A healthy well-balanced diet will help her to produce milk if she wants to breastfeed.

It is not necessary to have 'special foods', but the mother should make sure that she has a good balance of proteins, iron, calcium, fresh fruit and vegetables and plenty of fluids. One piece of good advice is to have three good meals per day, with plenty of snacks in between. These snack foods might include such items as milk, cheese, fruit, etc. Not only will they give her plenty of energy, they will also help to combat tiredness, particularly after the baby is born. It is also a good idea for the mother to have daily iron supplements at this time.

⊃ BREASTS AND BREAST MILK

During pregnancy, the mother's breasts change. They become enlarged and the glandular tissue within each breast develops to prepare them for the milk production. Milk production actually starts a few days after the birth.

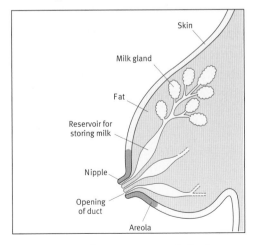

Figure 9.1 The structure of the breast

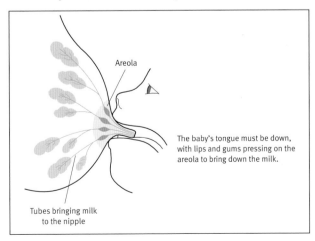

Figure 9.2 Baby breastfeeding

⟳ HOW BREAST MILK IS PRODUCED

Each breast contains between 15 and 20 sections of milk-secreting glands. Each gland is connected to the nipple by milk ducts. The milk is made within these glands. The dark area around each nipple is called the **areola.** During pregnancy, the expectant woman's placenta and ovaries produce very high levels of both oestrogen and progesterone. These two hormones work together to stimulate the milk glands to produce a substance called **colostrum.** This colostrum, when it is first secreted by the breasts, is very clear and almost colourless. Later on, it becomes yellowish in colour. The colostrum provides the baby with water, proteins, sugar, vitamins, minerals, and also antibodies to give extra protection from various infections.

The colostrum is produced at least 12 weeks before the end of pregnancy. When birth occurs, this is the signal for the breasts to stop producing colostrum, and to make a start on milk production. Milk production begins between three to five days *after* the baby is born. This process is called **lactation.**

When the breast content changes from colostrum to milk, the whole process is triggered by hormonal changes within the mother's body.

However, milk production is dependent on the baby sucking at its mother's breasts. When the baby sucks, the action stimulates nerve endings in the areola, and in turn, nerve endings in the **hypothalamus** in the brain.

Key Words

The **hypothalamus** is a very small area at the base of the brain, just above the pituitary gland. It is often called the *Appetite Centre.*

When the hypothalamus absorbs these signals, it sends out signals to the pituitary gland. These signals instruct the pituitary gland to release **prolactin** – a hormone which stimulates the milk production. As a result the baby's sucking is often known as the prolactin reflex. The pituitary glands also release another hormone known as **oxytocin**, and this makes the muscle fibres around the milk gland contract. As they contract, the milk is squeezed from the glands to the milk ducts. When the breasts are full of milk, the baby's sucking reflex stimulates the milk production, and as a result, the baby is fed. The diagram on page 207 shows you what happens when the baby is sucking.

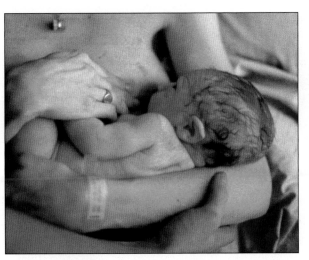

Figure 9.3 Breast feeding

The baby's lips put pressure on the areola, and squeeze the milk into the mouth through the openings in the nipple. The more the baby sucks, the more milk will be produced.

Every female is capable of breast feeding their baby regardless of the size of her breasts. However, it is a matter of personal choice as to whether she chooses to breast- or bottle-feed her baby.

Occasionally a baby may refuse to take breast milk. This often happens during the first few weeks after the birth. There could be many reasons, for example:

◆ the baby was not particularly hungry

◆ the breasts were too full of milk, making it difficult for the baby to suck.

Patience, time and encouragement are needed if the mother is determined to breast-feed.

⊃ Advantages of Breast-feeding to the Mother

◆ It gives the mother a chance to sit down during a busy day.

◆ Breast milk requires no preparation and no equipment.

◆ Immediately after the birth, breast-feeding may cause uterine contractions, which although may be painful, can also help the mother's womb return more quickly to its normal size. This is because breast-feeding stimulates the production of oxytocin.

◆ Breast-feeding can delay the return of menstruation after the birth, and for this, the mother might be very glad, particularly if her periods were painful.

◆ Some mothers find that breast-feeding (which uses up 300 calories per day) helps them to lose weight.

◆ It helps to increase the mother's natural bonding with her baby. It *should* be a satisfying experience for her.

◆ Breast milk is cheaper than bottle milk!

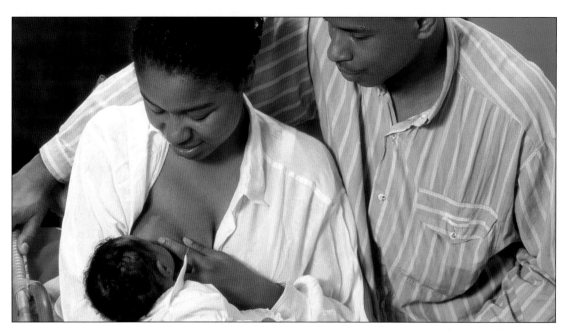

Figure 9.4 Breast feeding

Disadvantages of Breast-feeding to the Mother

◆ Breast-feeding is often tiring, and the mother is 'tied' to the baby. If the mother is tired, the baby will be upset.

◆ She may end up with sore or cracked nipples.

◆ What the mother eats or drinks will inevitably be passed on to the baby. She should therefore avoid alcohol (and drugs) and strongly flavoured foods.

◆ If the mother is tired or ill, or wants to go out without the baby, feeding could prove difficult.

◆ Some mothers feel too embarrassed to feed their babies in public.

Advantages of Breast Milk to the Baby

◆ Breast milk is an ideal food.

The fat in breast milk contains all of the essential fatty acids. The quality of the protein is excellent, even though there is very little of it. It has a low salt (sodium) content. There is no risk that the milk is too concentrated in one nutrient or another. Babies are born with a good iron supply which is stored in the liver.

◆ Babies are less likely to become obese (fat).

◆ Research suggests that babies' brains develop better if they have been breast fed.

◆ Breast milk does not need to be sterilised.

- Gastroenteritis and other common ailments of babies are less likely in babies who have been breast fed.
- Breast milk is less likely to give the baby eczema or nappy rash.
- Babies fed on breast milk are less likely to become allergic than those babies who are bottle-fed.
- Breast milk cannot be prepared wrongly, therefore its quality is always the same.
- Breast milk contains natural antibodies which help to ward off infections.
- Breast milk is easier for the baby to digest than bottle milk.
- Breast milk never causes indigestion.

Disadvantages of Breast Milk to the Baby

- Occasionally, the baby does not get enough milk from the breasts because the mother is tense and/or overtired.
- Some mothers breast-feed the child for 12 months or more. A baby who is fed entirely on milk after 6 months may, when weaning does begin, find it difficult to take to 'new' foods. If a baby has not been weaned by the time it is 9-10 months old, there is a danger that the baby may become anaemic, because it is no longer getting the iron from its mother's breast milk.

BREAST CARE

The breasts have to work hard while feeding a baby and a number of minor problems may arise. If these problems are identified quickly they will not develop further.

It is wise to keep the breasts and nipples very clean. They should be dried thoroughly by patting gently and always supported by a good bra. Women may find the breasts leak. Absorbent breast pads fit comfortably in the bra and soak up the excess milk.

Cracked Nipples

If the nipples become sore they may crack. When cracked it is painful when the baby suckles. To help prevent cracked nipples cream should be applied two or three times daily.

Engorgement

When breast-feeding becomes established the breast can become overfull, quite hard to touch and pain may be felt. If breasts are engorged the baby will find it difficult to latch on. If this is the case the mother should express some milk from the breasts before trying to feed the baby. A well-supporting bra is obviously important if breasts are engorged.

⟳ Mastitis

If a milk duct in the breast becomes blocked and is not treated it can lead to the breast becoming infected; this condition is known as mastitis. The breast will appear red and inflamed and should be emptied to relieve the pain. A doctor should be consulted, as often antibiotics are needed to clear the infection.

⟳ BOTTLE-FEEDING

Breast-feeding is not for everyone. These days, specially formulated baby foods are being manufactured, so that babies can be bottle-fed from birth.

There is no reason to suggest that a baby who is bottle-fed cannot be as healthy, and grow and thrive in the same way, as a baby who is breast-fed. Bottle-feeding is perfectly safe as long as the mother follows the manufacturer's instructions on how to make up the feed strictly and carefully.

Baby food, or infant formulas as they are sometimes known, usually come in two forms. They are either dried milk-based powders, or ready-to-use liquid products. Both types are vitamin- and iron-enriched, and are very carefully manufactured so that they resemble the mother's own breast milk as closely as possible. They are usually based on cow's milk, or soya. Cow's milk formulas are the most widely used, but some babies cannot tolerate the protein in cow's milk. This is where soya-based milk is useful.

If the mother is unsure which one to use for her baby, she should first consult her doctor, health visitor or midwife.

⟳ Advantages of Bottle-feeding to the Mother

- ◆ It is useful for those women who cannot breast-feed.
- ◆ Bottle-feeding can be reassuring because the mother can see exactly how much milk the baby has had.
- ◆ It can be useful for working mothers.
- ◆ Bottle-feeding affords a better quality of milk for those babies of women whose nutritional and dietary way of life is not very good.
- ◆ Some women find that they cannot physically cope with the demands of breast-feeding, especially if they find it painful.
- ◆ The bottle can be given by other people and that takes the pressure off the mother.
- ◆ The mother's breasts do not contain any milk. The breasts are not uncomfortable and cannot leak.

◆ The mother can feed the baby anywhere. Breast-feeding might make her feel embarrassed in public areas.

⊃ Disadvantages of Bottle Milk to the Mother

◆ It works out more expensive as the equipment and the milk formula have to be bought.

◆ It makes extra work for the mother, i.e. having to make up the feed carefully and having to sterilise the equipment thoroughly.

◆ The mother may find it difficult to work out the quantities of formula feeds, so the baby may be overfed or underfed.

⊃ Advantages of Bottle-feeding to the Baby

◆ Bottle feeds, although not perfect, are a good substitute for mothers unable to breast feed.

◆ Babies are extremely sensitive to the person giving the feed. A mother who is relaxed giving a bottle feed is better than a mother who is tense and anxious or afraid whilst breast-feeding.

Figure 9.5 Father bottle feeding

⊃ Disadvantages of Bottle Milk to the Baby

◆ Bottle milk does not have the same protection against allergies and infections as breast milk.

◆ The closeness between mother and baby may not be as intense whilst bottle-feeding.

- Babies who are bottle-fed tend to suffer more from constipation.
- Babies who are bottle-fed tend to swallow more air than breast-fed babies, and so they need to be 'winded' more often. Allowing baby to 'burp' or bring up wind is important whichever method of feeding is used. N.B. When babies 'burp', they may bring up a little of the milk. This is known as posseting.
- There is always a danger that babies who are bottle-fed may be left to feed themselves. Allowing this to happen might make the baby choke, and it also means that they, by not being supervised closely, could be sucking on a flattened teat or empty bottle. Either way, the baby is taking in air.

Feeding Equipment

Bottles

Babies' bottles come in a variety of shapes and sizes. There are tapered bottles, waisted bottles, easy grip bottles, disposable bottles. No one bottle has any great advantages over the others, it is just personal choice. However, it is sensible to choose a bottle made from clear material with graduated measurements on the side, a wide neck for easy cleaning and a cap to protect the teat.

Figure 9.6 Various feeding bottles

Teats

Again there are teats of varying shapes and sizes. The most important feature of a teat is the size of the hole. A hole which is the correct size will allow the milk to drip out rapidly without shaking the bottle. If the hole is too big the milk will flow too freely and could cause babies to choke as they try to swallow. If the hole in the teat is too small babies will have to suck harder. This will make them swallow a great deal of air and they may then have problems with wind.

⊃ Making up a Formula Feed

1 Boil a kettle and allow it to cool.
2 Wash hands thoroughly and
   dry with a clean towel.
3 Take a sterilized bottle,
   teat and lid.

4 Pour the correct amount of
   cooled boiled water into the
   graduated bottle. Check the
   measurement while the bottle is
   on a firm surface.

5 Put the required number of
   scoops of formula milk powder
   into the bottle. Each scoop
   should be levelled off using a
   straight bladed knife.
6 Put the teat and cap on to the
   bottle and shake well to mix
   together water and milk powder.

Remember

◆ **All equipment must be clean and sterile.**

◆ **Always read the instructions given on the formula milk container.**

◆ **Check the sell-by and use-by dates on tins of milk.**

◆ **Only use powdered milks produced for babies.**

⊃ WEANING

All babies are different in their needs, but they all depend on milk
(whether breast milk or bottle milk) to make them grow and develop,
particularly in the first few months of their lives. By the time babies are
about 4 months old, nearly all of the iron supply in their body has been
used up. Since iron is a vital nutrient, and it is *not* present in milk, babies
must be given food from other sources in order to provide iron and other
nutrients. Also, by this age babies are getting bigger and developing quite
fast, and they need more food.

This stage, when babies change from an all-milk diet to a milk and solids diet is called **weaning**. It should be a gradual process to allow the baby's digestive system to develop correctly. The age at which weaning occurs varies from baby to baby. Usual signs for the mother are if the baby:

◆ is still hungry after a milk feed

◆ wakes up hungry before the next feed is due.

However it is important to stress that it is not a good idea to start weaning before 4 months because it can lead to some allergies and digestive disorders.

⊃ **What is the purpose of weaning?**

Key Words

Weaning is the stage between a diet completely made up of milk, and a diet composed of milk and solid foods.

To make life easier for the mother, weaning is divided into three main stages. The first stage happens at around 3 months.

⊃ Stage 1 (3 to 4 months)

Suitable foods	Foods to avoid
◆ Puréed fruit and vegetables ◆ Mashed bananas ◆ Baby rice mixed up finely with either breast milk, bottled milk or water which has been boiled	◆ Foods containing **gluten** as it could trigger off **coeliac disease** ◆ Very sugary foods, because they could make a baby want sweet things all the time ◆ Nuts of any description, even if they have been crushed ◆ Salt, because a young baby is unable to get rid of too much salt in its kidneys ◆ Foods high in fibre ◆ Very fatty foods

Key Words

Gluten is the insoluble protein found in wheat.

Coeliac disease a food-related disorder where the lining of the small intestine is sensitive to gluten and, as a result, is damaged by it. Children who suffer from this disease tend to grow more slowly and either lose or fail to gain weight.

Stage 2 (5 to 6 months)

At this stage the baby can, with caution, eat the same as the rest of the family. However, the baby's portion should be removed before salt or seasoning is added to the family meal.

Suitable foods	Foods to avoid
◆ Eggs – hard boiled or cooked so the yolk is thoroughly cooked, to avoid salmonella poisoning	◆ Spicy foods, e.g. chillies, curries, etc
◆ Fish (no bones)	◆ Nuts of any description
◆ Baked beans, lentils, stews, casseroles – all mashed and well-puréed	◆ Fatty foods
◆ Milky puddings, e.g. rice, tapioca	◆ Foods high in sugar and salt. A little is fine, but no extra should be added
	◆ Bran- and wheat-based cereals, again to avoid Coeliac disease

Canned fish e.g. sardines or tuna can be used, but *all* bones must be removed.

Milk jellies and custards can also be given within moderation. Vitamin drops are suggested for children between the ages of 6 months and 2 years. This is to help prevent a vitamin D deficiency which can cause Rickets (bone malformation). Many of the foods given to children at this age are low in vitamin D and since they are developing quickly, they need extra vitamin D. Asian babies are particularly at risk.

Stage 3 (7 to 9 months)

Suitable foods	Foods to avoid
◆ Bread – different varieties, e.g. pitta	◆ Highly spiced food, e.g. curries
◆ Ordinary bread could be toasted and given as finger foods, e.g. soldiers dipped in egg	◆ Fatty and fried foods
◆ Small pieces of fruit and vegetables	◆ Babies of this age are beginning to like sweet flavours, so too much sugar, especially added sugar, should be avoided
◆ Citrus fruits, as long as they are not given too often	◆ Foods that contain too much salt
◆ Spreads such as peanut butter and Marmite are useful	

⊃ Food at 12 months

By 12 months babies are usually eating the same food as the rest of the family. Babies should never be force fed, and if they wish to play and finger the food, then the best option is to leave them alone, within reason. If babies get tired, help, otherwise let them feed themselves. Allow babies to eat with the rest of the family. It is good social training.

At 12 months children will be eating three meals a day, with midday drinks. This is the very best time to train children to eat healthily and have sound eating habits which hopefully will stay for the rest of their life.

During the next two years, the child's body develops very rapidly and will require plenty of body building as well as energy and protective foods. This is where a knowledge of all the nutrients are important (see Diet section in Preconceptual Care).

A nutritionally balanced diet for children is just as important as it is for an expectant mother. Babies should be allowed to experiment with textures and flavours. As we have already seen, a diet of milk is sufficient at the beginning, but as the need for solid food increases, the mother should pay close attention to the type and variety of food she gives her children.

On page 219 there is a table showing the Dietary Reference Values of a child from 0-5 years. N.B. Dietary Reference Values (DRVs) have replaced Recommended Daily Amounts (RDAs).

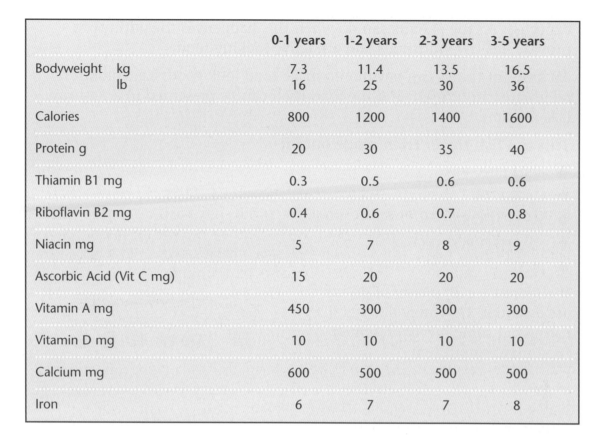

		0-1 years	1-2 years	2-3 years	3-5 years
Bodyweight	kg	7.3	11.4	13.5	16.5
	lb	16	25	30	36
Calories		800	1200	1400	1600
Protein g		20	30	35	40
Thiamin B1 mg		0.3	0.5	0.6	0.6
Riboflavin B2 mg		0.4	0.6	0.7	0.8
Niacin mg		5	7	8	9
Ascorbic Acid (Vit C mg)		15	20	20	20
Vitamin A mg		450	300	300	300
Vitamin D mg		10	10	10	10
Calcium mg		600	500	500	500
Iron		6	7	7	8

After children reach the age of 1 year, their appetite can begin to wander a little. This is because they are now becoming more fussy about likes/dislikes. Also, they are not so dependent on their mother for food every few hours, so while they play they may forget their hunger for a time.

⊃ Making food fun

> ### Remember
>
> In the first year, children eat what is given to them and always seem to be hungry. However, this hungry phase gradually gives way to children not always being hungry, and adopting a fussier attitude towards food. By now they know what they like and what they don't like. At this stage children will have 'food fads' where they will eat a certain food one day and refuse it the next.

As already mentioned, children should not be forced to eat what has been placed in front of them. Coaxing may help, but under no circumstances should sweets, chocolate or cakes be given as a bribe. Children will eat when they are hungry. They have smaller stomachs than adults, and can therefore only consume small quantities.

They also tend to change on a daily basis. One day they might eat a great deal, other days, hardly anything at all. Also, they will go through phases when for a little time, they will really like a specific item of food. When it suits them, they will go off the same item. This is natural and only to be expected. All the parents can do when this happens is to continue to provide healthy, nutritious and attractive looking food.

All kinds of things can be done to make food look good, e.g. colourful tableware can be used, and the food itself can be presented in a fun way (see picture).

This is a fish finger train made out of:

◆ FISH FINGERS

◆ CARROTS

◆ SWEETCORN

◆ MASHED POTATO

◆ PEAS

If children are ill, plenty of drinks are essential. They may not feel like eating but some nicely presented food may tempt them.

Figure 9.9 Fish finger train

⊃ Eating Fruit and Vegetables

Some tips for the mother to encourage her child to eat five portions of fruit and vegetables per day are:

◆ Drink a glass of fruit juice at breakfast

◆ Add a spoonful of dried fruit to morning cereal.

◆ Have a piece of fruit as a mid-morning snack.

◆ Add different fruit and vegetables to a casserole.

◆ Make a necklace or kebab out of a selection of fruit and vegetables. This may add 'fun' value to eating such foods.

A rough guide to portion sizes are:

Cooked vegetables	2 tablespoonfuls
Grapefruit	½ fruit
Apples/bananas/oranges	1 fruit
Grapes/cherries/strawberries	approx. 30-40g
Plums	2 whole fruit
Dried fruit	1 tablespoonful
Fruit juice	1 glass

Any 'new' food should be introduced without the child's knowledge. For example, courgettes could be placed either in a casserole, or covered by a sauce.

Other Food Matters

If children are overweight, parents should obtain professional advice. They will usually be advised to try to slow down the weight gain, rather than opt for a diet where the weight loss is going to be tremendous.

Parents often need help to ensure that children are receiving healthy foods, even though they may not like certain foods. The pie chart shows approximate quantities of foods least enjoyed by children.

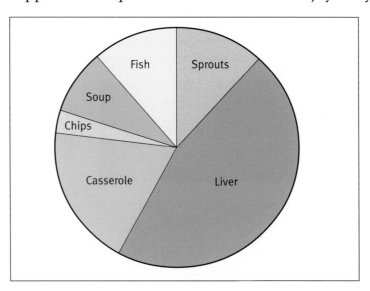

Figure 9.10 Pie chart showing foods least enjoyed by children

When this happens, the following guide might be useful.

◆ Give the child at least one pint of milk per day. If children do not like milk to drink, they can be given milk shakes, yoghurt, custards, cheeses, etc.

◆ One helping of fish, meat, poultry, cheese or beans per day. If they dislike any of these or are vegetarian, they can have eggs, peas, beans, lentils, etc instead.

◆ At least five portions of fruit and vegetables should be given daily. Vegetables are easy to disguise, but if fruit is disliked, juices can be given instead.

◆ Bread or whole grain cereals should also be tried daily.

By feeding children in this way, parents will know that they will be healthy. Parents can use a variety of cooking methods, e.g. if the child enjoys chips, try grilling them and keep the skin on, rather than frying them. This way the child is *not* getting too much saturated fat, and the fibre content of the diet is increased (potato skins).

⊃ Advertising and Junk Food

Some companies aim advertisements at children hoping they will get their parents to buy the products. There is nothing wrong with this, as long as the parents are happy that the food they are purchasing has some health-giving quantities (see labels of foods geared for children below).

Occasional foods are sometimes called **junk food**. They are fun foods and are loved by children.

Figure 9.11 Junk food labels show how advertisers target children

Junk foods usually contain a lot of fat, sugar and additives. Children should be discouraged from eating them, but this is often difficult when their friends are doing exactly the same thing.

Parents can help children avoid junk food by not buying it, and by making sure that they have access to healthy alternatives, e.g. pieces of fruit and vegetables.

Children can also be encouraged to become involved in the shopping and buying of foods; this way they can feel in control of what they eat. This may make it easier to keep them on a healthy diet.

Key Words

Additives in food can be flavours, preservatives, emulsifiers and stabilisers, colourings, sweeteners, anti-oxidants and flour improvers. Each one has a different function to perform but nearly all of them help to increase that particular food's safety in terms of taste, quality, etc.

Food allergy is a condition where a person has an intolerance towards certain foods.

Food aversion is a condition where a person cannot tolerate a certain food or foods for reasons best known to themselves.

Food intolerance is a condition where a person suffers a string of physical reactions, triggered off by a food, but not caused by any specific food. Some allergic responses may cause eczema or gastrointestinal problems (see Chapter II).

Junk food beefburgers, chips, crisps, cakes, processed pies. Foods children love!

Questions

Question 1

a) Give four advantages of breast milk to the baby.

b) Describe two disadvantages of bottle-feeding to the mother.

c) What precautions should you take when preparing bottle feeds?

Question 2

a) Give another name for the Hypothalamus.

b) What is the definition of weaning?

c) Describe briefly the three stages of weaning.

Question 3

a) Describe how a baby should be held for breast and bottle feeding.

b) Why is it so important to keep strictly to the manufacturer's instructions when preparing formula feeds?

c) What is the first milk which comes away from the mother called?

Question 4

a) Define healthy eating in three or four sentences.

b) What are the dietary guidelines and why are they important particularly in the under fives?

c) Give two suggestions for lunch or dinner for a child aged 4.

Question 5

a) If a baby has not been weaned by the time s/he is 9-10 months old, which mineral is the baby likely to be deficient in?

b) What is the point of being careful regarding gluten in wheat-based products?

c) What can be done by the mother when she knows that her child favours sugary/junk foods?

Question 6

a) What is a food fad?

b) Describe the difference between
   ◆ Food allergy
   ◆ Food intolerance
   ◆ Food aversion.

c) Why are sleep and exercise as important as a healthy diet?

10

Hygiene

In this section we will look at:
- all aspects of keeping babies clean
- the differences between modern and traditional nappies
- the importance of cleaning feeding equipment
- how to keep toys and equipment clean

BATHTIME

Bathtime for young babies and toddlers must be fun. New parents often fear bathtime but if everything is prepared and everyone is relaxed there should be no problems. There is no correct time to bath a baby but it is generally accepted that before a feed is best.

Bathing a Young Baby

Collect together all equipment and make sure the room being used is warm (18°C – 21°C is ideal). Prevent draughts by closing windows and doors. Remember new babies are not able to regulate their body temperature.

What do you need?

- baby bath (these are usually made from moulded plastic and can be used with a bathstand or placed on a firm surface – the floor is ideal)
- small container to use for cooled boiled water to clean eyes, nose, etc.
- cotton wool
- bath towels
- bath lotion
- waterproof apron
- a clean set of clothes
- a clean nappy

1 Always put cold water in the bath first and then add the hot water. Test the temperature of the water using the elbow or wrist. Keep the water shallow (5-8 cm is deep enough).

Figure 10.1 Testing bath temperature

2 Undress the baby, clean the nappy area and wrap the baby in a towel. Clean the face with damp cotton wool. Using cooled boiled water, damp a cotton wool ball and wipe each eye gently from the inner part to the outer part. Use a new cotton wool ball for each eye to prevent the risk of spreading any infections. Ears and noses clean themselves. They can be cleaned using moist cotton wool but never be tempted to poke in the ears or up the nose. The secretions which are there are for protection. If there is a build-up of secretions it is wise to consult a doctor.

3 Hold the baby carefully under one arm, supporting the back and head as below, and wash the baby's head. In the first few weeks it is not necessary to use lotions, shampoos or soap as these only **defat** the delicate skin.

> ### Key Words
> **Defat** to take the natural oils from the skin leaving it dry and uncomfortable

4 Unwrap the baby and lift the baby into the bath supporting the head, neck and bottom. Allow the baby to relax in the water. Let the baby kick and splash and talk to the baby and smile. This will make bathtimes happy times.

5 Keep one hand under the baby's shoulders so that the head is kept away from the water and gently use the free hand to wash the baby, paying particular attention to areas where there are folds and creases in the skin.

Figure 10.2 Washing the scalp

6 When the baby is clean lift the baby from the bath, wrap the baby in a warm towel and dry him thoroughly. Though babies do lose body heat quickly, if the room is warm they often like a few moments of freedom without their clothes before they are dressed.

Figure 10.3 Drying the baby on a towel

Some new babies do not like baths and are frightened. It is not wise to bath a frightened baby; instead he can be topped and tailed. As the baby gets older the parents should try to bath him again as the fear may have gone.

Bathing an Older Baby

It is highly likely that by the age of six months a baby will have outgrown a baby bath and will be ready to be introduced to a normal bath. To get babies used to this it is a good idea to put the baby bath in the 'big bath' so that they become familiar with the surroundings.

When using the bath, place a non-slip bath mat on the base of the bath. Add the cold water first and then top up with the hot. Check the temperature with an elbow. Keep the bath water relatively shallow (10-13 cm). Turn the taps off very tightly and cover the hot tap with a flannel. Touching a hot tap can burn little hands.

Do not let babies stand up in the bath. Apart from the obvious danger they may frighten themselves and not want to bath again. Children and toddlers must never be left alone in the bath.

Playing in the Bath

Once babies can sit up unsupported they will enjoy extra moments in the bath to play. There are many bath toys available on the market but an empty shampoo bottle or plastic cup will give hours of pleasure. Remember, however, that loose caps, etc., should be removed before being used as toys.

Figure 10.4 Playtime in the bath

⟲ TOPPING AND TAILING

It is not always convenient to bath a baby on a daily basis. Difficult times may be when travelling or on holiday, etc. On these occasions a baby should be 'topped and tailed'. This means cleaning the baby's face and nappy area thoroughly.

For topping and tailing you will need:

◆ a bowl of previously boiled water   ◆ a towel

◆ cotton wool balls   ◆ a face cloth

◆ a clean nappy

1   Undress the baby but leave on the baby's vest and nappy. Lay the baby on a towel.

2   Using the cool boiled water moisten a cotton wool ball and clean the baby's eyes. Remember to use one cotton wool ball per eye and wipe from the inside out as described in bathing a baby.

Clean the ears and nose with moistened cotton wool. Remember not to poke into ears and noses! Pat the face dry with a towel.

3   Using the facecloth gently wash the baby's hands and feet and towel them dry.

4   Remove the nappy and cleanse the nappy area with baby lotion/water and cotton wool or with baby wipes.

5   Put on clean nappy and dress the baby.

⟲ HAIR, NAILS AND TEETH

⟲ Care of the Hair and Scalp

A baby's hair/scalp should be washed daily if possible. It is not necessary to use soap or lotion for the first few weeks. Cradle cap is extremely common in small babies. This is when scaly patches, often red in colour, appear on the scalp. Cradle cap is harmless and will clear up without any special treatment. Do not be tempted to pick off the scales. Wash the scalp regularly and gently massage a little baby oil into the scalp. This loosens the scales and they will then wash off easily.

When shampoo or lotions are used for hair washing it is very important to use non-sting varieties and to ensure they don't get near the eyes. Only a small amount of shampoo is needed, which should be worked into a lather and rinsed away almost immediately. Adults usually apply two lots of shampoo, but one wash is enough for babies!

To dry the hair rub gently with a towel. Try not to cover the baby's face as he will be frightened. A good investment may be a shield which prevents water and soap running over the face while the hair is being washed.

Care of Nails

Babies have fast-growing nails. In order to stop babies scratching themselves nails should be kept short.

Using a small pair of blunt-edged scissors cut the nails when they are soft. The best time to do this is after bathtime. However, if you feel nervous or if it is difficult to keep the baby still, cut the nails when he is sleeping.

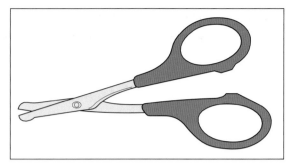

Figure 10.5 Nail scissors

Care of Teeth

As soon as babies are able to hold an object let them have a toothbrush. They will try to imitate others whom they have seen cleaning their teeth. Add a small amount of children's toothpaste to the toothbrush even if they have no teeth. This can still get rid of bacteria in the gums.

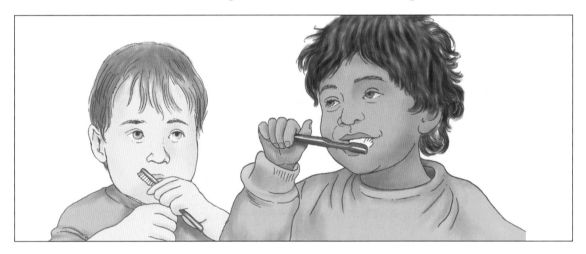

Figure 10.6 Child cleaning teeth

TOILETRIES

A trip to any local supermarket, chemist or baby store will reveal a vast array of baby toiletries. There is a very wide and confusing range available and it is certainly not necessary to have one of everything. Most mothers like to equip themselves with some form of the baby box in which to store toiletries, etc. The baby box can be specially designed for the job and is available from baby stores. However, a basket or general storage box is just as good.

The skin of new babies is delicate and it is not advisable to use soaps or wipes for the first six weeks as these products defat the baby's skin.

After six weeks special baby toiletries can be used as these are unlikely to irritate baby skin. Many are hypo-allergenic.

Figure 10.7 A range of toiletries

⊃ NAPPIES

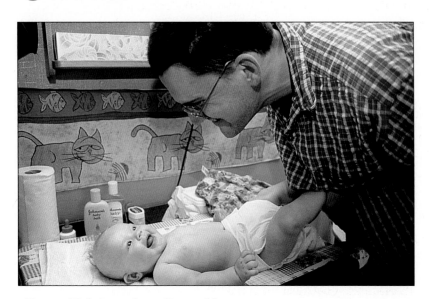

Figure 10.8 A modern disposable nappy

Nappies are available in a variety of materials, shapes and sizes, but they can be put into two main groups: disposable and reusable. In recent years many parents have been using disposable nappies but as people become more aware of environmental issues there is a move back to the classic terry towelling squares.

When choosing the type of nappy suitable for the baby, parents will need to think carefully and decide which is best and most convenient for them. Factors which may affect their choice may be:

- ◆ fashion
- ◆ trends
- ◆ availability
- ◆ cost
- ◆ environmental issues

There is a very wide and confusing range of disposable nappies available. The major manufacturers are constantly trying to improve their products.

⊃ Disposable Nappies

Disposable nappies are simple to use. There is no folding, no pinning and no plastic pants are needed. They are completely discarded when they are wet or dirty. Disposable nappies might appear expensive but remember there are no costs for water, detergents, sterilising solutions, etc.

Advantages	Disadvantages
◆ Very absorbent – the absorbent granules in the nappy attract urine away from the baby's skin	◆ They are expensive
◆ Very convenient – the soiled nappy is put in nappy bag and thrown away	◆ They are bulky to store
◆ No folding, no pinning, no liners, no plastic pants	

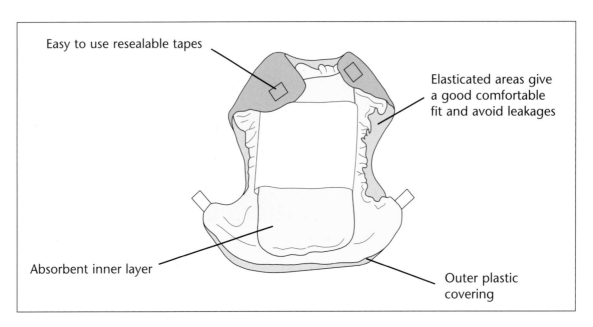

Figure 10.9 An opened out disposable nappy

Disposable nappies come in a range of sizes and can be for boys or girls.

⊃ Traditional Reusable Nappies

These nappies involve more work than disposable ones but they are kinder to the environment. It is wise to buy the best you can afford as these usually last longer and are more absorbent, and therefore more comfortable for the baby.

These nappies are generally used with nappy liners; they have to be pinned with nappy pins and plastic pants are also needed to prevent leakages. Terry nappies need to be sterilised and washed so nappy buckets, sterilising powders or liquids, washing machines and drying facilities are all essential.

Modern Reusable Nappies

Advantages	Disadvantages
◆ Cheaper in the long term	◆ Have to be sterilised and laundered
◆ Kinder to the environment	◆ Have to be folded and pinned
	◆ Need to be used with liners and plastic pants
	◆ Need to be changed more often than reusable because they are not absorbent
	◆ More difficult to use when away from home

On the market today there are more modern reusable nappies. These nappies are shaped and fitted and have a waterproof backing. They are fastened at the waist by Velcro strips, poppers, button or hooks and loops.

The advantages and disadvantages are much the same as traditional reusable nappies but the modern reusable nappies do not need folding, pinning or plastic pants. The initial outlay, however, can be quite expensive.

Changing a Nappy

As it is possible that a baby may need to be changed up to 12 times each day it is important that there is an area of the home which is warm and convenient to keep all the equipment needed close at hand.

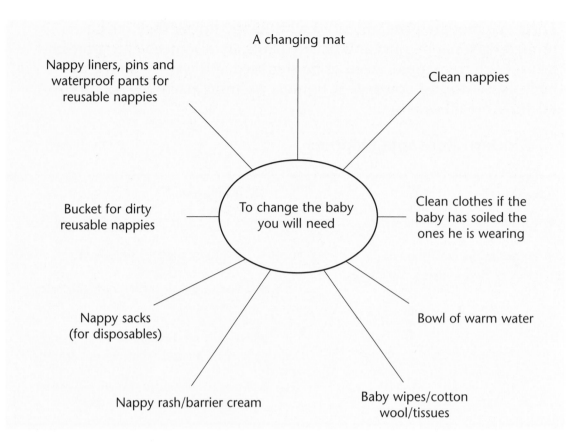

1 Make sure all equipment is at hand.

2 Wash your hands thoroughly.

3 Lay the baby on the changing mat and remove the soiled nappy by holding the baby's ankles with one hand and lifting the nappy away.

4 If the nappy is a dirty one, use cottonwool, tissues or wipes to clean the baby's bottom.

5 Use warm water and cotton wool to clean the bottom thoroughly.

6 Dry the bottom thoroughly and put on a thick layer of barrier cream.

7 Open out the new nappy and slide under the baby using your free hand to lift the baby's ankles.

8 Put the legs down then fasten the nappy securely with nappy pins, Velcro tabs, poppers, etc.

9 If using traditional nappies you will need to put a pair of plastic pants over the terry towelling nappy.

Figure 10.10 Baby on mat with equipment

Folding Fabric Nappies

Triple Absorbent Fold

This is the most suitable fold for a new born baby. The central panel gives excellent absorbency and is very small and neat.

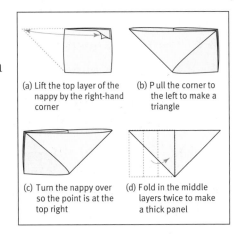

(a) Lift the top layer of the nappy by the right-hand corner

(b) Pull the corner to the left to make a triangle

(c) Turn the nappy over so the point is at the top right

(d) Fold in the middle layers twice to make a thick panel

Figure 10.11 Triple absorbent folding

Parallel and Kite Folds

These folds are suitable for larger babies and can easily be adjusted to the size of the baby.

Figure 10.12 Parallel folding

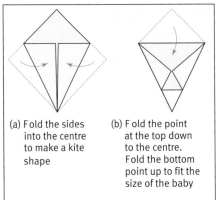

(a) Fold the sides into the centre to make a kite shape

(b) Fold the point at the top down to the centre. Fold the bottom point up to fit the size of the baby

Figure 10.13 Kite folding

Nappy Rash

Nappy rash (ammonia dermatitis) is a common skin complaint which affects the area covered by the baby's nappy. Nappy rash occurs when the tender skin of the baby is left in contact with urine and faeces. Bacteria in the faeces react with the urine and ammonia is released. This causes burning and irritation. The baby's skin becomes red and inflamed and is warm to touch.

Most babies have nappy rash at some stage in their first year. It is essential therefore that the nappy is changed regularly and the nappy region is washed and dried thoroughly.

Many babies do suffer from nappy rash, but the following factors increase the likelihood of the baby being infected.

◆ a few days after an immunisation injection
◆ a change of diet from breast to bottle
◆ if the baby has an upset tummy causing excessive bowel movements or diarrhoea
◆ if the baby is teething
◆ if the baby is generally 'off colour'

Most causes of nappy rash can be treated at home but if the soreness continues for more than a week it would be wise to consult the doctor.

Ways to Prevent Nappy Rash

◆ the baby's skin should be kept dry and aired and if reusable nappies are used they must be thoroughly washed and rinsed
◆ use nappy rash cream at the first sign of soreness
◆ do not wash the skin with soap and water as this defats the skin
◆ use a fairly thick application of barrier cream at each nappy stage
◆ try never to leave a baby in a wet nappy
◆ leave the baby without a nappy (lay on a towel) to let the air reach the skin

If nappy rash does develop, barrier cream should not be used until the bottom is no longer sore. It is advisable not to use talcum powder on babies' bottoms.

BOWEL AND BLADDER CONTROL

Children have no control over the bowel and bladder until well into the second year of their lives. Young babies may perform on their potties at a younger age but it is just luck. The age at which children are able to control the workings of their bladder and bowels varies considerably but it is generally accepted that bowel control develops before bladder control and girls are usually quicker to be completely clean and dry than boys. The most important fact when encouraging bladder and bowel control is to remember that a relaxed unhurried, undemanding, happy atmosphere will gain the best results.

The equipment shown below may be useful during the developing stages of 'potty training'.

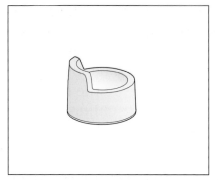

Figure 10.14 Traditional moulded potty

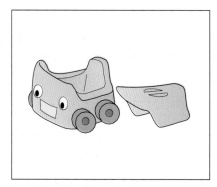

Figure 10.15 Fun potty

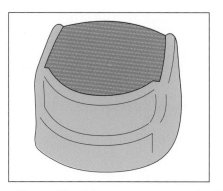

Figure 10.16 Step to put around toilet

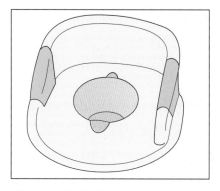

Figure 10.17 Trainer seat

Bowel and bladder control come gradually. Toilet training can properly begin only when children begin to realise they can control the muscles which open the bladder and bowel.

Bladder and bowel control usually follow a general pattern. It begins when children become aware they are passing urine or having a bowel movement. They will then indicate to their parents that they are wetting or soiling the nappy. Next, children will learn to indicate they are about to wet or soil the nappy. This allows the parents to put the child on a potty or the toilet.

Points to remember when helping children to gain bladder and bowel control:

◆ never force children to use a potty or the toilet. If they want to use the potty as a toy, let them. At some stage all children seem to like to use the potty as a hat

- ◆ always encourage and give praise. Be patient. Never chastise or ridicule children
- ◆ keep the potty handy. Take it with you when you go visiting or out in the car
- ◆ if children like to sit on the potty, sit and read with them. This will relax them and encourage them to relax
- ◆ accidents often occur. Make the minimum fuss and let children know it is not a problem

When children have complete bowel and bladder control in the daytime they may still need a nappy at night. Children can be encouraged to be clean and dry at night by putting them to bed without a nappy, making sure nightclothes are easy to remove, leaving the potty by the bed and cutting out drinks before bedtime. Some parents lift the children on the toilet or potty during the night. It is sensible to put a waterproof sheet under the ordinary sheet to protect the mattress.

CLEANING AND STERILISING EQUIPMENT

All equipment used for bottle-feeding has to be scrupulously clean to prevent any chance of the baby coming into contact with germs. Equipment should be first rinsed with cold water then thoroughly cleaned with hot soapy water. A bottle brush and teat cleaner are useful gadgets for this initial process.

The detergent should then be rinsed off the bottles, teats, caps, etc. and the equipment sterilised using one of the following:

- ◆ an electric steam steriliser
- ◆ a microwave steriliser
- ◆ a cold-water steriliser

Electric Steam Sterilisers

These are very convenient and easy to use, but storage may be a problem if you do not have a great deal of space in the kitchen. The steamers are electric and the cycle needed to sterilise bottles and teats takes approximately 10-15 minutes. All the carers have to do is add cold water and turn on.

Figure 10.18 Electric steam steriliser

Microwave Steam Sterilisers

In a microwave, sterilised water is added to the container and the equipment, the lid is then fitted and the steriliser put into the microwave. The microwave then needs to be operated on full power for about eight minutes.

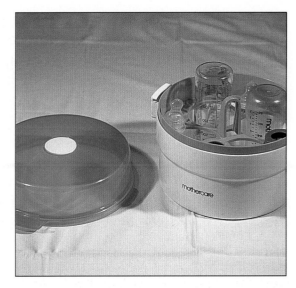

Figure 10.19 Microwave steriliser

Cold-water Steriliser

For this method of sterilising all equipment has to be submerged in cold water with sterilising tablets or sterilising solution for at least half an hour. Once made up the solution can be used several times. Cold, previously boiled water should be used to rinse the equipment just before use.

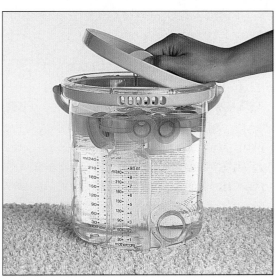

Figure 10.20 Cold water steriliser

STERILISING EQUIPMENT

Cleaning and sterilising is a vital part of the bottle feeding routine. If scrupulous hygiene rules are not followed, babies may come into contact with harmful bacteria that they cannot resist. This can result in tummy upsets or more seriously the baby may contract gastro-enteritis. Gastro-enteritis is an inflammation of the stomach and intestines which causes vomiting and diarrhoea. In a young baby this can cause excessive fluid loss and hospital treatment may be needed.

HYGIENE AND TEXTILES

Any textile items, e.g. clothing, bedding, toys and equipment need to be kept spotlessly clean to avoid germs and infections being transferred to the child. Clothing and bedding in particular can be soiled quickly and need to be laundered regularly.

Textile items when new will carry a label either sewn in or attached to the item which will give details of the fibre content of the item and care instructions, and it may also detail any special treatments or finishes which the item has undergone, plus sizing in garments.

Modern textile items are made from a wide and confusing range of fabrics. Different fabrics need different washing temperatures. To help keep textiles in good conditions the makers of detergents and washing machines have drawn up a guide. The guide is known as the International Textile Care Labelling Code (ITCLC), it is easy to understand and makes selecting the correct cleaning method easy. The care code appears on labels, washing machine and detergent packets.

The code is based on five symbols.

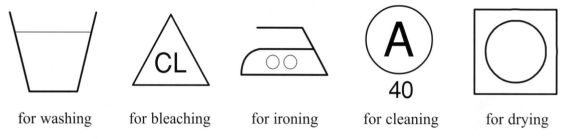

| for washing | for bleaching | for ironing | for cleaning | for drying |

Figure 10.21 The five symbols

The most common materials used in the manufacture of children's toys are plastic, wood and metal. The advantage of all of these materials is that they can be easily wiped clean or should they become heavily soiled they can be scrubbed. Many smaller toys can also be put through the dishwasher but do not use any detergent as the heat of the water will be enough to clean them thoroughly. If any detergents are used when cleaning toys make sure the toys are rinsed thoroughly before the child plays with them.

Questions

Answer the following questions:

1. What room temperature is ideal when bathing a baby?

2. Why is it sensible to put cold water into the bath first then add hot water?

3. Why must a clean piece of damp cotton wool be used to clean each eye?

4. If a baby does not like to be bathed, how can he be kept clean?

5. What is cradle cap?

6. Even if a child has no teeth he can be encouraged to use a toothbrush and toothpaste, of what benefit will this be?

7. What four factors affect the choice of nappies?

8. Give the approximate price of a modern reusable nappy.

9. What is the medical term used to describe nappy rash?

10. Give three methods which may be used to sterilize feeding equipment.

Match the beginnings to the ends

| 11 | Baby baths are usually made from moulded plastic |

| 12 | The skin of a baby is delicate and using soaps and wipes |

| 13 | Cool boiled water |

| 14 | Babies lose body heat quickly but if the room is warm |

| 15 | Empty bottles or plastic cups |

| can be used to clean around the eyes and nose. |

| can be used with a bath stand on a firm surface. |

| they often like to have a few moments of freedom without clothes. |

| can give much fun and pleasure. |

| may irritate the skin. |

Extension questions

16. Find out as much as you can about environmental issues concerning the use of disposable nappies. (Write up your findings try to include some graphs or pie charts. Useful places to look for information may be books, parent and baby magazines, newspaper articles, parents, teachers, health visitors nappy producers (e.g. Pampers, Huggies).

17. Try to arrange a visit to a local playgroup or toddler group, design a questionnaire to establish how many children are toilet trained. The aim of the questionnaire should be to prove or disprove the theory that girls are usually completely clean and dry earlier than boys.

⊃ HYGIENE WORDSEARCH

M	N	N	W	R	N	A	W	J	S	H	K	U	C	F
Z	A	B	C	F	E	P	Q	F	G	F	Z	B	X	U
I	S	E	O	N	N	U	M	H	A	B	S	O	R	B
G	G	L	R	B	V	D	S	J	J	I	G	I	S	V
C	D	B	V	C	I	A	L	A	T	L	N	B	H	H
D	H	A	G	T	R	P	X	I	B	E	B	E	T	M
A	N	S	W	Y	O	E	T	Y	P	L	T	A	D	X
I	V	O	P	L	N	A	I	Y	I	I	E	M	O	P
Q	A	P	K	D	M	A	T	R	I	I	X	P	N	K
B	A	S	R	R	E	D	P	M	R	Z	D	B	F	D
N	O	I	E	C	N	L	D	P	R	A	C	R	M	P
P	Z	D	E	C	T	L	I	M	Y	D	B	X	S	L
S	V	G	Y	E	E	B	Q	O	S	P	U	T	M	H
A	G	G	J	C	O	A	A	O	S	H	I	H	Y	U
Q	E	E	J	L	D	H	F	U	G	A	W	N	J	A

Absorb	**Nappy**
Barrier cream	**Nappy pin**
Dermatitis	**Nappy rash**
Disposable	**Reusable**
Environment	**Soiled**
Faeces	**Urine**
Fold	

11

Environment

In this chapter we will look at:
- ◆ how areas inside and outside the home can be made safer
- ◆ how to cope with accidents in and around the home
- ◆ the importance of fresh air, exercise and sleep
- ◆ choices for clothing and footwear

We tend to think that a home is the safest environment in which to bring up children. However, no home can be made completely foolproof and accident proof. Statistics show that the main causes of death to children under 5 and adults over 65 happen in and around the home.

It is understandable why these two age groups are most at risk – the under-fives are not aware of danger, and the over-65s are often **infirm.**

The following are accidents and preventative measures.

⊃ SAFETY IN THE HOME

⊃ The Kitchen

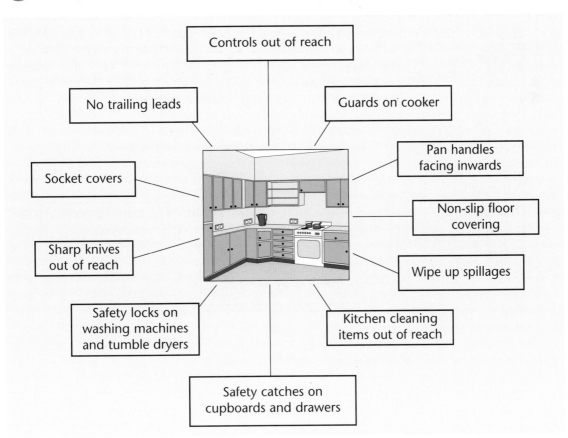

- Controls out of reach
- No trailing leads
- Guards on cooker
- Pan handles facing inwards
- Socket covers
- Non-slip floor covering
- Sharp knives out of reach
- Wipe up spillages
- Safety locks on washing machines and tumble dryers
- Kitchen cleaning items out of reach
- Safety catches on cupboards and drawers

The Bedroom

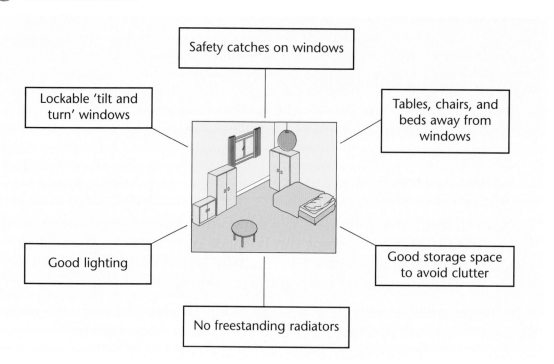

Safety catches on windows

Lockable 'tilt and turn' windows

Tables, chairs, and beds away from windows

Good lighting

Good storage space to avoid clutter

No freestanding radiators

The Bathroom

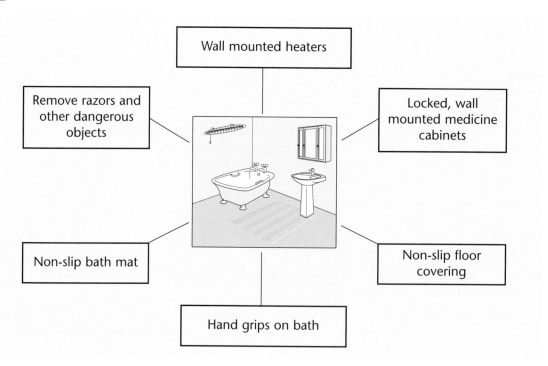

Wall mounted heaters

Remove razors and other dangerous objects

Locked, wall mounted medicine cabinets

Non-slip bath mat

Non-slip floor covering

Hand grips on bath

⊃ Living Room/Lounge

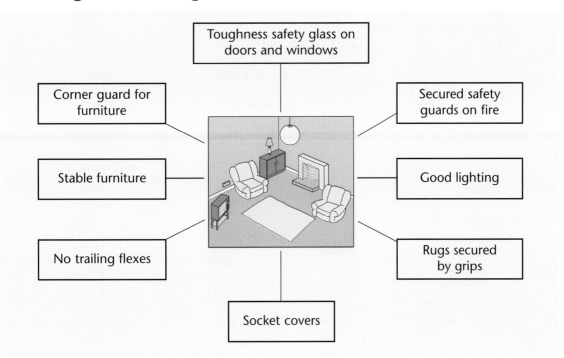

- Toughness safety glass on doors and windows
- Corner guard for furniture
- Secured safety guards on fire
- Stable furniture
- Good lighting
- No trailing flexes
- Rugs secured by grips
- Socket covers

⊃ Stairs/Landing

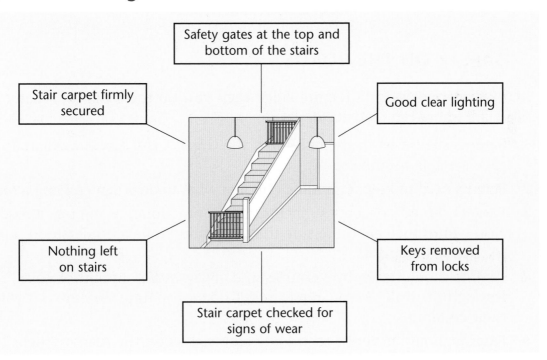

- Safety gates at the top and bottom of the stairs
- Stair carpet firmly secured
- Good clear lighting
- Nothing left on stairs
- Keys removed from locks
- Stair carpet checked for signs of wear

⊃ SAFETY IN THE GARDEN

⊃ Safety in the Garden/Patio, etc

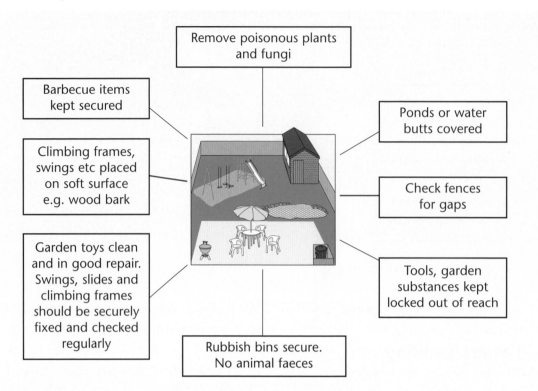

⊃ SAFETY ON THE ROADS

Many thousands of children are killed each year on the roads and many more are injured in road accidents.

1 Parents should teach their children the Green Cross Code, as soon as they are able to understand.

2 Parents need to keep reminding children what to do when crossing a road.

3 Parents should never allow their children out alone, or to cross a road alone, until they are quite sure that the children have understood how to cope with dangers.

4 Parents should teach by example, and always make a point of going through the drill of the Green Cross Code every time they are out with their children.

5 Parents should never be seen to be taking risks on the road by their children.

⊃ SAFETY IN THE CAR

Children should be strapped securely into their seat each time they take a car journey. It is against the law to sit a child on someone's lap, or to allow children to stand up while the car is moving. Parents should never allow children to put their arms or hands out of a window, and neither should they be allowed to lean out of any of the windows. All doors should have child-proof locks.

The following information on harnesses is important for the safety of children in cars:

1 Carry Cot Restraint Harnesses – strong webbing straps attached to the back seat. These fit around the cot to prevent it from sliding and being thrown forward (see page 246).

2 Car Safety Seats – special safety seats that clip to attachments in the back of the car. Suitable for children of 9 – 18 kg (see page 246).

3 Car Safety Harnesses – adjustable waist and shoulder straps with quick release fasteners. They fit on to the back seats and are suitable for children of 18 – 36 kg (see page 246).

4 Car booster seats are for children over 18 lbs in weight i.e. approximately four years of age. The car booster seat is secured firmly to the back seat. When the child is in place, the adult safety strap is fixed over the child and clipped firmly i.e. the child booster seat does not have straps of it own – it has to rely on the adult ones.

5 Parents can provide some toys to amuse children on a journey. Toys help to distract children from the boredom of a journey. Also, playing with toys prevents them from playing with door or window locks.

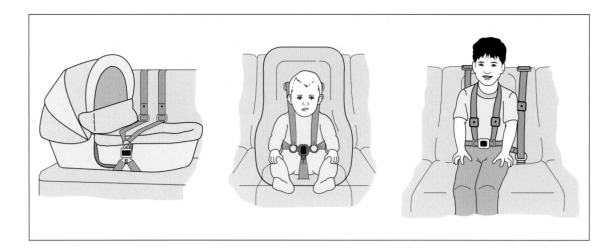

SAFETY AWAY FROM HOME

Children benefit from being taken out of the home environment for walks, park play or holidays. They learn from the different things they see, and the things people do. However, the world outside the home can be very dangerous to children but there are ways of preventing accidents.

1 Never lose sight of children – if they are very young, it might be a good idea to use a restraining harness to keep them close.

2 Supervise any type of play. All play equipment should have been checked for safety beforehand.

3 Never allow children to pick up anything off the floor.

4 Check whether there is an age restriction on the part of the park/open area where the children are playing. This will protect them from older, larger children.

5 Parents should teach their children to swim as soon as possible. It is a good idea to take babies to the local swimming pool to get them used to the water. This way they come to respect the water and not be afraid of it permanently.

6 Ensure that children are given water wings, floats, etc. to keep them afloat until they are older and more confident.

7 Do not allow children to paddle in dirty water.

8 If children go on a boat or canal boat, they and everyone else on board should wear lifejackets.

9 Supervise children on the beach at all times – watch out for strong currents, sand dunes, etc.

10 Do not allow children to play on ice covering a pond or lake.

All parents and carers should be able to recognise the following labels which indicate that certain equipment has been approved safe to use.

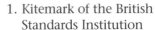

1. Kitemark of the British Standards Institution   2. European markings   3. BEAB mark of safety   4. British Gas

UNDERSTANDING THE NEED FOR SAFETY IN RELATION TO PETS

Very few health risks are attributed to pets, but the following points are important and everyone needs to be aware of them.

- Fleas and mites from cats and dogs can cause skin infections. Therefore, it is important to ensure that animals are regularly checked for parasites.

- Dogs/cats should be wormed regularly to avoid passing on diseases to the baby or toddler. For this reason, animals should be completely checked over, vaccinations given, etc., before a baby is born.

- Discourage a dog from licking a baby/toddler.

- When a baby begins to crawl teach the child not to go near the pet's food.

- Should the baby be placed in a pram outside the house e.g. garden, make sure there is a net over the child to prevent the cat from lying on the baby and causing suffocation.

- A good, fine net also has the added advantage of keeping flies and insects away.

DAY-TO-DAY ACCIDENTS/HEALTH PROBLEMS

Stings

Creams such as calamine, anti sting, anti histamine can be rubbed directly on to stings from insects, nettles etc. They help to prevent the child from scratching the affected part, and the itching which stings cause.

Something in the eye

A small visible foreign object, i.e. dust, at the corner of the eye or on the eye lid can be removed by using the corner of a clean cloth or washing the eye with an eye bath or eyedropper. Any other object which may be on the eyeball itself, should not be touched because of the danger of damaging the delicate surface of the eyeball. In these cases, take the child either to a doctor or an A/E hospital department, where professional advice may be sought.

Sunburn

At all times in a very sunny weather, a child should have shoulders and body covered as well as their head. Sunburn will begin to hurt several hours after the actual burning has taken place. A sun block (i.e. lotions/creams with a high SPF factor) should be rubbed into all other exposed parts, e.g. arms and legs, to avoid the child from being burnt by the sun's rays. At no time should the child's skin be exposed to the sun's rays for more than a few minutes per day. As the child gets older the amount of exposure time can be slowly increased. The lotions/creams with a high SPF factor should be rubbed into the child's skin both before and after contact with water.

See Chapter 13 for further information on child health.

GENERAL ADVICE

1 Every member of the household should know where the first-aid box is kept, its contents, and what they are used for.

2 Somewhere sensible, i.e. in a kitchen, there should be a list of useful telephone numbers, e.g. A/E department of the local hospital, doctor's telephone number, neighbour's telephone number, fire, police, ambulance.

3 It is a good idea to teach children how to ring emergency telephone numbers, i.e. how to give clear messages etc.

4 If a child has swallowed something, e.g. bleach or tablets, try to keep the evidence to show the doctor.

5 Try not to leave the patient, particularly if it is a child.

6 Never get panic stricken – you will only make everyone else nervous.

7 Never administer First Aid unless you are absolutely sure you know what you are doing.

8 Never give the patient anything to eat or drink until medical advice has been obtained. Keep them warm and keep reassuring them.

UNDERSTANDING THE IMPORTANCE OF FRESH AIR AND EXERCISE, REST AND SLEEP

Once a child is able to get about on his/her own, he/she should be allowed to play outside in the garden as much as possible. Cold weather should not be used as an excuse – all children should be encouraged to go outside whatever the weather. A child who is kept indoors, and inactive for long periods, will ultimately become bad tempered, possibly naughty and could lose their appetite. If there is no garden, the parents should ensure they take their child outside once a day for fresh air.

Parents with no gardens can still make every effort to take their child to a recreational area or a park or even to the shops. It will not only help give the child fresh air and exercise, but it can help to educate the child, especially if the parent is prepared to point things out to the child along the way. The fresh air and exercise will also help to make the child naturally tired and hungry, and this should help minimise both feeding and sleeping problems.

Babies and young children need to have adequate amounts of sleep. The sleep pattern of newborn babies is often determined by their weight and height, and their need for food. So generally, the less the baby weighs, the more often it will wake to feed. At this stage babies tend to sleep in four hour cycles and will often sleep as much during the day as they do at night – often sleeping more than 16 hours out of every 24!

As their feeding pattern changes, so does their sleep pattern – as the graph below shows.

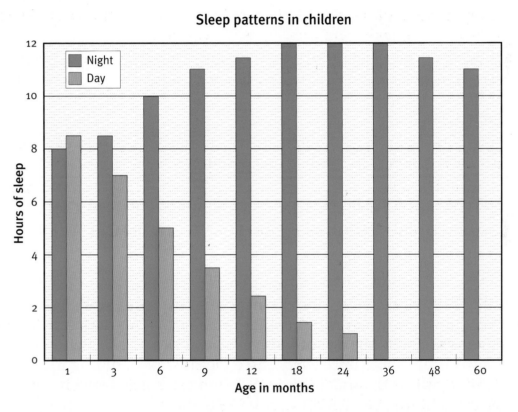

Sleep patterns in children

Gradually, the amount of daytime sleep will decrease, and they will sleep longer during the night, until by approximately 24 months they may sleep for 12 hours at night but only for a short time during the day. This daytime sleep will usually be a mid afternoon nap – in fact the child may not actually sleep at all but will be resting. This is just as beneficial – not just for the child! It also gives parents a break!

It is important that children also have a regular bedtime routine, so that getting children to bed and to sleep does not become a battle.

Suggested bedtime routine for a toddler

Routine	Reason
Have a regular bedtime every night	Child more likely to accept going to bed
Reduce the level of activity	Child will become calm and less excitable and more likely to sleep
Bath the child	A warm bath is relaxing. It also allows the child to spend quality time with parent(s).
Give the child a warm drink	This will help to calm and relax the child and may encourage sleep
Choose a suitable story to read	This is quality time for parent(s) and child – and the child may fall asleep during the storytime. However an active or frightening story may cause sleeplessness and anxiety.
Tuck child in and give a kiss and/or cuddle	This will increase feelings of security and child will settle easier.
Let the child have a favourite toy or comforter	This increases feelings of security and gives the child something to focus on.
Leave on a night light or lamp	Many children dislike the dark and become apprehensive.
Check on child regularly	Reduces 'separation anxiety'.

◯ KNOWLEDGE AND UNDERSTANDING OF THE CHOICE/ CARE OF APPROPRIATE CLOTHING AND FOOTWEAR

◯ Feet

A child's feet are extremely important in the first three years, because this is when growth is at its fastest. Feet grow about 2 – 2½ sizes each year until approximately the age of four years, and as a result, a child will outgrow his/her shoes once every three months. Also, during the first three years, this is the time when soft bones can easily be bent out of shape by ill-fitting shoes and/or socks. New shoes should therefore be fitted to leave 12-18 mm growing space between the end of the longest toe and the end of the shoe. Shoes should also be wide enough to allow the toes to wriggle inside. The following are useful points to be aware of when contemplating either buying shoes for the first time, or simply buying another pair of shoes.

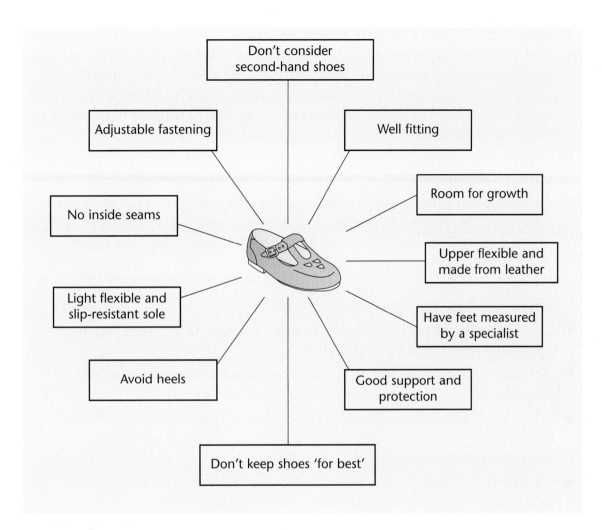

Other types of footwear

Previously we have dealt with correct day-to-day wear, but there may be circumstances where a toddler/child will wear other types of footwear, possibly to suit the weather, e.g. sandals/slippers, wellington boots or trainers. These named types of footwear are fine for short spells only, because they tend to be not particularly well fitting and can often prevent the feet from breathing.

Clothing

Clothing both for the toddler and the pre-school is just as important as clothing for the baby. Some general points are as follows:

◆ Children especially in their first three years grow very quickly, therefore the size of clothes should reflect this, both by buying slightly bigger sizes allowing for growth and ease of movement and also choosing fabrics for comfort and warmth. Common sense should prevail at all times, e.g. trousers that are far too long will inevitably catch on a child's shoes, similarly a hat or a cap that is too big will obstruct the child's vision.

◆ The choice of fabric should suit the purpose of the garment i.e. stretch fabrics allow for movement, denim or heavy cotton material for play etc. Natural fibres allow for perspiration and are therefore healthier. Often, however, a small amount of synthetic fibre is added to natural fibre to prevent the garment from creasing and stains are easier to remove where there is a combination of fibres.

◆ Unisex clothing is useful because it can be handed down from one child to another.

◆ Fastenings should be easy for both child and parent to operate – zip fasteners, Velcro and popper studs are much easier than buttons or ties. Waist and wrist bands are much easier to manage if they are elasticated. They are also often more comfortable.

◆ Children prefer very strong colours. This is fine because the darker the colour the less dirt will show.

◆ Clothing should be machine washable, dye fast and shrink resistant and need minimum or no ironing.

◆ As much clothing as possible should be flame resistant, especially nightwear.

◆ Children should have several warm layers of clothing on in winter, rather than just one or two heavy garments, to allow warm air to circulate between the layers.

◆ Home-made garments are a good idea, but they should still have all the safety features as if they had been shop bought.

◆ Badly fitting socks and tights are just as bad for a child's feet as badly-fitting shoes. The feet of the socks should be big enough without being stretched. Natural fibres are better than synthetic ones, to avoid the feet perspiring and to help prevent Athlete's foot. There should be enough length for the toes and width for the foot in the socks.

⊃ Underwear/Nightwear

◆ A young child should wear a vest which has an envelope or round neck. Many vests double up as a summer T-shirt and are best if made from ribbed cotton, thermal fabric etc.

◆ After the nappy stage the child can wear cotton briefs. At a later stage the boys can wear front opening briefs.

◆ Sleepwear should be soft and comfortable and suit the temperature. In all cases, the fabric should be flare free and flame resistant.

◆ A fleecy dressing gown with a zip opening is also useful.

⊃ **Outdoor wear – to include coats, anoraks, trousers etc.**

◆ These garments should be warm and protective without being heavy and bulky.

◆ Often, clothing which is lined, padded or quilted will add extra warmth.

◆ Knitted hats, gloves and scarves are a useful addition for cold weather.

◆ If it is raining/snowing garments should be waterproof, elasticised at the wrist and hoods should be fastened with either fasteners or zipped up under the chin, never with draw strings.

Questions

Question 1

a) How can parents who live in high-rise flats teach safety outdoors to a young child?

b) If you lived in the top flat of high rise building, list some things that you would do to ensure that children were safe inside the home.

Question 2

a) Name at least four dangers in each of the following rooms:

bedroom

living room/lounge

kitchen

bathroom

b) Name two ways of ensuring a cooker is safe.

c) Why is it so important to keep cleaning fluids and medicines in lockable cupboards?

Question 3

a) Do you consider it worthwhile to overprotect your child? Discuss your views.

b) Is there any stage in a child's life when parents can relax their complete protection? Give reasons for your answer.

Question 4

a) Why is it important to amuse a young child on a car journey?

b) Collect some leaflets on car safety seats/harnesses for a young child and describe the advantages and disadvantages of each one.

c) List and explain three things that can help reduce the chances of a child being badly injured during a car journey.

d) Why should young children never sit on someone's lap while the car is moving?

Question 5

a) If a small child had to spend some time at your house, describe what you would have to do in order to ensure that it was relatively safe for the child.

b) How can doors and windows be made safer?

c) Why is it important that everyone in the home knows where to find the first-aid box?

Extension Questions

a) What is the Green Cross Code?

b) How can parents ensure that very young children understand the importance of road safety?

c) List and describe situations that make it difficult for young children to cross the road safely.

12

Child Care Provision

In this section we will look at the wide variety of care which is offered for pre-school children in the United Kingdom.

We will examine:

◆ the roles of the staff who care for children

◆ the aims of the different types of provision

◆ the advantages and disadvantages of different types of provision

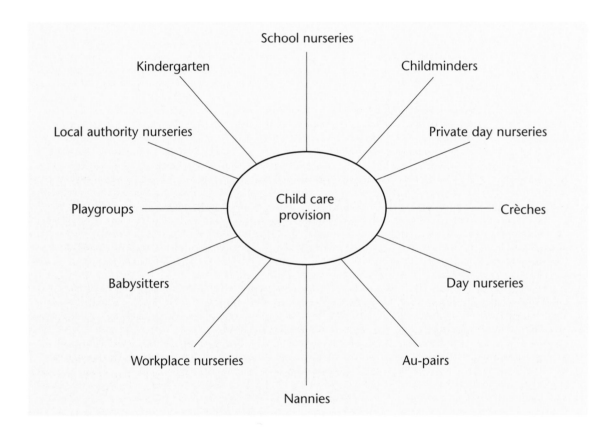

Most children under 5 are looked after by someone other than their parents before they are old enough to go to school. This could be grandparents, friends or babysitters who are giving the parents a break for a few hours. Increasingly, however, more parents are looking for someone to care for their children for longer periods because they both go out to work or are ill or studying. The range of child care provision is very varied and parents need to take into consideration many factors before deciding upon the right type of provision which will suit them and their child.

PROVISION OF CARE AND EDUCATION SERVICES IN THE UK

Provision	Time spent	Age of child	Cost for the family
Pre-preparatory schools, private nursery and schools	Usually about 9 am – 3.30 pm. Increasingly offer extra hours	2-4	The fees vary
Reception classes in primary schools	9 am – 3.30 pm during the school termtime	4	Free
Local education authority (LEA) nursery schools and classes	Usually morning or afternoon sessions, but some are full time. During the school term time	3-4	Free
Pre-schools (formerly known as playgroups)	Two or three sessions a week, usually. Sessions are usually 2 hours/ Some are full time	2½-4	Charge per session
Local authority day nurseries, children's centres, family centres	Some sessions are part time. Some are all day	0-4 (only a few children are 0-2)	This is means tested
Childminders	Usually all day	0-4	They vary widely
Workplace nurseries, partnership programmes and private day nurseries	Usually all day, but there is variation	0-4	Some places are subsidised
Combined nursery centres Centres of Early Years Excellence	Part time or all day. Open all year 8 am – 5 pm according to the needs of the family	0-4	Although education places are free, daycare is means tested
Family centres	Part time or all day	usually 0-4 but there is a variation	These vary
Holiday schemes and extended hours schemes, clubs and out of school clubs	During the school holidays. Before and after school	A wide range and increasing because of government initiatives	These vary

A framework for qualifications and training in early years education and child care

Who makes The provision?	Who are the staff?	Qualifications of staff	Adult: Child ratios	
Commercial organisations, private individuals	Not specified, but often NNEB, BTEC and NVQ 2/3	Not known	2 3-4 yrs 5+	1:5 1:8 1:20/30
Local education authority	Primary teachers. Sometimes a teaching assistant or a nursery nurse	Degree and PGCE/ Bed/BA (QTS) Diploma in Child Care and Education (formerly NNEB), BTEC, SNNB, SCOTVEC, NVQ	1:30/40 (1:15/20 if a trained nursery nurse is employed)	
Local education authority	Nursery teachers Nursery nurses	Degree and PGCE/ Bed/BA/(QTS) Diploma in Child Care and Education (formerly NNEB), BTEC, SNNB, SCOTVEC, NVQ	3-4 years	1:10/13
Parents and voluntary groups	Playgroup leader or pre-school leader	Diploma in pre-school practice	3-5 yrs	1:8
Local authority social services	Mostly nursery nurses	Diploma in Child Care and Education (formerly NNEB), DPQS, BTEC, SNNB, SCOTVEC, NVQ	0-2 yrs 2-3 yrs 3-5 yrs	1:3 1:4 1:8
Private arrangement	Registered childminder	No national requirements	0-5 yrs 5-7 yrs	1:3 1:6
Private individuals, organisations/employers	Some staff are untrained. Some nursery nurses	50% of the staff must be trained	0-2 yrs 2-3 yrs 3-4 yrs	1:3 1:4 1:8
Local authority education and social services usually, but sometimes voluntary organisations and health authorities	Nursery teachers Nursery nurses	Degree and PGCE/ BEd/BA (QTS) Diploma in Child Care and Education (formerly NNEB), BTEC, SNNB, SCOTVEC, NVQ		1:10/13
Local authority social services, health authorities, voluntary organisations	Nursery nurses, social workers, health visitors, wide range of staff	Very varied	This varies, and depends on the kind of work in the centre	
Schools, voluntary organisations. Departments of Leisure	Volunteers, community workers, playleaders	Not known	5-7 yrs	1:8

⟲ BABYSITTERS

Figure 12.1 A bedtime story

Babysitters usually care for children in their own homes for short periods so that parents can have a break. Many babysitters are young people who know the children and provide a service in exchange for pocket money, the term can be used for people of all ages.

It is important that the parents make sure that the babysitter is someone who is responsible and is able to act sensibly in a crisis. Sensible parents take time to go over important points which will help the babysitter if things go wrong or if the child is upset. Babysitters should always have details of the parents' proposed whereabouts and emergency telephone numbers in case they are needed. Since most babysitting is done in the evenings it is important that the babysitter understands the child's routine.

Bedtime routine	Babysitter's checklist
1 Does the child have a drink or snack before bed?	1 Where will the parents be?
2 Does the child have a bath?	2 Phone number where they can be contacted.
3 Is there any particular story or book they prefer?	3 When are the parents expected home?
4 Do they have a night-light?	4 Name and number of someone who may be contacted in an emergency, e.g. neighbours, grandparents.
5 Do they have any other special routine at bedtime?	5 Name and number of GP (family doctor).
	6 Details of any allergies suffered by the child.

⊃ CHILDMINDERS

Figure 12.2 A childminder at work

Childminders work in their own homes providing day care for families. Unlike nannies and au pairs, they must by law (The Children's Act 1989) be registered by the social services department of their local authority. The registration process is wide ranging and thorough, involving references, a health check and a police check on the childminder and all other adults in the family. The childminder's home is inspected to ensure that it provides a safe and suitable environment for young children.

Childminders are usually registered to care for up to three children under 5 and three 5 to 8 year olds, including their own children. These regulations are strictly enforced to allow children to have individual attention. Since childminders look after small groups of children their daily routine can be very adaptable and they can cater for individual dietary requirements and sleep patterns.

Childminders are flexible in the hours they work which can help parents who work shifts. Being cared for by a childminder gives children the opportunity to learn from real-life experiences. Everyday activities such as shopping trips, school runs, family meal times and visits to the park teach children life skills that they might not acquire so easily in nurseries.

These days many childminders make this their career and are undertaking training specific to the work they do, gaining qualifications such as those provided by the National Childminding Association (NCMA) which represents childminders in England and Wales in association with the Council for Awards in Children's Care and Education (CACHE) e.g. Basic Food Hygiene and First Aid Certificate.

AU-PAIRS

An au-pair is a girl or boy aged between 17 and 27 who comes to the UK primarily to learn to speak English and live for a time as a member of an English-speaking family. S/he will be expected to help with the housework and care of the children and in return she will receive her keep and pocket money. The great advantage to the family lies in her being educated, on-the-spot and flexible and prepared to work for less money than would be expected by professional domestic help.

The reasonable maximum time during which an au-pair may be expected to perform domestic tasks (including looking after children) is five hours daily, i.e. 25 hours per week, and she may be needed to babysit for up to two nights per week. She will be expected to help with such jobs as bed making, washing-up, tidying, dusting, babysitting, taking children to and from school and looking after them in the house; she should not be asked to do heavy housework.

NANNIES

The term nanny may be loosely applied to anyone who makes a career out of caring for a child in its family home. Unlike childminders nannies do not need to be registered with social services and they are not monitored by any outside regulatory body. There are no national requirements for nannies to have professional qualifications and some employers are more interested in the experience and personality of the person, while others will only employ those with recognised child care qualifications. Some nannies are particularly well qualified having undergone long periods of college training on how to care for children.

Figure 12.3 A trained nanny at work

Students attend a wide range of colleges such as the long-established private organisations which train Norland or Princess Christian Nannies. Other students attend courses in further education colleges to gain relevant qualifications such as CACHE Certificate in Childcare and Education or CACHE Diploma in Nursery Nursing (formerly NNEB).

Most nannies live with the family and care for the children when the parents are not there, while others come to the family each day and parents care for the children in the evenings and during the night.

⊃ NURSERIES

There are a number of different types of nursery provision in the UK:

◆ *Day nurseries:* these provide care for children aged 6 months to 5 years. They are open for long hours and during school holidays so they are good for working parents. They can be run by the state or privately.

◆ *Workplace nurseries:* which are organised by the employer and are usually on site. These may be subsidised by the employer.

◆ *Crèches:* care for children for short periods and are often found in large shopping centres. Staff will look after children under 8 and keep them safe while the parents go shopping.

◆ *Pre-schools or playgroups:* these are usually run by trained staff and managed by parents. They most usually care for children aged 2 to 4 years and sessions are up to three hours a day.

◆ *Kindergarten:* this word is made from two German words: Kinder (children) and garten (garden). It is used to describe pre-schools which follow the teaching methods of the German educationalist Froebel. Similarly, some pre-school groups may be called Montessori since they follow the teaching methods of Maria Montessori.

◆ *Nursery schools:* these can be run by the state or privately and are stand-alone schools offering care for 3 to 5 year olds. Children usually attend for five half days. Private nursery schools may follow a particular teaching method such as Montessori. Most nurseries and some other pre-school groups will have comprehensive **brochures** which will outline the **curriculum** and aims of the school.

◆ *Early years unit or reception class:* these are sometimes known as four-plus units and they are linked to a state primary school. They offer five half days of care a week for children aged 3 who will then go on to the primary school.

Most nurseries produce a leaflet or brochure for parents which outlines the aims and objectives of the school as well as detailing the school routine. It is important that parents examine the brochures carefully and visit the nursery before they enrol their child to ensure that they agree with its aims and are happy with the care provided.

This is an example of the aims of a nursery which appear in its school brochure:

1 *To create a stimulating, caring, safe environment for all children in our care.*

2 *To actively promote the development of positive self-image in each child, and foster physical, social, emotional, intellectual, cultural and moral growth.*

3 *To work as partners with parents/carers in an open and honest way, and encourage their input on all aspects of the running of the nursery.*

4 *To have an involvement with the local community.*

5 *To create a non-sexist atmosphere by introducing appropriate toys and activities to encourage equal opportunities and equal development of both sexes.*

6 *To eliminate racism throughout its whole structure by:*

   a *welcoming ethnic minority contributions to the nursery policies and practices*

   b *providing positive images of different ethnic minorities and cultures (e.g. posters, foods, clothing, toys and festivals).*

7 *To be available for regular informal discussions with parents.*

8 *To provide places for special needs children, if appropriate, with staff who are trained to give the child and parent/main carer support.*

9 *To encourage parents/carers to visit the nursery at any time.*

10 *To provide an atmosphere which makes the child and the parent/carer feel happy and comfortable within the nursery.*

Reproduced from the brochure of The Farmhouse Nursery School, Witney in Oxfordshire.

The education of under-5s is taken very seriously these days and nurseries are independently inspected by **Ofsted** (Office for Standards in Education) to ensure that high quality educational nursery care is being provided. Inspection teams look at the six Early Learning Goals (these used to be called 'Desirable Outcomes') which are designed to prepare children with key learning skills in these areas before they start school.

The six Early Learning Goals are:

1 Personal and social development

2 Language and literacy

3 Mathematics

4 Knowledge and understanding of the world

5 Physical development

6 Creative development

⊃ Points to Observe if Visiting a Nursery

◆ Is there a secure entry system to the premises?

◆ Do the members of staff know the children's names?

◆ Do they seem to make the children welcome when they arrive?

◆ Are the children playing happily?

◆ Is there a wide variety of toys and equipment?

◆ Is the equipment in good condition?

◆ Do staff notice if children need help?

◆ Are children praised and encouraged?

◆ Is there anywhere for the children to play outdoors?

◆ Is the atmosphere calm?

◆ What happens if parents are late?

⊃ ADVANTAGES AND DISADVANTAGES OF CHILD CARE OPTIONS

⊃ In-home child care

A nanny, babysitter or any other child care worker comes to the family home and cares for the child full or part time, or on a flexible schedule.

ADVANTAGES	DISADVANTAGES
For the child	**For the child**
◆ the comfort of familiar surroundings	◆ fewer opportunities to socialise
◆ one-to-one care from the same person each day	◆ risk of confusion – if the parent works long hours the child may come to see the nanny as the parent figure
◆ more personal attention	◆ possibility of a sense of loss if the nanny leaves suddenly
◆ less time commuting (travelling to another place)	
◆ less possibility of contact with childhood illnesses	**For the parent**
	◆ problems of sharing the home with another person
For the parent	◆ higher cost when compared to au-pairs and nurseries
◆ fewer problems about getting to work on time	◆ competition for the child's affection
◆ no worries about picking up the child if delayed	◆ do not need to be registered with social services
◆ no need to take time away from work if the child is unwell	◆ are not monitored
	◆ worries about qualifications
	◆ lack of back-up if the nanny is ill

⊃ Child minders (Family Day Care)

A childminder cares for a small number of children in her own home.

ADVANTAGES	DISADVANTAGES
For the child	**For the child**
◆ a cosy home-like atmosphere	◆ more possibility of infection than with in-home care
◆ less exposure to infection than in a large centre	◆ health and safety problems may arise although these should have been picked up during social service checks
◆ more individualised care	◆ high turnover of children

ADVANTAGES continued	DISADVANTAGES continued
For the child	**For the child**
◆ the opportunity to be with other children	◆ may have to compete for attention if the childminder's own children are present
For the parent	**For the parent**
◆ relatively low cost	◆ lack of back-up if the childminder is ill
◆ more flexibility regarding hours	◆ worries about competence of the childminder
◆ registered and monitored by social services departments	◆ worries about health and safety issues

⊃ Group Day Care/Day Nursery

Groups of young children spending all or part of the day together in formal care looked after by teachers or nursery nurses.

ADVANTAGES	DISADVANTAGES
For the child	**For the child**
◆ quality care from trained and experienced staff	◆ more exposure to illness
◆ a programme of activities for the correct age and level of development	◆ possibly less individual care
◆ opportunities to play with other children of the same age	◆ possibility of high ratio of children to teachers
◆ a wide variety of toys and equipment	**For the parent**
◆ usually some government regulation of health and safety	◆ less flexibility over hours
For the parent	◆ fairly high cost
◆ sufficient staff	◆ problems if the child becomes ill
◆ qualified staff	
◆ all aspects of the nursery can be monitored	

⊃ Pre-school

Classes of children who spend half or full days under the care of teachers in a formal situation to enable them to be ready for school.

ADVANTAGES	DISADVANTAGES
For the child	**For the child**
◆ care given by experienced staff	◆ the programme may be too demanding for the child
◆ a wide range of experiences available	◆ more exposure to infection from other children
◆ a formal programme geared to the child's age and maturity	
◆ children can be challenged academically	**For the parent**
◆ opportunities to socialise with a group of children of the same age	◆ less flexibility over hours
◆ children can be schooled in essential skills	◆ can be expensive if privately run
◆ a varied range of play equipment	◆ some pre-schools are available only in term time
◆ health and safety standards monitored	
For the parent	
◆ staff with recognised qualifications	
◆ reliability – substitute found if teacher is ill	

Key Words

Brochure a book or leaflet outlining the work done by a particular establishment such as a nursery, its aims, structure, organisation and codes of practice, etc.

Curriculum the activities and experiences that help children learn

LEA Local education authority. The LEAs fund nursery classes within schools

Material provision In the context of pre-school provision; this would include painting materials, paper, toys and play equipment

CACHE Certificate in Child Care and Education or CACHE Diploma in Nursery Nursing (formaly NNEB).

Ofsted Office for Standards in Education which provides inspection teams to ensure that nursery schools provide high quality educational nursery care

Private sector nurseries which make a profit from the services they offer

Statutory service any service provided by central or local government such as social services

Things to do

Activity 1

If possible, visit some form of pre-school group. Using the checklist given as a guide add other points which would help parents to decide whether this would be a suitable place for their children.

Note: This would be a good exercise to complete if the child you are using for your study attends a pre-school group. If you are not able to visit you could use the checklist as the basis for an interview with the parents for the research aspect of one of your observations.

Activity 2

If you are able to visit a nursery try to decide which of the activities you have seen the children undertake that would enable Ofsted inspectors to judge whether the nursery is providing high quality care. Use the six Early Learning Goals as a guide.

Activity 3

In the following scenarios parents are looking for child care provision to suit their family's needs. Using your knowledge of the range of places available try to match the child to the placement which will be most suitable. Take into consideration all the factors that a parent would need to consider, e.g. cost, flexibility, distance, and discuss the advantages and disadvantages in each case.

i Duncan is an only child who is 10 months old. His mother wishes to return to work part time and needs to be flexible about the hours she works. She is anxious that Duncan should be in a family environment where he can meet other children.

ii Lucy is 20 months old and she is looked after by an excellent childminder when her mother is teaching for three days each week. The family is very happy with the care Lucy receives and would like her to continue to have contact with her childminder. However the childminder will soon be looking after two young babies as well as Lucy. The family feels that when Lucy reaches the age of 2 she would benefit from spending some time with children of her own age.

iii Jake is 3 and his parents are highly paid executives who often work long hours. They sometimes need to work abroad for short periods. Until recently Jake has been looked after by his grandparents but they are no longer able to help.

iv Grace is 3 and lives with her father and her 5-year-old sister, Rosie. Her father has cared for both girls since they were babies and now that Rosie has started school he has been offered work with a firm which is close to their home. Unfortunately this means that he will need to work until 5.30 pm. He needs help for both girls if he is to be able to accept the post and he is anxious that both girls should have some contact with females.

Questions

Answer the following questions:

1 Give 5 reasons why parents may need child care provision for their under fives.

2 What is the difference between the role of a nanny and that of an 'au-pair'?

3 Why is it important for a babysitter to know about the child's bedtime routine?

4 What do we mean by the term 'Early Learning Goals'?

5 a) Which law governs the work of a child minder?

   b) How is this law enforced?

   c) What is involved in the registration of a childminder?

13

Child Health

In this section we will look at:

◆ the health of children from birth

◆ the causes of childhood illness and diseases

By the time babies are about 9 months old, they have already experienced their first cold or sniffles. Most parents are capable of dealing with this, whereas the onset of a rash might make them feel less confident.

⊃ SIGNS OF GOOD/POOR HEALTH

Good Health	Poor Health
◆ Good sound eating habits	◆ Poor appetite
◆ Alertness	◆ Signs of apathy
◆ Normal opening of bowels	◆ Constipation
◆ Always interested in surroundings	◆ Being miserable, crying, whinging
◆ Contented child	◆ Miserable, unhappy
◆ Breathing normally through the nose	◆ Breathing difficulties
◆ Very bright eyes	◆ Dull eyes
◆ Sleeping well	◆ Very poor sleeping habits
◆ Good, clear and firm skin	◆ Skin has a pallor, almost white-looking
◆ Well-developed muscles	◆ Muscles tend to be flabby
◆ No constantly runny nose	◆ Constantly runny nose
◆ 'Normal' progress and development for the age group	◆ Child not progressing and developing as expected
◆ Weight and height 'average' for the age group	◆ Below average weight and height for age group

If children show signs of good health, it is fairly safe to assume that they are progressing normally. From time to time young children will suffer from colds, flu, upset stomach, earache, toothache, etc., but these can usually be dealt with by the parent. However, it is as well to remember these points:

Young children, when really ill, will show some of the following signs and symptoms. These are in addition to those mentioned previously.

- pains and stiffness of the joints
- diarrhoea
- inflammation/swelling of glands
- rashes on various parts of the body
- headache, earache
- raised temperature
- vomiting
- difficulty breathing
- perspiration

Young children can often recover from illness very quickly indeed. They can be seriously ill one day and well on the way to recovery the next, giving the impression that nothing untoward has happened.

> ### Remember
>
> Very young children will rarely, if ever, pretend to be ill. Therefore the parent should consult the doctor if any of the above symptoms persist.

⊃ WAYS OF PREVENTING ILLNESS

No parent can be fully prepared for a child's illness, but they can go a long way to ensure good health by helping to prevent the illness in the first place. This can be done by ensuring that children have a healthy diet. They should be encouraged to eat a variety of nutritious foods for both growth and development. The current dietary goals should be followed as far as possible, i.e.:

- few *sugary* foods – helps with prevention of dental caries
- little junk food which contains a lot of *salt*.
- few fatty foods – children's fat intake should be the same as for adults, i.e., no more than 35% of their food energy should come from fat
- increasing intake of fibre (NSP = Non-Starch Polysaccharide); fibre-rich foods include wholemeal bread, beans, potatoes in their jackets, brown rice and brown pasta
- eating at least five portions of fruit and vegetables per day

Figure 13.1 Eating healthily

Remember

Good eating habits should always be started when children are young. Hopefully they will stay with them for the rest of their lives. It is widely recognised that an unhealthy diet will lead to obesity (being overweight).

Parents also have a duty to keep their children clean, and always to prepare food in a hygienic manner. By keeping children, the environment, and the children's food clean, parents are doing all they can to help prevent later health problems.

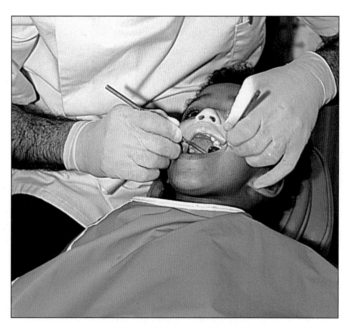

Figure 13.2 Regular visits to the dentist are important

◆ It is not always possible to keep children away from other children and adults. However, parents can keep their children away from people who they know to be suffering from infectious diseases.

◆ All children should be given regular medical and dental check-ups.

◆ No parent should ignore any of the symptoms already mentioned, particularly if any of them persist.

◆ Parents should be aware of symptoms of diseases as well as immunisation information and schedules in their area. Not all parents want their children to be immunised, but whatever their decision, they should be given the opportunity to discuss such matters with their family doctor.

⟳ DICTIONARY OF KEY WORDS RELATING TO ILLNESSES

Despite taking some or all of the precautions mentioned, most children will still contract an illness or disease. It is noticeable that once disease is mentioned, particularly in children, a great many words are used, e.g., infections, viruses, etc., and all too often, such words only cause confusion. Below is a list of such words and their definitions:

> ### Remember
> Microbes do not have to be bacteria, but bacteria are always microbes.

Key Words

Microbes these are often known as germs or pathogens. This is a collective name only. There are thousands of different microbes, but they can be divided into two main groups:

◆ *pathogenic (patho = disease, genic = causing)*

Pathogenic microbes always cause diseases in humans. There are many different types of pathogenic microbes, but the main ones causing diseases are:

◆ *bacteria* – these are one-celled organisms. They have a very simple make up. Some can be seen by a microscope. Many of these bacteria are fine and live naturally on the skin, vagina, stomach, etc. and as long as the person is healthy they are quite harmless. However, should the person feel ill or stressed or just under the weather, these bacteria will multiply very quickly, and in so doing give rise to infections such as sore throats, etc. Examples of disease-causing bacteria are streptococci and straphylococci.

◆ *viruses* – These are parasites and are extremely small. They cannot even be seen by a microscope. Because they are parasites they live and reproduce in other living cells, and the way that they operate is by breaking down these cells. Viruses cause influenza, measles, etc., and cannot be treated by any type of antibiotic.

◆ non-pathogenic – These are really harmless to humans. However, they can be very useful, for example, when converting milk into cheese, or breaking down organic matter, e.g., leaves, etc., into fertilizer.

As well as bacteria and viruses, there are other organisms which cause diseases in humans.

These are:

Key Words

Protozoa: these are simple one-celled animals such as amoeba, which can cause diseases like dysentery

Metazoan Parasites: tiny creatures which live on other living material, known as a host. Such parasites produce tapeworms, fleas and lice. These three, for instance, feed on the human body and that way cause infections

Fungi: these are small plant organisms which cause irritations and conditions such as athlete's foot, ringworm, etc.

⊃ Other Terms

◆ **Contact:** every day, people touch someone else, or kiss them, or use other people's towels, which have been in contact with a disease. When a person picks up an infection by any of the above means, we say that they have been in *contact* with an infected person

◆ **Contagious diseases:** diseases that spread from one person to another by contact are known as contagious diseases

◆ **Symptoms:** symptoms act like signposts, because they signal that something is wrong, e.g., a sore throat, a rash, etc.

◆ **Infectious stage:** this is when germs can spread form one person to another

◆ **Infectious diseases:** diseases which are caused by either bacteria, viruses, fungi or protozoa.

◆ **Epidemic:** this is when a disease spreads extremely quickly by infecting large numbers of people.

◆ **Antibodies:** substances which the body produces to try to control/destroy the disease.

◆ **Immunity:** this is a person's ability to resist infection. There are three types of immunity. If a person is able to resist the infection completely, i.e., the antibodies destroy the germs, this is known as *total immunity*. If a person contracts the disease, because they did not have enough immunity, but the disease is not severe, it is called *partial immunity*. *No immunity* means that the germs have nothing to fight them, and so a person will contract an infection

◆ **Antigen:** this is a substance which helps to stimulate the production of antibodies. Antigens can be pollen, germs, some foods, vaccines, etc.

◆ **Vaccines:** a vaccine usually has to be administered medically. It can be a dose of dead germs or live microbes. A different vaccine is required for each disease. Vaccines work by making the body produce the correct antibodies to help destroy the infection/disease

◆ **Immunisation:** is a way of trying a help prevent the infection or disease. This could be through the use of vaccines.

◆ **Incubation:** this is the time between germs entering a person's body and the appearance of the first symptoms.

◆ **Allergy:** this is a condition which occurs when a person overreacts to a substance. Such substances could be food (chocolate, cheese, nuts), detergents (washing powder, soap), medicine (penicillin) or dust. Reactions include rashes, breathing difficulties and stomach-upsets.

◆ **Droplet infection:** when a person sneezes or coughs, minute droplets of the sneeze or cough are sprayed into the atmosphere.

◆ **Carriers:** these are people who 'carry' germs, or who have infectious microbes on their own bodies, but do *not* suffer the infection themselves. They show no symptoms of the disease, and most are unaware that they are carrying the germs at all. This is often the case with typhoid, Hepatitis B, AIDS, etc.

◆ **Vector:** vector is the name given to animals and insects which transmit diseases.

◆ **Isolation:** usually refers to *one* person infected with a disease who is kept away from people who are not infected.

◆ **Contamination:** sometimes food or water or both are harbouring germs. When this happens we say that it is contaminated. Diseases such as food poisoning, cholera and dysentery are usually the result of contaminated food or water.

◆ **Oral:** given by mouth.

As well as good health, good diet and regular medical check-ups, a very high standard of hygiene should be kept at all times, both in and out of the home. All children should be taught basic hygiene rules, and throughout the child's life, these rules should be reinforced over and over again, so that infectious diseases can be kept to a minimum. Some of the more obvious rules for hygiene are:

◆ Always wash hands after visiting the lavatory.

◆ Hands should be clean before and during food preparation.

◆ If it is possible, hands should be washed after blowing one's nose, doing messy jobs, emptying the bin, etc.

◆ As far as is possible, children should be kept away from infectious diseases, such as measles, skin diseases, etc.

◆ Take care with pets and animals. If they are stroked or touched, hands should be washed immediately, particularly if the person is then going to prepare food. Pets' feeding dishes should be kept quite separately from those of the rest of the family.

◆ Clean teeth, regularly, and always after food has been consumed.

♦ Long hair should be tied back if preparing food.

♦ All utensils, equipment, etc., connected with food should be washed in extremely hot water and left to dry. Strictly speaking, tea towels should not be used.

♦ Nails should be kept clean and preferably short so that germs cannot harbour in them.

⊃ CHILDHOOD ILLNESSES

Earlier in this chapter we looked at the various ways in which infections and diseases are brought about. In this next section, *all* of the infections and diseases are mentioned according to their principal cause, e.g., bacterial. Also included are the symptoms, incubation periods and treatment, including present/up-to-date preventative measures.

⊃ Bacterial Infections

Disease	Symptoms	Incubation (In days)	Infectious stage	Other information	Immunisation
Diphtheria	A white layer forms on the throat which may block the airway; it produces poison which damages heart and nervous system	2-5	Usually for about two weeks after onset	Uncommon. It can occur in children who have not been immunised	Vaccines against diphtheria, whooping cough and tetanus are often given together as *triple vaccine* (DPT vaccine). Three injections are needed between the age of 3 and 12 months. *Booster doses* of vaccine for diphtheria and tetanus are given at 5 years and again between 15 and 19 years. Further doses of tetanus vaccine may be given at five-yearly intervals
Whooping Cough (Pertussis)	Long bouts of coughing which may end with a 'whoop' and vomiting	7-12	A few weeks before onset to four weeks after onset	Whooping cough vaccine prevents the disease or makes it much less severe	
Tetanus (Lockjaw)	Muscles of the neck, back and limbs tighten and the jaw may lock	4-21	Cannot be passed directly from one person to another	Germs exist in soil and enter the body through cuts and scratches	
Tuberculosis (TB)	Usually coughing and damage to lungs. Swollen glands in the neck	28-42	Variable	Most people who are infected with TB germs do not develop TB, but they develop natural immunity to TB	Vaccination of young children and teenagers who are at risk of infection

Disease	Symptoms	Incubation (In days)	Infectious stage	Other information	Immunisation
Typhoid (Salmonella typi)	Fever, constipation, dry mouth	About 14	Variable. A few people become permantent carriers	Can be prevented by proper sewage disposal, clean water supply, clean food handling	Two injections of vaccine with an interval between them of not less than seven days. A booster dose required every one to three years
Cholera	Violent diarrhoea, dehydration and collapse	1-5	A few days after recovery		Immunisation every six months for those exposed to risk of infection
Scarlet Fever	Sore throat, temperature, swollen glands, sickness rash of small red spots - skin flakes off. Tongue very red ('strawberry tongue')	2-5	N/A	N/A	Paracetamol to reduce fever. Course of penicillin (or other antibiotic if child is allergic to penicillin)
Poliomyelitis (Polio)	Infection of the spinal cord which may result in paralysis	3-21	From three days after infection to six weeks or longer after onset	Immunisation has almost eliminated this disease from Britain	Polio vaccine is given by mouth Three doses are required and are given at the same time as DPT vaccine. Booster doses are given at 5 years and again between 15 and 19 years
Measles	Fever, severe cold and cough. four to five days later a red rash appears on face and spreads downwards	10-15	From onset of cold symptoms to five days after rash appears	More serious in infancy than in older children	A single dose of combined measles, mumps and rubella vaccine (MMR) is given at 15 months. Rubella vaccine is offered to all girls between the age of 11 and 13 years who have not already had German Measles
Mumps	Painful swelling near the Jaw on one or both sides	12-18 (usually about 18)	Until the swelling goes down	Mumps in males over the age of 11 may affect a testis but rarely results in sterility	
German Measles (Rubella)	A mild disease with a red rash and usually with swollen glands	10-21	From onset to end of rash	Dangerous to the baby in the first four months of pregnancy	
Chicken Pox (Varicella)	Small red spots which turn to blisters then scabs	10-21	Two days before the spots appear until a week after	A mild disease in children. More severe in adults. The same virus causes shingles	N/A

Disease	Symptoms	Incubation (In days)	Infectious stage	Other information	Immunisation
Rabies (Hydrophobia- fear of water)	Fever, delirium, convulsions, paralysis. The throat muscles tighten so that it is impossible even to drink	Variable, usually one to two months	Rabies can only be caught from the saliva of an animal with rabies after being licked, scratched or bitten	Rabies can infect all mammals - foxes, bats, etc. - but is only a serious risk to people if domestic animals are infected, hence the need for quarantine of dogs and cats entering the country	A course of six injections – no longer painful – starting immediately after possible infection (active immunity). Passive immunity can be obtained by an injection of gamma globulin

Other Common Childhood Ailments

Ailment	Symptoms	Treatment
Asthma	Breathing difficulties because air passages are temporarily narrowed. May be caused by allergies or infection. Many children grow out of it	Anti-allergy and other drugs and inhalers
Bronchitis	Inflammation of the bronchial tubes. Causes cough, excessive mucus	Consult doctor who will probably prescribe antibiotics
Cold sores (Herpes)	Caused by a virus which makes the skin itch and causes a watery blister. Easily passed from person to person. Blister will dry and scab over	Cold sore lotion or ointment from a chemist's. See doctor if sore is severe
Colic	Usually occurs after feeds with some babies and disappears after the first six months	Severe cases can be treated by drugs
Conjunctivitis	Inflammation of the eye, making the eye red, sore and itchy	Very contagious, so use separate towels for the child. Doctor will prescribe drops or ointment
Pneumonia	This is the infection of the tissues of the lungs. The child will have a high temperature, a cough and difficulty with breathing	Usually responds to antibiotics
Stomach upsets	Usually caused by unsuitable food or bacteria which has infected the food	The child should be given plenty of fluids to avoid dehydration, and special attention given to personal hygiene
Thrush	Caused by a fungus and affects the mouth and sometimes the nappy area. It appears as a thick white fur on tongue and gums	Easily cured with Nystatin preparations, which will be supplied by the doctor
Constipation	Usually caused by poor diet. The child may pass hard stools containing blood	Give child more roughage, fresh fruit, prunes and more liquid. See doctor before giving any laxatives

Ailment	Symptoms	Treatment
Convulsions (fits)	Usually accompany high temperatures and fevers. Child becomes unconscious and twitches violently. Must not be left as they may vomit and choke	Call a doctor
Coughs	Usually a sign of bronchitis or an infectious disease	See doctor
Cradle cap	A thick layer of scurf which forms on the scalp of some babies. It is harmless but unsightly	May be softened with warm olive oil and removed
Croup	Affects the child's breathing, giving him a barking cough and a tight chest	Consult doctor
Earache	May be after-effects of a cold or infectious disease. Results in inflammation of the tubes of the ear	Doctor will give immediate treatment with antibiotics. Hearing must be checked when the infection is cleared up
Eczema	Infantile eczema is related to hay fever and asthma and seems to run in families. It produces a scaly, red rash on the face, behind the knees and elbow creases. It is very itchy and children make it worse by scratching.	There is really no cure, but it is generally outgrown after three or four years
Epilepsy	There are two main types – *petit mal* and *grand mal*. During a petit mal attack the child may lose consciousness for a second, become vacant and pale, then continue as if nothing has happened. With a grand mal attack, the child has convulsions, falls unconscious and may bite the tongue, shake violently and grind the teeth	There is no cure for the complaint, but medication does help to control it, and is generally very successful in preventing convulsions
Headaches	These are common in children. May be due to over tiredness, worry, anxiety, or even due to an infection e.g. tonsillitis, meningitis etc. It can often be confused with the fact that the child does not want to go to school and therefore the headache is used as an excuse.	Treatment is dependant on the age of the child, and the severity of the headache. If the headache is accompanied by a sudden change in the mood of the child, or a fever, vomiting, stiff neck or a bulging soft spot in a baby, then a doctor should be consulted. Any sudden severe headache or a headache lasting for more than 2 days demands medical attention. Also, a child with a headache on waking should see a doctor. In all cases it is sensible for the parent to try simple cures first i.e. a) reassure the child b) get the child to lie down in a darkened room. c) dependant on the age of the child, he/she can be given aspirin or paracetamol, having first made sure of the recommended dose. Again if these strategies have not relieved the pain medical advice can be sought.

Ailment	Symptoms	Treatment
Meningitis	This condition is the result of inflammation of the *meninges* (covering of brain and spinal cord), caused by a virus or bacterial infection. Symptoms include fever, convulsions, sickness, apathy and a distinctive rash	Treatment with antibiotics must be quick as the acute illness is dangerous. It can leave permanent deafness. A new anti-meningitis vaccine known as Preynar is now recommended to all children under the age of 2 years in the United States. This vaccine helps to protect against pneumococcal illness including meningitis and severe ear infections.
Nose bleeds	Usually caused by children damaging the nose while playing, or picking their nose	The head should be held over a bowl and the nose firmly pinched at the sides to stop the bleeding. If there are frequent nose bleeds the child should see a doctor
Vomiting	When the baby is bringing back large amounts of milk it could indicate inflammation of the stomach, etc. Shows signs of sunken eyes, dry nappies, dark coloured urine	Call doctor or Health Visitor who may well give the baby a rehydrating solution e.g., Dioralyte
Diarrhoea	Watery stools, often accompanied by vomiting	Best to call the doctor if the diarrhoea has continued for more than a few hours. Doctor may well take a stool sample, and give the baby some rehydrating solution, as above
Toothaches	By far the commonest cause is tooth decay. At first, the decay eats through the hard outer enamel, and this causes no pain at all. As soon as the decay reaches the living centre of the tooth, pain sets in. It is made worse by eating very hot or very cold food and often seems worse at night.	The only real treatment has to be carried out by a dentist. However, as a short-term measure, the child (dependant on age) can be given the recommended dosage of asprin or paracetamol. Oil of cloves is also useful as a short-term measure to try and deaden the pain.

⊃ Parasital Infections (Animal Parasites)

A parasite is a creature which lives on or in another creature. Parasites feed on the creature they live on, in order to develop and to be able to multiply. These parasites pass easily from person to person, and they do not cause a great deal of harm. However, they are a nuisance because they can make a person itchy, scratchy and they disturb one's sleep. The following are the most common animal parasites:

- fleas
- lice
- bed bugs
- itch mites

- roundworms
- threadworms
- tapeworms

Fungal Infections

Ringworm

This is not a worm but a fungus which infects the skin. When it just appears, it starts at a point, and works its way outwards, hence the name *ring*worm. If it invades the scalp, hair is usually lost. If it invades the feet it is known as:

Athlete's Foot. It grows in damp, warm places, and the only cure is not to touch infected areas, e.g., bathmats, towels, etc., and to apply anti-fungal sprays.

THE SICK CHILD AT HOME

Many of the conditions mentioned above can be treated at home. However children will need to be entertained while they are getting better. Bear in mind that they may need to be kept in bed for a time and will need to change activities regularly so they don't get bored. Such activities (depending on the age of the child) could be:

- games
- television/radio
- building bricks
- books/stories
- knitting/lace making
- dominoes
- making shapes from odd bits which the parents give, e.g., cotton reels, etc.

- crosswords
- jigsaws
- construction games
- Lego
- number games
- Monopoly

Of course, children will also enjoy having different people to talk to and play with. So the parents can enlist the help of siblings, grandparents and other friends and relatives.

THE SICK CHILD IN HOSPITAL

Should children have to go into hospital, the following suggestions might help to make the situation easier – both for the children and the parents.

◆ Children should be prepared (unless it is an emergency) for this new situation. Actually going into hospital can be traumatic and an emotional upheaval for anyone, so parents who prepare their children for this upheaval may find they cope better with it.

◆ If possible, try to get children admitted to either a children's hospital, or a children's ward in a general hospital, and preferably where the staff is especially trained to deal with children.

◆ Children can be prepared for hospital in many ways:

   ◆ discuss the hospital with them

      a explain to the child that he/she is only going to the hospital to get better, and that everyone who goes to hospital, *always* comes out of there feeling well again

      b tell them that they will not be alone – there will be lots of other children for them to play with

      c describe how the doctors and nurses will make him/her feel better

      d as well as taking in his favourite toys, reassure the child that in hospital there will be lots more toys to play with

      e describe how the child will be made to feel so important, because he/she may have his food in bed

      f show him/her books about being in hospital

      g when he actually goes into hospital his parents should take him, undress him, show him where the toilets are (if he is old enough) and they should stay with the child as long as possible

   ◆ tell them positive stories about the hospital

   ◆ make a guessing game with all the different types of people they are likely to meet, e.g., doctor, paediatrician, nurse, etc.

   ◆ if possible, try to visit the hospital beforehand

   ◆ role play at being doctors and nurses

   ◆ let children pack their own suitcases and allow them to take their favourite toys

   ◆ when children actually go into hospital, the parents should stay with them until they are competely settled in – accommodation is also often available

   ◆ parents can tell children beforehand exactly when they will be visiting

   ◆ reassure children that they are missed at home

Questions

Question 1

a) What is the difference between pathogenic and non-pathogenic microbes?

b) Can you name any other two types of microbes which cause infectious diseases?

c) What are toxins?

Question 2

a) What is the main difference between bacteria and a virus?

b) What is a contagious disease?

c) Describe how droplet infection works.

Question 3

a) Define the following words:

- contact
- infectious diseases
- antibodies
- epidemic

b) How does vaccination work?

c) Give four ways of helping to prevent illness in a young child.

Question 4

a) Name two common childhood ailments and describe them.

b) What is whooping cough and how is it treated?

c) How are measles, mumps and rubella treated, and when?

Question 5

a) Why is it important to prepare a child going to hospital for the first time?

Question 6

a) What is the chief difference between an antibody and an antigen?

b) Using a flow diagram describe how antibodies work.

c) Which vaccines are given orally?

d) What advice would you give to a mother who notices a rash on her 9-month-old baby?

⊃ SIMPLE FIRST AID/BASIC FIRST AID – THEY ARE ONE AND THE SAME

First aid is exactly what it says it is and nothing more. It is a means of administering help to a person, who has had an accident; and it is hoped that help, however small, will keep the person alive until professional medical help arrives. It is simple or basic because it is the first help which is given hence the words first aid, i.e. first help. The three golden rules to remember about first aid are:

A – check airways.

B – check if the patient is breathing.

C – check circulation.

⊃ THE CONTENTS OF A FIRST-AID BOX

It is a good idea for anyone, not just parents, to keep a first-aid box in the home and in the car. From time to time everyone has to deal with minor cuts, scalds, scratches, etc., so it is both useful and necessary to have the following equipment handy in a box clearly marked with the words *First Aid*. A well-kept box should include:

- cotton wool
- plasters
- gauze dressings
- tweezers
- crepe bandage
- cream for insect bites, etc.
- sling for supporting someone who may have damaged their arm

- paper tissues
- bandages
- safety pins
- scissors
- calamine lotion
- pair of cheap thick plastic gloves

Questions

The following questions are on First Aid.

Question 1

a) What do the words first aid mean?

b) What do the letters A, B and C stand for when dealing with patient who appears to be unconscious?

c) List the contents of a first aid box.

Question 2

Draw or collect some 'safety approved labels' found on different pieces of toys.

Extension questions

Research will be required to answer the following questions.

Question 3

a) What is the usual cause of a bruise?

b) What type of treatment would you suggest?

Question 4

Describe the first aid treatment for:

a) a child whose hand has been scalded with hot water

b) a child who is having a minor epileptic fit

c) a minor cut/wound to the leg

d) a child who is choking

Question 5

a) How does first aid treatment for a graze differ from the treatment of severe bleeding?

b) Would you use sticking plaster or antiseptic oinment on a small cut?

c) What should never be placed on a burn and why?

Question 6

a) Why do you think you should never prick a blister?

b) How would you treat a child complaining of severe pains in his/her arm after falling off a high step?

Question 7

a) What is concussion?

b) How would you recognise if a person/child had just been concussed?

c) Give your list of treatment procedures.

⟲ HEALTH WORDSEARCH

M	N	N	W	R	N	A	W	J	S	H	K	U	C	F
N	V	B	A	I	R	E	H	T	P	I	D	B	S	L
A	O	V	A	C	C	I	N	E	F	Q	A	A	P	E
D	C	I	E	P	I	D	E	M	I	C	H	M	V	F
G	D	R	T	W	S	Y	M	P	T	O	M	S	T	O
C	P	U	A	A	N	N	E	E	M	K	E	E	L	V
L	K	S	P	U	Z	O	R	R	H	R	T	H	Q	V
O	T	U	E	D	C	I	I	A	U	A	G	N	S	R
A	N	I	W	K	A	T	N	T	N	E	A	C	E	J
H	P	C	O	O	R	A	I	U	C	D	F	C	B	Q
G	E	A	R	G	R	L	S	R	M	E	A	O	O	E
L	D	B	M	Q	I	O	K	E	S	M	F	J	R	M
L	S	E	S	A	E	S	I	D	R	A	I	N	C	R
T	E	C	M	X	R	I	K	X	G	J	C	P	I	W
I	I	Z	M	D	L	L	L	I	K	O	H	X	M	K

Bacteria

Carrier

Diptheria

Diseases

Epidemic

Immunisation

Infection

Isolation

Microbes

Symptoms

Tapeworms

Temperature

Tetanus

Vaccine

Virus

Part Three
Development of the Child

In Part Three we will look at how children acquire the skills which will help them to progress through life.

No matter which skills are being acquired, there is a recognised pattern of development. However, the speed and rate at which children will achieve these skills will be as individual as the child itself.

There are four main areas of development and these often overlap:

physical   intellectual   social   emotional

How a child develops will depend on a number of factors.
These are often referred to as:

Nature	**Nurture**
Genetic inheritance	Environmental influences

Examples of factors influencing development:

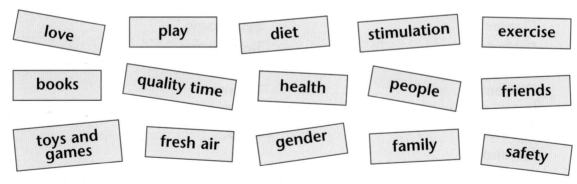

love   play   diet   stimulation   exercise

books   quality time   health   people   friends

toys and games   fresh air   gender   family   safety

Remember

◆ all children will develop at their own pace
◆ all areas of development are interlinked

14

Physical Development

During their first five years, children grow and develop more than at any other stage in their life.

In this section we will look at how children develop physically using

- fine motor skills
- gross motor skills
- sensory skills

We will also look at the importance of providing children with

- opportunities to explore, discover and experiment
- suitable activities to encourage physical development

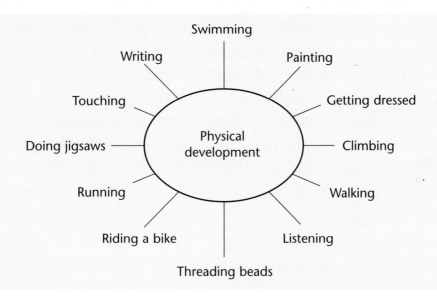

Physical development is one of the easiest aspects of development to observe and recognise in children – however – it is closely linked to all other aspects of development.

These are two separate strands to physical development:

- ◆ **growth** is about the physical changes in the child – the increase in size, height and weight
- ◆ **development** is about how children begin to gain control over their physical actions, so that they can do more complex activities

Growth and development are very closely linked, because the ability to develop and improve skills will very much depend on size and muscular strength.

⊃ LOOKING AT GROWTH

Growth is about size, height and weight. It is easy to recognise, easy to measure and easy to record. Throughout their early years, health visitors and doctors will measure children's height and weight, and record and compare this using standard charts, known as percentile, or more usually **centile** charts (see below). By doing this, children's pattern of growth can be checked and any problems can be detected and dealt with.

Children usually grow at around the same rate – sometimes referred to as the **norm**. For example, a newborn baby will measure, on average, 50 cm; by 1 year old he will have grown to about 75 cm and by 5 years old will have more than doubled in length/height to 110cm.

⊃ Percentile and Centile Charts

These are the charts used by health professionals to compare the growth patterns of individual children with those of other children in the same age range.

Different charts are used for boys and girls as boys tend to grow slightly taller than girls, and are usually heavier at birth.

⊃ Using Centile Charts

Each chart shows the normal range of weight or height for girls and boys.

Each chart has three lines marked.

◆ **The middle line (red)** is known as the 50th centile. This means that 50 per cent of children have a weight or height around this line.

◆ **The top line (yellow)** is known as the 98th centile. This means that 98 per cent of children have a weight or height below this line.

◆ **The bottom line (blue)** is known as the 2nd centile. This means that only two per cent of children have a height or weight below that line.

Therefore, only four per cent (four in every 100) of all children will not follow a normal growth pattern.

How tall children grow largely depends on the genes they inherit from their parents.

Weight may also depend on genetic inheritance, but will also be influenced by:

◆ diet

◆ exercise

◆ environmental factors

Recording a Child's Height Using Centile Charts

1 Find the child's age in years and/or months along the bottom axis.
2 Identify the child's height along the vertical axis.
3 Where the two lines cross is the child's height in comparison to other children of that age.

In the example, the boy is aged 3 years 6 months and measures 100cm. This falls on the 50th centile line, so the child is of average height for that age.

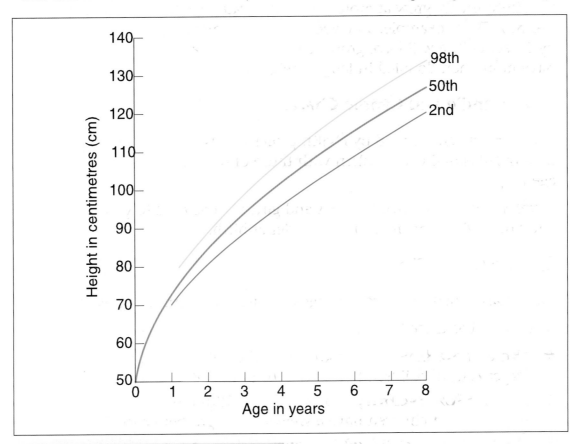

Key Words

Centile charts another name for percentile charts

Development the ability to use more complex skills

Growth a change in size

Percentile charts charts used to compare the growth of individual children with expected average growth

⊃ Teeth

From around the age of 6 months,
a child's primary (milk) teeth will
start to appear.
There are three different types.

Incisors	These are mainly used for biting and are 'chisel shaped' with sharp edges.
Canines	These are used to tear food into manageable pieces. They are sharp and pointed.
Molars	These are used to grind and crush food to make it easy to swallow. They are strong and have a wide flat surface area.

There are 20 primary teeth, and they usually appear in the following order.

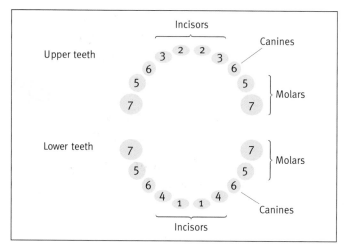

Figure 14.1 The primary teeth

Occasionally, a baby may be born with a tooth already through.
Usually children will have all 20 teeth by the time they are 3 years old.

Permanent teeth usually begin to come through at around 6 years of age, and there are 32 of these.

From an early age it is important to care for, and encourage children to care for, their teeth.

As soon as teeth appear they need to be cleaned. If they are not **plaque** will stick to the teeth and begin to cause them to decay.

Parents should use a soft toothbrush and from about 1 year old, children can be taught to brush their own teeth. But it is a difficult skill and they will need help and supervision.

For teeth to grow and stay healthy, children need to eat the right sort of foods.

They need foods with a lot of calcium, phosphorous, fluoride, vitamins A, C and D and foods which are crisp and need biting and chewing, such as carrots, apples and celery.

Sugar causes decay and can damage the teeth before they come through. Parents should avoid giving sweets as treats, and especially not give sweet drinks in baby bottles and feeders. This concentrates the sugar on the teeth as the drink is taken.

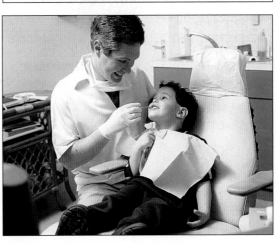

Regular visits to a dentist are a must. If children start these early:

◆ they are less likely to be afraid

◆ any problems can be dealt with immediately.

Children should visit the dentist every six months from the age of 3.

⊃ LOOKING AT DEVELOPMENT

Physical development is a much more complex process and much more difficult to measure and record.

As children's bodies become more mature they gradually learn to control and use different muscles and make different movements. In doing so, they learn to do more complicated and difficult physical tasks more skilfully and easily. But this control may be learnt at different rates by different children – so one child may learn to walk at 9 months, another at 12 months and another at 18 months. So instead of using charts and norms for development, professionals tend to refer to **Milestones** – points at which a child masters a skill which can be broadly linked to an age.

Newborn babies have little control over their bodies. They are born with a number of **involuntary reflexes** (see p.183) which are designed to keep them alive, and which they cannot control. As they get older, these reflexes disappear and the baby begins to develop **voluntary skills** – movements it can control.

To gain complete control, children need to master three different types of skills:

◆ gross motor skills
◆ fine motor skills
◆ sensory skills.

⊃ Understanding Gross Motor Skills

Children need to learn to control the muscles which are used for balance and large movements, such as walking, climbing and kicking a ball.

These are known as **gross motor skills**. Control develops from the head down to the shoulders and arms and finally to the legs.

ALL THESE REQUIRE STRENGTH, STAMINA, BALANCE, CO-ORDINATION, DETERMINATION AND CONFIDENCE

Key Words

Gross motor skills the use and control of the whole body and larger muscles

Involuntary movement an automatic movement which cannot be controlled

Milestone a point or stage where an average child should have mastered a skill

Voluntary movement a movement which can be controlled

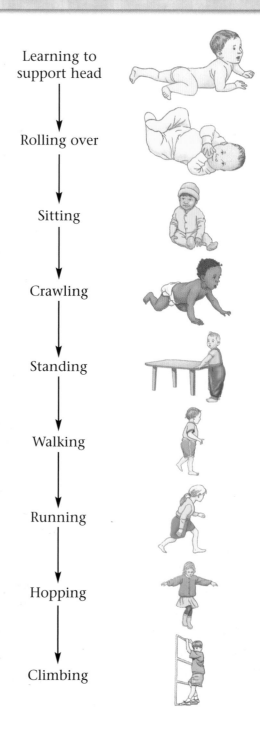

Learning to support head
↓
Rolling over
↓
Sitting
↓
Crawling
↓
Standing
↓
Walking
↓
Running
↓
Hopping
↓
Climbing

⟳ Understanding Fine Motor Skills

At the same time as they are learning to control the larger body muscles, children also have to learn to develop and control the smaller muscles of the hands and fingers (and feet) so that they can do more delicate tasks, such as drawing, fastening buttons and threading beads. These are the **fine motor skills**.

In doing this they use a variety of different grips and grasps until the **mature pincer grasp** is developed at about 4 years.

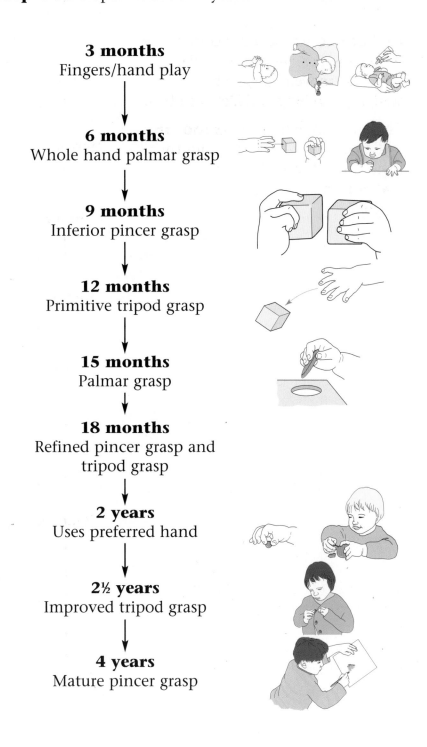

3 months
Fingers/hand play

↓

6 months
Whole hand palmar grasp

↓

9 months
Inferior pincer grasp

↓

12 months
Primitive tripod grasp

↓

15 months
Palmar grasp

↓

18 months
Refined pincer grasp and tripod grasp

↓

2 years
Uses preferred hand

↓

2½ years
Improved tripod grasp

↓

4 years
Mature pincer grasp

CHILDREN LEARN TO CO-ORDINATE INWARDS TO OUTWARDS – SO THEY LEARN TO CONTROL ARMS, THEN HANDS, THEN FINGERS

Age	Gross Motor Skills	Fine Motor Skills
3 months	◆ when lying on front, can lift head and turn from side to side ◆ when lying on front can push up on arms and raise shoulders ◆ can kick legs strongly ◆ can hold a rattle	◆ looks at and plays with fingers
6 months	◆ can lift head and chest clear of floor, supported by arms ◆ can sit for long periods if supported by cushion ◆ can sit for short periods without support but will 'topple' over ◆ may be able to roll over from back to front ◆ may try to crawl ◆ when lying on back, grasps legs and puts into mouth	◆ puts all objects to mouth ◆ grabs toys using whole hand **palmar grasp** ◆ will pass toys from hand to hand
9 months	◆ tries to crawl by rocking backwards and forwards ◆ can pull into a standing position, by going on to knees first ◆ may begin to **'cruise'** (side-step) around furniture ◆ may begin to crawl upstairs ◆ can sit unsupported for long periods of time	◆ uses **inferior/primitive pincer** grasp to pick up small objects ◆ cannot voluntarily 'let go' of toys ◆ will look for dropped or fallen objects which are out of sight ◆ uses **pincer grasp** (thumb and first finger) to pick up small objects ◆ uses index finger to point
12 months	◆ becoming very mobile – either by crawling, shuffling, bearwalking or bottom shuffling ◆ may be walking ◆ can sit unsupported for long periods ◆ tries to crawl upstairs forwards and downstairs backwards ◆ pulls up to a standing position and then sits back down ◆ can sit down without falling	◆ uses **neat pincer grasp** (thumb and first finger) to pick up small objects, e.g. rattles, small toys ◆ points to objects with index finger ◆ uses both hands but may begin to show preference for one ◆ puts small objects into a container, e.g. bricks into a beaker ◆ drops and throws toys deliberately ◆ uses **tripod grasp** to hold and bang together bricks

Sensory skills	Suitable toys and activities	How parents/carers can help
◆ finds hands and brings them to mouth	Baby gyms Rattles and squeaky toys Pram toys Activity mats with different textures Bath toys to kick	Give baby time and opportunity to lie on back and kick, and to lie on front to strengthen neck and back. Play finger and hand games. Give time for bath play time.
◆ looks around curiously ◆ if a toy falls out of sight will not look for it	Stacking beakers/blocks Bricks to hold and bang Rattles Simple picture books Teething rings Mirrors Textured (feely) toys	Because baby is learning through using the senses he needs toys and activities which will encourage this. For example: ◆ textured/feely toys ◆ peek-a-boo ◆ finger rhymes ◆ clapping games
◆ looks in correct place for fallen toys	Any object which will encourage sensory skills: Bricks Safe household objects Plastic bath toys Squeaky toys	Play simple games, e.g. peek-a-boo. Point to toys and objects. Give baby time to explore toys on floor.
◆ watches people, animals and moving objects for long periods ◆ drops and watches falling toys ◆ looks for lost/hidden toys ◆ recognises familiar people ◆ turns to sound of own name	Rattles Stacking beakers/bricks Push and pull toys Wheeled toys Large balls Cardboard books Baby swings Shape sorters	Allow baby the time and opportunity to develop gross motor skills. Play games with baby which will help fine motor skills, e.g. playing with shape sorters or building with bricks. Give lots of praise and encouragement.

Age	Gross Motor Skills	Fine Motor Skills
15 months	◆ walks independently using arms to balance ◆ can crawl downstairs, feet first ◆ throws a ball but may fall over ◆ can kneel without support ◆ can get into a standing position without using the help of people or furniture	◆ claps hands together ◆ can build a tower of two blocks ◆ can drink from a cup using two hands to hold it ◆ makes a mark with crayon using a **palmar grasp** ◆ tries to turn pages in a book but will turn several at once ◆ tries to eat with a spoon but will turn it upside down
18 months	◆ can walk confidently without using arms to balance ◆ can pick up toys by bending from waist ◆ can 'squat' to look at things without losing balance ◆ can roll and throw a ball ◆ may be able to walk up and down stairs without adult help ◆ runs, but sometimes bumps into obstacles ◆ can push and pull toys when walking	◆ can turn knobs and handles on doors ◆ can build a tower of three cubes ◆ can string together four large beads ◆ uses **mature pincer grasp** ◆ beginning to use the **tripod grasp** when using pencils and crayons ◆ can pull off shoes
2 years	◆ can walk up and down stairs confidently, two feet to a step ◆ enjoys climbing on to furniture ◆ can kick a ball that is not moving ◆ enjoys toys which are put together and pulled apart, e.g. duplo, sticklebricks ◆ runs safely ◆ pushes and pulls large wheeled toys	◆ can turn the pages of a book one by one ◆ has good hand-eye co-ordination ◆ can build a tower of five or six bricks ◆ uses **mature pincer grasp** to pick up and place small objects ◆ holds a pencil firmly and can form circles, lines and dots ◆ can zip and unzip a large zipper
3 years	◆ can walk and run forward with precision ◆ can walk on tip toe ◆ can kick a ball forwards ◆ can throw a ball overhand ◆ can catch a large ball between extended arms ◆ can pedal and steer a tricycle ◆ can walk upstairs with one foot on each step ◆ can hop on one foot	◆ holds a crayon and can draw a face ◆ can eat with a spoon without spilling ◆ can wash and dry hands without help ◆ can put on and take off coat ◆ can build a tower of nine or ten bricks ◆ cuts with toy scissors

Sensory skills	Suitable toys and activities	How parents/carers can help
◆ looks with interest at pictures in a book and pats them ◆ stands at a window and watches what is happening for long periods of time ◆ beginning to understand ◆ **object permanence** – things exist even if they cannot be seen	Picture books Shape sorters Large chunky crayons and paper Musical toys Cause and effect toys, e.g. Jack-in-the-Box	Spend time playing with children and showing them how toys work.
◆ picks up small objects, such as beads, on sight with **delicate pincer grasp.** ◆ enjoys simple picture books ◆ recognises and points to boldly coloured items on a page ◆ recognises familiar people at a distance	Push and pull toys Threading toys Picture books in card or fabric Simple tricycles Rocking horse	Children like to spend time playing alone so need to be allowed to do this. They will enjoy repetitive games, e.g. putting small objects such as bricks into a box. They are becoming more independent and like to try to take off shoes, socks, etc. They need to be allowed to do this.
◆ enjoys picture books ◆ recognises fine detail in favourite pictures ◆ recognises familiar adults in photographs	Ride on and sit on toys Large Duplo/Sticklebrick construction toys Bricks Crayons and paper Play dough Picture books	Parents need to provide children with a wide variety of toys to play with and explore, especially as concentration spans are limited. Children are beginning to have favourite toys and activities.
◆ knows names of some colours ◆ can match two or three primary colours, usually red and yellow ◆ listens eagerly to favourite stories and wants to hear favourite ones over and over again	Large outdoor toys such as swings, slide and climbing frames Paints and crayons Tricycles Dressing up clothes Sand and water	Children are becoming more social and willing to play with other children. They may be ready for play or nursery school. They will enjoy practical activities such as baking.

Age	Gross Motor Skills	Fine Motor Skills
4 years	◆ can walk or run alone up and down stairs, in adult fashion ◆ can walk along a straight line ◆ hops on one foot ◆ climbs ladders and trees ◆ pedals and controls a tricycle confidently ◆ is becoming increasingly skilled at ball games – can throw, catch, bounce, kick and use a bat	◆ can build a tower of ten or more cubes ◆ can build three steps with six bricks if shown ◆ controls a pencil with a **mature pincer grasp** ◆ can fasten and unfasten buttons and zips ◆ can put together simple, large piece jigsaw puzzles
5 years	◆ can skip with a rope ◆ very skilful in climbing, sliding, swinging, jumping, etc. ◆ can use a variety of large equipment confidently ◆ can throw a ball to a partner, catch, hit a ball with a bat with accuracy ◆ can balance on one foot for several seconds	◆ dresses and undresses with little help ◆ can complete more complex jigsaw (20+ pieces) ◆ cuts out shapes using scissors more accurately ◆ can colour in pictures neatly

⊃ Understanding Sensory Skills

While all this is happening, children are also learning to develop and use their **sensory skills** – the skills of taste, touch, vision, hearing and smell.

During their first two years especially, children will use all of these senses to find out about their world.

In particular vision is closely linked to **fine motor skills** and the development of **hand-eye co-ordination** and hearing to **language developments**, taste and touch to **intellectual development** and smell to **social and emotional development**.

Key Words

Fine Motor Skills the use and control of hands and fingers

Hand-eye co-ordination the ability to use hand and eye together to make precise movements

Palmar grasp using the whole hand

Pincer grasp using thumb and first finger

Sensory to do with sight, hearing, touch, taste and smell

Tripod grasp using the thumb and two fingers

Sensory skills	Suitable toys and activities	How parents/carers can help
◆ matches and names four primary colours correctly ◆ follows story books with eyes and identifies words and pictures	Any materials or objects for creative activities, e.g. collage, junk toys Paints and crayons Jigsaw puzzles Construction toys, such as Lego Climbing frames, slides and swings	Children at this age are more independent and need less help from parents. They can play with other children, usually co-operatively. They still need a wide variety of opportunities for playing.
◆ matches 10-12 colours ◆ vision and hearing developed to adult level	Bicycle with stabilisers Balls Rollerblades Creative materials Construction toys Board games	Children are now beginning to understand and enjoy games with rules – but they need adult help, both to explain and act as a peacemaker! They will play independently and make up their own games.

⟳ A CLOSER LOOK AT PHYSICAL DEVELOPMENT

Children's physical development usually follows the same sequence, although the age may vary. However, there are some children who may grow at the same rate as other children, but whose control and development does not follow the expected pattern – perhaps because of some disability (see Chapter 18).

Figure 14.5 'Making tea'

Figure 14.6 Building with bricks

Figure 14.7 Reading books

Figure 14.8 Dressing up

ENCOURAGING PHYSICAL DEVELOPMENT

Almost every toy, game and play activity, will involve some sort of physical movement, and will therefore help, in some way, to encourage different physical skills. (See Chapter 17 Play and Toys)

However, more toys and games tend to be used indoors, and therefore concentrate on children's fine motor skills. As children grow and become more mobile, they usually have lots of energy, which some of these games and activities will not use up. Parents need to give children the chance to run around and burn off this energy, while at the same time allowing them to explore their own, and new, environments, and to learn more about the world around them.

So it is important for lots of reasons to give children time to play outdoors – even on a cold day.

➲ Why Outdoor Play is Important

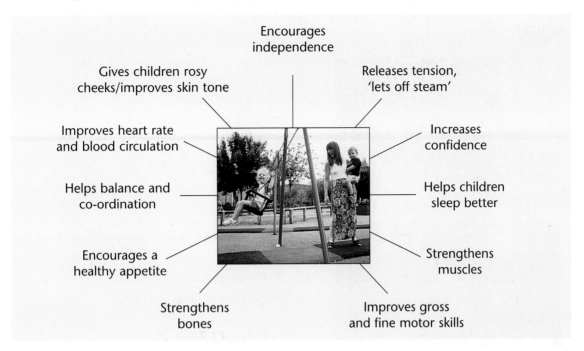

Equipment for outdoor activities, such as swings, slides and climbing frames, can be expensive and take up a lot of space. It also needs to be safe, secure and checked regularly (See Chapter II Environment). However, this sort of equipment is usually readily available at parks and play areas. Regular visits to these with parents will provide good play opportunities, and children will get a lot of pleasure from just having the freedom to run around. It will also help parents and children to bond, may provide opportunities for social development and a chance to explore a new environment.

⟩ Ideas for Outdoor Play

Activity	How it helps

Riding bicycle/tricycle

- ◆ Helps to develop leg muscles and strengthen bones
- ◆ Improves balance
- ◆ Builds up stamina
- ◆ Helps co-ordination
- ◆ Increases confidence

Playing hide and seek/tig/chasing game

- ◆ Develops co-ordination and balance
- ◆ Builds up stamina
- ◆ Promotes spatial awareness
- ◆ Helps develop social skills

Hopping/skipping/jumping/trampoline

- ◆ Develops leg muscles
- ◆ Develops co-ordination and balance
- ◆ Improves stamina
- ◆ Builds up confidence

Playing with balls and bat

- ◆ Develops hand-eye co-ordination
- ◆ Develops hand, arm and leg muscles
- ◆ Encourages co-operative play

Climbing

- ◆ Improves balance and co-ordination
- ◆ Develops leg and arm muscles and strength
- ◆ Increases confidence and independence
- ◆ Promotes spatial awareness

When the weather is bad, and 'playing out' is not possible, parents can still provide opportunities to allow children to 'let off steam' by taking them swimming, or to organised play groups where there is still space to run around, or even planning a disco.

And should it snow – there are endless opportunities for all sorts of physical development, and to explore a totally new world!

Remember

Physical growth and development are very closely linked – being able to learn and improve a new physical movement or skill will depend a lot on size and muscular strength.

Questions

Answer the following questions:

Question 1

a What is the difference between *'growth'* and *'development'*?

b i Suggest *two* factors which might affect the growth of a child.

ii Suggest *three* factors which might affect the development of a child.

c Explain how and why growth and development are closely linked.

d What are *'centile charts'* and how are they used?

Question 2

a i What is another name for *milk teeth*?

ii How many milk teeth do children have?

iii There are three different types of milk teeth.

Name and describe them and explain how each are used,

b List the main nutrients that are needed for the growth and maintenance of healthy teeth.

c Suggest *four* suitable foods which could be given as snacks to young children which will encourage the development of healthy teeth.

d Why should sugary snacks be avoided?

Question 3

a When measuring development, it is usual to talk about *'milestones of development'*.

i What is meant by a *'milestone of development'*?

ii Why should care be taken when using 'milestones' to assess children's development?

b What is the difference between an *'involuntary movement or reflex'* and a *'voluntary movement'*?

Question 4

a i Explain the difference between *'gross motor skills'* and *'fine motor skills'*.

ii Give *three* examples of each.

b Gross motor skills develop from the head downwards.

Explain what this means and at what age each stage is achieved.

c Name and describe *three* different grasps a young child might use when playing with toys.

d Which of the following are examples of gross motor skills, and which are examples of fine motor skills?

Skipping: doing a jigsaw puzzle: painting: fastening a button: cutting shapes with scissors: swimming: riding a tricycle: reading a book: building with lego: playing with a shape sorter

Question 5

a What are sensory skills?

b How are the different senses linked to physical, intellectual, emotional and social development?

Question 6

a Playing out of doors is important in helping children's physical development.

Suggest *eight* reasons why.

b Suggest *four* different toys or activities which would help to encourage the development of fine motor skills in a *three year old* child. Explain how.

c i In your own words describe the stage of physical development of a *two year old* child.

ii Suggest *three* toys or activities which would be suitable for a child of this age. Give reasons.

⊃ PHYSICAL DEVELOPMENT WORDSEARCH

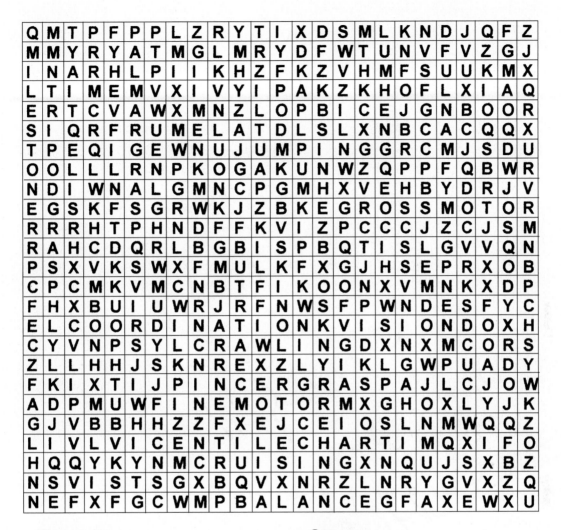

Q	M	T	P	F	P	P	L	Z	R	Y	T	I	X	D	S	M	L	K	N	D	J	Q	F	Z
M	M	Y	R	Y	A	T	M	G	L	M	R	Y	D	F	W	T	U	N	V	F	V	Z	G	J
I	N	A	R	H	L	P	I	I	K	H	Z	F	K	Z	V	H	M	F	S	U	U	K	M	X
L	T	I	M	E	M	V	X	I	V	Y	I	P	A	K	Z	K	H	O	F	L	X	I	A	Q
E	R	T	C	V	A	W	X	M	N	Z	L	O	P	B	I	C	E	J	G	N	B	O	O	R
S	I	Q	R	F	R	U	M	E	L	A	T	D	L	S	L	X	N	B	C	A	C	Q	Q	X
T	P	E	Q	I	G	E	W	N	U	J	U	M	P	I	N	G	G	R	C	M	J	S	D	U
O	O	L	L	R	N	P	K	O	G	A	K	U	N	W	Z	Q	P	P	F	Q	B	W	R	
N	D	I	W	N	A	L	G	M	N	C	P	G	M	H	X	V	E	H	B	Y	D	R	J	V
E	G	S	K	F	S	G	R	W	K	J	Z	B	K	E	G	R	O	S	S	M	O	T	O	R
R	R	R	H	T	P	H	N	D	F	F	K	V	I	Z	P	C	C	C	J	Z	C	J	S	M
R	A	H	C	D	Q	R	L	B	G	B	I	S	P	B	Q	T	I	S	L	G	V	V	Q	N
P	S	X	V	K	S	W	X	F	M	U	L	K	F	X	G	J	H	S	E	P	R	X	O	B
C	P	C	M	K	V	M	C	N	B	T	F	I	K	O	O	N	X	V	M	N	K	X	D	P
F	H	X	B	U	I	U	W	R	J	R	F	N	W	S	F	P	W	N	D	E	S	F	Y	C
E	L	C	O	O	R	D	I	N	A	T	I	O	N	K	V	I	S	I	O	N	D	O	X	H
C	Y	V	N	P	S	Y	L	C	R	A	W	L	I	N	G	D	X	N	X	M	C	O	R	S
Z	L	L	H	H	J	S	K	N	R	E	X	Z	L	Y	I	K	L	G	W	P	U	A	D	Y
F	K	I	X	T	I	J	P	I	N	C	E	R	G	R	A	S	P	A	J	L	C	J	O	W
A	D	P	M	U	W	F	I	N	E	M	O	T	O	R	M	X	G	H	O	X	L	Y	J	K
G	J	V	B	B	H	H	Z	Z	F	X	E	J	C	E	I	O	S	L	N	M	W	Q	Q	Z
L	I	V	L	V	I	C	E	N	T	I	L	E	C	H	A	R	T	I	M	Q	X	I	F	O
H	Q	Q	Y	K	Y	N	M	C	R	U	I	S	I	N	G	X	N	Q	U	J	S	X	B	Z
N	S	V	I	S	T	S	G	X	B	Q	V	X	N	R	Z	L	N	R	Y	G	V	X	Z	Q
N	E	F	X	F	G	C	W	M	P	B	A	L	A	N	C	E	G	F	A	X	E	W	X	U

Fine motor

Climbing

Palmar grasp

Milestone

Gross motor

Cruising

Tripod grasp

Centile chart

Sensory

Crawling

Balance

Vision

Jumping

Pincer grasp

Coordination

Things to do

Activity 1

Plan an activity which you think will encourage the fine motor skills of a three year old child.

Explain what the aim of the activity would be and what you expect the child to learn from it.

Describe how you would organise the activity (remember to include safety points) and what materials and equipment you would need.

Activity 2

If possible, carry out the activity you planned (see Activity 1).

Write up your observations.

Evaluate how successful your planning and the activity was.

Did the activity encourage other aspects of development?

Explain how.

Activity 3

Try to observe a child playing with a wide range of toys or doing some activity which involves using fine motor skills (e.g. painting, collage).

Look particularly at how the child uses his hands/fingers.

Try to identify the different groups used.

Write up your observations (you could do this as a chart) and compare these with the 'norms' for the age of the child.

Activity 4

Plan and make a book or jigsaw with the child you are studying.

You could use photographs, pictures from magazines, or get the child to do some drawings.

This will help you to look at fine motor skills, as well as other areas of development.

Activity 5

Plan a 'feely bag' or box.

You will need a cardboard box or a bag – preferably a cloth one, such as a shoe bag.

Put a number of different objects inside – both familiar and unfamiliar (choose items suitable for the age of the child).

Try to include items of different textures.

Encourage the child to talk about and describe what they can feel.

This will help both language and sensory skills.

Activity 6

Plan an indoor treasure hunt for the child you are studying.

Activity 7

Set up a simple obstacle course in the garden (make sure it's on a soft area such as grass).

Observe the child you are studying, and note the way in which gross motor skills are used.

Activity 8

Within your class, carry out a survey into when different people reach 'milestones' in physical development.

Present your information as a chart or graph and write up your conclusions.

Intellectual Development

Intellectual development is about learning – about how we use and organise our minds, thoughts and ideas to understand and make sense of the world we live in. In this section we will look at the ways in which children learn:

◆ to think
◆ to reason
◆ to understand

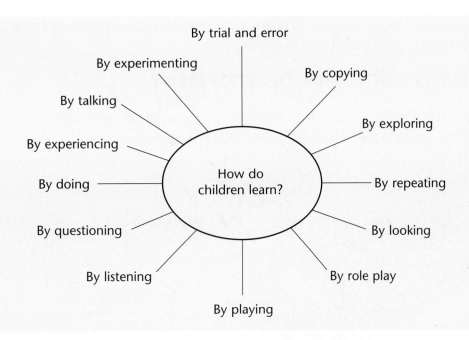

Understanding how children learn, how their thoughts and ideas develop, is very complicated. The spider diagram above shows some of the different ways children might 'learn' – and in any one day, they could use all of these different ways (and more) at some time.

This means that it is sometimes difficult to separate intellectual development from the other areas of development.

◆ Children learn through their **senses** – by touching, tasting, listening and through active play – all **physical** experiences

◆ Children play and relate to other children and people **socially** and **emotionally**

◆ Children also need **language** and **communication skills**, the important tools of intellectual development

The two main strands of intellectual development are:

LANGUAGE DEVELOPMENT	COGNITIVE DEVELOPMENT
the way children acquire the skills of communication	the way children acquire the skills of communication

There is a strong and clear link between the two strands, and it is almost impossible to understand children's cognitive development without looking at how their language skills develop (see page 315). Language is the tool which enables us to make sense of our world. It helps us to organise our thoughts, knowledge and understanding into **concepts** – these can be simple such as size, shape, colour or complex and abstract such as time, silence and space. Language helps us to make connections, and to ask questions about what we see. It helps us to develop and progress from simple understanding to more complex ideas.

⊃ WHAT IS COGNITIVE DEVELOPMENT?

Cognitive development is about how we use our minds, and organise our thinking to understand our world and our place in it.

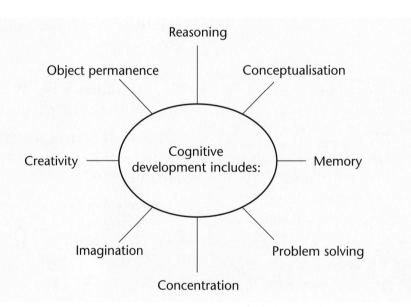

Imagination is the ability to picture things when they are not in front of us, or when they do not exist.

Children use their imaginations to play pretend games and to tell stories. They also use it when drawing, painting, reading, dancing, making models and dressing up.

Problem solving is the ability to solve both simple and complex problems, e.g. shapes in a shape sorter and riding a bike. The ability to solve problems tends to follow a set pattern.

Trial and error

↓

Identify the problem

↓

Work out a solution

↓

Predict what might happen (hypothesise)

Creativity is the ability to express imaginative ideas in an individual and unique way.

Children are creative when they paint, make collages and junk toys, dance, make music, etc.

Conceptualisation is the ability to understand and use concepts. These are ideas we use to help organise information into an understandable form.

Children need to begin to learn to understand concepts of number, colour, shape, time, volume, speed, etc.

Memory is the ability to store and recall information, ideas and events. We have both

◆ short-term memories – this allows us to remember things as we need to e.g. shopping lists

◆ long-term memories, which allows us to store information until it is needed. We often need a 'trigger' to 'jog' our long-term memories e.g. a smell, a name, a picture.

Concentration is the ability to pay attention on one particular task.

Children tend to concentrate more on things in which they are interested.

Children need to be able to concentrate so that they can learn, store and sort information.

Object permanence is the ability to understand that something still exists even when it is out of sight.

Children show their understanding of this when they play hide and seek, hunt the thimble, etc.

Reasoning is the ability to understand that whatever actions we take have a cause and effect

If you press the button on the toy, the animal pops up.

THE NATURE V NURTURE DEBATE

Are children born intelligent or does the 'environment' they are born into and grow up in develop their intelligence? This is the basis of what people call the **'nature v nurture'** debate, and influence how they believe children learn.

Some people believe that intelligence is determined at conception through the **genes** inherited from the parents. Others believe that the quality of the child's **environment**, including the people the child comes into contact with (especially when they are very young) has a greater influence on how their intelligence develops.

Initially, it was believed that children were born with a fixed level of intelligence, and that this would never change – however that view is no longer accepted, and it would seem that both 'nature' and 'nurture' have their part to play in the development of learning and understanding). Over the years psychologists (specialist in human behaviour) have studied the way children think and learn and produced some theories, which help us to understand cognitive development.

Theories about how children learn

There are three types of theory

◆ The social learning theory
◆ The behaviourist theory
◆ The developmentalist theory

Social Learning Theory

This theory was first developed by Alfred Bandura. He believed that children learn by looking at the behaviour of adults, and other people they see, and copying what they have seen (see Chapter 16).

Behaviourist Theory

Behaviourists are groups of psychologists who believe that learning takes place though actions and experiences, and that we will repeat actions and experiences which are enjoyable and avoid those which are not. The psychologist Burrhas F. Skinner believed that praise and reward (positive reinforcements) would encourage children to repeat the experience and develop learning (see Chapter 16).

Developmentalist Theory

Some psychologists have based their theories on the belief that learning is linked very closely to defined stages of development, and that children will go through these stages but at varying speeds. Perhaps the most influential of these psychologists was Jean Piaget (1896-1980).

As well as studying his own children, Piaget was involved with carrying out intelligence tests with young children. Through these, he discovered that children's answers followed a logical pattern, but that this was different to adults, and seemed to be based on their own experiences. He called these answers **schemas**.

He also believed that as children learned new concepts and had new and different experiences, they would adapt or change their schema. He called this **assimilation** (adapting) and **accommodation** (changing). From this Piaget decided that children went through four very different, but distinct, stages of learning, and that these stages could be linked to approximate ages. He also believed that children would not move from one stage to another before they were ready, and would not 'skip' a stage.

Piaget's Stages

Stage	Age	Title	Description of Learning
1	0-2 yrs	Sensory Motor	At this stage children: ◆ learn mainly through the **senses**, especially touch, taste and hearing. ◆ are **egocentric** – they see the world only from their own point of view. ◆ begin to be aware of **object permanence** – that a person or an object they cannot see still exists. This usually happens at about 8 months. ◆ learn through trial and error. ◆ have only limited language skills.
2	2-7 yrs	Pre-operational	At this stage children: ◆ still learn through the sense of taste and touch, but hearing becomes more important now. ◆ are still egocentric. ◆ have better language skills and begin to use these to ask questions and put their thoughts, ideas and feelings into words. ◆ use symbols in play – so teddy becomes a baby or a bus driver (pretend play see page 356). ◆ believe that objects and animals have the same thoughts and feelings as themselves – **animism**. As children get towards the end of this stage they: ◆ begin to learn about **concepts**. ◆ become more involved in pretend play. ◆ begin to understand right and wrong, but in a very simple way. ◆ use symbols more – in play, language and drawing.

Stage	Age	Title	Description of Learning
3	7-11 yrs	Concrete operational	By now children: ◆ can see things from other people's point of view – they can **decentre** ◆ begin to develop more complex reasoning skills – but they will still need to use objects to help them to understand and solve problems ◆ understand that things are not always what they seem – they can **conserve** ◆ understand that non-living things do not have feelings.
4	12-adult	Formal operational	At this stage children: ◆ can think logically ◆ can think abstractly – that is they can manipulate ideas in their head and don't need to use objects to help them solve problems. ◆ Understand more complex concepts.

⊃ More about Concepts

Concepts are ways in which we organise our knowledge, information and thinking, so that we can understand and make sense of the world we live in. They are also important, because they allow us to communicate with other people and share ideas and opinions.

We need to **learn** concepts.

Some are quite simple and easy to understand, such as colour, size and shape, and children will learn these quite early. Others are more complex and will take a long time to understand, such as the concepts of space and time. Some concepts we may never fully understand!!

Colour is one example of a concept.

Look at the pictures on page 310. The coat, bus, umbrella, bicycle, ball and flowers are all yellow, although they are all different shades, and we recognise them as yellow.

But – if we tried to explain how we *know* that they are yellow or what it is that makes them yellow, or what exactly 'yellow' means, we would find it very difficult. We just know that they are yellow!

This is because as adults we have stored and sorted different pieces of information and ideas in our memories which help us to recognise and identify yellow as yellow – whatever the shade!

⤷ Learning about Concepts

Children need to learn many different concepts.

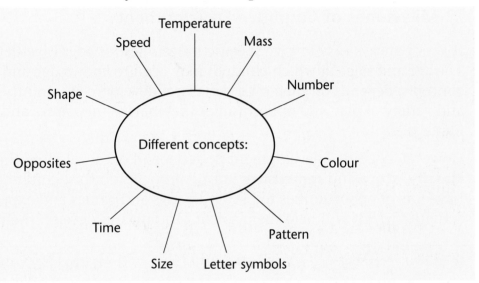

Children learn about some concepts just by seeing and experiencing, but to understand others, they need the help of adults. It is important that parents, families and other adults who deal with children, such as carers and teachers, support or **facilitate** children's learning. They can do this by making sure that children have lots of opportunities to explore, discover and investigate, to play with different toys, games and activities. They also need to spend time playing with children, talking to them and answering their questions, and offering praise and encouragement.

Remember

Intellectual development has two main strands – cognitive skills and language skills. However it is also closely linked to physical, social and emotional development. Intellectual development can be helped by parents spending time with children and giving them lots of opportunities to play, investigate and explore.

Key Words

Animism belief that objects and animals have the same feelings as humans

Cognitive to do with thinking and understanding

Concept a way of organising knowledge and information so it can be understood

Conservation understanding that even if material changes shape or form, the actual amount remains the same e.g. water in different size/shape containers

Decentre seeing things from other people's point of view

Egocentric self centred

Facilitate make easy or easier

Nature the talent and abilities we might inherit

Nurture outside factors which can influence development

Object permanence understanding that objects and people still exist even when out of sight

Milestones of Cognitive Development

It is not always easy to give specific milestones for cognitive development. The age and stage at which children may acquire knowledge and understand concepts, depends on their own pattern of development, and the range and variety of play and opportunities they have – the nature and nurture idea again.

However, cognitive development does depend on developing the ability to **classify**, **store** and **remember** information. To do this, children need to have lots of opportunities to play with toys and games and experience other activities which will help them to concentrate and develop their memories.

Age	Stage of Development	Suitatble toys and activities
0-12 months	◆ uses mouth and touch to explore ◆ watches and copy adults ◆ repeats actions e.g. dropping a rattle or brick ◆ looks for an object which has been taken away ◆ finds an object which has been seen and hidden ◆ places an object such as a brick in a container when asked	◆ Rattles ◆ Teething rings ◆ Soft squeaky toys ◆ Finger rhymes and actions ◆ Activity centres ◆ Mobiles ◆ 'Feely' toys ◆ Peek-a-boo game
12 months- 2 years	◆ points to parts of the body ◆ learns about things through trial and error ◆ recognises and points to a named picture or object ◆ scribbles on paper ◆ can take out objects one by one from a container	◆ 'Feely' bags and boxes ◆ Activity mats ◆ Paper and large crayons ◆ Building bricks ◆ Musical toys ◆ Cause and effect toys e.g. 'Jack in the box'

Age	Stage of Development	Suitable toys and activities
2–3 years	◆ begins to show some reasoning skills but still learns mainly by trial and error ◆ can copy a circle ◆ can complete a simple 3–5 piece puzzle ◆ recognises and matches different textures ◆ can stack beakers in order ◆ matches three colours ◆ uses everyday objects in pretend play e.g. wooden spoon may be sword, a cardboard box, a car	◆ Any safe household items ◆ Simple games and large puzzles ◆ Paints, crayons, paper ◆ Construction toys e.g. Lego ◆ Dressing up clothes ◆ Any toys or objects for imaginative play ◆ Alphabet games ◆ Playdough/plasticine ◆ Simple cooking activities ◆ Trips to new places e.g. zoos, farms ◆ Visits to library ◆ Musical instruments
3–4 years	◆ asks lots of questions ◆ can sort out simple objects ◆ recognises long or short objects ◆ knows and names three shapes ◆ can count ten objects with help ◆ recognises letters, numbers ◆ knows primary colours ◆ can say which of two objects is heavy and light ◆ can repeat a simple story	◆ Jigsaw puzzles ◆ Magnetic boards with letters and numbers ◆ Toys for imaginative play e.g. dolls ◆ House, farms, garages ◆ Construction sets ◆ Books ◆ Dressing up toys ◆ Water and sand play
4–5 years	◆ can pick up a number of objects if asked e.g. 4 sweets ◆ can name 5 textures ◆ can name 8 colours ◆ begins to understand use of symbols e.g. letters and numbers in reading and writing ◆ can count up to 20 by rote ◆ uses reason based on experience ◆ can understand simple rules in games ◆ can name times of day e.g. bedtime	◆ Board games ◆ More complex jigsaw ◆ Matching games ◆ Simple card games e.g. snap ◆ Dominoes ◆ Cardboard boxes to create cars, furniture, cartons etc. ◆ Items to make 'dens' ◆ Visits to zoos, museums, theatre, cinema ◆ Simple scientific toys e.g. magnifying glass, binoculars

⟳ Toys, Games and other Activities

As we have already seen, cognitive development depends on the ability to be able to group, sort, remember and recall information. Therefore it is very important for parents not to just buy toys and games because they look attractive and interesting, but to think about how they will help children to learn. They also need to plan different games and activities that will encourage these skills, and above all, spend time playing and working with the child.

Look at some of the following activity. It shows how something as simple as threading beads can help cognitive development as well as helping children to concentrate and develop memory skills.

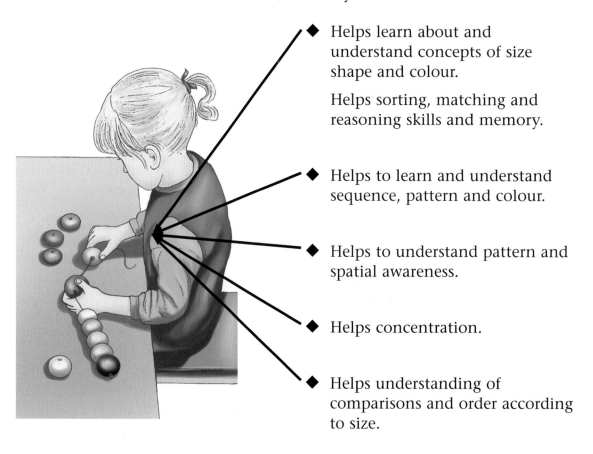

Helps learn about and understand concepts of size shape and colour.

Helps sorting, matching and reasoning skills and memory.

Helps to learn and understand sequence, pattern and colour.

Helps to understand pattern and spatial awareness.

Helps concentration.

Helps understanding of comparisons and order according to size.

Remember

Toys, games and activities need not always be expensive or bought. Playing with safe household items will give lots of opportunities for cognitive development (see Chapter 17).

Cognitive development can be hindered by

◆ frequent illness

◆ absence from school

◆ defective eyesight

◆ defective hearing

◆ lack of verbal communication

◆ lack of stimulation

◆ feelings of insecurity

◆ poor concentration

◆ lack of confidence

◆ lack of contact with other people

⊃ HOW DOES LANGUAGE DEVELOP?

In this section we will look at:
- why language is important
- how language skills are acquired
- the stages of language development
- factors which may affect development

⊃ The Importance of Language

As in all development the acquisition of language follows a distinct pattern, but the rate of progress will depend on the individual child. This often depends on the (chronological) age of the child but the opportunities they have to work, to experiment with and to use language are very important.

Language is very closely linked to cognitive development. The world is a complex place – to be able to make sense of it we need to be able to organise our thinking from more than simple understanding of what is there. We need to be able to predict and hypothesise – language allows us to talk about things that are concrete and abstract, e.g. silence.

All humans are born with a need to communicate – language is the tool which allows them to do this. It begins very simply with crying sounds used to tell parents how the baby is feeling and builds up quickly until by the age of 5 the child can use a huge range of words, put together in complex sentences to describe, question, discuss, express feelings etc.

⊃ Learning to talk

Language has to be learnt. All babies babble in some way, even deaf babies. Language development begins at birth – a new mother's initial reaction when first holding her baby is to hold her close, look directly into her face and talk to her. This is the surest way to give her a good start.

To be able to make speech sounds babies must learn to control many different muscles. They need to practise pushing lips and tongue forward and backwards, up and down while at the same time taking in air.

Most children pass through two distinct phases of language development: **pre-linguistic** and **linguistic.**

Pre-linguistic

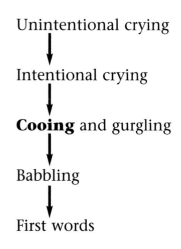

Unintentional crying

↓

Intentional crying

↓

Cooing and gurgling

↓

Babbling

↓

First words

This phase usually lasts from birth to 12 months. During this time babies cry, smile, use facial expression and make sounds such as cooing and grunting to attract attention. This is how they begin to communicate.

Linguistic

First words

↓

Holophrases

↓

Jargon

↓

Telegraphic sentences

↓

Complex sentences

This usually begins between 12 and 15 months. It is the phase when children begin to use recognisable words to communicate. They use these words as labels for familiar objects, e.g. dog, cup, ball, then gradually progress to simple, then more complex sentences.

Approximate Age	Level of Development
Birth	Involuntary crying
4 weeks	Voluntary crying to show tiredness, hunger, boredom, etc. May smile and stop crying when spoken to. Begins to make guttural sounds
6 weeks	Coos and gurgles to show contentment
8 weeks	Moves eye and head towards direction of sound
3 months	Raises head when sound attracts attention being to control muscles of lips, tongue and voice box. May being to babble
6 months	Cooing may cease Babbling is more repetitive, e.g. da,da,da and more tuneful (echolalia) Laughs, chuckles and squeals Screams with annoyance

Approximate Age	Level of Development
9 months	Repeats syllables, e.g. dad,dad mum,mum ba,ba Uses sound deliberately to express emotions Imitates sounds, e.g. smack lips, blows raspberries May understand simple words, e.g. own name, no, bye-bye
12 months	Imitates simple words Begins to point, usually at the beginning of a word, showing understanding Words are symbolic Understands simple commands Babbling becomes more tuneful and reflects the intonation of speech Develops first words (active vocabulary) They understand more than they can vocalise (passive vocabulary) Talks incessantly in their 'own' language (Jargon) Can understand and act upon simple instructions, e.g. 'Say bye-bye'
15 months	Uses several words which carers understand Points using single words to indicate items Acquisition of new words may slow down as physical development accelerates
18 months	Active vocabulary increases Can point to named object, e.g. nose, ball, teddy Words are used to mean more than one thing, e.g. 'cup' may mean 'Where is my cup?' 'I want my cup', 'I've dropped my cup' (holophrase) Echoes and repeats words
2 years	New words learnt quickly May use short, telegraphic sentences, e.g. 'Me want ball' Begin to use pronouns, e.g. me, I, you Frequently asks questions, e.g. Where Teddy? Begins to use negative, e.g. 'No Teddy'
3 years	Vocabulary is large Sentences longer and close to adult speech Often holds imaginary conversations Begins to use language to express thought, ideas and feelings Can describe past and present experiences Incessantly asks questions: Why? Where? What? How? May use incorrect word ending, e.g. drawed, sheeps
4 years +	Vocabulary now very extensive Sentences longer and more complex Uses language to socialise, argue, and show feelings, give explanations and predict what may happen (hypothesise) Enjoys telling jokes Play involves running commentaries Enjoys telling long stories but may confuse fact and fantasy Speech is more grammatically correct

Key Words

Active vocabulary the words a child is able to use

Cooing the earliest sounds used to show contentment

Crying until one month the only real sound made. Changes in tone may indicate hunger, boredom, discomfort, etc

Holophrase where one word may be used for more than one thing depending on the intonation

Jargon the child's 'own' language which may be understood only by those close to them

Monosyllabic babbling the repetition of single syllables with no meaning, e.g. ba ba ba ba. This is sometimes called echolalia

Motherese is used to describe the way in which adults speak to a baby in a simple, slow, clear rhythmic manner. It is not baby talk.

Passive vocabulary the words a child may understand but cannot yet use

Polysyllabic babbling long strings of different syllables, e.g. do-da-dee-do. This is sometimes known as scribble talk when changes in tone and pitch may sound like conversation.

Telegraphic speech when sentences are used without the linking words, e.g. 'Me want drink'

All children need to be talked to, listened to, praised and encouraged. They need to be given the chance to practise their skills and make mistakes.

Parents can help by:

- using different intonation
- speaking clearly
- speaking slowly
- always answering
- listening
- asking questions
- correcting sympathetically
- being patient

There are some children who, in spite of all normal efforts, support and encouragement, do not begin to speak or whose speech is distorted. This could be due to emotional pressure and/or disabilities (see chapter 18 Special Children).

⟳ READING

Reading is one of the most important skills a child needs to learn. In this section we will concentrate on examining:

- why reading is important
- how parents can begin to prepare children for reading

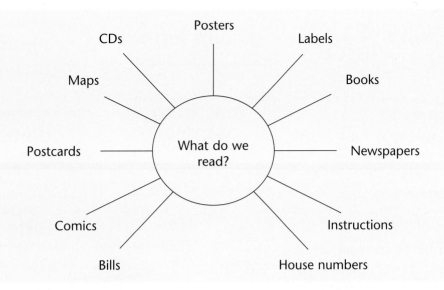

Babies are born into a world where they are surrounded by words and symbols. Learning to read means being able to recognise, interpret, and understand hundreds of symbols and combinations of symbols in a meaningful way.

As with other aspects of development this process is gradual and continuous, beginning with:

◆ the recognition of picture symbols

◆ then linking alphabet symbols to picture symbols

a

◆ and finally recognising combinations of alphabet symbols and linking these to a picture symbol

apple

This process takes time and 'real' reading, i.e. recognising and correctly interpreting the symbols, may not begin fully until a child is 4+. Learning to read goes hand in hand with other aspects of development. Looking at books is, of course, an important way of encouraging children to read.

However, there are many other fun activities which parents could share with a child which would make the process easier.

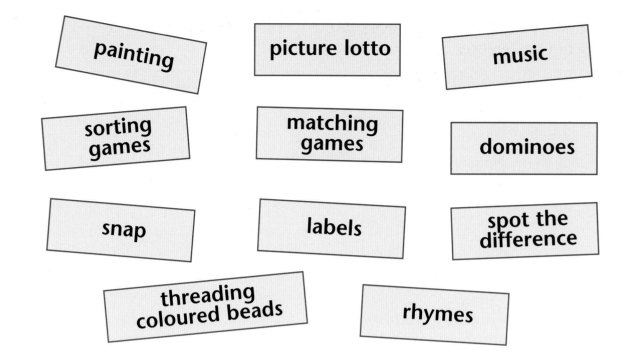

painting

picture lotto

music

sorting games

matching games

dominoes

snap

labels

spot the difference

threading coloured beads

rhymes

All of these activities will help a child to develop the sort of skills and understanding they need for reading.

Children need to understand that symbols on paper have meaning.

Children need to acquire the **visual discrimination** to be able to identify differences and similarities.

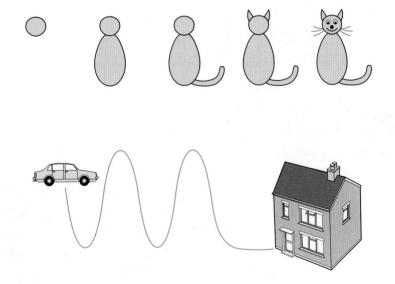

Children need to recognise the importance of order and sequence.

Children need to be helped to learn more practical skills:

◆ begin at the top of the page
◆ hold book the right way up
◆ read from left to right
◆ turn page from right to left

⊃ The Importance of Books

Books are the obvious and most effective tools we can use to help children to learn to read. It is, therefore, important that from a very early age children have access to books. However, these are of little value if parents do not spend time with their children looking at pictures, telling stories, asking questions and having fun together.

It is important that books are well chosen. (See The Importance of Books in Chapter 17 Play and Toys.)

Just as when learning to walk and talk, some children find reading easier than others. Children will learn to read when they are ready and must be allowed to progress at their own pace. There should be no pressure from parents since this may lead to a reluctance to learn.

> ### Key Words
> **Visual discrimination** the ability to recognise similarities and differences

⊃ DRAWING AND WRITING

> This section will examine
> ◆ how children develop drawing and writing skills

Most children love to draw and paint, and from an early age toddlers will enjoy making marks on paper although they will not represent any real meaning. Encouraging children to handle crayons, paint brushes and pens will develop fine manipulative skills and good hand–eye co-ordination. Through trial and error they will eventually develop good pencil control and the drawing symbols will represent their thoughts more clearly. This process shows the foundation of sound writing skills where a child will be able to hold a pencil effectively, form recognisable letters, write their own name and form simple sentences.

As with all other areas of development children will develop at their own rate and the ages stated are simply a guideline to the child's progression. A number of factors may affect a child's interest and development in drawing and writing:

- encouragement and praise from parents, guardians and siblings
- a wide variety of drawing implements available, e.g. chunky wax crayons, crayons, washable felt tip pens, chalk
- lots of cheap paper
- suitable table and chair
- copying good examples of how to hold a pencil
- good pencil control can be assisted with books containing exercises, e.g. joining dots, copying patterns, letter formation
- letting the child paint freely with a protective apron
- colouring-in books encourage skilful pencil control
- allowing a child to choose the preferred hand for writing
- white/blackboard
- making it fun
- using an easel
- playgroup, nurseries and childminders could encourage drawing

⊃ Sequence of Drawing and Writing Skills

Approximate Age	Drawing	Crayon Control
15 months		Grasps crayon half way up, with the palmar grasp with either hand. Scribbles to and fro.
18 months		May still use either hand to draw. Could be showing preference for one hand or the other. Could demonstrate a primitive tripod grasp (thumb and first two fingers). Scribbles and dots.
2 years		Attempts to hold the pencil close to the point in a primitive tripod grasp. May make a letter V. Vertical lines and circular scribble forming

Approximate Age	Drawing	Crayon Control
2½ years		Improved tripod grasp. Recognisable circle. Horizontal lines and circles. May produce a V and T.
3 years		Has quite good control of the crayon between first two fingers and thumb. Shows preference for left or right hand. Can copy a circle but it does not always join up. May write V,H,T. draws a person and head with one or two features.
4 years		Holds a pencil like an adult with quite good control. Can colour in pictures but not always with the lines. V,H,T,O may be copied. Begins to trace shapes, letters and numbers formed by dots, e.g. draws a potato person with head, legs and trunk, may no have arms and legs with digits. Names drawings.
5 years		Good control of a pencil. Can copy circles, squares, triangles and T,H,O,X,C,A,C,U,Y. May write own name and simple words. Can draw a house with windows, door, chimney and roof. Pictures now have a background, i.e. sky. Can colour in a picture and stay within the outline.

Once children have mastered the art of drawing a recognisable circle, they will then begin to represent a person by making markings within the circle which represents two eyes, nose and a mouth resembling a potato person. This will progress to more features representing arms and legs from the head. At first there will be no body mass. Finally a body appears and the legs have feet and toes. Clothes are then added to represent characters that are familiar to the child's environment. Eventually drawings will become more recognisable and will contain more complex detail.

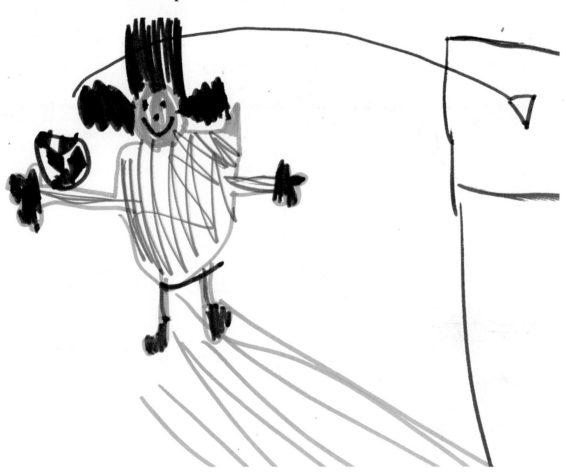

From the age of 5 drawings of houses look recognisable. Pictures usually have sky and grass with a simple tree. Animals look more realistic with tails and have their feet on the ground.

Also from the age of 5 children will have gained good pencil control and their writing will be more recognisable. At this stage children spell phonetically (how the word sounds literally) and their writing reflects this.

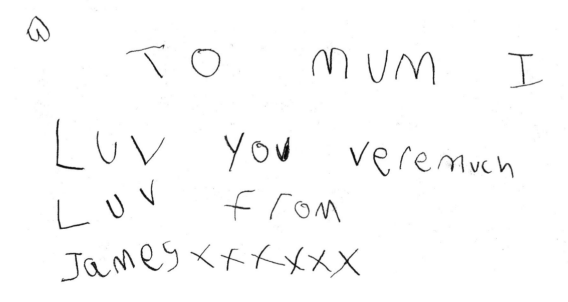

Questions

Question 1

a   Describe what is meant by *intellectual development*.

b   Intellectual development involves two main strands.

   Name and describe the two strands of intellectual development.

c   Children will learn in lots of different ways.

   List *eight* ways in which children might learn.

d   Why is language development so important for cognitive development?

e   Explain how intellectual development is closely linked to physical, social and emotional development.

Question 2

Cognitive development involves several different aspects.

Name and describe *eight* aspects of cognitive development.

Question 3

a   What is meant by the *'nature v nurture'* debate?

b   i   Name and briefly describe the *three* main theories about how children learn.

   ii   According to Piaget, children aged between 2 and 7 years are at the *pre-operational stage* of development.

Describe how you would expect a child to act and learn at this stage.

c   i   What is a *concept*? Why are concepts so important?

   ii   Name *two* simple concepts.

   iii   Name *two* more complex concepts.

Question 4

Parents and other adults, such as carers and teachers need to *'facilitate'* children's learning.

a   What does this mean?

b   How could this be done?

Question 5

a   Describe the stage of intellectual development you might have expected the following to reach

   i   12–24 month old toddler

   ii   3–4 year old child

b   Suggest *three* different types of toys or activities which would help the children in part a. Give reasons.

Question 6

List six reasons why intellectual development might be hindered.

Things to do

Activity 1

Design and make a simple game using only basic materials paper, card, coloured pens/pencils etc., which would help a child to develop one or more of the following concepts:

numbers
colour
shapes
time

In your planning, identify a suitable age for the game.

Explain your reasons by referring to normal stages of intellectual and physical development. Explain how and why your game would work.

Activity 2

If possible, try to arrange to play the game with a child. It would be best if the child was the same age as the age you planned it for.

Was the game successful? Explain how and why.

What changes might you make to it? Why?

Activity 3

Organise and play a game of "Simon Says" with the child you are studying (and possibly with a friend of the child's).

This will help you to look at language and understanding as well as social skills.

Activity 4

Try to organise a visit to a nursery.

Draw a plan of the nursery showing the different areas and activities provided.

From your plan and observations, identify which aspects of intellectual development are being encouraged and how.

Activity 5

Use a TV guide and identify the programmes offered for the under 5's during and one day/week.

Produce a chart of your results, showing such things as:

– Title
– Type of programme cartoon, puppet, activity etc.
– Time of programme
– Length of programme
– Content

Evaluate your findings.

Activity 6

Try to arrange to watch two different kinds of children's TV programmes and carry out a programme review.

Give details of the programme (title, time on, length etc.) and a resumé of the content and how it was presented.

Evaluate its suitability for the age range, both as entertainment and as learning.

⊃ INTELLECTUAL DEVELOPMENT WORDSEARCH

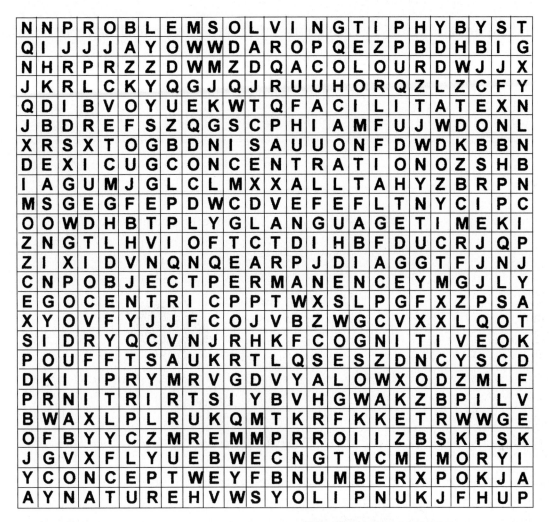

N	N	P	R	O	B	L	E	M	S	O	L	V	I	N	G	T	I	P	H	Y	B	Y	S	T
Q	I	J	J	J	A	Y	O	W	W	D	A	R	O	P	Q	E	Z	P	B	D	H	B	I	G
N	H	R	P	R	Z	Z	D	W	M	Z	D	Q	A	C	O	L	O	U	R	D	W	J	J	X
J	K	R	L	C	K	Y	Q	G	J	Q	J	R	U	U	H	O	R	Q	Z	L	Z	C	F	Y
Q	D	I	B	V	O	Y	U	E	K	W	T	Q	F	A	C	I	L	I	T	A	T	E	X	N
J	B	D	R	E	F	S	Z	Q	G	S	C	P	H	I	A	M	F	U	J	W	D	O	N	L
X	R	S	X	T	O	G	B	D	N	I	S	A	U	U	O	N	F	D	W	D	K	B	B	N
D	E	X	I	C	U	G	C	O	N	C	E	N	T	R	A	T	I	O	N	O	Z	S	H	B
I	A	G	U	M	J	G	L	C	L	M	X	X	A	L	L	T	A	H	Y	Z	B	R	P	N
M	S	G	E	G	F	E	P	D	W	C	D	V	E	F	E	F	L	T	N	Y	C	I	P	C
O	O	W	D	H	B	T	P	L	Y	G	L	A	N	G	U	A	G	E	T	I	M	E	K	I
Z	N	G	T	L	H	V	I	O	F	T	C	T	D	I	H	B	F	D	U	C	R	J	Q	P
Z	I	X	I	D	V	N	Q	N	Q	E	A	R	P	J	D	I	A	G	G	T	F	J	N	J
C	N	P	O	B	J	E	C	T	P	E	R	M	A	N	E	N	C	E	Y	M	G	J	L	Y
E	G	O	C	E	N	T	R	I	C	P	P	T	W	X	S	L	P	G	F	X	Z	P	S	A
X	Y	O	V	F	Y	J	J	F	C	O	J	V	B	Z	W	G	C	V	X	X	L	Q	O	T
S	I	D	R	Y	Q	C	V	N	J	R	H	K	F	C	O	G	N	I	T	I	V	E	O	K
P	O	U	F	F	T	S	A	U	K	R	T	L	Q	S	E	S	Z	D	N	C	Y	S	C	D
D	K	I	I	P	R	Y	M	R	V	G	D	V	Y	A	L	O	W	X	O	D	Z	M	L	F
P	R	N	I	T	R	I	R	T	S	I	Y	B	V	H	G	W	A	K	Z	B	P	I	L	V
B	W	A	X	L	P	L	R	U	K	Q	M	T	K	R	F	K	K	E	T	R	W	W	G	E
O	F	B	Y	Y	C	Z	M	R	E	M	M	P	R	R	O	I	I	Z	B	S	K	P	S	K
J	G	V	X	F	L	Y	U	E	B	W	E	C	N	G	T	W	C	M	E	M	O	R	Y	I
Y	C	O	N	C	E	P	T	W	E	Y	F	B	N	U	M	B	E	R	X	P	O	K	J	A
A	Y	N	A	T	U	R	E	H	V	W	S	Y	O	L	I	P	N	U	K	J	F	H	U	P

Language	**Object permanence**
Nature	**Facilitate**
Number	**Concept**
Memory	**Colour**
Reasoning	**Concentration**
Cognitive	**Problem solving**
Nurture	**Egocentric**
Time	

Children are born into a world that they have to share with others.
In this section we will look at:
- how children learn to share, respect and understand others
- how children learn to cope with feelings and emotion
- the importance of self-image and self-esteem

Social development and **emotional development** are very complex processes, and are very difficult to separate. For example, adults are expected to have more control over their own behaviour and feelings than children. Yet the way some adults act, behave and treat others can depend on may different factors such as, whether they feel happy or sad, what someone has said to them and how it affected them, whether they feel ill or tired, or even what the weather is like.

All of these factors, and many more, can affect how we act. Learning to balance and control feelings and behaviour is a skill which children need to develop – and this learning will go on throughout their childhood and adult life.

⊃ THE THEORIES

There are many different theories about how and why children develop their personalities and relationships with others. The three main ones are:

- The Social Learning Theory of Albert Bandura
- The Psychoanalytical Theories of Sigmund Freud and Erik Erikson
- The Attachment Theory of John Bowlby

The Social Learning Theory

This theory is often used to explain how children act and behave (See Behaviour Page 344-350). It is also used to explain how children's **personalities** develop, suggesting that children will copy and take on the characteristics of their parents. So, if parents are happy, outgoing and friendly, children will be more likely to develop similar characteristics.

The Psychoanalytical Theories

These theories are more complicated. In very simple terms, Freud and Erikson believed that children's personalities and behaviour are shaped both **consciously** and **unconsciously** by their experiences at different stages of their development, and how they cope with the experiences.

Freud believed that physical needs were the main influence, while Erikson felt that stages of development were more linked to intellectual and social development. Erikson also believed that personalities carry on developing and changing all through life.

The Attachment Theory

This suggests that children's main need is to have a strong and stable relationship with their **primary carer** – usually their parent(s). Their ability to develop and relate to other people is dependent on how secure this relationship is. Originally, this theory was used as the basis for the belief that mothers should not work, and should stay at home with their children. However, it has developed from this, and it is now accepted that even very young children can have *more* than one close relationship, and as long as this exists, their social and emotional development will be secure.

THE IMPORTANCE OF BONDING

Bonding describes the close two-way feelings and relationships that develop between a baby and an adult. Once the bond is made and becomes strong, the child will want to stay close to that adult, and be cared for by them. When that adult is not with them, or leaves them, children may suffer from **separation anxiety**. They will become emotionally upset and distressed, because they think that the adult will not come back.

Bonding is a very important factor in a child's social and emotional development, and forms a main part of John Bowlby's Attachment Theory (see above). Bowlby believed that babies had a biological instinctive need to form an attachment to the person who fed and cared for them – initially the mother. His theory was developed further to show that babies could, in fact, form several attachments, and needed to, for successful social and emotional development.

⊃ Factors Which can Encourage Bonding

Although physical bonding will only begin at birth, there are other factors which can help, both before and during the actual birth process.

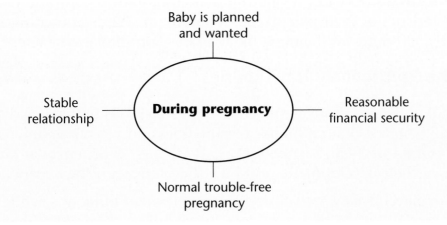

Baby is planned
and wanted

Stable
relationship — **During pregnancy** — Reasonable
financial security

Normal trouble-free
pregnancy

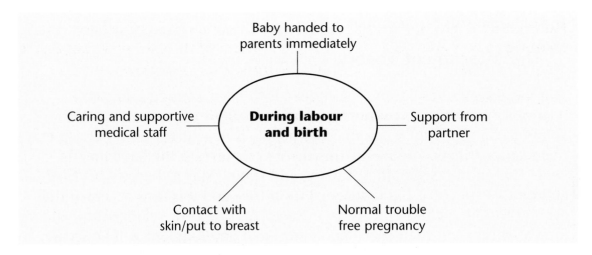

Baby handed to
parents immediately

Caring and supportive
medical staff — **During labour
and birth** — Support from
partner

Contact with
skin/put to breast — Normal trouble
free pregnancy

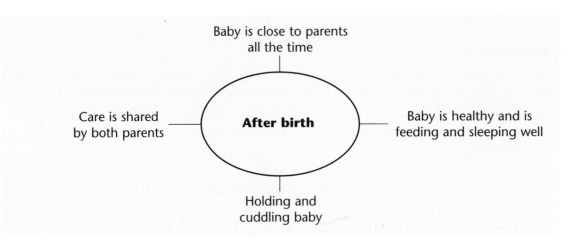

Baby is close to parents
all the time

Care is shared
by both parents — **After birth** — Baby is healthy and is
feeding and sleeping well

Holding and
cuddling baby

STAGES OF SOCIAL AND EMOTIONAL DEVELOPMENT

Although there are different and definite stages of social and emotional development, and although ages can be given as a guideline, the actual age at which children will reach each stage will vary greatly and depend on many factors.

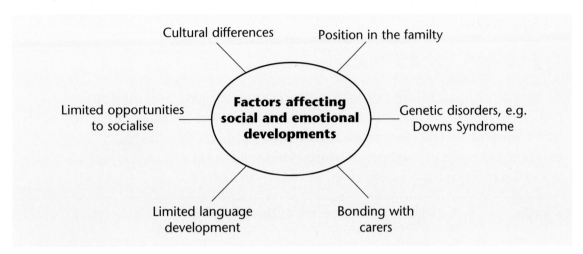

Birth to 1 Year

During this stage children are solely dependent on others. They are learning to communicate their needs and learning through play. Contact is sensory through touch, eye contact, by cries, smiles and coos.

1 month	◆ watches parent's/carer's face
3 months	◆ will smile and coo to show pleasure and enjoyment ◆ likes to be cuddled
6 months	◆ will enjoy being played with ◆ laughs
9 months	◆ can tell the difference between family and strangers ◆ will show fear of strangers
12 months	◆ will show affection for parents and family ◆ will want to be close to familiar people ◆ will play on their own (**solitary play**) ◆ will wave bye-bye

Between 1 and 2 Years

At this age children are very **egocentric** – this means that they see things only from their own point of view. They are often very demanding and can be defiant. They want their own way, and they want it now.

15 months	◆ will be more adventurous and want to explore **BUT**
	◆ will still need a familiar adult near
	◆ will begin to use words to communicate
	◆ will have a stronger feeling of being an individual
18 months	◆ will show strong and different emotions – fear, anger, happiness
	◆ will have a greater vocabulary so can communicate more easily
	◆ will still be shy of strangers and need a familiar adult close to them

⟃ Between 2 and 3 Years

At this age children are becoming more independent and adventurous, but because they still don't have total control over language and physical skills they are often frustrated at not being able to do what they want to do. Emotions are strong and temper tantrums frequent, although they do occur less frequently as the child gets to 3 years old.

2 years	◆ will play near other children (**parallel play**)
	◆ will act out ideas and feelings through pretend play
	◆ will copy and imitate adults
	◆ are prone to tantrums and show strong emotions
	◆ still very egocentric
	◆ will have a strong sense of their own identity
3 years	◆ are beginning to understand gender and age
	◆ will begin to show interest in other children and to play with them
	◆ show feelings and concern for others
	◆ becoming less egocentric and may not demand immediate and full attention from adults

⟃ Between 4 and 5 Years

At this age children are usually friendlier, more confident and more trusting. They are usually more social, and are beginning to make friends and lasting friendships.

4 years	◆ will be very affectionate towards family, friends and people they see often
	◆ will begin to play with others (**co-operative play**)
	◆ will play on their own for long periods of time without adult attention
	◆ will share toys
5 years	◆ are beginning to choose their own friends
	◆ can understand rules and fair play
	◆ will play happily with other children (**co-operative play**)
	◆ are more confident
	◆ will take turns in play activities
	◆ will respond to reasoning
	◆ may start to play more with own sex

⊃ ENCOURAGING SOCIAL DEVELOPMENT

Giving children opportunities to mix and meet with other people, in different environments and situations, is very important for their social development. It gives them confidence, helps them to learn how to respect and be sympathetic to other people's views and feelings, to communicate, to share, and to become independent. Initially parents, close family and any regular carers e.g. child minders, are the main influence on a child's social development. From them children begin to learn the attitudes, values and behaviour patterns which are socially acceptable.

However, as they get older children need wider social experiences. They need to be given opportunities to develop friendships of their own, mix with peers, have contact with young and old alike, experience contact with other cultures and those with special needs in situations where they will see broad gender roles. All of these will help children grow into socially developed adults.

⊃ Examples of Social Experience

◆ Holidays
◆ Mother/Toddler groups
◆ Activity clubs
◆ Parks
◆ Beach

◆ Shopping trips
◆ Swimming pool
◆ Playgrounds
◆ Visit to zoo
◆ Nursery classes

⊃ People are Important

From the moment they are born, babies are aware of other people and will spend a lot of time watching them, although at this stage they don't understand about other people. However, they respond to the actions and feelings of parents and carers – smiling when they smile. When they start to 'babble' they will become very excited when parents respond and talk back to them.

At the age of 5/6 months, babies will enjoy being in the company of other babies or young children, even if they are not actually 'playing with them'. However, they will love 'peek-a-boo' games and will take turns in doing this – in a limited way. At this stage they are still very reliant on close family for emotional support, and will begin to show 'separation anxiety' (see page 331).

From six months onwards, children begin to notice and be more sensitive to, the actions and feelings of other people in their family. Separation anxiety can become greater and they become very afraid of strangers. This can last until children are two or three years of age, but does become easier as children become more confident, and know that parents will not leave them permanently.

As children become more mobile and confident, they begin to respond more positively to other people – they will love playing to an audience, will play alongside other children (parallel play), may offer toys or sweets to others – but are likely to grab them back! This is their first real attempt at socialisation.

By two to three years of age, children are becoming more skilful. They can usually feed themselves, use the toilet independently, wash and dress themselves (in a fashion). They are also becoming more independent, wanting to try things for themselves, and are very easily frustrated when things don't work out, or they are told they cannot do something. The role of adults at this stage is very important – they have to try and make sure that children are successful but at the same time allow them to fail at times without damaging their self esteem (see page 338). So, providing children with clothes, shoes that are easy to put on/take off – a step to the toilet etc. will aid success. Being supportive and loving and not laughing at failures will prevent damage to children's confidence.

From three years onwards, children are much more aware of other people, and their social circle needs to be much wider. Now is the time for them to attend playgroup or nursery on a regular basis. They need to learn how to react and respond to others, to be co-operative, to take turns, to share, to consider other people. They can only do this if they are around others regularly – but they will still need parent and family support and help.

Friendships and Sharing

From around three years of age friendship will become increasingly important, and children will in many ways become less socially dependant on parents, family and carers.

They will begin to choose their own friends – by three years of age children can usually play co-operatively, although at this stage the actual play activity is more important than the other people playing it. By four years of age stable friendships are now being formed, and 'having a friend' is very important. At this age, children will begin to choose same sex friends, and will become very attached to these. Some friendships made now will last a lifetime, some only a few days, some will cause tears and tantrums, some will give lots of hours of pleasure – all are important to the learning process.

Alongside developing friendships, grows the ability to share – ideas, toys, attention, other people. This is hard for children to do, as initially children are naturally **egocentric**. This means they want everything for themselves – if another child, even a brother or a sister picks up a toy which belongs to them they may well throw a tantrum and become aggressive – even if they don't want to play with it.

It takes time to learn how to share, and they need to be with other children and adults to be able to learn this concept. Initially they may only be able to share for very short periods of time

⊃ Factors which might hinder social development

- ◆ problems with language development
- ◆ problems with physical development
- ◆ limited opportunities to meet others
- ◆ weak bond of attachment
- ◆ learning difficulties
- ◆ cultural differences
- ◆ poor role models

⊃ PLAY

Children use play as a way of learning how to get along (socialise) with other children. Most children will go through the following stages as they learn to play together.

⊃ Solitary Play

This is playing alone, and from the age of 0–2 this is often the only type of play observed.

However, older children will continue to have times when they will enjoy playing alone.

⊃ Parallel Play

By the time children are 2 years old, they will begin to enjoy parallel play. This is where they play *alongside* other children but not with them.

⊃ Looking-on Play

Looking-on play occurs from about 3 years old. It is when children will be happy to watch other children as they play, and may copy them. At this stage they are often ready for nursery/playgroup.

⊃ Co-operative Play

This also happens at about 3 years old; children will be happy to play together, share activities and takes on roles. But arguments will occur.

⟲ SELF-IMAGE AND SELF-ESTEEM

How we relate to other people is very much affected by how we feel and think about ourselves.

Children's social and emotional development is very closely linked to their **self-image** and **self-esteem**.

Self-image and self-esteem can, and often do, affect how we behave, how successful we are, how we are able to get on with others and how we react to problems.

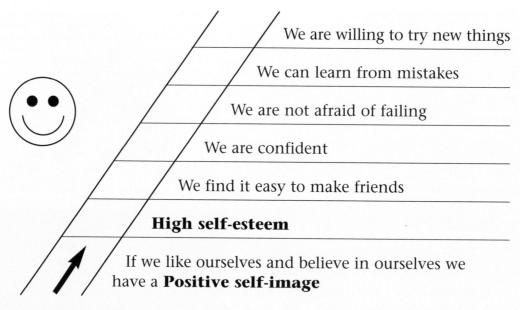

We are willing to try new things

We can learn from mistakes

We are not afraid of failing

We are confident

We find it easy to make friends

High self-esteem

If we like ourselves and believe in ourselves we have a **Positive self-image**

SELF IMAGE:

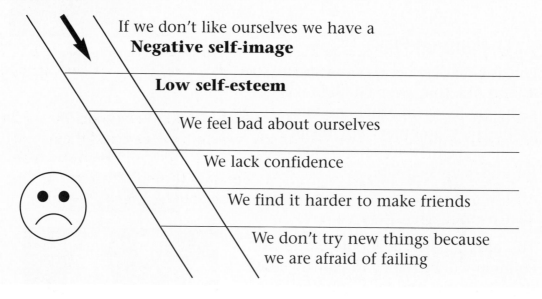

If we don't like ourselves we have a **Negative self-image**

Low self-esteem

We feel bad about ourselves

We lack confidence

We find it harder to make friends

We don't try new things because we are afraid of failing

Children learn about themselves and develop a self-image based mainly on the way in which adults treat them, talk with them and react to them. It is therefore very important that parents and carers encourage children to grow up feeling loved, valued and respected.

There are lots of different ways in which parents can do this.

◆ **Praise and encourage** children when they do something well and succeed, AND when they try!

◆ Have **realistic expectations** of children, remembering their age and stage of development.

◆ Give lots of **love and affection** so that children know they are loved and valued.

◆ Give children **opportunities to be independent**, to make mistakes and fail without criticism.

◆ Try to provide a **WIDE variety of toys and games**, especially those which encourage imaginative role play and feelings.

◆ Try to make sure children are brought up in a **positive atmosphere** – laugh with them but not at them.

◆ Make sure children have lots of **opportunities to socialise** with other children and make friends.

◆ Avoid attitudes, behaviour and experiences which promote **stereotyping**.

All of these factors work **together** to help children develop a positive self-image which, in itself, will influence their behaviour, feelings and attitude towards others.

Above all, it must be remembered that children will often model themselves both **consciously** and **unconsciously**, on the adults around them, and copy what they say (see later section on Behaviour) so parents need to be very careful what messages they give to children through their own behaviour. In particular, parents should try to avoid any activity which might encourage **stereotyping**.

⊃ WHAT IS STEREOTYPING?

Stereotyping is the expectation people may have of themselves, and others, based on age, gender, race or disability.

Once children get to about 3 years old, they become more aware of their gender, and need to work out for themselves, what 'being a boy' or 'being a girl' is all about. They can do this in lots of ways, but are mostly influenced by adults and their attitudes and behaviour. They see and copy.

Why is Stereotyping Harmful?

Stereotyping can damage children's development and self-esteem in many ways. It can stop children from achieving their full potential, because they may believe that they should not or cannot do something because of their gender.

- It can make them start to behave in certain ways that they think are expected of them. Girls are always expected to be caring and gentle, boys boisterous and adventurous.
- It may make boys afraid of showing affection or that they care and girls afraid of being strong and daring.
- It can reinforce superior and inferior roles and attitudes towards others.
- It can make it difficult for children to mix with and relate to members of the opposite sex.

How Can Stereotyping be Avoided?

- Allow boys and girls to play together.

- Do not buy gender-biased toys e.g. dolls, prams and kitchens for girls, train sets, tractors for boys.
- Check books for gender-bias i.e. girls in 'caring role' looking after home, or boys having adventures, climbing trees.

- ◆ Share roles and jobs in the home.
- ◆ Avoid letting children watch TV programmes which reinforce gender roles.
- ◆ Try not to dress children differently–especially colour choices e.g. girls in dresses, boys in jeans, pink and blue.

⊃ LOOKING AT EMOTIONS

Emotions are the feelings we have for and about people, objects, situations, etc. Everyone experiences strong feelings and emotions throughout their life, however, adults can use words to try to explain how they feel and this helps them to understand their feelings and control them. Children cannot do this so easily – they cannot understand themselves and they don't always have the words to be able to explain how they feel.

So

- ◆ they hit out when angry and frustrated
- ◆ they cry, scream and kick when they are refused
- ◆ they shriek with happiness

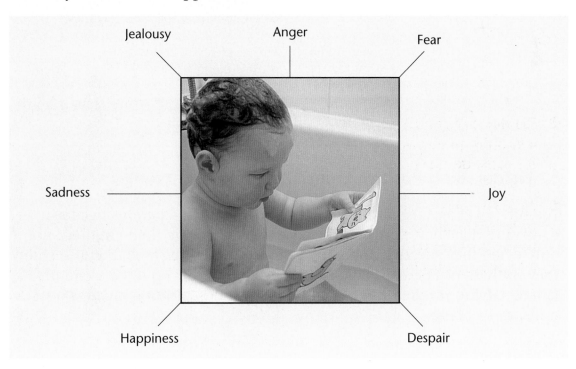

Jealousy   Anger   Fear

Sadness   Joy

Happiness   Despair

Emotions such as happiness are **positive emotions**, and parents need to work to encourage these feelings.

Emotions such as anger and sadness are **negative emotions**, and need to be handled carefully, in a positive way – getting angry with a child who is angry will not work.

⊃ Coping with Negative Emotions

Emotion	Cause	Ideas for coping
Jealousy	Often occurs if there is a new baby because they feel insecure and not loved. It is one of the hardest emotions to control–even for adults.	◆ Give children love, attention and cuddles ◆ Be patient ◆ Try to respect how they are feeling ◆ If old enough, talk about feelings
Fear	Children often develop irrational fears for no apparent reason so it's often hard for adults to understand	◆ Try to show that you understand the fear, and accept that it is real ◆ Give lots of love ◆ Reassure them ◆ Avoid 'scary' stories or TV programmes
Anger	This is one of the most common emotions and can be caused by lots of situations	◆ Sometimes best to try to 'ignore' ◆ Try to stay calm ◆ With a young child try to distract with a toy or activity ◆ Talk firmly but gently to the child about how they are feeling and why ◆ Give time and space to 'cool down'
Sadness	This can also happen for no apparent reason – it may be because something hasn't worked, or because a game has been lost, not won, or because a pet has died	◆ Give plenty of love and attention ◆ Help them to talk about what has caused the sadness ◆ Try to distract with an interesting activity

⊃ Encouraging Positive Emotions

Too often we can take positive emotions for granted – parents need to make sure that they consistently praise and encourage their children, not only when they succeed, and when they do something well, but also when they try hard but perhaps fail. Then they won't grow up to be afraid of failure! Giving children lots of cuddles and smiles, pinning pictures on walls, can all help.

⊃ FEEDING, WASHING AND DRESSING

The social skills of feeding, dressing, washing and going to the toilet, are also part of social and emotional development.

Age	Skill Development
6 months	◆ drinks from a cup which is held for them
12 months	◆ uses fingers to feed themselves ◆ may try to help with feeding by holding the spoon ◆ may drink from a feeding cup themselves ◆ may help dressing by holding out leg/arm
15 months	◆ can hold a cup and drink from it without help ◆ can eat using a spoon but may spill some ◆ may be beginning to understand when they want to empty bladder but cannot control muscles ◆ will need help with dressing and undressing but will try themselves
18 months	◆ can use a cup and spoon well ◆ can take off clothing quite easily and help to dress themselves ◆ can give warning that they need the toilet, by words, or action
2 years	◆ can feed without spilling a lot ◆ can lift up a cup and put it down without spilling ◆ can put on some clothing themselves ◆ can say when they need the toilet and manage to get the potty themselves ◆ may be dry at night
2½ years	◆ can use a spoon well ◆ can pour themselves a drink ◆ can unfasten buttons, zips and buckles ◆ will be dry during the day ◆ may be dry at night
3 years	◆ can use a fork and spoon to eat ◆ will go to the toilet on their own during the day ◆ should be dry at night ◆ can wash their hands, but not dry them properly ◆ becoming independent, wanting to dress themselves
4 years	◆ can feed themselves skillfully ◆ can dress and undress themselves ◆ can wash and dry hands and face and clean teeth
5 years	◆ uses a knife and fork well ◆ can easily dress and undress themselves ◆ may be able to tie shoelaces

Remember

Social and emotional development depends on lots of factors, Above all, children need to be praised and encouraged, and brought up in a positive atmosphere. This will help them to develop a positive self-image and self-esteem.

Key Words

Bonding the close feeling which develops between a baby and an adult

Co-operative play playing together and sharing/taking turns

Egocentric self-centred

Emotional Development learning to handle and control feelings

Looking-on Play watching other children and copying them

Parallel Play playing alongside other children but not with them

Self-concept another phrase for self-image

Self-esteem how we feel about ourselves

Self-image what we think of ourselves

Separation anxiety emotional distress children feel when away from parent/primary carer

Social development learning to live with others

Solitary play playing alone

Stereotyping expecting people to behave and act in a certain way – usually based on gender, race or disability

⊃ BEHAVIOUR

As well as learning how to share, co-operate and respect other people, children also have to learn to behave in a way that is acceptable to others.

In this section we will look at:
- ◆ expectation about behaviour
- ◆ how children learn to behave
- ◆ coping with unacceptable behaviour

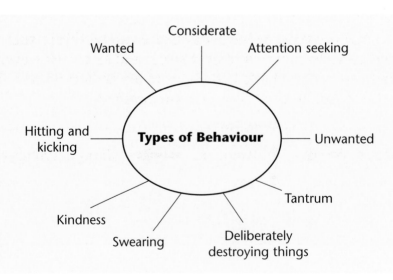

Learning to behave is a gradual process – children are not born with self-control.

How children are expected to behave will vary, and can depend on lots of factors such as:

◆ cultural beliefs and traditions   ◆ parent's attitudes
◆ country   ◆ position in family

Also the way children are expected to behave changes with time – 50 years ago children were expected to be seen but not heard, especially when with adults. Nowadays, children are expected and allowed to have views, opinions and show their feelings freely.

What is Good Behaviour?

Again this will vary from family to family and from society to society, but in general good behaviour means thinking of the feelings and needs of others, as well as our own. It means being able to share, take turns, listen to others and be helpful and kind.

How Do Children Learn to Behave?

Different people have different theories (views) on how children learn to behave. The most common theories are

◆ the **Behaviourist Theory**
◆ the **Social Learning Theory**
◆ the **Self-Fulfilling Prophecy Theory**

The Behaviourist Theory

This theory developed by B.F. Skinner is based on the idea that if good behaviour is recognised and rewarded in some way, children will learn that it is acceptable, and will repeat it.

Rewards are called **positive reinforcers**, and can be things such as attention from parents, praise, a treat, a sweet and so on. However, children can sometimes use unacceptable behaviour to attract attention – this should be ignored. This is called **negative reinforcement**.

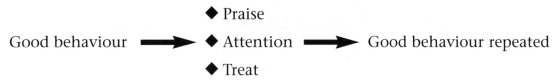

Good behaviour ➡ ◆ Praise ◆ Attention ◆ Treat ➡ Good behaviour repeated

The Social Learning Theory

This theory developed by Albert Bandura suggests that children learn to behave (as they do lots of other things) by watching and copying what happens around them, so they will learn to behave from their parents, or primary carers. Therefore, if a child is brought up by parents who swear and are aggressive, they will see this as 'normal' and copy. If, however, parents are polite, calm and considerate, then children will copy this, and behave in a similar way.

The Self-fulfilling Prophecy Theory

This theory suggests that the way adults **think** about their children will influence how the children behave. So, if a parent thinks a child is 'good' and 'kind' the child is likely to behave in that sort of way. If, however a parent thinks the child is 'naughty' then the child is more likely to behave in that way. This theory shows that **negative labelling** of children can be very harmful (see page 338).

Putting the Theory Into Practice

None of these theories is perfect. However, all can give parents ideas about how they can help children to learn and show 'wanted' behaviour. Parents can do this by:

◆ staying calm
◆ creating a positive atmosphere and environment where children can see and feel that they are important and valued
◆ being a good role model
◆ praising and rewarding wanted behaviour, and ignoring unwanted behaviour
◆ having realistic expectations of children, depending on their age and stage of development
◆ being consistent in what is acceptable and unacceptable
◆ setting clear guidelines and boundaries about what is acceptable
◆ letting children know that they are loved, unconditionally
◆ being consistent in using any sanctions
◆ treating all children in the family the same

Even normally well behaved children will misbehave at times and act in an unacceptable way.

⟳ Handling Unwanted Behaviour

It takes a long time for children to learn how to control their feelings, and to 'behave', and sometimes it is impossible for them to do so.

Often, sudden changes in children's lives can affect their behaviour – sometimes it may be something as simple as tiredness. How much their behaviour is affected, will depend on their age, their level of understanding and the attitudes and support of their parents.

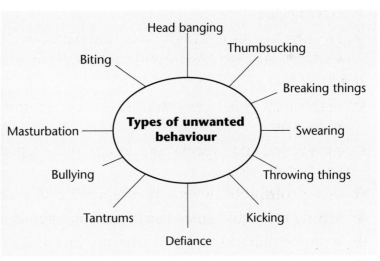

Sometimes behaviour is **regressive** – children begin to behave in a way which is much more like that of a younger child.

◆ bed wetting
◆ clinging to parents
◆ refusing to communicate
◆ talking 'baby' talk
◆ wanting to be fed

Sometimes behaviour is **aggressive** – children may try to hurt themselves or others.

◆ headbanging

◆ kicking

◆ biting

Although the behaviourist theory suggests that unwanted behaviour should be ignored, sometimes this isn't possible, especially when there is a danger that the child may harm themselves, and/or others. Parents need to know how to cope, and may feel that they want to use some sort of sanction or punishment.

How they cope will depend on many factors, and may vary according to the type of behaviour being shown, the age of the child, the place where the behaviour occurs, their own values and beliefs and even their own mood and feelings.

⊃ Ways of Coping

Say No!	If said firmly this will often stop unwanted behaviour, especially if eye contact is made.
By distracting the child	Younger children will not always be able to understand that what they are doing is unacceptable, or why. Offering a different activity will take their attention and defuse the situation.
Setting clear rules and boundaries	Making children aware of what is acceptable and not acceptable behaviour and sticking to it.
Explaining to the child	If the child is old enough, unwanted behaviour can be stopped by explaining why it is wrong, or what harm they might do by continuing
Using sanctions	Sometimes parents may feel that taking away a favourite toy or not having a story before bed time is a fitting punishment Sanctions are always negative, and parents should use these only in extreme cases. However if a sanction is threatened and then not used, children learn that they can get away with certain things and will do it again and again. Any sanction chosen should be appropriate to the behaviour.
Using eye contact and facial expressions	Sometimes a 'look' is enough to tell children that what they are doing is not acceptable – and once the unwanted behaviour has stopped this can be re-inforced by praise.

Under no circumstances should any sort of physical punishment be given. Smacking, no matter how 'gentle', is not an option, and under the 1989 Children Act, is illegal.

Comfort habits

Many children, instead of behaving in an aggressive or regressive way, develop comfort habits to help them cope with difficult situations. Some may have imaginary friends, and will talk to them or blame them for something they themselves have done wrong. Others will use comforters, blankets, favourite toys which they will take with them all the time but mainly when they go to bed, or into an unknown situation or a situation where they may be separated from their parents.

Separation anxiety

This is the term given to the feelings children have, especially very young children, when they are separated from their parents and/or close family. This usually begins at 5–6 months – at this stage children do not yet fully understand that even if they cannot see their parents, they still exist. So if the parent goes out of sight they think they have lost them and will become upset. At the same age, children also become fearful of strangers.

Can Toys and Games Help?

As with all other forms of development, toys, games and other activities are important in helping children to cope with and express their feelings, and to get rid of negative emotion (see Chapter 17).

Toy/game/activity	How it helps
Hammer toys	Children love to hammer and bang and this helps them to get rid of tension and destructive feelings.
Drawing and painting	Children often don't have enough language or know enough words to say how they feel and to get rid of anger Painting and drawing is a way in which they can show their feelings both through what they paint, how they paint and the colours they use.
Play dough	This can be squeezed, squashed, battered and flattened. Handling it can be a way of soothing or of getting rid of tensions.
Role play	Children love to take on roles and play pretend games with others. They can act out their fears, feelings and emotions.
Chasing	Running around allows children to 'let off steam'.

Toy/game/activity	How it helps
Soft toys such as teddy bears 	Playing with soft toys can give comfort and allow children to learn to care and show their feelings.

Things to do

Activity 1

Try to arrange a visit to a nursery or a playgroup. If this is not possible, visit a play area or park where young children and their parents go.

Try to observe the different activities and games enjoyed by the children, and the types of social play (solitary, parallel etc.).

How do children express their emotions?

Write up your observations. Try comparing them with the development charts.

Activity 2

During your child study visits, try to make a list of all the signs shown by the child when happy (both verbal and non-verbal).

Now make a similar list for when the child is unhappy.

Think about what sort of incidents make the child feel happy/unhappy.

Activity 3

Look at a range of children's books and list any ways in which they might present people in stereotypical ways.

Activity 4

Over the next 24 hours, try to be aware of, and make a note of, any examples of stereotypical behaviour or images – either at school, home, on TV, in magazines etc.

Discuss your findings as a group.

Activity 5

Sometimes the way we talk about and think about children is stereotypical.

Look at the following words:

- strong
- loyal
- attractive
- petit
- kind
- caring
- pretty
- small
- loving
- tough
- friendly
- emotional
- artistic
- gentle
- trendy
- affectionate
- trustworthy
- timid

Under the headings *Boys* and *Girls*, make a list of the words you might use to describe them.

Look at your lists carefully.

Activity 6

Try to arrange to interview people from different generations e.g. parents, grandparents and, if possible, from different cultures, about ways in which children have been/are treated depending on whether they are boys or girls.

Evaluate your results.

Questions

Question 1

a Why are social and emotional development difficult to separate?

b Name and briefly describe three different theories of social and emotional development.

Question 2

a What is meant by *bonding*? Why is it so important?

b Describe how bonding can be helped

   i during pregnancy

   ii during labour and birth

   iii after birth

Question 3

Describe six factors which might affect social and emotional development.

Question 4

a What is meant when a child is described as '*egocentric*'?

b How might this affect a child's behaviour?

c Describe the stage of social-emotional development of

   i a 12 month old baby

   ii a 2 year old

   iii a 4 year old

Question 5

a Parents need to make sure that children have plenty of opportunities to meet and mix with other people.

Suggest *six ways* in which they could do this.

b Why would this be especially important for an only child?

c At what age might children start to choose their own friends?

Question 6

Describe *six* factors which might limit social-emotional development.

Question 7

Name and describe *four* different types of social play.

Question 8

a What is the difference between '*self-image*' and '*self esteem*'?

b Suggest eight ways in which a parent could help a child to develop a positive self image.

Question 9

a What is meant by *stereotyping*?

b Why might stereotyping be a problem?

c Suggest six ways in which parents could help prevent stereotyping.

Question 10

a i Give *three* examples of positive emotions.

   ii Give *three* examples of negative emotions.

b How can parents help to encourage positive emotions in children?

Question 11

At what age might you expect children to have the following social skills.

   i use fingers for feeding

   ii take of clothes easily and help to dress themselves

   iii unfasten zips

   iv be dry at night

   v wash and dry hands and face.

Question 12

a List *four* factors which might influence how children are expected to behave.

b According to the Behaviourist Theory, how do children learn to behave?

c Suggest *eight* ways in which parents can encourage '*wanted*' or '*desirable*' behaviour.

d List *eight* different types of unwanted behaviour.

Question 13

a Suggest *six* reasons why children might behave badly.

b List ways in which parents could handle unwanted behaviour.

c Suggest with reasons, *three* toys or activities which might help children to express their feelings, and get rid of negative emotions.

⊃ SOCIAL AND EMOTIONAL DEVELOPMENT WORDSEARCH

P	P	I	V	Y	X	V	J	N	Z	T	F	C	O	M	F	O	R	T	E	R	T	E	X	Q
O	G	U	Y	Q	S	X	B	L	E	V	C	T	Q	N	N	W	D	N	G	Q	D	T	N	P
C	Q	R	I	P	W	S	Q	N	A	O	Q	G	K	O	P	R	C	A	P	T	H	U	B	O
O	U	Q	K	N	A	J	G	P	O	S	T	I	V	E	E	M	O	T	I	O	N	S	V	W
O	K	V	O	I	Q	R	B	P	F	Q	P	F	V	K	D	P	C	M	J	K	G	D	W	O
P	M	Y	A	B	H	S	A	M	L	B	P	P	Z	Y	V	M	G	P	Y	B	H	J	B	Z
E	X	K	G	C	I	V	U	L	P	U	R	R	K	F	T	M	T	I	W	K	J	M	T	I
R	F	Q	X	N	S	D	M	W	L	V	S	Z	X	H	G	M	X	R	F	M	G	R	T	R
A	P	F	H	G	E	P	F	M	X	E	Q	J	T	L	C	M	A	E	S	Y	G	Q	A	I
T	V	H	T	B	L	X	U	Z	W	I	L	L	Y	A	S	P	I	R	E	S	T	H	K	X
I	B	S	N	W	F	X	N	Q	W	J	K	H	S	D	N	X	J	E	L	J	D	S	I	M
V	P	C	H	Y	I	S	O	L	B	U	L	D	O	T	A	M	G	W	F	N	R	A	N	S
E	X	I	E	I	M	W	O	E	V	G	A	N	B	Q	P	W	S	U	E	P	W	D	G	S
L	V	D	Q	M	A	F	E	E	A	S	Y	E	H	C	V	Q	H	T	S	P	Z	N	T	O
U	T	E	Q	X	G	F	E	J	M	Z	I	V	M	O	L	Q	F	O	T	T	G	E	U	L
M	H	P	X	L	E	M	F	X	D	J	S	H	B	Q	R	Q	F	X	E	Z	Z	S	R	I
K	X	M	E	R	U	I	D	O	S	D	Q	J	H	Y	H	K	L	V	E	Q	C	S	N	T
J	F	A	N	H	A	P	P	I	N	E	S	S	G	Y	G	O	J	X	M	D	N	E	S	A
U	C	I	P	V	N	E	G	A	T	I	V	E	E	M	O	T	I	O	N	S	J	A	U	R
V	E	E	C	M	E	Z	B	Z	M	D	B	O	H	A	S	B	J	Z	I	G	Y	G	V	Y
V	P	W	J	E	A	L	O	U	S	Y	R	D	K	U	S	S	M	Q	P	F	P	A	F	C
Z	Z	Q	H	M	S	E	P	A	R	A	T	I	O	N	A	N	X	I	E	T	Y	S	K	N
W	J	R	H	C	C	R	B	B	M	H	M	R	S	H	A	R	I	N	G	N	Q	Z	K	G
V	S	H	T	E	M	P	E	R	T	A	N	T	R	U	M	S	A	I	E	D	B	D	N	J
M	J	Z	T	Z	A	M	S	Y	A	K	Q	P	D	F	T	A	K	X	T	I	A	C	G	J

Positive emotions	Happiness
Parallel	Sharing
Comforter	Solitary
Self image	Temper tantrums
Taking turns	Self esteem
Negative emotions	Sadness
Cooperative	Jealousy
Separation anxiety	

17 Play and Toys

Play is something that children do instinctively – it is something they spend most of their time doing and it takes up a large part of their lives.

In this section we are going to look at:

- ◆ why children play
- ◆ how play helps children's development
- ◆ different types of play

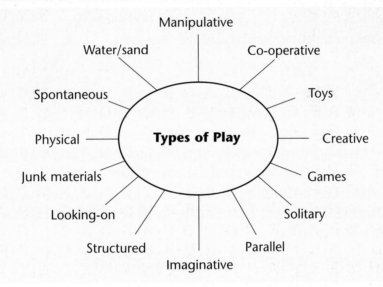

Children spend most of their waking time playing. During this time they will move from activity to activity and show different levels of concentration, enthusiasm and determination. Play is something that children tend to choose for themselves. Parents may try to suggest ideas, but if children don't want to play at that particular activity, they won't. However, parents do have a role to play:

- ◆ they need to make sure that children have lots of opportunities and time to play with different activities and in different situations
- ◆ they may need to give help and guidance when it is needed
- ◆ they may need to act as a referee.

⟳ WHY DO CHILDREN PLAY?

Children play:

- ◆ to learn and practise the different skills that they will need later in life
- ◆ to learn to understand concepts such as time, space, number and shape
- ◆ to have fun

◆ to allow them to explore, experiment, to try and to fail–but in a non-threatening way.

For most of their time, and certainly at home, children play in their own way, and at their own pace – they use the toys and materials around them in lots of different and imaginative ways. So, a large cardboard box can become a car, a space ship or a cooker – depending on the game. This is often called **spontaneous** play. In nurseries and play groups, play may be more **structured**. Here, it is planned by adults to help children to develop certain skills or knowledge.

No matter what type of play, or kind of play, children are involved in, they will be having fun and learning.

PHYSICAL
◆ develops fine motor skills
◆ develops balance and co-ordination
◆ develops senses – sight, sound, hearing, touch, taste
◆ exercises body and limbs

SOCIAL
◆ learns to share
◆ learns to co-operate and take turns
◆ learns rules
◆ develops social skills

How Play Can Help Children's Development

INTELLECTUAL
◆ develops language skills
◆ learns about the world
◆ develops memory and concentration
◆ learns to experiment and test
◆ learns concepts
◆ discovers new things
◆ develops imagination and creativity

EMOTIONAL
◆ gives pleasure
◆ prevents boredom
◆ gets rid of tension
◆ lets off steam
◆ develops confidence and independence
◆ acts out feelings
◆ acts out roles

STAGES OF PLAY

Very young children are quite happy to play on their own, as long as they know that there is an adult close by. As they become older, they become more interested in playing with other children – this is known as **social play** and is divided into four main stages:

- ◆ solitary play
- ◆ parallel play
- ◆ looking-on play
- ◆ co-operative play

Descriptions of these stages of play can be found in Chapter 16.

DIFFERENT TYPES OF PLAY

Just as children can learn to play together in different ways socially they will also, at different times, be involved in different **types** of play.

There are four main types of play:

- ◆ imaginative or pretend play
- ◆ creative play
- ◆ physical play
- ◆ manipulative play

These different types of play are often associated with particular activities and particular skills. However, it must be remembered that all the different types of play will allow children to use and develop a wide range and variety of skills covering all aspects of development. For example, dressing up games are a form of imaginative play which allow children to take on roles and act out feelings. They also help social and emotional development, language development and often physical, fine motor and gross motor skills.

CREATIVE PLAY

What is it?

Creative play takes place when children use different materials to make something from their own ideas and imagination.

It allows them to explore and experiment and to use their senses to find out what can and cannot be done.

The end result may not be too recognisable to an adult! However, it is important that it is praised and not laughed at.

CREATIVE PLAY

Types of activities

◆ painting, drawing and printing
◆ collage
◆ making 'junk' toys
◆ sand and water play
◆ play dough and plasticine

How it helps development

Creative play very often helps physical development, especially the development of fine motor and sensory skills and hand-eye co-ordination. It can also help language skills and it allows children the chance to express their ideas and feelings without using words – therefore it is important for emotional development. It develops the imagination, helps children learn about different materials and properties and helps them to understand different concepts. If done with other children it can develop social skills.

IMAGINATIVE (PRETEND) PLAY

What is it?

Imaginative, or pretend, play takes place when children act out being somebody or something else. They will often use toys and objects as 'props' and will enjoy dressing up for their part. This sort of play can also be called **role play**

Types of activities

◆ dressing up to be a nurse, pop star, footballer
◆ playing 'mums and dads', 'shops'
◆ making dens
◆ making cars, trains, rockets out of cardboard boxes and going on exciting adventures
◆ puppet shows

How it helps development

Depending on the type of activity, it will develop children's language skills, imagination and confidence, help them to learn how to share and think about others, allow them to act out their fears, encourage fine and gross motor skills.

PHYSICAL PLAY

What is it?

Although most play is physical in some way, physical play takes place where children are using their whole bodies, and their large muscles. It is usually very active, and involves lots of running around allowing children to use up all their energy. It usually takes place out of doors as lots of space is needed.

Types of activities

◆ playing team games, such as football

◆ hopscotch/skipping

◆ playing on slides, swings, climbing frames

◆ riding bicycles, tricycles

◆ rollerblading

◆ trampolining

◆ swimming

How it helps development

Physical play helps the development of gross motor skills, co-ordination and balance, as well as fine motor skills. It can help children to develop concepts of size, speed and spatial awareness, as well as helping them to learn about the outside world. When children are playing together, it will encourage language development and social development – taking turns, sharing. Emotionally it helps children 'let off steam', boost self-confidence and be adventurous.

MANIPULATIVE PLAY

What is it?

Manipulative play involves children in developing their fine motor skills and hand-eye co-ordination. It is important because it helps them to begin to be more confident and competent in using all the different tools and equipment needed in life. Manipulative play usually involves children in building or fitting things together.

Types of activities

◆ jigsaws

◆ using Duplo, Lego or stickle bricks

◆ playing with shape sorters

◆ playdough

Almost any activity which involves handling small toys or games will help manipulative skills.

MANIPULATIVE PLAY

How it helps development

Although this type of play mainly helps to develop fine motor skills and hand-eye co-ordination it will also help all other areas of development

Intellectually, it encourages language development and helps children with problem solving because it encourages them to think logically. It will also develop their understanding of concepts (such as shape, size and volume) and spatial awareness.

Emotionally it can build up confidence and give children a feeling of pleasure and the chance to succeed and cope with failure in a fun way. It can also help social skills if children are playing together.

Key Words

Creative play where children make something original from their own ideas

Imaginative play where children act out ideas from their imagination

Manipulative play where children are involved in using hands, fingers and hand-eye co-ordination

Physical play where children use their whole body, large muscles

Pretend play another name for imaginative play

Role play another form of imaginative play

Spontaneous play play which is unplanned

Structured play which is planned to develop contact skills

Remember

Play is the way children learn – it is something they do naturally, and it needs very little adult help. What adults must do, however, is make sure children have time, opportunity and a range of toys, materials, equipment and space to do it.

⊃ TOYS AND OTHER PLAYTHINGS

The dictionary defines a toy as 'a plaything, especially for a child', (Chambers Dictionary, new ed.)

In this section we are going to look at:

- ◇ what toys are
- ◇ what makes a good toy
- ◇ toys for different stages and ages
- ◇ toy safety

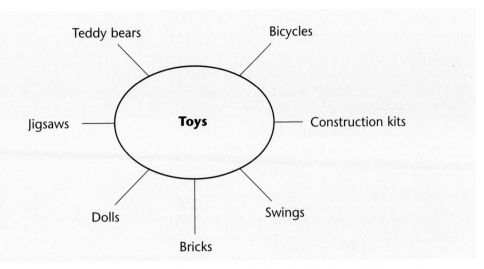

What is a toy?

We have already looked at how children learn through different types of play. When playing, they will use different objects in different ways to help them to investigate and learn about the world around them. Some of these will be bought toys, such as dolls, Lego sets or paints, some will be household objects, such as empty packets, pans or wooden spoons.

Strictly speaking children don't need 'toys' as we understand them – they will use their imagination to make even the simplest of items into the most exciting of objects. A twig from a tree will become a sword, or a laser gun, or a magic wand; an empty cardboard box becomes a space ship, a train or a boat.

However, purpose-built toys, although not really essential for play, can have an important role both in helping children to explore, investigate and experiment, and in encouraging imaginative and creative skills. The Trading Standards Toy Safety Regulations 1995 defines toys as 'any product or material which is clearly intended for play by a child under the age of 14 years' – so for this purpose, a toy is something which has been specifically designed and made for a child to play with.

Choosing Toys

Parents often spend hours trying to choose toys for their children – they will think about what their child enjoys, how safe it is, if it's colourful, fun, how it works, what it will help the child learn, and, of course, how much it costs. Then they buy it and the child ignores it, or uses it in a way it was intended, or gets more fun out of the box and packaging!

The fact is that it is almost impossible to buy the perfect toy for your child – and certainly price is no guarantee of success. Sometimes the best toys are the cheapest, and they are often the ones a child will want to use over and over again – but that will depend on the individual child.

However, there is no doubt that well designed and well-chosen toys can give hours of pleasure. The following points can help when choosing and buying toys.

1. The toy should be appropriate for the child's age and stage of development (see page 361). Children grow and develop very quickly, especially during the first three years. If a toy is too simple, the child will become bored very quickly. If it is too complicated, the child may not know how to play with it and become frustrated.

2. The toy should be safe to use (see page 365)

3. The toy should be stimulating and interesting for the child. The child should want to play with it – it should be exciting, colourful and fun, and what the child likes, not bought because the parent thinks the child **should** like it, or because it is 'educational'.

4. The toy should have good play value. In other words, it should be simple enough and versatile enough to be used in different types of play for different purposes.

5. The toy should be colourful both to attract and hold attention and, especially for babies, should be in primary colours.

6. All new toys and equipment should have safety marks on them. If they do not, they might be dangerous, have small parts or sharp corners, or may fall apart. Look for

    a The Lion Mark **b** The CE logo **c** The Kite mark

7. The manufacturer's age recommendations and instructions for use must be read. This will help to avoid buying a toy which might be dangerous for a child of a certain age.

⊃ Linking Toys with Ages and Stages of Development

Age	Development	Toys for Indoors	Toys for Outdoors
0-1 year	Development at this age tends to be mainly physical – children move from involuntary to voluntary control. They use hands and mouths to explore, and are becoming more mobile. They need to have toys which are easy to handle, safe to go in the mouth, washable, sensory and unbreakable.	Rattles Activity centre Soft fluffy toys Card or fabric books Bricks Teething rings	
1-2 years	Children's physical skills are developing very quickly – both fine motor and gross motor skills. They need toys which will help them to develop and strengthen muscles, help balance and co-ordination. Play is solitary.	Push-and-pull toys Shape sorters Building bricks Simple books Simple jigsaws Cause-and-effect toys	Small swings and slides Paddling pools
2-3 years	At this age children's physical skills are quite well developed and they can move and handle things confidently. This is a stage when intellectual development is speeding up – their language skills are growing fast, and they are very curious and adventurous. However, they cannot concentrate for long periods and are easily frustrated. Moving towards parallel play.	Cuddly toys and dolls Playdough Books Jigsaws Paints and crayons Pretend toys Dressing up toys	Paddling pools Slides and swings Simple climbing frames Sit and ride toys Tricycle
3-4 years	Children's physical skills are now well advanced and controlled, and language skills are good. They particularly enjoy creative and imaginative play as they are moving quickly from parallel play to co-operative play. They need larger toys to encourage gross motor skills, and toys and games to stimulate imagination and understanding of concepts.	Construction toys Toys to develop imagination such as Playworld, Fisher Price Water and sand Playdough Paints and crayons Dressing up Activity books	As above plus: climbing frame Bicycle with stabilisers Balls of different sizes
4-5 years	By this stage children are confident at all sorts of gross motor skills – climbing, running, using large equipment–and they do so well with great co-ordination and balance. Intellectual skills are developing quickly–they are imaginative, love to discover and explore and are curious about everything. They can usually take turns and follow rules.	Paints and crayons Paper More complex jigsaws Construction toys Simple board games Material for modelling and making Story books	As above plus: Skipping ropes Rollerblades Bats Balls Gardening tools Obstacle courses

No single toy will ever help only one type of development, and as children grow and develop more skills, many are not used and need to be replaced. However, some toys will be used over and over again, and give children hours of pleasure – although even they may need to be replaced when worn out or the child grows too big to play with them or on them.

Intellectual development
Helps to develop creative and imaginative skills as children use them for building and construction. Can help colour recognition, size, shape and number

Language skills can also be developed

Fine motor skills
Children learn to grasp, hold, fit together and build with them

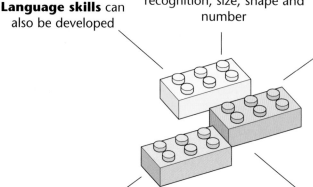

Social development
As children get older they may play co-operatively at construction and building activities

Emotional development
Children will experience pride and pleasure in what they have made, especially if praised

Intellectual development
Helps children to recognise shapes and colour – can also help with object/number/letter recognition depending on

Fine motor skills
As children get older they develop more refined grasps, moving from palmar to tripod to pincer. Help hand-eye co-ordination

Language skills
Will help to increase vocabulary

Emotional development
Children get pleasure from complex puzzles

Intellectual development
Helps children to develop an understanding of size, speed and spatial awareness

Gross motor skills
Children build up and strengthen legs and muscles – develop co-ordination and balance

Emotional development
Children can experience a lot of different emotions – pleasure, excitement, happiness. Can help children overcome fear, and gain confidence

Social development
Children usually play with friends

Intellectual development
Children can cuddle them, get comfort from them. Can help children learn to be caring, think of others. Children can act out fears and feelings

Physical development
Playing with dolls and teddies can help fine motor skills and hand-eye co-ordination, especially when toys include dressing and undressing. Helps sensory development

Social development
In imaginative play can help children to learn how to look after others. Helps to encourage co-operative play. Can help children learn skills of fastening, dressing and washing, etc.

Intellectual development
Helps to encourage imagination and creativity

Language skills
Children often talk to themselves as they play with these toys – even young babies

⊃ Things other than toys

Children can be given the chance to play in exciting and imaginative ways without having to buy lots of expensive toys. All it takes is a little planning and imagination!

Collect empty cartons, yoghurt cartons, food boxes, biscuit tins, plastic bottles →	These can be used to make junk toys, musical instruments, play 'shops', cars	Have a box to put in old, but clean clothes, hats, shoes and jewellry →	Children will become pop stars, pirates, spacemen, and so on
Keep some large cardboard boxes close by →	These can be made into ships or cars or aeroplanes	Let children have access to sheets and blankets, boxes →	They will quickly create 'dens' and 'houses' from them
Buy rolls of old wallpaper or lining paper →	These can be used for painting and printing	A washing up bowl filled with water and bubbles and plastic cups →	Children will play for hours, learning concepts such as empty full, floating, sinking

Toy Libraries

Many areas have centres where families can borrow toys, rather like borrowing books from libraries. They are often found in health centres, day nurseries and playschools. Sometimes play buses offer similar opportunities.

These centres:

◆ let children play with a greater variety and range of toys
◆ let parents see what sort of toys their child likes to play with
◆ allow families to borrow toys
◆ save families money

⊃ Toys and Safety

It is very important that parents and other carers make sure that the toys they buy children, and the ways in which they are used, do not put children in danger.

> ## *Remember*
>
> ◆ **Children under 2 are likely to put things in their mouth**
> ◆ **Young children will play with older children's toys**

⊃ Some points for safety

◆ Toys regularly handled and put into children's mouth should be washed regularly.

◆ All new toys should have appropriate safety marks (see figs 8.10-8.12) – toys without could be dangerous.

◆ Buy toys from reputable shops – where the 'Lion' sign is displayed.

◆ If buying toys second hand, from car boot sales or market stalls, check carefully.

◆ Avoid toys with small easily detached pieces which could easily be swallowed.

◆ Follow manufacturers' instructions for the use and care of toys.

◆ Look for age recommendations on toys – and use them!

◆ Check toys regularly for wear and tear.

◆ Check that furry, fluffy toys are washable – and wash regularly.

◆ Avoid metal toys.

◆ Throw out broken toys

◆ Keep toys for young children in their reach – it will stop them from climbing up and perhaps falling off.

◆ Avoid toys with loose hair or fur on which children could choke.

⊃ BOOKS

Perhaps one of the most important things that parents can do for their children is to encourage an interest in, a love of, and a respect for, books.

In this section we are going to look at:

◦ the importance of books
◦ choosing books for different ages and stages
◦ encouraging an interest in books

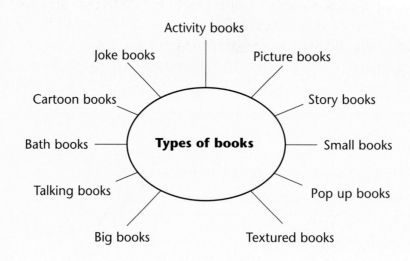

The Importance of Books

Books can, and should be, a source of great enjoyment and pleasure. They are crucial in helping to develop children's language skills, by increasing their vocabulary and giving them a good start with learning to read.

But listening to stories, reading and sharing books with parents does much more than this.

But, best of all, books are fun.

Different Types of Books

Books come in all shapes and sizes and styles:

Children need to be given the chance to handle, look at and read as many different types and styles of books as possible so that they can begin to decide for themselves what they prefer. They also need to be given books from a very early age – even as young as 8-9 months, when they become fascinated with pictures and images.

Although some books are more appropriate for different ages and stages of development than others, a good range and variety should be available for children to use as and when they want. These can be:

- picture books
- factual books
- story books
- feely books
- pop-up books
- activity books
- joke books
- poetry/rhyme books
- counting books
- bath books

Choosing Books for Children

There are no hard and fast rules for choosing books for children as the choice may depend on:

- the age of the child
- the stage of development
- the interests of the child
- the purpose of the book
- the amount of money available

However, there are one or two general rules which can help. Books for young children should:

- be colourful
- have large clear pictures
- have large clear print
- be of everyday objects
- use lower case letters
- have uncluttered background
- have few words on each page
- be easy to hold
- be strongly made

Books for older children should:

- be colourful
- match the child's interest
- be suitable for the age of the child
- be suitable for the child's stage of development
- be a suitable length

Books should be chosen for the child, not because the adult thinks the child should like it.

Above all, books should show positive images of people, and avoid stereotyping (see Chapter 16)

Age 6–12 months

At this stage children can hold and handle objects. They like to point to objects. They recognise objects in their own life.

Few pages

Pictures are simple

Everyday objects

Bright and colourful

Made from thick card or fabric

No words

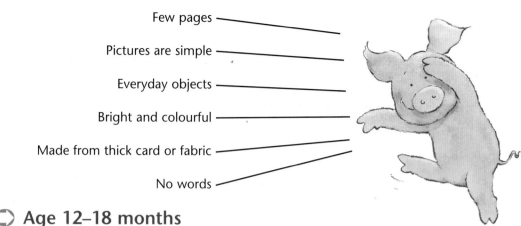

⊃ Age 12–18 months

By this stage children can recognise familiar objects and memory skills are developing. They can turn the pages in a book, although sometimes several at a time.

Few pages

Simple alphabet or number books

Clear Letters

Lowercase letters

Colourful

Touch and feel

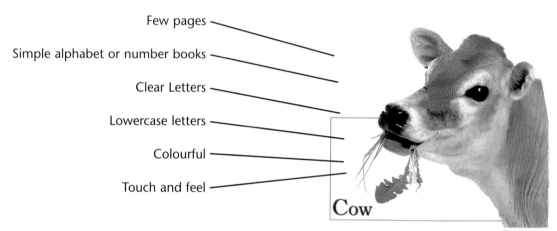

Cow

⊃ Age 18 months to 2 years

Children will enjoy books which involve joining in activities – especially and clapping and nursery rhymes.

Pictures can be more detailed and children quickly learn to join in.

By the age of 2 children will be able to sit for longer periods and listen to quite long stories.

Short, simple stories

More details in pictures and background

Colourful

Easy to turn pages

Activity stories let children join in

Stories to encourage imagination

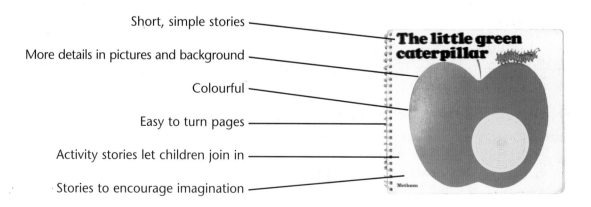

The little green caterpillar

Methuen

Age 3 to 4 years

Children will love to listen to stories, and will want the same ones repeated over and over again.

They will want to choose books for themselves.

They will often know stories off by heart.

Stories can help children to deal with everyday problems.

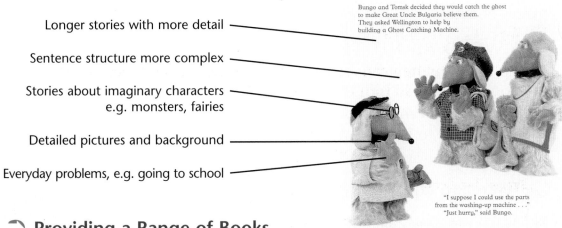

Longer stories with more detail

Sentence structure more complex

Stories about imaginary characters e.g. monsters, fairies

Detailed pictures and background

Everyday problems, e.g. going to school

Bungo and Tomsk decided they would catch the ghost to make Great Uncle Bulgaria believe them. They asked Wellington to help by building a Ghost Catching Machine.

"I suppose I could use the parts from the washing-up machine . . ." "Just hurry," said Bungo.

Providing a Range of Books

Buying books can be expensive, especially when they are part of a large series, and children want to collect them all. However, they do give good value for money.

To build up a good collection of books:

◆ make books with children
◆ go to book sales or car boot sales
◆ join book clubs
◆ ask relatives to buy books for birthdays
◆ give books as special 'treats' or 'rewards'

How to Encourage an Interest in Books

◆ always have books and comics within reach of children, i.e. on low shelves
◆ let children see that you read
◆ plan regular times to read books with children, especially but not only at bedtime
◆ allow plenty of time to 'read' with the child
◆ encourage the child to take part and ask questions
◆ answer questions

- take children on regular visits to a library
- cuddle up with the child
- switch off television or radio when reading

Talking Books

These are books which have a cassette tape to accompany them. They are useful if a child is ill in bed, or likes to listen to stories on their own, but they should not be used too frequently. They cannot take the place of a parent or adult.

A WORD ABOUT TELEVISION, VIDEOS AND COMPUTERS

Television, videos and computers are now a very big part of everyday life, and hard for us to ignore. All can be educational and all can be enjoyable, <u>IF</u> used sensibly.

Television and videos

The benefit children will get from watching television and videos, very much depends on how they are used.

If children are allowed to watch television and videos on their own and for a long period of time, they may grow up not knowing how to play or how to mix with others.

If however parents spend **time** with their children watching **suitable** programmes, and for **limited** time, and if they **talk about** what they have seen, or follow it up with activities such as painting, making models, playing games, reading books, pretend play, they can be good educational tools.

TV and videos may help children to:

- learn number recognition
- learn to count
- learn about different places in the world
- learn to read
- improve observation skills
- learn to understand concepts such as time and space
- understand and use technology
- develop creative skills
- concentrate – improve memory

TV and videos may also prevent children from:

- developing social skills
- developing language skills
- developing physical skills (both fine and gross motor skills)
- developing their own creative and imaginative skills
- writing and reading
- asking questions
- developing problem solving skills

Definitely don't

◆ use television and videos excessively

◆ use them as a replacement for parent company

◆ let children watch unsupervised

Remember

Many programmes, even during daytime viewing, deal with issues which are not suitable for young children. Programmes and adverts on television can reinforce gender-stereotyping, bad language is often normal and violence acceptable.

Computers

Computers and computer games are enjoyed by many children. They can be entertaining, they can be educational and they can help children to know and experience the wider world.

As with television and video, their use needs to be monitored. Too long spent in front of a computer screen can, as with television and videos, limit social, physical (gross motor skills) and language development – and children can become addicted.

However, using a keyboard can benefit children – it helps develop fine motor skills, and recognition of numbers and letters. Computers with concept keypads and pressure pads are also of great value to children with disabilities.

TOYS AND PLAY FOR SPECIAL NEEDS CHILDREN

Children with special needs are no different from other children when it comes to toys and play – they need lots of them. But what they often need more of, is parents time, as they tend to need more help and involvement from other people. It is sometimes a mistake to think that they need 'special' toys. Children under five are just that – children! They need toys and lots of opportunities to play, just like all children. They will still go through the same stages it's just that they may do so more slowly (or in the case of gifted children, more quickly) or they may get stuck at one stage.

However, care in the choice of toys for some conditions can help children develop more quickly.

Autism and Asperger's Syndrome

When choosing toys and activities for children with autism or Asperger's Syndrome, its important to remember that complex toys will be confusing for them and make them withdraw even more. Basic simple toys are best such as those based on reality and everyday life e.g. train sets, farms, cars and garages etc. It's also helpful if these can be linked to visits, books, videos, so that children can relate the toys to their lives.

Autistic and Asperger's Syndrome children may become 'fixated' by one particular toy, so they need to be encouraged to handle and play with others. It is important to introduce them to other toys, but slowly, and in a structured way – perhaps setting aside a time in the day when a box of special toys is brought out and played with.

Care also needs to be taken when decorating children's bedrooms – they should be quite simply decorated. There needs to be toys and posters around, but wallpaper, curtains that are too busy and with lots of posters pinned on top of them can cause confusion.

Cerebral Palsy

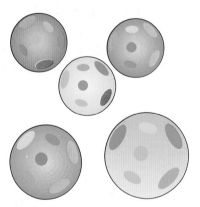

Children with cerebral palsy find it difficult to play naturally, because they may have little movement and little control.

From birth, it is important to give these children lots of sensory stimulation – especially sight, sound and touch. A mobile over the cot and musical mobiles are especially good for these children. Pictures stuck to the ceiling where they can be looked at, beds close to bright curtains, toys on shelves at eye level will all help to stimulate senses. As children get older, any musical toys will help, and textured objects, such as books, soft squeezy toys, and 'feely' bags. Textured balls which can be stroked will encourage children to use their hands and extend their fingers as they tend to normally have clenched fists. Also a towelling facecloth in the cot will introduce a new texture to a young baby.

⊃ Down's Syndrome

Children with Down's Syndrome need similar toys and stimulation to those with cerebral palsy. They tend to learn by accident – to roll over, hand-eye co-ordination, head control. Until they are 3 or 4 years old; joints tend to be lax, and they will need physiotherapy. However it is important to know that baby walkers are not a good idea, as they damage ligaments.

Down's Syndrome children learn by 'mouthing' – they use their mouths and tongues to explore toys, so it's important to make sure that toys are made of materials suitable to put into the mouth and be kept clean. Also, because some Down's Syndrome children may have a heart condition, big physical activities are not always possible. As they get older, they tend not to play a lot imaginatively.

⊃ Cystic Fibrosis

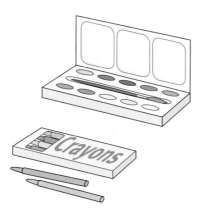

Children with cystic fibrosis are often very intelligent and usually very artistic – they often love reading and excel at music and art, so any toys or activities related to this are important.

Because children with cystic fibrosis have problems with their breathing, active physical games are not always suitable but should be encouraged where possible.

⊃ Sensory Impairment – Visual and hearing

In general if a baby or young child cannot use one of its senses to find people or objects, then such things as colour, sound and movement need to be exaggerated.

Children with visual impairment tend to develop more slowly – because they have limited vision, there is not as great a need for head control, so control of arms, body and legs will also be slowed down.

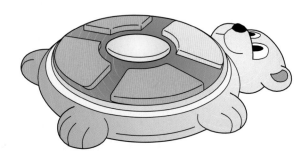

Choosing suitable toys and activities will very much depend on the level of impairment – how much vision the child has. However toys which make sounds and have flashing lights, glitter sticks, mirrored toys and brightly coloured toys will all help. Holographic paper can be used to make lots of things for children and will stimulate vision. Using holographic tape on the edges of tables and chairs can also help their spacial awareness.

If children have very little vision, black and white images are often easier for them to follow. Colour tracking is needed to identify colours which children can see and then toys, books, decorations in a room can be chosen to encourage this.

From an early age children with visual impairment often need to be encouraged to use their hands – because they cannot see, the touch of new and unknown textures and objects can be frightening.

Children with hearing impairment need lots of different toys to keep them interested and alert. Toys need to be colourful and bright, and toys that move, light up, or make noise when the child makes a sound can help them to realise when they are making sounds. Musical toys and instruments are of great value as they help to develop motor skills and a sense of rhythm, and can help children identify certain sounds through vibrations.

⊃ Muscular Dystrophy and Spina Bifida

Children with Spina Bifida will have little or no use of their lower limbs and as they grow older may need to use a wheelchair. Muscular dystrophy may also result in children being confined to a wheelchair in later life. As a result activities using gross motor skills may be restricted or increasingly difficult. Other than this toys and game bought for these children will be no different from those for other children – except they will have to be brought to the child's level.

Questions

Question 1 a Give two reasons why children need to play.

b List ways in which play can specifically help a child's physical, intellectual, emotional and social development.

c What is the different between *spontaneous* play and *structured play*?

Question 2 a Name and describe *four* main types of play.

b For each type of play, suggest two different suitable activities.

c Describe how each type of play will help a child's development.

Question 3 a Give a simple definition of a toy.

b Suggest *seven* points to remember when choosing and buying toys for children.

c List *ten* safety points to remember when buying used toys.

Question 4 Suggest with reasons, suitable toys for the following

i a six month old baby

ii a $2\frac{1}{2}$ year old toddler

iii a $4\frac{1}{2}$ year old child.

Question 5 Toys can be expensive

a Suggest *four* which parents could give children to play with that would be cheap or easily available at home.

b For each of the items suggested in (a) describe how they would help a child's development.

Question 6 a i List *six* ways in which TV, videos and computers might help development.

Things to do

Activity 1

Plan and organise a play activity for a four year old child which would encourage either:

   a creative play

   b imaginative play

In your planning, indicate what materials and equipment you might need, where the activity would take place, and preparation needed and safety factors.

Identify what sort of areas of development this activity might provide for the child.

Activity 2

If possible, carry out the activity with a child of that age.

Write up your observations and evaluate your planning.

Comment on how successful the activity was in helping the child to develop skills.

Activity 3

Ask the parents of the child you are studying if you can look at the range of toys they have provided.

Evaluate the range and type of toys.

Analyse the toys looking at:

◆ type (give a description)

◆ cost

◆ how they would be used

◆ type of play they would encourage

◆ child appeal

◆ safety

You could write this up as a chart, using ICT if possible.

Write up your conclusion.

Activity 4

Try to organise a visit to a nursery or playgroup.

Draw a detailed plan of the area, showing the different activities provided.

From your plan and observations, identify the different types of play being encouraged (you could also interview the teacher or playgroup leader about how and why the area is set up as it is).

Activity 5

Carry out some research into the opportunities offered for different types of play, at home and at nursery.

You could do this as a questionnaire.

Activity 6

Investigate how toys have changed over the past 50–100 years.

You could write to museums, interview parents and grandparents, look on the internet etc.

Compare the type of toys available and the range (and cost).

Look at the sorts of skills they were designed to develop, and compare them with the sorts of toys children have to play with nowadays.

What are your conclusions about how toys have changed?

⊃ PLAY AND TOYS WORDSEARCH

Imaginative	Books
Pretend	Concepts
Parallel	Physical
Games	Social play
Experiment	Toys
Creative	Discover
Roleplay	Sharing
Co-operative	

Special Children

In this section we will examine:
- the meaning of the term special needs
- different types of conditions and impairments
- the needs of children with special needs and their families

The term' special needs' covers a wide range of conditions. Not all children with special needs have a recognised disability. Any child may be said to have special needs when they need help to satisfy one or more of the most basic human needs. There are many different conditions or impairments which special needs children may have and when these are known the correct term should be used rather than labelling a child as 'disabled' or 'handicapped'.

⊃ CATEGORIES OF SPECIAL NEEDS

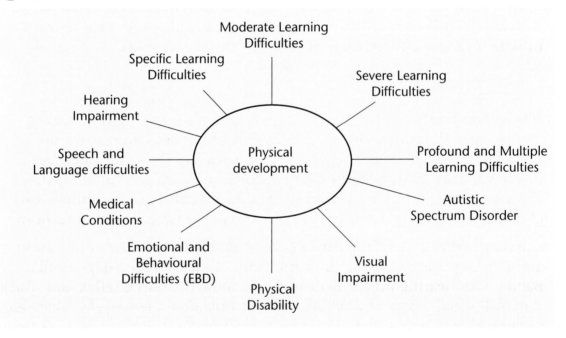

⊃ Moderate Learning Difficulties

This includes children who have difficulties in all areas of learning. Their rate of progress may be very slow. They attend mainstream schools unless they also have additional significant difficulties.

Severe Learning Difficulties

This term is used to describe children who show a global developmental delay in all areas of physical, intellectual, social and emotional development. Their rate of progress is less than half the rate of other children of the same age. These children will be given **Statements of Special Educational Needs**. They will attend mainstream school wherever possible. If they have additional needs, they are more likely to be placed in a special school or nursery.

Profound and Multiple Learning Difficulties

This term is used to describe children whose combination of physical, sensory and intellectual impairment is profound. They are usually identified soon after birth. They will have special provision from an early age and are most likely to attend a special school or nursery.

Specific Learning Difficulties

This term is used to describe children who appear to be within the average range of intelligence and who often make a good spoken contribution but who have significant difficulties in learning to read, write, spell or use numbers. These children will attend mainstream schools.

Hearing Impairment

Hearing impairment may not be immediately obvious in a young baby; parents may think the child is merely slow or uncommunicative. Few children are totally deaf. Partial deafness is usually the result of illness or injury whereas total deafness is a congenital problem present at birth. The causes of hearing impairment could be: infections of the middle ear, glue ear, birth injury, heredity, rubella, severe jaundice or viral infections.

Children with hearing impairments have problems with communication and language development since they do not pick up everyday sounds. Babies with hearing impairment may not show the startle reflex and whilst they will usually begin to babble this will stop after a few weeks. There are currently government plans to introduce testing for deafness within 48 hours of birth under national screening standards.

Most children with hearing difficulties go to their local mainstream school but those with a significant hearing impairment may have a **Statement of Special Educational Needs**. Those with the most severe hearing difficulties may need to be placed in a special resource for hearing impaired children. Oral/aural and signing methods of teaching are used according to the needs of individual pupils.

Visual Impairment

Only 18 per cent of the visually impaired are totally blind; others have varying degrees of sight or awareness of light and darkness. Causes of visual impairment could be cataracts, damage to the optic nerve, abnormal development of the retina, tumour of the retina or glaucoma (this is rare in children).

Most children who have difficulties with their eyesight will go to mainstream schools and nurseries where an advisory teacher for visually impaired children will be available to offer help and advice. If the condition is particularly severe and they need to use Braille or access to specialist teaching materials and equipment they may attend a special resource centre for the visually impaired.

Physical Disability

This term is used to describe conditions in which children have problems with co-ordination or mobility. Muscular dystrophy, cerebral palsy and spina bifida can all be placed in this category. Some children have mild problems and others have very severe difficulties. Many physically disabled children attend local schools and nurseries but if their disability is greater they may go to a mainstream school that has been specially adapted and resourced for their needs e.g. doorways are wider to allow wheelchairs to pass and ramps and lifts allow access to all areas of the building. Most children with severe physical difficulties will have a **Statement of Special Educational Needs**.

Medical Conditions

Generally children with a specific medical need will go to their mainstream school. If the child needs to be an in-patient at a hospital for any length of time he or she will have lessons in a hospital school. Some children need to go to a hospital school on a daily basis. Children suffering from cystic fibrosis or those who need kidney dialysis often use hospital schools. These children may have a **Statement of Special Educational Needs**.

Autistic Spectrum Disorder

Autism is a condition that affects the development of a child's social, communication and imagination skills. Autism can be found in people from those with average or high general intelligence (this is usually known as Asperger's Syndrome) to those with severe intellectual impairment. Some children can also be severely affected in one of three impairments i.e. difficulty with communication, social interaction and imagination, but not necessarily in all. Autism can also vary in intensity from relatively mild to severe.

For these reasons the phrase 'Autistic Spectrum Disorder' is commonly used.

Many children on the autistic spectrum stay in their local nursery or school. The most severely affected are likely to have a **Statement of Educational Needs** and may be placed in a specialist autism resource or special school.

Emotional and Behavioural Difficulties (EBD)

Emotional and behavioural difficulties describes a wide range of difficulties and includes children who are very withdrawn, children who are hyperactive, children with mental health problems, children who are unable to control their temper and those who are aggressive or disruptive. Most children with EBD attend their local mainstream school. Those with the most extreme needs are likely to have a Statement and, for some, placement in a special school may be considered appropriate.

WHY ARE SOME CHILDREN DISABLED?

There are three main reasons why a child may be disabled:

◆ **Genetic** (inherited) causes: this may be because the sperm or the egg may have contained genetic material which was imperfect. If there is a serious imperfection then usually the mother has a miscarriage. Some genetic conditions may not always be obvious at birth, however some, like Down's Syndrome, will be obvious at birth, other conditions may only show up when the child is a few months old.

◆ **Congenital disorders:** this means that the child has been born with the condition. It may have been inherited. However not all congenital disorders are inherited. If the child has been damaged in the womb or at the time of birth then the problem may be congenital but not inherited.

◆ **Other causes:** some chronic problems or disorders are caused by events after birth. Injuries due to infections or accidents, particularly those which affect the brain are the most common.

DIFFERENT TYPES OF CONDITIONS AND IMPAIRMENTS

Autism

Autism is a rare developmental disorder that occurs in children before the age of three. An autistic child has difficulty in relating to other people. Autism is a lifelong disability. It is believed that the child is born with the condition but symptoms do not show until later.

An autistic child may:

◆ pay more attention to objects than people

◆ have problems with speech and language

◆ lack awareness of other people

◆ have learning difficulties

◆ lack the ability to play

◆ repeat activities

◆ become upset when unfamiliar things occur.

Autistic children can be helped by highly structured education which involves skills training in situations which are structured, organised and distraction free.

Some children are diagnosed as suffering from **Asperger's Syndrome**. This condition is considered as a sub-group within the autistic spectrum.

Children suffering from Asperger's Syndrome may:

◆ lack empathy

◆ find difficulty in making friends

◆ have poor non-verbal communication

◆ be clumsy and ill co-ordinated

◆ be naïve

◆ become intensely absorbed in certain subjects or activities

⊃ Cerebral Palsy

Cerebral palsy is a disorder resulting from damage to a child's developing brain before, during or after birth. This disorder affects around one in 500 babies with some children being more severely affected than others.

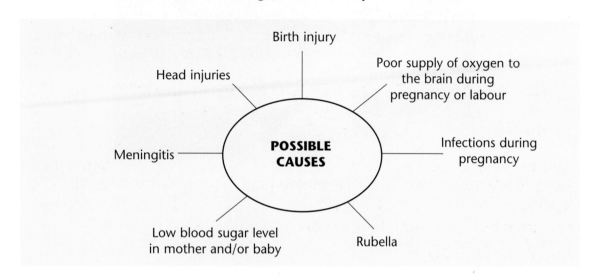

Cerebral palsy jumbles messages between the brain and the muscles. In some people, cerebral palsy is barely noticeable but others will be severely affected. No two people will be affected in quite the same way.

The damage to the brain may cause:

◆ speech and hearing difficulties
◆ problems with co-ordination and balance (ataxia)
◆ sight problems
◆ floppy limbs (athetosis)
◆ jerky movements (spasticity)
◆ possible epilepsy
◆ possible learning difficulties

Physiotherapy is a branch of medicine that uses physical methods including manipulation, exercise and massage to help manage cerebral palsy. Occupational therapists work with CP children and advise on specialist equipment which will help.

Figure 18.1 This is Katy aged 4, who has cerebral palsy. She is sitting in her specially adapted chair which enables her to sit and holds her head upright.

Cystic Fibrosis (CF)

Cystic Fibrosis (CF) is a hereditary condition which affects the lungs and digestive system. In this condition all the glands which discharge their secretions directly into the body are affected. The secretions are thick and sticky instead of being runny so they block up some of the connecting tubes in the body's system.

One in twenty people carry the CF gene but it is only when both parents are carriers that there is a one in four chance that the child will have CF.

What are the effects of CF?

◆ breathing difficulties
◆ chest infections
◆ food is not digested and absorbed properly
◆ the child fails to gain weight

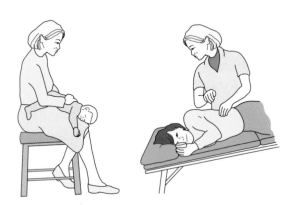

Children who suffer from CF need daily physiotherapy to help their breathing.

⊃ Down's Syndrome

Down's Syndrome is a genetic condition which causes a number of distinctive characteristics and some learning difficulties which vary from child to child. This condition is caused by the presence of an extra chromosome making 47 chromosomes in total. The possibility of having a baby with Down's Syndrome increases as the mother gets older.

Figure 18.2 The chromosome pattern of a boy with Down's Syndrome – note the presence of the extra chromosome

Signs of Down's Syndrome

◆ eyes which slant upwards and outwards
◆ eyelids with an extra fold
◆ the back of the head may seem to be flatter than usual
◆ the tongue may seem to be too large, causing feeding problems
◆ a single crease running across the palm of the hand
◆ lower birth weight and slower growth rate

There are a number of health problems associated with Down's Syndrome such as heart, chest and sinus conditions, but with advances in medicine today children with Down's can and do grow up to live long and happy lives. Babies with Down's Syndrome need extra love and attention since they take longer to reach their developmental milestones. They may need extra support when they go to school. If they are given the correct help and opportunities they can go to school and some can go on to employment.

⊃ Haemophilia

This an inherited disorder which causes problems with the clotting of the blood and spontaneous bleeding occurs. Children with haemophilia vary a good deal in how many times they bleed spontaneously – in some it occurs several times a week and in others only two or three times a year. The bleeding often occurs into the joints which may become painful and stiff and then red, swollen and tender. The disease is passed on through the mother but affects only her sons. A man with haemophilia will only pass on the gene to his daughters who will in turn become carriers. It is important that parents are more watchful especially with toddlers but there is no reason why children should not go to playgroup or nursery and the vast majority go to ordinary schools.

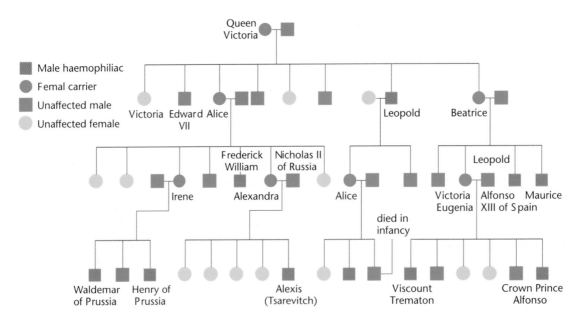

Figure 18.3 Queen Victoria's family tree showing how haemophilia is passed through the mother

⊃ Muscular Dystrophy

This a condition which causes muscle tissue to weaken. This rare condition becomes noticeable between the ages of two and five years. The child will usually not learn to run and will have difficulties in climbing. The muscles become steadily weaker and the child's walking is affected so that he may begin to stumble, fall or have difficulty with stairs. The most common type, Duchenne muscular dystrophy, affects only boys and, as with haemophilia, it can be passed by a mother to her son if he inherits the faulty gene.

⊃ Spina Bifida

This a condition in which the spine fails to develop properly before birth. Children with spina bifida will nearly always need special help, for example from physiotherapists, paediatricians, orthopaedic surgeons or urologists to make them as mobile as possible. Depending on where the defect is some will need wheelchairs, others will be able to get around with callipers or even without any special aids.

A full description of this condition is included in Chapter 4.

Remember

Each of the disorders listed can cause problems which mean that the children will need special help, hence the term Special Needs.

◑ CHILDREN WITH SPECIFIC EDUCATIONAL NEEDS

◑ Specific Learning Difficulties

The term specific learning difficulties is used to describe children who have difficulty in learning to read, write, spell or do mathematics. They do not have difficulty learning other skills.

◑ Dyslexia

The term dyslexia covers a wide range of difficulties ranging from mild problems with spelling to a total inability to read and write. Early identification of the problem can reduce the problems and strategies can be used to help children within school.

◑ ADHD

Attention Deficit Hyperactivity Disorder is a specific learning difficulty since children with this disorder show behaviour traits which prevent them from learning. They may have difficulty sharing and taking turns, they often talk excessively, they are easily distracted and appear restless.

Gifted Children

Gifted children may not have a physical disability but they can have problems with socialisation. They may be academically more advanced than other children but they still need to have friends of their own age. Wherever possible parents of gifted children are advised that they should have opportunities to extend their ability by means of a specially adapted curriculum without being separated from their friends since this can cause social and emotional problems.

PROFESSIONALS INVOLVED WITH CHILDREN WITH SPECIAL NEEDS

Many professionals can be involved in caring for children with special needs. Severe medical problems will call for the work of medical staff, behavioural problems will need the help of psychologists and all will need the help of educationalists. The amount of involvement from professionals will depend upon the severity of the disability but some children will need help from many sources.

Family Doctors	Physiotherapists	Health Visitors
Occupational Therapists	Dieticians	Psychologists
Speech Therapists	Play Therapists	Paediatricians
Social workers	Community Nurses	Special Needs Teachers
Nursery Nurses	Respite carers	Family Support Workers
Orthopaedic Surgeons	Neurologists	

THE NEEDS OF SPECIAL CHILDREN

Every child is a 'special child' but those with special needs require a good deal of understanding. It is important to remember that all children may reach stages, or milestones of development at different ages. Children who have a disability are often made to feel that they are younger than they are because they have not reached 'normal 'milestones. The basic needs of all children are stability, security and protection. Sometimes special children, especially those with obvious disabilities, find that their special needs override their ordinary needs. It is important to see the individual child first and then the special need or disability if the child is to develop to its full potential. Like all children, special children need to be helped to become as independent as possible. This can be achieved by carers and friends by:

- having patience, especially if the child has problems with communication
- using praise and rewards for effort rather than achievement
- showing respect for the child's personal dignity and privacy
- making sure that whenever possible the child is involved with other children (integration)
- showing empathy rather than sympathy
- responding positively to things over which the child has control
- allowing the child to make decisions

THE NEEDS OF PARENTS AND CARERS

Children with special needs can bring much love and happiness to a family but there can be difficulties depending upon the nature of the impairment suffered by the child. All parents of young children need help and support because of the extra work needed in caring for young children but families with special needs children need even more support.

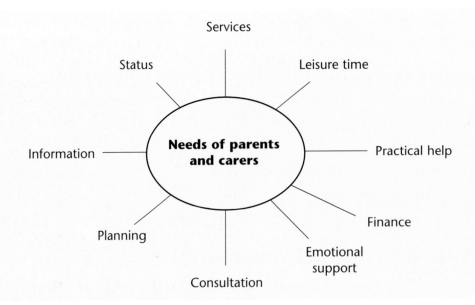

- **status:** the number of professionals involved in caring for a special child can be so large that parents need to be given recognition that usually they are the ones who know the child best and that they have the most important role to play in the care of their child and should not be undermined or overwhelmed by the professionals
- **services:** everyone has the right to help and parents should be made aware of the opportunities and services open to them

- ◆ **leisure time:** looking after special children takes up a good deal of time and parents should not feel guilty about making time for their own needs and the needs of their family

- ◆ **practical help:** this could be help in the home, respite care, help with transport and mobility

- ◆ **information:** parents have the right to be given full information about their child's condition

- ◆ **planning:** parents should be involved in all aspects of planning for their child's future education or care

- ◆ **consultation:** parents opinions should always be taken into consideration

- ◆ **emotional support:** some parents may need help in adjusting to the change in their own lives and help in finding pleasure in their child

- ◆ **finance:** help may be needed to cover the costs of special equipment, aids and adaptations to the home or frequent trips to hospitals

The Needs of Siblings

It is often difficult for brothers and sisters of children with special needs because, however much they love their sibling they will see that the child needs, and gets, much more attention than normal. Hospital appointments, special equipment, professional helpers can disrupt the normal routine of any home. Parents and carers need to make sure that brothers and sisters do not feel left out. Sometimes other children can be cruel about children who are different and this can hurt siblings.

Case Study: Jemma, Jade and Jack

Jack is a very handsome boy who lives with his parents and his sisters Jemma and Jade. When Jack was a baby all was well but as he grew older the family became aware that he was not progressing as he should. He was often ill and his speech did not continue to develop as it had.

Eventually Jack was diagnosed as having autism and whilst the family were shocked they loved him very much and did all they could to make him happy. This was not easy because in common with most children with autism Jack found it difficult to show any feeling and seemed indifferent to everyone even his own family.

The parents felt that the girls were coping well with Jack's problems until Jemma explained that her friends at school did not understand about Jack and that she too wanted to know why Jack was different. In the following passage Jack's mum explains how she came to write a book for Jemma and Jade to help them understand. When the book was complete they took it to Jemma's school so that her friends could understand too. The book was so successful that it has been published by The Autistic Society and has been translated into many different languages to help brothers and sisters like Jemma and Jade.

The reason I wrote 'My Brother is different' was because my daughter Jemma wanted to know why it was that whenever she got any games out he ruined the game by sweeping the lot onto the floor in a satisfying heap, or why it was that when she did something wrong herself, a 'telling off' followed or even worse punishment or banishment to the bedroom was dealt out, <u>but</u> if Jack did anything wrong the same did not apply. He was told gently but firmly which was the right way to behave. Things like this must have seemed so unfair in Jemma and Jade's eyes. Why did they have to go to bed at 7.30pm when Jack was younger and allowed to stay up until past midnight?. Very unfair! Why did Jack, in Waitrose, wait until he was positioned behind a frail old lady leaning over the freezer counter, give a high pitched squeal at the top of his voice and not get told off when she fell in, like they would have done? It was very hard for them to see that he got a very satisfying reaction from everybody in the shop from that one squeal, while the managers were pulling her out of the frozen sausages. In their eyes he was just being naughty and embarrassing.

I asked Jemma about all the things that Jack did that upset her and we wrote them down and I wrote down next to them why he did those particular things to help her understand a little of what was going on in Jack's head. But a lot of it is still guesswork!

Louise Gorrod

A STATEMENT OF SPECIAL EDUCATIONAL NEEDS FOR A YOUNG CHILD

Obtaining a '**statement of special educational needs**' (also known as statementing) is the key to gaining specialist help a child might need.

1   Local Education Authorities have a duty to provide suitable education for children from the pre-school years. Children who have a disability are first given a 'statutory assessment' usually between the ages of two and four. This helps the Local Education Authority (LEA) to decide whether it can meet the needs of the child in their local school.

2   If the local school is unsuitable for the child the LEA must provide a '**statement of special educational needs**' which states the child's condition and details any extra educational requirements, equipment or special help which will be needed. The statement will state whether the

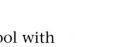

child is to be educated at a special school, a mainstream school with extra help, or at home. It will also detail non-educational needs such as transport to and from school.

3 The parent will have the opportunity to see the statement before it is complete so that they may comment and give any opinions they might have on the choice of school.

4 The finished statement will state the type and amount of support which is to be provided by the school and the LEA, any special equipment required plus educational targets and a list of suitable schools. The LEA must provide transport as long as the school chosen is the closest suitable school to the child's home.

Questions

Question 1
What is the difference between a child with moderate learning difficulties and one with specific learning difficulties?

Question 2
List some of the causes of hearing impairment in young children.

Question 3
Give 3 examples of conditions which may cause physical disability.

Question 4
Why may it be necessary for some children to attend a hospital school?

Question 5
What are the main differences between congenital and genetic disorders?

Question 6
How may a child who suffers from cerebral palsy be affected?

Question 7
What is the cause of Down's Syndrome?

Question 8
Why are gifted children sometimes considered to have special needs?

Question 9
What problems might the siblings of children with special needs have?

Things to do

Activity 1
If you can visit a nursery or playgroup try to decide what problems there might be for a three year old in a wheelchair who wishes to join in the activities. Suggest ways in which the staff can make this possible.

Activity 2
Use your own school timetable to decide what problems might there be for a child in a wheelchair if they were to attend your school. Suggest adaptations which could be made to the building to make it wheelchair friendly.

Activity 3
Look at the table which lists some of the professionals who may be involved in the care of children with special needs and use your school or local library to research the work that they do.

NB For information on play for disabled children see Chapter 17 on Play and Toys.

Part Four
Key Skills/ Coursework/ Exam Preparation

The following three chapters will help you develop the Key Skills you will need, as well as give tips on successful coursework. Finally, techniques for dealing with exams are given to boost confidence.

19

Key Skills

⊃ COMMON QUESTIONS AND ANSWERS

⊃ 1 What are Key Skills?

Key Skills are skills that can enable you to perform well in education, training and life in general.

⊃ 2 What Key Skills are available?

There are three 'main' Key Skills

◆ Communication
◆ Application of Number
◆ Information Technology (IT)

There are also three 'wider' Key Skills

◆ Working with Others
◆ Improving Own Learning and Performance
◆ Problem Solving

The main Key Skills are those which lead to a recognised Key Skills Qualification. You can also gain a certificate for passing each of the wider Key Skills.

⊃ 3 At what level are they available?

Each of the Key Skills is available at four levels (1 to 4). Levels 1 and 2 relate to GCSE.

⊃ 4 What do Key Skills look like?

Each of the six Key Skills is made up of three parts.

Part A	What you need to know
Part B	What you must do
Part C	Guidance

5 What must I do to achieve a Key Skills qualifications?

For the 'main' Key Skills you will be assessed in two ways:

1 You must compile a portfolio of evidence, which your teacher will assess.

2 There will be an external test, task, or assignment which you must also pass or complete successfully.

6 How can my Child Development course help?

This course offers you opportunities to generate evidence of achievement in each of the Key Skills. The work you produce can form part, or even all of the portfolio for each Key Skill.

7 Must Key Skills be delivered through this specification?

No, Key Skills apply to a wide range of courses and studies. So Key Skills will assist you in your work whatever the subject or specification. However, it is always worth thinking about how they might apply to this particular course.

SIGNPOSTS OF KEY SKILLS IN HOME ECONOMICS (CHILD DEVELOPMENT)

Activity

Go to http://www.qca.org.uk/nq/ks/ and find the Key Skills specifications link on that page. Print out the main Key Skills (Application of Number, Communication, and IT) for Level 1 and Level 2.

Use your print out to match Key Skills opportunities to the Child Development activities that follow.

⊃ SECTION 1 THE FAMILY

⊃ Application of Number Levels 1 and 2

Child Development activity	Opportunities to develop key skills evidence	
	Level 1	Level 2
● consider the financial implications of planning a family and present findings	N1.1 N1.2	N2.1 N2.2
● analyse the composition of a healthy diet during pregnancy	N1.3	N2.3

⊃ Communication Levels 1 and 2

Child Development activity	Opportunities to develop key skills evidence	
	Level 1	Level 2
● discuss/present a relevant topic, e.g. variations of family type including the roles within the family and cultural variations	C1.1	C2.1a C2.1b
● investigate the anatomy and physiology of reproduction	C1.2	C2.2
● report on maternal health including ante-natal care, routine checks and specialised testing	C1.3	C2.3

⊃ Information Technology Levels 1 and 2

Child Development activity	Opportunities to develop key skills evidence	
	Level 1	Level 2
● use the Internet, CD-ROMs and databases to find and select information, e.g. medical advice on pregnancy	IT1.1	IT2.1
● present results from an investigation into the stages of pregnancy from conception to birth	IT1.2	IT2.2 IT2.3

SECTION 2 CARE OF THE CHILD

Application of Number Levels 1 and 2

Child Development activity	Opportunities to develop key skills evidence	
	Level 1	Level 2
• calculate amounts of formula milk feed or nutritional requirements in relation to age and present findings	N1.1 N1.2	N2.1 N2.2
• compare the development of children against physical norms	N1.3	N2.3

Communication Levels 1 and 2

Child Development activity	Opportunities to develop key skills evidence	
	Level 1	Level 2
• discuss/present findings from research on a topic, e.g. hygiene, safety within a child's environment	C1.1	C2.1a C2.16
• investigate childhood illnesses and diseases	C1.2	C2.2
• report on the medical needs of a child, including vaccination and immunisation	C1.3	C2.3

Information Technology Levels 1 and 2

Child Development activity	Opportunities to develop key skills evidence	
	Level 1	Level 2
• use the Internet, CD-ROMs and databases to find and select information, e.g. on the variety of child care provision	IT1.1	IT2.1
• make a presentation of the results of investigations, e.g. into the choice and care of appropriate clothing and footwear	IT1.2	IT2.2 IT2.3

Key Skills

opment

Application of Number Levels 1 and 2

Child Development activity	Opportunities to develop key skills evidence	
	Level 1	Level 2
• investigate growth, height and weight patterns of a child's physical development and present findings	N1.1 N1.2	N2.1 N2.2
• analyse the child's development	N1.3	N2.3

Communication Levels 1 and 2

Child Development activity	Opportunities to develop key skills evidence	
	Level 1	Level 2
• discuss/present findings from research on factors which help or hinder the intellectual, emotional and social development of a child	C1.1	C2.1a C2.1b
• produce a written piece of work on the causes and effects of a physical or mental disability	C1.2 C1.3	C2.2 C2.3

Information Technology Levels 1 and 2

Child Development activity	Opportunities to develop key skills evidence	
	Level 1	Level 2
• use the Internet, CD-ROMs and databases to find and select information, e.g. on toys and books suitable to a child's stage of development	IT1.1	IT2.1
• present findings in a suitable format, e.g. using graphical or photographic evidence to illustrate the use/benefits of toys	IT1.2	IT2.2 IT2.3

COURSEWORK

Application of Number Levels 1 and 2

Child Development activity	Opportunities to develop key skills evidence	
	Level 1	Level 2
• use statistical information in planning, testing or interpreting elements of the coursework	N1.1	N2.1
• carry out calculations e.g. the costs of providing suitable equipment for a playgroup	N1.2	N2.2
• present findings using numbers, graphs, charts and diagrams	N1.3	N2.3

Communication Levels 1 and 2

Child Development activity	Opportunities to develop key skills evidence	
	Level 1	Level 2
• discuss/plan how to investigate a topic, e.g. deciding upon the focus for research during observational visits	C1.1	C2.1a C2.1b
• read and analyse information relevant to the proposed child study	C1.2	C2.2
• present/summarise written findings in a portfolio	C1.3	C2.3

Information Technology Levels 1 and 2

Child Development activity	Opportunities to develop key skills evidence	
	Level 1	Level 2
• use the Internet, CD-ROMs and databases to find and select information on a particular topic, e.g. guidance on healthy diets for children	IT1.1	IT2.1
• present the findings from research/coursework using appropriate IT software, e.g. using text, images and numbers to illustrate the physical development of a child	IT1.2	IT2.2 IT2.3

20

Coping with coursework

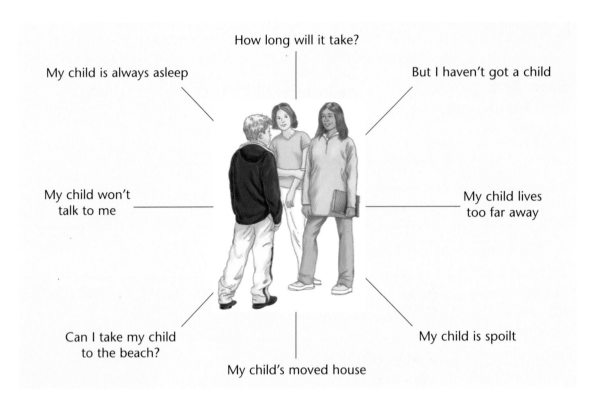

How long will it take?

My child is always asleep

But I haven't got a child

My child won't talk to me

My child lives too far away

Can I take my child to the beach?

My child is spoilt

My child's moved house

⟁ THE CHILD STUDY – WHAT IS IT?

This is what the specification says:

◆ The Child Study should take place over a period of six months minimum.
◆ The Child Study will involve research/investigation and observational visits of a single child between 0-5 years on which candidates should spend approximately 30 hours.

This sounds scary! But it doesn't have to be.

> This section will guide you through the coursework and your teacher will be there to help you!

FIRST: Find a child to study!

Remember

- Babies do little more than sleep and eat.
- You need to have the parents' permission to visit the child.
- Ideally the child should not live too far away.
- The child must be under five years of age at the beginning of the study.

Now: Arrange your introductory visit but think carefully. What do you need to find out?

Name:
Age:
P
I
E
S
Environment:
Personality
Interests
Look for possible areas of research

You can do this by:-

- ◆ chatting with parents/carers
- ◆ chatting and playing with the child
- ◆ watching the child

Remember

You need to look for ideas for your research and investigation so try to find out what the child likes to do.

This information needs to be written on A4 paper. Now you have completed your introductory visit! WELL DONE!

⊃ BACKGROUND RESEARCH

Choosing an area of research is difficult, but don't worry as your teacher will help you with this.

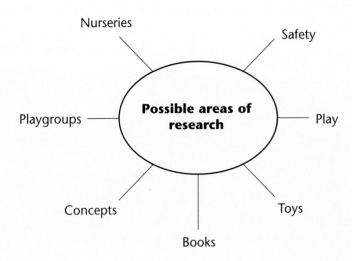

You need to research the topic. Here are some suggestions

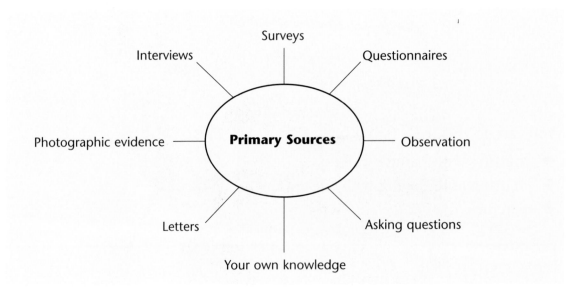

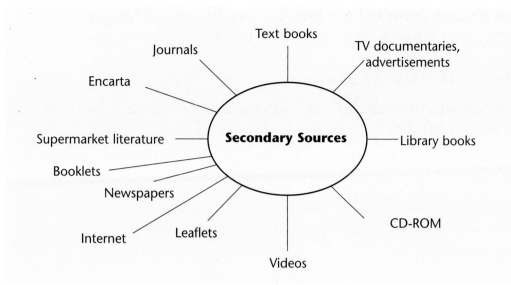

Journals

Encarta

Text books

TV documentaries,
advertisements

Supermarket literature — **Secondary Sources** — Library books

Booklets

Newspapers

Internet   Leaflets   CD-ROM

Videos

Remember

Be selective – you don't have to use everything you find out.

So far so good...

Focus on your

Area of

Research   **(FAR)**

Choose something which is suitable to your child and give your reasons.

Think about how you can use your research in at least three of your visits (Action Plan?)

NOW It's time to visit the child again!

Remember

You will be making six visits over at least the next six months. These will need to be planned.

⤵ **How do I write up my visits? What should it look like?**

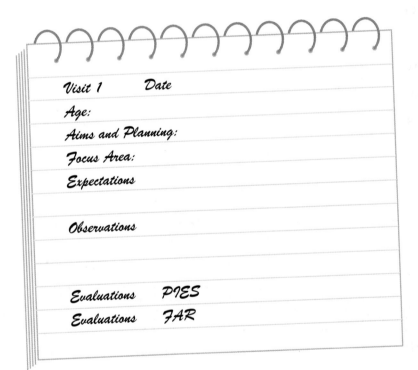

Almost there!   Don't give up now!

⊃ FINAL CONCLUSIONS!

◆ Tell us what you have done
◆ Look back and read your introduction
◆ Write about the changes you have seen
◆ Don't forget to link these to theory
◆ Have you included some personal opinions?
◆ Comment on your research.
◆ Was it useful? What did you find out?

Remember

Have you done your bibliography?
This is a list of books and other resources you have used.

FINALLY

One last check:

Have I got...	✓
Introductory visit	
Background research	
Focus area of research	
Visit 1	
Visit 2	
Visit 3	
Visit 4	
Visit 5	
Visit 6	
Final Evaluation	
Bibliography	

FINISHED – Didn't you do well!

NOW – All you have to do is hand it in to your teacher!

⊃ WEB SITES

Many students write letters to charities and other organisations or firms asking for information to help with their coursework and are disappointed if they do not receive a reply. Most charities would like to help but postage and administration makes this very costly. Charities and other organisations have web pages which contain lots of information therefore using the Internet can be a useful tool. This will also give you the opportunity to generate evidence on which you may be assessed in IT which is one of the main Key Skills and help you to access the wider Key Skill of Improving your own Learning Performance.

Tips on using the Internet for information

1　You can type in the web site to get information directly from an organisation.

2　If you do not know the website name search for sites which might be close to what you want by using a search engine such as www.google.com.

3　You can guess at a web site by typing in the name of the organisation and try adding .com or .co.uk. Even if you don't find exactly what you want you will be searching through information and discovering facts for your research.

4　Collect web sites by looking at magazines etc.

The following are a few of the many web sites which are concerned with Child Development.

www.babycentre.co.uk	Good for downloading information on stages of development and milestones reached
www.babyworld	Detailed information on all aspects of feeding
www.bedtime-story.com	A story is printed off with illustrations to colour
www.b4baby.com	Pre-conceptual care, pregnancy and the new baby stage
www.cdipage.com	Child development, parenting safety, disabilities. Excellent charts on PIES
www.family.go.com	Child health A–Z, baby growth and development checklists
www.growthspurts.com	Good charts and databases (careful of American spelling)

www.lalechleague.org	Advice on breast feeding
www.motherandbaby.co.uk	Pregnancy, birth, health issues and development of child up to age of three
www.nannyknowsbest.com	Put in a query and a simple explanation is given on child behaviour
www.\\nsc.org\1rs\lib\facts.htm#CHILD	
	National Safety Council factsheets
www.rospa.co.uk\childsaf.htm	Information on child safety
www.wiganmdc.gov.uk\pub	Information on toy safety regulations

⊃ MORE USEFUL WEB SITES

Vegetarian Society
www.vegsoc.or.uk

Vegan Society
www.vegansociety.com

The Institute of Food Science and Technology
http://www.easynet.co.uk/ifst/resource.htm

Berrydales Publishers (special diets and food tolerance)
www.insidestory.com

British Diabetic Association
www.diabetes.org.uk

British Nutrition Foundation
www.nutrition.org.uk

The Coeliac Society
www.coeliac.co.uk

Hyperactive Children's Support Group
www.hyperactive.force9.co.uk

British Heart Foundation (special diets and healthy eating)
www.bhf.org.uk

The Real Nappy Association (environmentally sustainable nappies)
www.realnappy.com

Healthy Eating and Pregnancy (Sainsbury's leaflet)
www.sainsburys.co.uk

Healthy Eating Before, During and After Pregnancy
(The University of Sheffield Department of Obstetrics and Gybaecology –
Centre for Pregnancy Nutrition)
Pregnancy
Nutrition@Sheffield.ac.uk

National Dairy Council
http://www.milk.co.uk
http://www.ndc.co.uk

Boots
http://www.boots.co.uk

MAFF (National Food Survey)
http://www.maff.gov.uk

Exam Preparation

No one really enjoys exams! Unfortunately, to get qualifications, they usually need to be done.

Remember

No one is trying to trick you or deliberately make you fail. The exam is your chance to show what you <u>know</u> and <u>understand</u> about child development.

So ...

◆ you have got this far

◆ you have handed in all the coursework

◆ why not give it your best shot?

This needs to begin with ... REVISION. OK ... it might be boring, but it's the only real way to succeed in exams.

⊃ TOP REVISION TIPS

⊃ Tip 1

PLAN – both your time and what you need to do. You will have lots of subjects to revise for, so you need to work out how to fit everything in. A bit like doing a jigsaw.

⊃ **Tip 2**

Choose a revision style that suits <u>you</u>!

> We revise together

> I like to write everything out over and over again

> I write keywords and phrases on postcards

> Highlighting words helps me

> I tape my notes and then play them back on my personal stereo

> I stick notes and keywords on my computer and desk

⊃ **Tip 3**

Have regular breaks and give yourself a treat to aim for as a target when you have finished one section. You will learn more in several short periods than you will in one long one.

⊃ **Tip 4**

Do lots of practice questions – your teacher will give you these from old exam papers <u>BUT</u> – when you get your work back, don't just look at your mark but <u>read</u> the comments made. This will show you how to improve.

⊃ **Tip 5**

Don't miss out huge chunks of revision. The exam paper has to include questions to cover <u>all</u> the specification in some way.

⊃ **Tip 6**

Don't leave it all to the night before the exam – or on your way to the exam!

So, you have done your revision – now, on to the exam.

Don't worry! When you first open an exam paper it's not unusual to think you don't know anything and can't answer anything.

Learn how to make the exam paper work <u>for</u> you.
Look for the clues.

Clue 1	Spend a few minutes reading through the whole paper – sometimes words and phrases used in one question might give you ideas for others.
Clue 2	Try to answer all parts of the same question at the same time – they are often about similar or related topics.
Clue 3	Look for any words in **bold** type or *italic* – underline these. These will give you an idea of what is needed in your answer.
Clue 4	Underline any key words and/or phrases. As the words suggest, key words can help you to 'unlock' and understand the question. There may be two types of key words:

- those used by the examiner to tell you what sort of answer is expected (see Keywords below)

- those which tell you what your answer has to be about – the topic

Key Words

<u>Describe</u>: to give information in an accurate and detailed way.

<u>Discuss</u>: to describe and give an opinion about something, usually looking at different points of view. You will need to use facts and knowledge to back up your ideas and opinions.

<u>Explain</u>: to make something very clear, usually by giving facts and reasons.

<u>Identity</u>: to give factual information about something.

<u>Illustrate</u>: to give examples to explain something more clearly.

<u>List/Name</u>: to give facts in a simple, clear way.

<u>Suggest</u>: to put forward an idea. Often you will be asked to give reasons.

⊃ Key words telling you what the question is about

Carefully-chosen toys and games can help a child's **physical, intellectual, social and emotional development**.

Discuss this statement, using the age ranges given below.

Give examples for each.

from birth to 1 year

from 1 year to 3 years

from 3 years to 5 years

Key words telling you what sort of answer is expected

Clue 5	Look at the number of lines given for each part of the question. This will give you some idea about how much detail or information you need to give. <u>But remember</u> – IF YOUR WRITING IS BIG, you may need to continue on extra paper!
Clue 6	Look at the number of marks for each question. Generally, the more marks, the more detail is needed – this might mean giving reasons, explanations or personal opinions which you support with facts.
Clue 7	Are there any illustrations, charts, graphs etc? These might give you clues about the question.

⊃ What kind of questions might you be asked?

Some questions are <u>short, factual questions</u> and are worth a small number of marks. These often say 'list' or 'name' or 'give' and may give you a set number of points.

Give **three** reasons why a baby might need to be induced.

1..

2..

3.. (3)

Some questions are more <u>structured</u> and give you more guidance.

They may be split into different parts.

Each part will have a set number of marks.

2 The diagram below is of identical twins.

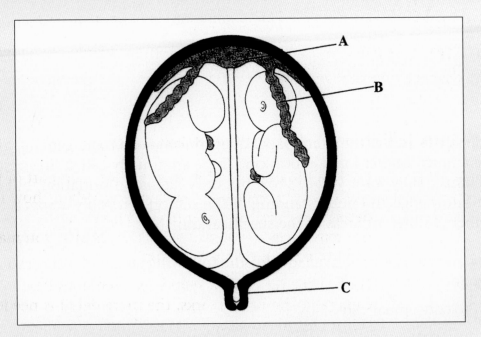

(a) Give another name for identical twins.

....

(1)

(b) Explain how identical twins are formed.

....

....

....

(2)

(c) Name the parts labelled A, B and C.

A..

B..

C..

(3)

(c) (i) Outline <u>two</u> functions of amniotic fluid.

....

....

(2)

(ii) Outline <u>three</u> functions of the placenta.

1...

2...

3...

(3)

Towards the end of the exam paper questions may be more general, and have a much higher mark allocation. These are usually called 'free response questions'. They want you to show not only factual information, but also your knowledge and understanding of the subject, probably across a number of different areas of the specification.

What advice should be available for the following stages of a successful pregnancy?

(i) Pre-conceptual care.

(ii) Ante-natal care.

(iii) Post-natal care.

Explain how each can safeguard the health and development of both mother and baby. (20)

These sorts of question will often give you a lot of space for your answers – so you need to think about them carefully.

Make sure you:

◆ read the questions carefully

◆ underline the keywords and phrases

◆ plan your answer. Examiners like to see this, so use some of the space available to jot down ideas.

In your answers try to have

◆ a brief introduction to show you understand what the question means

◆ sound, factual well reasoned and explained information related to the topic of the question

◆ a conclusion.

In writing up your answer, the following words might be useful.
They either CONNECT or START sentences.

First(ly)..... Second(ly).... Then.... ...and then.... ...after(wards).... Meanwhile.... During.... Whenever.... Eventually.... Finally.... In addition.... Furthermore..... Therefore..... Consequently.... ....because/as.... Accordingly.... ...as long as... Also.... Moreover.... As a result....	Equally..... Similarly.... Likewise.... In the same way.... As with.... However.... ....but.... Nevertheless... Alternatively.... Despite this.... ...instead... Whereas.... Although...	In particular...... Above all.... Notably.... Specifically..... ....especially.... For example.... ....such as.... Clearly.... ....of course.... ...the following... In brief..... On the whole.... To sum up.... In conclusion.

⊃ Running out of time?

Use bullet points – they can

◆ give information in a clear and quick way

◆ help you pick up marks

⊃ FINALLY

In answering many questions, it's not just enough to know lots of facts. The examiner is looking for your '<u>knowledge and understanding</u>'. This means that you have to show that you can use lots of facts and information to support and explain different ideas. Much of this information will come from the text books you have used - this one for example. It will also come from discussion in your lessons when you have listened to the ideas and views of others.

But it could also come from your own experiences of being part of a family, from babysitting, reading magazines, talking to family and friends, watching TV and videos and even watching soaps!

So use all of this to give you ideas.

⊃ KEY TERMS USED BY THE EXAMINERS

⊃ Terms used in written papers

Describe:
recall facts, events, processes etc., in an accurate and detailed way; give an account of what something looked like or what happened

Discuss:
describe and give an opinion, refer to different points of view; give facts or reasons to support opinions

Examine:
look closely at a statement or issue, discuss its truth or accuracy and give an opinion or conclusion, with reasons

Explain:
make something clear or state the reasons for something

Identify:
select or list examples from something

Illustrate:
provide examples to explain something

⊃ Terms used in coursework

Analyse:
break down issues/ideas into parts and examine how the parts are related

Assess:
make an informed judgement about how good/effective something is based on an awareness of strengths and weaknesses; present a reasoned analysis

Evaluate:
give a judgement or opinion as to the worth of something; judgements should be reasoned and whenever possible be supported by arguments or facts from books, articles etc.

Outline:
offer a summary, e.g. a brief description of planned research/methods

⊃ What about your other subjects?

Child development is probably one of many subjects you are studying – don't ignore the other ones. Something you may have studied in Science, R.S., Social Studies etc. might be useful and relevant, so use that information as well!

> ## *Remember*
>
> ◆ revise thoroughly
> ◆ read questions carefully
> ◆ underline keywords and phrases
> ◆ look at the space available for answers
> ◆ look at the marks available
> ◆ use illustrations and other information given to help

GOOD LUCK !

Index

Picture Credits

The authors and publishers would like to thank the following copyright holders for their permission to reproduce photographs in this book:

Bubbles for p.82 and 140 left (© Loisjoy Thurston); p.118 bottom; p.140 right (© D. Howells); p.151 (© Pauline Cutler); p.164, 341 top (© Jennie Woodcock); p.174 (© Anthony Dawton); p.210 (© Perry Joseph); p.289 (© Toni Revan); p.385 (© Angela Hampton)

Corbis for p.81; 259

Format for p.5, 260 top, 270 top, 288, 297 left, 298 left and right, 300 (3), 320 top, 337 top, 340, (© Maggie Murray), p.7, p.9 and p.21, 260 bottom, 299, 337 bottom (© Lisa Woollett); p.35, 93 and 118 top, 193; 194; 195 top; 196 (© Paula Glassman); p.50, 205, 258, 297 right (© Judy Harrison); p.53 and p.106 bottom, 190, 229, 233 (© Paula Solloway);
p.137 (© Rebecca Peters); p.172 right , 261, 301(© Jackie Chapman); p.195 middle 1 (© Sacha Lehrfreund); p.195 middle 2, 337 middle 2, 341 bottom (© Joanne O'Brien); p.200 (© Sheila Grey); p.213, 270 bottom, 300 (1) (© Ulrike Preuss); P.300 (4) (© Bruno Zarri); p.300 (5) (© Brenda Prince); p.320 bottom (© Sally Lancaster); p.354 and 381 (© Karen Robinson)

Sally Greenhill for page 25, 28; 86; 117; 154; 156; 169; 236, 300 (2); 337 middle 1; 347; 388

Life File for p.214, 237 top (© Emma Lee)

Mary Evans Picture Library for p.10

Mother and [obscured] p.146; 237 bottom

Muscular [obscured] © Pete Jones)

National [obscured] ddle and p.186 top and bottom

Science [obscured] Dr Yorgos Nikas/SPL);
p.79 top [obscured] (© Professor P.M. Motta et al/SPL);
p.83 (© Sa [obscured] , 96 and 99 top right
(© Biophoto [obscured] top left and bottom right;
p.103 bottom le [obscured] p.99 bottom left
(© Gary Watson/S [obscured] bottom right (© Neil Bromhall/SPL);
p.104 (© Stephani [obscured] tient, [obscured] SPL);
p.105 (© Mehan Kulyuk/SPL); p.173 (© Bruce Mireyless/SPL)

Wellcome Photo Library for p.106 top, p.155, p.158, p.160; p.172 left, 179; 181; 185 top; 187; 189 top; 189 bottom; 191; 195 bottom; 204, 209 (© Anthea Sieveking)

Wellcome Trust for p.185 bottom

Every effort has been made to obtain the necessary permission with reference to copyright material. The publishers apologise if inadvertently any sources remain unacknowledged and will be glad to make the necessary arrangements at the earliest opportunity.

Artworks created by Chartwell Illustrators and Peter Bull.